Tributes
Volume 19

From Quantification to Conversation
Festschrift for Robin Cooper
on the occasion of his 65th birthday

Volume 9
Acts of Knowledge: History, Philosophy and Logic.
Essays dedicated to Göran Sundholm
Giuseppe Primiero and Shahid Rahman, eds.

Volume 10
Witnessed Years. Essays in Honor of Petr Hájek
Petr Cintula, Zuzana Haniková and Vítězslav Švejdar, eds.

Volume 11
Heuristics, Probability and Causality. A Tribute to Judea Pearl
Rina Dechter, Hector Geffner and Joseph Y. Halpern, eds.

Volume 12
Dialectics, Dialogue and Argumentation. An Examination of Douglas Walton's Theories of Reasoning and Argument
Chris Reed and Christoher W. Tindale, eds.

Volume 13
Proofs, Categories and Computations. Essays in Honour of Grigori Mints
Solomon Feferman and Wilfried Sieg, eds.

Volume 14
Construction. Festschrift for Gerhard Heinzmann
Solomon Feferman and Wilfried Sieg, eds.

Volume 15
Hues of Philosophy. Essays in Memory of Ruth Manor
Anat Biletzki, ed.

Volume 16
Knowing, Reasoning and Acting. Essays in Honour of Hector J. Levesque.
Gerhard Lakemeyer and Sheila A. McIlraith, eds.

Volume 17
Logic without Frontiers. Festschrift for Walter Alexandre Carnielli on the occasion of his 60th birthday
Jean-Yves Beziau and Marcelo Esteban Coniglio, eds.

Volume 18
Insolubles and Consequences. Essays in Honour of Stephen Read.
Catarina Dutilh Novaes and Ole Thomassen Hjortland, eds.

Volume 18
From Quantification to Conversation. Festschrift for Robin Cooper on the occasion of his 65th birthday
Staffan Larsson and Lars Borin, eds

Tributes Series Editor
Dov Gabbay   dov.gabbay@kcl.ac.uk

From Quantification to Conversation
Festschrift for Robin Cooper
on the occasion of his 65th birthday

edited by
Staffan Larsson
and
Lars Borin

© Individual author and College Publications 2012. All rights reserved.

ISBN 978-1-84890-091-2

College Publications
Scientific Director: Dov Gabbay
Managing Director: Jane Spurr
Department of Computer Science
King's College London, Strand, London WC2R 2LS, UK

http://www.collegepublications.co.uk

Cover created by Laraine Welch
Printed by Lightning Source, Milton Keynes, UK

All rights reserved. No part of this publication may be reproduced, stored in a retrieval system or transmitted in any form, or by any means, electronic, mechanical, photocopying, recording or otherwise without prior permission, in writing, from the publisher.

Contents

Introduction *Staffan Larsson and Lars Borin*	1

Quantification and underspecification

Constant operators: Partial quantifiers *Dag Westerståhl*	11
Expressive completeness and computational efficiency for underspecified representations *Chris Fox and Shalom Lappin*	37
Storage in deterministic dependency parsing *Joakim Nivre*	59
Licensing by modification: The case of Brazilian Portuguese distributive-universal quantifiers *Esmeralda Vailati Negrão*	71

Formal semantics and logic

Quantification, the reprise content hypothesis, and type theory *Jonathan Ginzburg and Matthew Purver*	85
What is in a concept? How adjectives might help *Nick Braisby*	111
Situation types subatomically *Tim Fernando*	129
Robust VP ellipsis resolution in DR theory *Johan Bos*	145
The symbiosis between computational linguistics, logic and computer science *Bengt Nordström*	161

Language Technology

Example-based grammar writing 173
Aarne Ranta

Some general problems in machine translation of Swedish 193
noun phrases to English
Anna Sågvall Hein and Eva Pettersson

Computing word similarities for ontologies 213
Martin Volk, Hans Hjelm and Henrik Oxhammar

Objects and relations in the world of microbiology: 227
Information extraction from biological texts
Barbara Gawrońska

Conversation

Dialogue for one 253
Rodger Kibble

A question of cost 269
Ian Lewin

To be or not to be, isn't that a question? 281
Lars Ahrenberg

Attitude reports in spontaneous dialogue: Uncertainty, 297
politeness and filled pauses
Merle Horne

Modelling speech synthesis for human interaction 309
Rolf Carlson

Conversational Interactions: Capturing Dialogue Dynamics 325
Arash Eshghi, Julian Hough, Matthew Purver,
Ruth Kempson and Eleni Gregoromichelaki

Introduction

Staffan Larsson and Lars Borin

This collection of papers[1] offers an overview of current research in formal and computational linguistics with a focus on semantics, i.e., the study of meaning. The topics covered range from fairly abstract theorising about quantification phenomena in natural language to quite concrete issues in language technology and dialogue systems. This indicates the wide scope of formal and computational semantics, and also gives an indication of the historical development and shift in focus of formal semantics over the last three-or-so decades, since its modern origin in the work of Richard Montague in the early 1970s. In a development which could hardly have been predicted given its ivory-tower beginnings, formal semantics has recently started to become of practical (and thus commercial) interest, and is beginning to have effects on our everyday lives in the form of language technology.

Firstly, computational semantics has has recently been touted as a fundamental prerequisite to the next step in the development of the internet, the "Semantic Web" (see the contributions by Volk et al. and Gawrońska in this volume). Secondly, conversational human-computer interfaces (commonly referred to as *dialogue systems*) is a fast-growing sector in industry as well as in academia, and there is a general realisation that these systems need a proper account of semantics to move beyond the simple slot-filling dialogues of present-day commercial systems.

While the more abstract topics of early formal semantics has never quite dropped out of sight for academics, these recent developments have arguably lead to a resurgence of interest in the theoretical puzzles related to quantification and situational interpretation in natural language. Formal and computational semantics are thus very much alive, and the future looks bright.

There is an additional common thread running through this collection: The contributors are all colleagues, collaborators or/and former students of Robin Cooper, one of the leading figures in the field of formal and computational semantics. Hence, the present volume reflects Robin's wide range of interests in topics related to formal semantics, language technology, and dialogue systems. Robin's career is in many ways a reflection of the development of formal and computational semantics and language technology over the last three decades. The invention of so-called *Cooper storage* as a solution to the problem of underspecification of quantificational scope was one of his major early achievements, and from there he moved on to making important contributions to the tradition of Situation Semantics. In recent years he has contributed to the development of the *Information State Update* approach to dialogue management, just to mention a few of the highlights of his career.

Robin has always been careful to anchor his theorising in concrete examples, and in the move towards practical language technology he has combined an aptitude for clever solutions to abstract problems with a concern for their practical usefulness. This, together with his theoretical sophistication and his openness to new tools, technologies and theories, has set a great example for his students and collaborators. In joining forces to put this collection together, we wish to show our gratitude to Robin for the positive influence that his work has had on formal and computational semantics, as well as on language technology and dialogue systems research, and more specifically for the great positive influence that he has had on our own work in these areas.

This collection is divided into four sections. The first, *Quantification and underspecification*, contains four articles building on the work by Robin Cooper and others on underspecification and quantification in natural language.

Starting from the notion of "partial quantifiers" introduced in the seminal paper by Barwise and Cooper (1981), the article *Constant operators: Partial quantifiers* by Westerståhl uses simple type theory to investigate formally the notion of constancy, as part of an effort to understand the notion of a logical constant. Constancy is the idea that a logical operator "means the same" over different universes. Notions of constancy in various kinds of simple type theory are explored – are types functional (as in Montague grammar) or relational? Are they types of total or partial (as in Barwise and Cooper) objects?

In *Expressive completeness and computational efficiency for underspecified representations*, Chris Fox and Shalom Lappin follow Westerståhl in addressing underspecification using type theory, amd in particular, underspecified scope representations. There are serious problems with existing accounts in that they either suffer from expressive incompleteness, or generating the full set of scope readings results in combinatorial explosion. Operating in the framework of PCTC (Property Theory with Curry Typing), Fox and Lapping provide an account of underspecified scope which retains expressive completeness, yet reduces computational complexity, using so-called *filters*.

The remaining two papers in this section are primarily geared towards syntax than semantics. However, both an appreciation of the virtues of semantics as well as a concern with computational complexity continue in Joakim Nivre's article *Storage in deterministic dependency parsing*. The framework is Deterministic Dependency Parsing, and the problem is, as ever, ambiguity. The two naive strategies for dealing with ambiguity are (1) brute force enumeration, which leads to serious efficiency problems, and (2) deterministic disambiguation – resolve each ambiguity as it arises – which can lead to erroneous decisions because of early commitment. More sophisticated techniques avoid early commitment by representing possible interpretations without enumerating them. A well known example of such a technique from semantics is, of course, so-called "Cooper Storage" introduced by Cooper (1975). Nivre discusses a storage mechanism inspired by Cooper Storage which uses storage-like mechanisms to postpone certain disambiguation decisions. The goal of this research is to efficiently deal with structural ambiguity and underspecification.

The final paper of this section, by Negrão, examines the interaction between syntax and semantics in scope-ambiguity sentences in Brazilian Portuguese (BP). Negrão observes that modification by relative clauses tends to license structures that would otherwise be ungrammatical. Specifically, Negrão's article aims at understanding the contribution give by modification by a relative clause in the licensing of two different Distributive Quantifier Phrases of BP: those formed by *todo* (Eng. 'all' or 'every') and those formed by *cada* (Eng. 'each' or 'every'). Arguing against a purely syntactic analysis, Negrão argues that the observed differences can be accounted for by differences in the semantic contributions by *todo* and *cada*.

The theme of the second section, *Formal semantics and logic*, is rather more general than that of the first (and in fact can be said to properly subsume it).

The article *Quantification, the reprise content hypothesis, and type theory* by Jonathan Ginzburg and Matthew Purver provides a bridge between the two first sections of this book by placing scope ambiguity issues in a wider context of a formal semantics of dialogue. Based on evidence from dialogue, and in particular the so-called Reprise Content Hypothesis (RCH), they argue against the notion of Generalized Quantifiers and Montagovian higher-order properties of properties as NP denotations. Instead, they sketch an alternative account based on a type-theoretical framework including records. The RCH in a strong version says that a nominal fragment reprise question queries exactly the standard semantic content of the fragment being reprised. The RCH requires that we do not postulate any part of a semantic representation which cannot be observed via a reprise question.

In *What is in a concept? How adjectives might help* Nick Braisby takes an experimental approach to the issue of compositionality by investigating the semantics of non-intersective noun-noun combinations of English (*a fish frog*) and the (supposedly) intersective adjective-noun combinations (*a red car*). It is noted that not all adjective-noun combinations are intersective (*a potential leader, a beautiful dancer*). Braisby distinguishes three kinds of adjective-noun combinations: prototype affirming (*a yellow lemon*), prototype denying (*a blue lemon*) and prototype neutral (*a waxed lemon*). A further distinction is made between two kinds of interpretation – property mapping (intersective) interpretations, and relational (including transformational, e.g. *a brown banana*) interpretations. The hypothesis is that prototype affirming combinations yield predominantly property mapping interpretations, whereas prototype denying combinations yield relational interpretations. Incidentally, this work has interesting connections to Robin's recent work on word meaning, compositionality and the "generative lexicon".

Tim Fernando's article *Situation types subatomically* investigates Cooper's (1998, 2005) proposal to analyse NL semantics as types of situations. Fernando relates Cooper's type-theoretical formulation to "subatomic semantics", whose main hypothesis is that simple sentences of English contain subatomic quantification over events (Parsons 1990). In trying to bring out temporal matters essential to subatomic semantics, situations as structured objects, built from temporal formulas.

In *Robust VP ellipsis resolution in DR theory*, Johan Bos operates within the DRT framework, designed to extend the coverage of Montagovian formal semantics from single sentences to discourse. However, unlike most if not all work in "traditional" formal semantics, the focus is not on a constructed and restricted fragment but on wide coverage parsing of real text. The concrete problem dealt with in this article is VP ellipsis, as in *Carlo hates his boss and so does Marco*. While such sentences are typically argued to have one strict and one sloppy reading, inspection of real data shows the latter to be is very rare, and it is ignored in this analysis. Bos proposes a robust algorithm for VP ellipsis resolution, which includes VPE detection, antecedent location, and resolution.

Bengt Nordström takes a bird's-eye view in *The symbiosis between computational linguistics, logic and computer science*. Nordström regards logic as the mother of Computational Linguistics and Computer Science. Logicians were studying how to mechanically compute something long before we had modern computers, and computers are still based on the same architectural principles as Turing's ideas in Logic. Nordström also observes that Montague's view – taken from Logic – of English as a formal language has a correspondence in Computer Science, where Scott, Strachey and Plotkin borrowed ideas from Logic to analyse programming languages. Deduction rules and computation rules come in many disguises in Logic, Computational Linguistics and Computer Science.

The theme of the third section is *Language technology*. Language technology has been a major preoccupation of Robin's as head of the Swedish National Graduate School of Language Technology (GSLT).

The first article, *Example-based grammar writing* by Aarne Ranta, addresses problem of designing grammars for dialogue systems. This work requires three different kinds of knowledge: domain-specific vocabulary knowledge, practical knowledge of how to express things correctly in the language used, and finally theoretical knowledge of rules and formalisms for expressing syntactic rules. Ranta shows how the notion of *libraries* help in modularising expertise and simplifying the grammar design task. Still, some level of expertise in formal grammar is needed by domain vocabulary expert. This too can be alleviated through example-based grammar writing, where the author gives examples of sentences and the system generalises over phrases (mainly NPs) and learns general syntactic patterns. This minimises the need for the application grammar builder to write grammar rules by hand.

Some general problems in machine translation of Swedish noun phrases to English by Anna Sågvall Hein and Eva Pettersson explores rule-based machine translation of noun phrases from Swedish to English in technical text. Generally, definiteness is not affected by translation (true for 98% in the corpus). However, some NPs which are definite in Swedish are translated into indefinite NPs in English, e.g. *felkoderna* → 'fault codes'. This is especially true for certain contexts such as headings. The authors formalise transfer rules for NPs for shifting from definite to indefinite forms in certain contexts and show how these rules improve translation quality.

While both Ranta and Sågvall Hein and Pettersson used rule-based methods for language technology, statistical and hybrid approaches are utilised in *Computing word similarities for ontologies* by Martin Volk, Hans Hjelm and Henrik Oxhammar. An ontology can be defined as a resource representing the conceptual model underlying a certain domain. Ontologies are useful for many practical language technology tasks, e.g. Query expansion and Cross-language Information Retrieval (CLIR). A major problem, however, is the manual construction of ontologies. The goal of the research reported in this article is to facilitate ontology construction through ontology learning. In a first study, different ways of fleshing out a hand-coded ontology are compared. The task is to classify company profile texts from the web with regard to product type, and the baseline classifier uses the hand-coded Common Procurement Vocabulary (CPV). The authors compare the results using different automatically fleshed-out ontologies produced using different ways of computing word similarities.

In a second study, a new ontology is induced from a parallell corpus.

The theme of using hybrid approaches combining statistical and rule-based methods in information retrieval continues in *Objects and relations in the world of microbiology: Information extraction from biological texts* by Barbara Gawrońska. The motivation for language technological research in bioinformatics is that a large part of the accumulated knowledge in molecular biology is represented in NL texts. Gawrońska utilises text mining methods to integrate information from different sources, in the form of relations between biological objects. This involves several steps of processing, including named entity recognition, syntactic parsing, and semantic interpretation. Problematic constructions include long ambiguous coordinations with multiple conjunctions; in such cases, syntactic and (domain-specific) semantic knowledge turn out to be very useful. The semantic interpretation process is inspired by Situation semantics: matching situation described in the text against a standardized set of "situation types".

The final section of this festschrift takes up the theme of *Conversation*, to which Robin's research has become increasingly oriented over the last decade or so.

In *Dialogue for one*, Rodger Kibble explores the implications of adopting the slogan "Communication as the basis for rational interaction". Kibble shows how extended argumentative or explanatory monologue can be reconstructed as the outcome of an "inner dialogue", where some dialogue moves are implicit. On this account, the ability to reason requires the ability to participate in argumentative dialogue. Using an Information State Update (ISU) model of dialogue moves where the IS contains acknowledged, pending and disputed commitments, dialogue coherence and rhetorical relations between utterances are reconstructed as sequences of explicit and implicit dialogue moves.

Some themes in dialogue management are pondered by Ian Lewin in *A question of cost*. Lewin focuses on the problem of selecting the next dialogue move, i.e. of deciding what to do next, in the case where the system's previous questions was not answered but instead followed by unsolicited but relevant information from the user. A general method is to provide a preference ordering over all subsets of possible moves, and to choose the move which maximises value of some selection function. Lewin argues for taking into account the estimated costs of next moves when selecting moves, rather than using a static protocol of interaction. He also asks: what is the status of the ignored question? Is it rejected? Is a superordinate goal (subsuming the question) being pursued? Should it be popped off the question stack? This depends on several factors. Could it be used as context for an elliptical followup question? What can the system do? For example, can it choose to just acknowledge the user's response and see what the user does? This option should be included in set of possible next moves, according to Lewing. Finally, does unsolicited information or counter-questioning always indicate that the speaker does not know the answer, or is being uncooperative? No, according to Lewin. Selecting next moves on the basis of a preference ordering over a set (including not taking any intitative at all) may well lead to leaving many questions unanswered but nevertheless efficiently achieving the overall goal. Lewin proposes to explore these issues further in the ISU approach.

In *To be or not to be, isn't that a question?*, Lars Ahrenberg notes that while Ginzburg & Sag (2000) provide an HPSG analysis of English questions, they do not mention *alternative questions*, e.g. *Did Bo or Mo leave?* or *Did Bo leave or stay?*. Ahrenberg sketches an analysis of alternative questions as x-questions (wh-questions) plus a set of Answers Of Interest (AOI), thus generaling from the account of negotiative dialogue in Larsson (2002). This provides the basis for a refined analysis of polar questions, as it turns out that some polar questions are best analysed as polar alternative questions, e.g. *Are you coming or not?* and *Are you coming? Yes or no?* and even Hamlet's *To be or not to be...?*. Additionally, some (non-alternative) polar questions invite *accommodation* of an x-question (a framing question). While polar and alternative questions give rise to framing questions via accommodation, and propose one AOI, x-questions are framing questions, and do not propose an AOI.

While the three papers just discussed dwelled on issues of dialogue management, the next two papers are dedicated to the interplay between phonetics and conversation. In *Attitude reports in spontaneous dialogue: Uncertainty, politeness and filled pauses*, Merle Horne notes that propositional attitude reports have been studied in Situation Semantics and are important for the analysis of spontaneous discourse since they give important information about speaker's attitude to propositions. The attitude of *uncertainty* can be expressed by propositional attitude verbs, mood-related pragmatic particles and prosodic hedging devices. As an example of the latter, glottalized (creaky) filled pause typically expresses uncertainty. However, the uncertainty does not concern propositional content but rather regarding how to best express something. The creaky filled pause can thus function as a kind of *procedural* attitude report. (Non-glottalized filled pauses do not have this function.) Uncertainty regarding coding can depend on minimal common ground, which fits with the observation that creaky filled pauses often occur in conversation between strangers.

In *Modelling speech synthesis for human interaction*, Rolf Carlson presents two investigations of acoustic correlates to perceived upcoming utterance boundaries. Human-like speech includes natural breaks and disfluencies, and the goal of this research is the synthesis of human-like speech for use in dialogue systems. It has been shown that users prefer synthesis with a "prosodic profile" similar to their own. In a first study on human perception of upcoming boundaries, listener groups were able to detect upcoming boundaries based on acoustic and prosodic features rather than syntactic and semantic features. The second study was an experiment in the synthesis of disfluencies using KTH parametric synthesis, where variation in pause duration, final lengthening, creakiness, and F0 were modeled and synthesised. Combined effect of pause and final lengthening turned out to be the strongest cue to hsitation, while F0 and creakiness had some effect.

Following these two excursions into phonetics and conversation, the final paper in this collection discusses the relation between dialogue, grammar and parsing. In "Conversational Interactions: Capturing Dialogue Dynamics", Eshgi et. al. set out the case for combining the Type Theory with Records framework with Dynamic Syntax in a single model (DS-TTR). This framework allows incremental parsing into, and generation from, TTR record types. Interpretations for substrings of utterances can be accessed by dialogue managers, parsers and generators equally, allowing the articulation of syntactic and semantic dependencies across parser and generator modules. In the words of the authors, "with this move, the nesting of the language faculty into a coherent cognitive system at last becomes possible, opening up radical new perspectives on philosophy of language, psychology and cognition." What better way to end this festschrift than with this bold proclamation?

It is our very great pleasure to present this eminent collection of articles in celebration of Robin on the occasion of his sixty-fifth birthday.[2] Congratulations (again), Robin!

Notes

1. The editors wish to thank Robert Adesam for helping out with the LATEX typesetting of this volume.
2. Actually, an earlier version of this book, without the final chapter by Eshghi et. al., was presented to Robin in electronic format already on his sixtieth birthday. One might think that we are thus in breach of the rule that one should not give the same gift twice. However, we would argue that things are a bit more complicated than that. In TTR-inspired words, one could say the type corresponding to this book has two subtypes, and what is to count as "the same" book is a matter of semantic coordination and negotiation. We take this to sufficiently confuse matters so as to allow us to present this book as a different gift from the previous one.

Quantification and underspecification

Constant operators: Partial quantifiers

Dag Westerståhl

1. Introduction

This paper concerns a small part of a larger project to do with the notion of *logical constants*. A background idea is that this notion is not necessarily unitary, but contains distinct ingredients. One such ingredient is often called *topic neutrality*, and made precise in the form of requirements of *invariance* under various transformations between models. Such invariance has been the object of several recent studies (Feferman 1999, van Benthem 2002, Bonnay 2006) and is rather well understood. Another ingredient may be called *constancy*; in one version, it is the idea that a logical operator 'means the same' over different universes. It is less clear how this idea should be made precise, and the project mentioned deals with just that.

The goal is to treat operators of any *type*. By "type" we mean type in a simple type theory à la Church. There are several familiar versions of this theory, and in many cases it is just a matter of convenience which version one chooses. It seems, however, that notions of 'constancy' are somewhat sensitive to this choice. For example, does one use *relational* or *functional* types? Also, are they types of *total* or *partial* objects? To begin, at least, one needs to look at what 'constancy' could amount to in each of these cases. In particular, the introduction of partial objects appears to complicate matters. It may be that much of this complication is spurious or unnecessary, but if so, that is something that needs to be established.

First-order generalized quantifiers, or just *quantifiers*, are a paradigmatic kind of operators, well studied in logic as well as language (see, for example, Peters and Westerståhl 2006 for an overview). The issue of which of these operators are logical constants has often been raised: The logician's $\forall$ and $\exists$ are of course prime examples, but what about something like *most* or *each other*? Quantifiers are often presented in a relational framework, but some prefer a functional one, finding that it better reflects the compositional function-argument structure commonly ascribed to the syntax of natural languages. Usually, quantifiers are seen as total, but in their pioneering paper on generalized quantifiers in natural language, Barwise and Cooper (1981), who worked in a functional framework, actually used partial quantifiers; more precisely, quantifiers that were *undefined* for certain arguments.

This paper focuses on one aspect of what 'constancy' could mean for quantifiers in a partial framework, with a view to extend the results to (a) operators of other first-order types (such as the denotations of many adjectives), and eventually, (b) arbitrary types. More precisely, it focuses on the condition of *extension* (EXT), familiar from generalized quantifier theory. Since quantifiers are ubiquitous in logic and language, intuitions about them are stronger than in other cases, and might lead to insights about those cases. Of course, the insights may be negative: perhaps first-order quantifiers (i.e. quantifiers over individuals) form a very special class, and the senses in which they are constant will not transfer to other types. Some such issues will be discussed here.

Apart from Barwise and Cooper (1981), little has been written about partial quantifiers, and Barwise and Cooper did not deal with the issue of 'constancy'. Not did they use the full power of partial quantifiers, as partial functions whose *arguments* may also be partial. The observations in the present paper are preliminary and exploratory. I first present and compare some main versions of simple type theory, and then discuss how quantifiers fare in these systems.

2. Versions of simple type theory

A type theory usually comes with (i) a set of *types*, (ii) a definition of the *objects* of the various types, (iii) a *language* in which one can talk about these objects, and (iv) a *logic* for this language, described both semantically in terms of what its expressions *denote*, and proof-theoretically in terms of a formal deduction system for how certain of these expressions can be *inferred* from others. Here I will only be concerned with the first two of these aspects, and will therefore talk of *type systems* rather than type theories.

The use of type theory in model-theoretic semantics (aspects (i) – (iii) above) began with Montague (see Montague 1974). There are the basic types e of *individuals* and t of *truth values*. Montague wanted to handle *intensional* phenomena and so he had another type s for possible worlds or *indices*, which however was not quite on a par with the other basic types. His type theory, and the accompanying language and intensional logic *IL* did what he wanted them to do, but from a mathematical point of view they had some idiosyncracies (which, for example, resulted in the fact the Church-Rosser theorem did not hold for *IL*). Indeed, Barwise and Cooper (1981) said that Montague Grammar "looks a bit like a Rube Goldberg machine" (p. 204). It was later realized that by using a more standard format of simple type theory, only with an extra basic type s, the idiosyncracies disappear but the usefulness for semantics remains (cf. Gallin 1975, van Benthem and Doets 1983, Muskens 1989a). Another observation was that s played little role in parts of the theory — the extensional part — and in practice most of the theory of quantifiers developed within the Montague framework used only the extensional part.

The type systems to be considered here all have e and (when needed) t as basic types. However, nothing seriously turns on that; everything we say is adaptable to the presence of other basic types.

2.1. Universal operators

Let Θ be a type system where the set T^Θ of types is generated inductively from the basic e and (possibly) t. For each universe M, $M_e^\Theta = M$ and M_t^Θ is a fixed set of truth values (usually $\{T,F\}$). Further, M generates for each $\tau \in T^\Theta$ (by a definition following the one for the types) the *domain* M_τ^Θ of objects of type τ. (We leave off the superscript $^\Theta$ whenever possible.)

> **Definition**: Let $\tau \in T^\Theta$. A *universal operator in* Θ *of type* τ is a function(al) u that with each universe M associates a unique object u_M in M_τ^Θ.

Various natural language expressions, in particular determiners and noun phrases, are naturally taken to denote universal operators. It is for such operators that the issue of 'constancy', or logicality, is raised.

2.2. Standard functional type systems

Let TFT be the type system whose types are given by

(a1) a basic type (e and t) is a type

(a2) if σ and τ are types, so is $\langle \sigma, \tau \rangle$

and the corresponding objects by (dropping the superscript ^{TFT})

(b1) $M_t = \{T, F\}$

(b2) $M_e = M$

(b3) $M_{\langle \sigma, \tau \rangle}$ = the set of all total functions from M_σ to $M_\tau = [M_\sigma \longrightarrow M_\tau]$

This is probably the most widely used (simple) type system. Sets and relations are rendered as characteristic functions. Note that all functions are unary. To deal with functions of several arguments one uses *currying*, based on the natural bijection between $[X \times Y \longrightarrow Z]$ and $[X \longrightarrow [Y \longrightarrow Z]]$. However, curried types tend to get rather complex, and moreover the bijection fails for *partial* functions (see Muskens 1989b), to be considered later. Therefore, we focus on a variant of TFT that allows multi-argument functions; call this system TFT$^+$:[1]

(c1) a basic type is a type

(c2) If $\sigma_1, \ldots, \sigma_n$ and τ are types, so is $\langle \sigma_1 \ldots \sigma_n, \tau \rangle$ $(n \geq 1)$

(d1) $M_e = M$

(d2) $M_t = \{T, F\}$

(d3) $M_{\langle \sigma_1 \ldots \sigma_n, \tau \rangle} = [M_{\sigma_1} \times \cdots \times M_{\sigma_n} \longrightarrow M_\tau]$

Every type τ in TFT$^+$ can be uniquely written as

$$\tau = \langle \sigma_{11} \ldots \sigma_{1k_1}, \ldots, \langle \sigma_{n1} \ldots \sigma_{nk_n}, \tau_0 \rangle \ldots \rangle$$

where τ_0 is e or t $(n \geq 0)$. Following the terminology in van Benthem (1989) (for TFT), we call τ *individual* if $\tau_0 = e$ and *Boolean* if $\tau_0 = t$. Boolean types are relations but their arguments need not be; cf. $\langle \langle e, e \rangle, t \rangle$. The *strictly relational* types of TFT$^+$ are defined (inductively) as follows:

Definition: τ is *strictly relational* iff τ is either primitive or of the form $\langle \sigma_1 \ldots \sigma_n, t \rangle$, where each σ_i is strictly relational.

(e is included for convenience here.) It is easily seen that τ is strictly relational if and only if no occurrence of a right bracket $\rangle$ in τ is immediately preceded by an occurrence of e or of another right bracket.

We end by noting the following characteristic fact about TFT$^+$; it does not hold for relational or partial types (see below).

Fact 1
If $\tau \neq \tau'$ in TFT$^+$, then $M_\tau \cap M_{\tau'} = \emptyset$, provided the truth values do not belong to any M_σ except M_t.

Proof. Induction. It is clear that

$$\tau \neq e \implies M_\tau \cap M_e = \emptyset$$

$$\tau \neq t \implies M_\tau \cap M_t = \emptyset$$

For the induction step, suppose $f \in M_\tau \cap M_{\tau'}$, where $\tau = \langle \sigma_1 \ldots \sigma_n, \tau_0 \rangle$ and $\tau' = \langle \sigma'_1 \ldots \sigma'_n, \tau'_0 \rangle$. It follows that

$$dom(f) = M_{\sigma_1} \times \cdots \times M_{\sigma_n} = M_{\sigma'_1} \times \cdots \times M_{\sigma'_n} \neq \emptyset$$

and thus $M_{\sigma_i} = M_{\sigma'_i}$, $1 \leq i \leq n$. By induction hypothesis, $\sigma_i = \sigma'_i$, $1 \leq i \leq n$. Now take $a \in dom(f)$. Then

$$f(a) \in M_{\tau_0} \cap M_{\tau'_0}$$

Again by induction hypothesis, $\tau_0 = \tau'_0$, and so $\tau = \tau'$. □

2.3. Relational types

Although Montague Grammar uses a functional type system, many of its operators, and in particular quantifiers, have an essentially relational character. More exactly, their functional types (in TFT$^+$) are strictly relational in the above sense. Muskens (1989a) concludes from this and other arguments that Montague Grammar is more simply formulated in a framework that is relational by definition. Let RT have the following types and objects:

(a1) The only primitive type is e.

(a2) If $\tau_1, \ldots, \tau_n$ are types ($n \geq 0$), so is $(\tau_1, \ldots, \tau_n)$.

(b1) $M_e = M$

(b2) $M_{(\tau_1, \ldots, \tau_n)} = P(M_{\tau_1} \times \cdots \times M_{\tau_n})$

Here it is stipulated that the cartesian product of the empty sequence () of sets is $\{\emptyset\}$. Thus, $M_{()} = P(\{\emptyset\}) = \{\emptyset, \{\emptyset\}\} = \{0, 1\} = \{F, T\}$, so () corresponds to the type t in TFT.

It is not hard to establish that there is an isomorphism between RT and the strictly relational part of TFT$^+$ (cf. Muskens 1989b):

Fact 2
The mapping π from the RT-types to strictly relational TFT$^+$-types given by

$$\begin{cases} \pi(e) & = e \\ \pi(()) & = t \\ \pi((\tau_1, \ldots, \tau_n)) & = \langle \pi(\tau_1) \ldots \pi(\tau_n), t \rangle \quad (n \geq 1) \end{cases}$$

is a bijection. Moreover, it extends naturally to bijections π_M from M_τ^{RT} to $M_{\pi(\tau)}^{TFT^+}$, in such a way that for $R \in M_{(\tau_1,\ldots,\tau_n)}^{RT}$ and $a_i \in M_{\tau_i}^{RT}$,

$$(a_1,\ldots,a_n) \in R \iff \pi_M(R)(\pi_M(a_1),\ldots,\pi_M(a_1)) = T$$

Accordingly, π further extends to a bijection from universal operators u in RT to universal operators in TFT$^+$ over strictly relational types, letting

$$\pi(u)_M = \pi_M(u_M)$$

The mappings π_M should really be indexed for types as well, writing $\pi_{M,\tau}$, but we leave that index out for perspicuity. To see the need for it, note that the domains in RT are *not* in general disjoint; for example $\emptyset$ belongs to all M_τ^{RT} for $\tau \neq e$, $\{\emptyset\}$ belongs to $M_{((e))}^{RT}$, $M_{(((e)))}^{RT}$, etc. So π_M maps the empty set to different objects depending on which type we are considering; more exactly, to the 'empty' characteristic function in that type. But this does not prevent each $\pi_{M,\tau}$ from being a bijection.

2.4. Going partial

Muskens (1989a) argues that partiality naturally belongs to a formal semantical framework; the most obvious reasons coming from apparent truth value gaps and lack of denotation of certain terms. There are also purely conceptual advantages.

For one example, take the denotation of the predicate *prime* (number). Arguably, only natural numbers can be prime or non-prime; there is something amiss with asking, for example, if the dog Fido is prime. We could of course introduce a new basic type for the natural numbers, but if we prefer to stick with e and t (while treating treat numbers as individuals, not sets), another option is to stipulate that the set $\mathbb{N}$ of numbers is the 'range of significance' of the predicate *prime*, or, more precisely, that in each universe of discourse M, that range is the set of numbers *in M*.

Similarly, consider the *successor function*, $S(n) = n+1$, taken to be of type $\langle e,e \rangle$. This function is only defined for natural numbers, so in an arbitrary universe M, S_M is naturally taken to be a partial function. Its domain is not quite the set of numbers in M; rather

$$dom(S_M) = \{n \in M \cap \mathbb{N} : n+1 \in M\}$$

(Not only the arguments but also the values must belong to M.)

How can we modify a type system to take care of partiality? In RT, it is fairly clear what to do. A predicate generally gets a *positive* and a *negative extension*, i.e. two sets P^+ and P^- of objects of the appropriate type. Their union is the range of significance; in the example above, P^+ is the set of primes in that range, and P^- the set of non-primes; Fido belongs to neither.

In full generality, let (following Muskens 1989a) a *partial relation* be a pair of ordinary relations, the first member of which is its *positive part*, or *extension*, and the second its *negative part*, or *anti-extension*. In the corresponding type system, which we call PRT, types are as in RT but the objects of each type are defined as follows:

(a1) $M_e = M$

(a2) $M_{\langle \tau_1,\ldots,\tau_n \rangle} = (P(M_{\tau_1} \times \cdots \times M_{\tau_n}))^2$

A partial relation in $M_{\langle \tau_1,\ldots,\tau_n \rangle}$ is *coherent* iff its negative and positive parts are disjoint, and *classical* iff its negative part is the complement of its positive part. Let PRT-3 be the version of PRT which constrains partial relations to be coherent, and PRT-2 the one which constrains them to be classical (the choice of labels will become clear below). RT is clearly isomorphic to PRT-2.

For the functional type systems, there are essentially two ways to 'go partial': either consider partial functions instead of total ones, or keep total functions but add an extra truth value. Modifying TFT^+ in the first way is extremely simple: just take the set of all partial functions from X to Y instead, which we will denote $[X \hookrightarrow Y]$. That is, PFT^+ is the type system which has the same types as TFT^+, and whose objects are given by:

(c1) $M_e = M$

(c2) $M_t = \{T, F\}$

(c3) $M_{\langle \sigma_1 \ldots \sigma_n, \tau \rangle} = [M_{\sigma_1} \times \cdots \times M_{\sigma_n} \hookrightarrow M_\tau]$

This will be our main candidate here for a partial version of functional type theory.[2]

Note that distinct domains in PFT^+ are not disjoint, since every non-primitive type now contains a *null object*: the function (of the type in question) with empty domain, which can be identified with the empty set. This must of course not be confused with the various (total) characteristic functions of the empty set.

Fact 3
For all τ, $M_\tau^{TFT^+} \subseteq M_\tau^{PFT^+}$.

Proof. Induction. The base step is immediate. Consider $\langle \sigma_1 \ldots \sigma_n, \tau \rangle$ and suppose $M_{\sigma_i}^{TFT^+} \subseteq M_{\sigma_i}^{PFT^+}$, $1 \leq i \leq n$, and $M_{\tau}^{TFT^+} \subseteq M_{\tau}^{PFT^+}$. An object F in $M_{\langle \sigma_1 \ldots \sigma_n, \tau \rangle}^{TFT^+}$ is a *total* function from $M_{\sigma_1}^{TFT^+} \times \cdots \times M_{\sigma_n}^{TFT^+}$ to $M_{\tau}^{TFT^+}$. Thus, F is a *partial* function from $M_{\sigma_1}^{PFT^+} \times \cdots \times M_{\sigma_n}^{PFT^+}$ to $M_{\tau}^{PFT^+}$ (cf. note 2). □

Corollary 4
Every universal operator in TFT^+ is also a universal operator in PFT^+.

We may now expect PRT to correspond to the strictly relational part of PFT^+. Before looking at this, however, we should consider the other way of partializing TFT^+, i.e. by introducing extra truth values. Actually, there are two ways to go about this. Let TFT_3^+ be just as TFT^+ except that

$$M_t = \{T, F, N\}$$

and let TFT_4^+ be like TFT^+ except that

$$M_t = \{T, F, N, B\}$$

(The notation is from Belnap 1977; 'N' stands for 'neither' and 'B' for 'both'.)

The main idea, of course, is that instead of saying that a function F with values in M_t is *undefined* for a certain argument a, we stipulate that $F(a) = N$ (or $F(a) = B$). Note that this works only for functions with values in M_t. More generally, it extends to the strictly relational part of TFT^+, but not to a type like $\langle e, e \rangle$. But what about the fourth truth value?

TFT_3^+ and TFT_4^+ essentially commit us to a 3-valued or 4-valued logic, respectively. It turns out that for many purposes, the 4-valued version is quite natural, and mathematically more elegant. This can be seen already from PRT. In the general case, a partial relation splits the domain into *four* parts; only if we add the coherence requirement do we get three.[3]

Muskens (1989a) gives a clear and informative account of 3- and 4-valued logic, and the generalization to type theory. In particular, he shows that, as one would expect, there is a tight connection between PRT and the (strictly) relational part of TFT_4^+.[4]

It should be fairly obvious by now how to map (isomorphically) the objects in M_{τ}^{PRT} to the the objects in $M_{\pi(\tau)}^{TFT_4^+}$; we omit the details. Likewise, one sees how PRT-3 maps isomorphically onto the strictly relational part of TFT_3^+.

Note also that Fact 1 holds (with the same proof) for TFT_3^+ and TFT_4^+.

Now, what about partial sets and relations in PFT^+? If we restrict attention to *coherent* relations, they are already there; more exactly, their *partial characteristic functions* are. The positive part of such a relation is mapped to T, the negative part to F, and the mapping is *undefined* on the remaining part. It is easy to see that in this way one obtains an isomorphism between PRT-3 and the strictly relational part of TFT_3^+. Similarly, the strictly relational part of TFT_3^+ and PFT^+ are isomorphic; we omit details.

PFT^+ admits a 3-valued logic but doesn't necessitate one. Of course one needs to make a decision about what to make of a sentence "*c* is *P*" when *c* denotes an object for which the characteristic function denoted by *P* is undefined. Farmer (1990) stipulates that the sentence is false in this case (thus preserving a 2-valued logic), arguing that this fits best with *mathematical* practice.[5] Since our concern is type systems rather than type theory, we shall not pursue this further here.

2.5. Summing up

We have looked at a variety of similar but not equivalent formulations of simple type theory. Which of these one prefers can be a matter of usefulness for the purpose at hand, but also a matter of taste. In the context of the present paper, the following considerations can be made:

1. We are eventually interested not only in the (strictly) relational types but also in the purely functional types, such as $\langle e, e \rangle$.

2. As to partial relations, the coherence constraint seems natural.

3. One main source of intuition are generalized quantifiers, which are relational.

Therefore, among partial systems we focus on PFT^+, and among total ones, RT and TFT^+.

3. Monotonicity and related properties

Let Θ be a type system of the kind considered here. On issue that turns out to be important to the matter of 'constancy' (but is rarely considered in the literature, as far as I know), is to what extent the domains of a given type τ can *overlap* for different universes of individuals. In particular, if you extend the universe (of discourse), do you then also extend the corresponding domain M_τ^Θ? If you do, we say that τ is *monotone*. The main result in this section is a characterization of the monotone types for each of the type systems in section 2. We use the following terminology.

Definition: A type τ in a type system Θ is

(a) *monotone* iff $M \subseteq M'$ implies $M_\tau^\Theta \subseteq M_\tau'^\Theta$;

(b) *distinct* iff $M \neq M'$ implies $M_\tau^\Theta \neq M_\tau'^\Theta$;

(c) *disjoint* iff $M \neq M'$ implies $M_\tau^\Theta \cap M_\tau'^\Theta = \emptyset$.

For example, we have seen that types in RT are not disjoint, since each domain (except M_e) contains the empty set. We need one more

Definition: A type τ in a type system Θ is *truth-functional* if (the expression) τ does not contain e.

The domain of a truth-functional type does not depend on M, so these types are trivially monotone and non-distinct.

Theorem 5 *All types in RT, PRT, PRT-3, and PFT$^+$ are monotone. All non-truth-functional types in these systems are distinct.*

Proof. Use induction. Obviously, t and e are monotone. Among the relational systems, consider PRT (the others are similar). Suppose $M \subseteq M'$. If (dropping the superscript) $M_{\tau_i} \subseteq M'_{\tau_i}$, $1 \leq i \leq n$, and $(R_1, R_2) \in M_{(\tau_1,\ldots,\tau_n)}$, then

$$R_j \subseteq M_{\tau_1} \times \cdots \times M_{\tau_n} \subseteq M'_{\tau_1} \times \cdots \times M'_{\tau_n}$$

$j = 1, 2$. Thus $(R_1, R_2) \in M'_{(\tau_1,\ldots,\tau_n)}$.

For PFT$^+$, consider $\langle \sigma_1 \ldots \sigma_n, \tau \rangle$. $F \in M_{\langle \sigma_1 \ldots \sigma_n, \tau \rangle}$ is a partial function from $M_{\sigma_1} \times \cdots \times M_{\sigma_n}$ to M_τ. If $M \subseteq M'$ then, by induction hypothesis, $M_{\sigma_i} \subseteq M'_{\sigma_i}$, $1 \leq i \leq n$, and $M_\tau \subseteq M'_\tau$. Therefore, F is a partial function from $M'_{\sigma_1} \times \cdots \times M'_{\sigma_n}$ to M'_τ.

This proves the first claim of the theorem. For the second claim, consider again the relational type systems first. e is trivially distinct, and it is clearly enough to show that

$$M_{(\sigma_1,\ldots,\sigma_n)} = M'_{(\sigma_1,\ldots,\sigma_n)} \text{ implies that } M_{\sigma_i} = M'_{\sigma_i} \text{ for } 1 \leq i \leq n$$

for all RT-types $\sigma_1, \ldots, \sigma_n$. Consider PRT; the other cases are similar. Fix i between 1 and n and suppose $(R_{i1}, R_{i2}) \in M_{\sigma_i}$. Take any $(R_{j1}, R_{j2}) \in M_{\sigma_j}$ for $1 \leq j \leq n$, $j \neq i$. Then

$$((R_{11}, R_{12}), \ldots, (R_{n1}, R_{n2})) \in M_{\sigma_1} \times \cdots \times M_{\sigma_n}$$

Thus

$$\{((R_{11}, R_{12}), \ldots, (R_{n1}, R_{n2}))\} \in M_{(\sigma_1,\ldots,\sigma_n)} = M'_{(\sigma_1,\ldots,\sigma_n)}$$

It follows that $(R_{i1}, R_{i2}) \in M'_{\sigma_i}$. This shows that $M_{\sigma_i} \subseteq M'_{\sigma_i}$, and by a symmetric argument we see that $M'_{\sigma_i} \subseteq M_{\sigma_i}$.

For PFT$^+$ one shows instead that

$$M_{\langle \sigma_1 \ldots \sigma_n, \tau \rangle} = M'_{\langle \sigma_1 \ldots \sigma_n, \tau \rangle} \text{ implies } M_{\sigma_i} = M'_{\sigma_i} \text{ for } 1 \leq i \leq n, \text{ and } M_\tau = M'_\tau.$$

The proof of this is similar. □

This result fails for PRT-2 (since the complement of a relation increases when the universe is extended). But that is an artifact of attempting to present RT in the format of PRT. In practice one would use RT instead.

The situation as regards monotonicity is very different in the total functional type systems. We need one final

Definition: A TFT$^+$-type τ is *extended truth-functional* if it is either truth-functional or of the form

(1) $\langle \sigma_{11} \ldots \sigma_{1k_1}, \ldots, \langle \sigma_{n1} \ldots \sigma_{nk_n}, e \rangle \ldots \rangle$

with each σ_{ij} truth-functional. (This includes the case $n = 0$, i.e. $\tau = e$.)

Theorem 6 *The monotone types in TFT$^+$, TFT$_3^+$, and TFT$_4^+$ are exactly the extended truth-functional types. All other types are disjoint. The same holds for TFT and its 3- and 4-valued variants.*

Proof. The claim for TFT and its variants follows from the one for TFT$^+$ and its variants by restricting attention to TFT-types, so we can focus on types in TFT$^+$. The following argument works for any one of TFT$^+$, TFT$_3^+$, and TFT$_4^+$. Clearly, a truth-functional type τ is monotone, since then M_τ is independent of M. Suppose τ has the form (1), where each σ_{ij} is truth-functional. An element F of M_τ can be seen (using currying!) as a function from the product

$$M_{\sigma_{11}} \times \cdots \times M_{\sigma_{nk_n}}$$

to M. If $M \subseteq M'$, then $M_{\sigma_{ij}} = M'_{\sigma_{ij}}$ for each i, j, since σ_{ij} is truth-functional, and it follows that $F \in M'_\tau$. So τ is monotone, and we have verified the first part of the claim. To prove second part, we start with a number of observations:

(2) If at least one of the τ_i is distinct, then $\langle \tau_1 \ldots \tau_n, \sigma \rangle$ is disjoint for any type σ.

The assumption entails that if $M \neq M'$, then $M_{\tau_1} \times \cdots \times M_{\tau_n} \neq M'_{\tau_1} \times \cdots \times M'_{\tau_n}$. But then, if $f \in M_{\langle \tau_1 \ldots \tau_n, \sigma \rangle}$ and $g \in M'_{\langle \tau_1 \ldots \tau_n, \sigma \rangle}$, $dom(f) \neq dom(g)$, so $f \neq g$.

(3) If τ is distinct, then $\langle \sigma_1 \ldots \sigma_n, \tau \rangle$ is distinct for any types $\sigma_1, \ldots, \sigma_n$.

To see this, take $b \in M_\tau - M'_\tau$. There is some $f \in M_{\langle \sigma_1 \ldots \sigma_n, \tau \rangle}$ such that for some $a \in M_{\sigma_1} \times \cdots \times M_{\sigma_n}$, $f(a) = b$. Then $f \notin M'_{\langle \sigma_1 \ldots \sigma_n, \tau \rangle}$.

(4) If τ is disjoint, then $\langle \sigma_1 \ldots \sigma_n, \tau \rangle$ is disjoint for any types $\sigma_1, \ldots, \sigma_n$.

This is because a function in $M_{\langle \sigma_1 \ldots \sigma_n, \tau \rangle}$ and a function in $M'_{\langle \sigma_1 \ldots \sigma_n, \tau \rangle}$ cannot have common values (since τ is disjoint), and so cannot be identical.

(5) τ is distinct if and only if it is not truth-functional.

Proof: Clearly truth-functional types are not distinct. In the other direction, use induction over τ. If $\tau = e$ it is distinct. Suppose $\tau = \langle \sigma_1 \ldots \sigma_n, \tau_0 \rangle$. Since τ is assumed not to be truth-functional, at least one of $\sigma_1 \ldots \sigma_n$ and τ_0 is not truth-functional, and hence distinct, by induction hypothesis. But then it follows from (2) and (3) that τ is distinct. This proves (5).

Now we can prove the second part of the proposition. Every type τ has the form

$$\langle \sigma_{11} \ldots \sigma_{1k_1}, \ldots, \langle \sigma_{n1} \ldots \sigma_{nk_n}, \tau_0 \rangle \ldots \rangle$$

where τ_0 is either e or t. If each σ_{ij} is truth-functional, then τ is extended truth-functional, and hence monotone by the first part of the proof. Suppose instead that some σ_{ij} is not truth-functional, and hence distinct, by (5). Then

$$\sigma = \langle \sigma_{i1} \ldots \sigma_{ik_i}, \ldots, \langle \sigma_{n1} \ldots \sigma_{nk_n}, \tau_0 \rangle \ldots \rangle$$

is disjoint by (2). Therefore, $\langle \sigma_{i-11} \ldots \sigma_{i-1k_{i-1}}, \sigma \rangle$ is disjoint by (4). Repeating this argument, it follows that τ is disjoint. This completes the proof. □

4. EXT for standard quantifiers and beyond

The quantifiers we consider are first-order in the sense that they quantify over individuals (*not* in the sense of being definable in first-order logic!). More generally, let the *level* of a (functional or relational) type be the maximal number of *nestings* of angle brackets, or parentheses, that occur in it. Then quantifiers have level 2. Lindström (1966) introduced a practical type system tailor-made for quantifiers, which is still normally used in this context, but here we shall stick to relational or functional types as before. Thus, let the *first-order relational types* be those of the form $\langle e \ldots e, t \rangle$ (in TFT$^+$ or PFT$^+$) or $(e \ldots e)$ (in RT). A *quantifier* is then a universal operator of type $\langle \sigma_1 \ldots \sigma_n, t \rangle$, or $(\sigma_1 \ldots \sigma_n)$, where each σ_i is a first-order relational type (in the respective system).

For standard quantifiers, there is a familiar notion of 'constancy' over varying universes, usually called *extension* or EXT. It says that if you extend M to M', the quantifier remains the same on arguments over M. For example, it rules out a quantifier meaning *some* on universes with less that 10 elements and *every* on other universes. In fact, EXT is easily defined for arbitrary types in RT:

Definition: A universal operator u of type $(\sigma_1, \ldots, \sigma_n)$ is EXT if $M \subseteq M'$ implies that $u_M = u_{M'} \upharpoonright M$ $[= u_{M'} \cap (M_{\sigma_1} \times \cdots \times M_{\sigma_n})]$.

This works because RT-types are monotone. Since RT is isomorphic to the strictly relational part of TFT$^+$, EXT is defined for arbitrary strictly relational types in TFT$^+$ as well. But note that in TFT$^+$ it is almost *never* the case that $u_M = u_{M'} \upharpoonright M$, in the sense of ordinary function restriction, since the arguments of u_M are functions with domain M (when u is a quantifier), whereas $u_{M'}$ has arguments with domain M' (cf. Fact 1). The reformulation of EXT for strictly relational types becomes clumsier in TFT$^+$, precisely because types in TFT$^+$ are not monotone.

Eventually we want to generalize in three directions from the case of quantifiers: (1) to arbitrary (strictly) relational types (for EXT this was done above), (2) to other functional types, and (3) to partial types. It is then convenient to take the functional type systems as a starting-point, even when dealing with quantifiers. If we need to go back to the relational case (to RT) we use the mapping π from Fact 2.

Here our focus is on (3). Remaining with the types of quantifiers, we consider the corresponding partial objects. That is, we look at universal operators of these types in PFT$^+$, or in other words, *partial quantifiers*.

5. Partial quantifiers

A partial quantifier q of type $\langle \sigma_1 \ldots \sigma_n, t \rangle$ may exhibit partiality in two ways: q_M may itself be a partial (characteristic) function, and it may take partial (characteristic) functions as arguments, i.e. the domain of q_M could be the whole $M_{\sigma_1}^{\text{PFT}^+} \times \cdots \times M_{\sigma_n}^{\text{PFT}^+}$ (or any subset of it). As noted, Barwise and Cooper (1981) considered the first kind of partiality. A quantifier like *the three* was only defined for those (characteristic functions of) subsets of M having exactly three elements. The intuition was that a sentence like *The three boys failed the exam* has no truth value unless there are exactly three boys in the (discourse) universe. For now, however, we must allow both kinds of partiality. To simplify notation we often consider the case of type $\langle ee,t\rangle$ below (type $((e,e))$ in RT, or $\langle 2\rangle$ in the standard typing of quantifiers), but everything we say generalizes to arbitrary quantifier types (and some of it to arbitrary strictly relational types).

Even if our main objects are characteristic functions, it is convenient to have a notation for the sets they correspond to. The following definition is formulated for the case of $\langle ee,t\rangle$ but works for any first-order relational type. For $f \in M_{\langle ee,t\rangle}^{\text{PFT}^+}$, let

(6) $f^{+M} = \{(a,b) \in M^2 : f(a,b) = T\}$
(7) $f^{-M} = \{(a,b) \in M^2 : f(a,b) = F\}$

f^{+M} and f^{-M} together determine f. That is, we have the following

Fact 7
If $f^{+M} = g^{+M'}$ and $f^{-M} = g^{-M'}$, then $f = g$ (and hence $dom(f) \subseteq (M \cap M')^2$).

Experience with partial quantifiers in the full sense seems limited, but one obvious source is 'partial versions' of already familiar total quantifiers.

5.1. Total quantifiers as partial quantifiers

By Corollary 4, an ordinary total quantifier Q (in TFT$^+$) already *is* a quantifier in PFT$^+$. The switch to PFT$^+$ is a change of perspective on the *same* object. What does this switch amount to for EXT?

Roughly, EXT in TFT$^+$ says that, for arguments f of Q_M, the universe outside f^{+M} is irrelevant. Using the *same* condition in PFT$^+$ we get the following property:

>**Definition:** q is p-EXT^{gq,s} if, whenever $f \in dom(q_M)$, $g \in dom(q_{M'})$, and $f^{+M} = g^{+M'}$, it holds that $q_M(f) = q_{M'}(g)$.[6]

(p' stands for 'partial', 'gq' for 'generalized quantifier', and 's' for strong; cf. below.) One easily sees that we have:

Fact 8
A quantifier in TFT$^+$ is EXT if and only if it is p-EXT^{gq,s} as an operator in PFT$^+$.

However, in the partial case it seems at least as natural to consider the weaker condition that everything outside f^{+M} and f^{-M} is irrelevant:

Definition: q is p-EXT^{gq} if, whenever $f \in dom(q_M)$, $g \in dom(q_{M'})$, $f^{+M} = g^{+M'}$, and $f^{-M} = g^{-M'}$, it holds that $q_M(f) = q_{M'}(g)$.

Using the fact that f^{+M} and f^{-M} determine f we can find a simpler formulation of this requirement:

Fact 9
q is p-EXT^{gq} if and only if it has the following property:

(8) *If $f \in dom(q_M) \cap dom(q_{M'})$ and $M \subseteq M'$, then $q_M(f) = q_{M'}(f)$.*

Proof. That (8) follows from p-EXT^{gq} is immediate. In the other direction, given the assumptions in p-EXT^{gq}, use Fact 7, and apply (8) to M and $M \cup M'$, and to M' and $M \cup M'$. □

(8) no longer mentions f^{+M} or f^{-M}. It is thus a putative formulation of EXT for arbitrary types in PFT$^+$. Indeed, it is a slight strengthening of what is perhaps the most obvious candidate for EXT in a partial functional framework:

Definition A universal operator u of type $\langle \sigma, \tau \rangle$ in PFT$^+$ is p-EXT if $M \subseteq M'$ entails $u_M = u_{M'} \restriction M$.[7]

p-EXT is stronger than (8), since $u_M = u_{M'} \restriction M$ entails that $dom(u_M) \subseteq dom(u_{M'})$, which does not follow from (8). As an example, consider, the successor function S mentioned earlier, taken as a universal operator of type $\langle e, e \rangle$, such that for each M, $dom(S_M) = \{n \in M \cap \mathbb{N} : n+1 \in M\}$. S is clearly p-EXT.

But we have already observed that a condition like p-EXT can never hold in a total functional framework. More precisely, we have:

Fact 10
For any universal operator in TFT$^+$ of type $\langle\langle \tau_1 \tau_2, t \rangle, t \rangle$ (where τ_1, τ_2 are strictly relational), when seen as an operator in PFT$^+$, p-EXT^{gq} trivially holds. Also, p-EXT trivially fails, except when the type is truth-functional.

Proof. Suppose $M \subseteq M'$. If Q is such an operator, $dom(Q_M) = M^{TFT^+}_{\langle \tau_1 \tau_2, t \rangle}$, and $dom(Q_{M'}) = M'^{TFT^+}_{\langle \tau_1 \tau_2, t \rangle}$. Now consider two cases.

Case 1: At least one of τ_1 and τ_2 is not truth-functional. Then, since both are strictly relational, it follows that the type $\langle \tau_1 \tau_2, t \rangle$ is not extended truth-functional. Hence, by Theorem 6, if $f \in dom(Q_M) \cap dom(Q_{M'})$, then $M = M'$, and p-EXT^{gq} holds trivially. Similarly, if M is a proper subset of M', it can never hold that $u_M = u_{M'} \restriction M$, so p-EXT fails.

Case 2: Both τ_1 and τ_2 are truth-functional. Then the arguments of Q_M do not depend on M at all, so p-EXT^{gq} again holds trivially (use the formulation (8)), and so does p-EXT. □

It follows that we shall never get any interesting examples of p-EXT^{gq}, but not p-EXT^{gq,s}, quantifiers if we restrict attention to quantifiers in TFT$^+$. But perhaps the conclusion we should draw from this is that even though every total quantifier Q is also a partial quantifier, it isn't really Q itself that is its closest 'partial version'. There are indeed other such versions, which *extend* Q to a partial quantifier.

5.2. Partial version of total quantifiers

A total quantifier Q of type $\langle\langle ee,t\rangle,t\rangle$, say, puts, for any M, a condition on (characteristic functions of) relations $R \subseteq M^2$, or, more exactly, on R and its complement. An obvious way to extend Q to a partial quantifier is to put the *same* condition on relations corresponding to partial characteristic functions f. But now we have a choice whether to take the complement with respect to the whole M^2, or with respect to the possibly smaller set $dom(f)$. Note that in both cases, there seems to be no obvious reason to limit attention to some partial characteristic functions and not to others. Thus, the resulting partial quantifiers will have all of $M^{\text{PFT}^+}_{\langle ee,t\rangle}$ as their domain, for each M.

Let us formulate this precisely, generalizing to the case of a universal operator Q in TFT$^+$ of type $\langle\langle \tau_1 \tau_2,t\rangle,t\rangle$, where τ_1 and τ_2 are strictly relational. It is somewhat more perspicuous to use the RT-framework here. Letting $\sigma_i = \pi^{-1}(\tau_i)$, $i = 1, 2$, $\pi^{-1}(Q)$ is thus of RT-type $((\sigma_1, \sigma_2))$.

Corresponding to Q we define a global binary relation $\mathbf{R}_Q$ between relations between objects of type σ_1 and objects of type σ_2, as follows:

Definition: For any relations S, R of the above kind:
$\mathbf{R}_Q(S,R) \Leftrightarrow \exists M[R \subseteq M^{\text{RT}}_{\sigma_1} \times M^{\text{RT}}_{\sigma_2} \,\&\, S = (M^{\text{RT}}_{\sigma_1} \times M^{\text{RT}}_{\sigma_2}) - R \,\&\, \pi^{-1}(Q)_M(R)]$

Fact 11
For all M and all $R \subseteq M^{\text{RT}}_{\sigma_1} \times M^{\text{RT}}_{\sigma_2}$,

$$\pi^{-1}(Q)_M(R) \iff \mathbf{R}_Q((M^{\text{RT}}_{\sigma_1} \times M^{\text{RT}}_{\sigma_2}) - R, R)$$

Moreover, every such global relation $\mathbf{R}$ corresponds to a universal operator $Q_{\mathbf{R}}$ in TFT$^+$ such that $\mathbf{R}_{Q_{\mathbf{R}}} = \mathbf{R}$.

Proof. We proof the first part and leave the second to the reader. The left-to-right direction is obvious from the definition of **R**. In the other direction, take $R \subseteq M_{\sigma_1}^{RT} \times M_{\sigma_2}^{RT}$ and suppose the right-hand side of the claim holds. Then there is a universe M' such that $R \subseteq M_{\sigma_1}^{\prime RT} \times M_{\sigma_2}^{\prime RT}$, and $(M_{\sigma_1}^{RT} \times M_{\sigma_2}^{RT}) - R = (M_{\sigma_1}^{\prime RT} \times M_{\sigma_2}^{\prime RT}) - R$, and $\pi^{-1}(Q)_{M'}(R)$.

Now take $(a,b) \in M_{\sigma_1}^{RT} \times M_{\sigma_2}^{RT}$. If $(a,b) \in R$, then $(a,b) \in M_{\sigma_1}^{\prime RT} \times M_{\sigma_2}^{\prime RT}$ by the above. If $(a,b) \in (M_{\sigma_1}^{RT} \times M_{\sigma_2}^{RT}) - R$, then again $(a,b) \in M_{\sigma_1}^{\prime RT} \times M_{\sigma_2}^{\prime RT}$. Thus, $M_{\sigma_1}^{RT} \times M_{\sigma_2}^{RT} \subseteq M_{\sigma_1}^{\prime RT} \times M_{\sigma_2}^{\prime RT}$, and from a similar argument we conclude that $M_{\sigma_1}^{RT} \times M_{\sigma_2}^{RT} = M_{\sigma_1}^{\prime RT} \times M_{\sigma_2}^{\prime RT}$. Thus, $M_{\sigma_1}^{RT} = M_{\sigma_1}^{\prime RT}$, and it then follows from Theorem 5 that $M = M'$. Hence, $\pi^{-1}(Q)_M(R)$. □

So these global relations are just another way to present universal operators of this type, and, generalizing, any total operator of strictly relational type; in particular, any (total) quantifier. We use this presentation to extend from total to partial operators, going back, however, to the case of a quantifier Q of type $\langle\langle ee,t\rangle,t\rangle$ in TFT$^+$.

Definition

Define two quantifiers in PFT$^+$ of the same type, Q^{p1} and Q^{p2}, by letting, for each M and each $f \in M_{\langle ee,t\rangle}^{\mathrm{PFT}^+}$,

$$Q_M^{p1}(f) = \mathrm{T} \text{ iff } \mathbf{R}_Q(M^2 - f^{+M}, f^{+M})$$

$$Q_M^{p2}(f) = \mathrm{T} \text{ iff } \mathbf{R}_Q(dom(f) - f^{+M}, f^{+M}) \text{ iff } \mathbf{R}_Q(f^{-M}, f^{+M})$$

This is taken to mean that when the right-hand side is false for f, the operators get the value F.

By Fact 11, it is clear what Q^{p1} means, given Q. The effect of Q^{p2} is the following:

Fact 12
For all $f \in M_{\langle ee,t\rangle}^{\mathrm{PFT}^+}$, $Q_M^{p2}(f) = \mathrm{T} \iff \exists A \subseteq M[dom(f) = A^2 \;\&\; \pi^{-1}(Q)_A(f^{+M})]$

Proof. By Fact 11, we see that $Q_M^{p2}(f) = \mathrm{T}$ iff there is a set A such that $f^{+M} \subseteq A^2$, $A^2 - f^{+M} = dom(f) - f^{+M}$, and $\pi^{-1}(Q)_A(f^{+M})$. Therefore, it is enough to show that the right-hand side entails that $dom(f) = A^2$. If $(a,b) \in dom(f)$, then either $f(a,b) = \mathrm{T}$ or $f(a,b) = \mathrm{F}$, so $(a,b) \in f^{+M}$ or $(a,b) \in f^{-M} = dom(f) - f^{+M}$, and in both cases it follows that $(a,b) \in A^2$. In the other direction, if $(a,b) \in A^2$, then $(a,b) \in f^{+M}$ or $(a,b) \in A^2 - f^{+M}$, and in both cases we have $(a,b) \in dom(f)$. □

To see some examples, consider first the simplest type of a quantifier, $\langle\langle e,t\rangle, t\rangle$ (type $\langle 1 \rangle$ in the standard notation). For $Q = \exists_{\geq 2}$ we have, when $f \in M_{\langle e,t\rangle}^{\mathrm{PFT}^+}$,

$$(\exists_{\geq 2}^{p1})_M(f) = \mathrm{T} \iff |f^{+M}| \geq 2 \iff (\exists_{\geq 2}^{p2})_M(f) = \mathrm{T}$$

This quantifier just says something about the size of the set f^{+M}, so the complement doesn't matter, and the two partial versions of $\exists_{\geq 2}$ coincide. The reason is that $\exists_{\geq 2}$ is EXT. The partial version is p-EXT^{gq,s}. On the other hand, take the Rescher quantifier Q^R, which is not EXT:

$$(Q^R)_M^{p1}(f) = \mathrm{T} \iff |f^{+M}| > |M - f^{+M}|$$
$$(Q^R)_M^{p2}(f) = \mathrm{T} \iff |f^{+M}| > |f^{-M}|$$

It is clear that $(Q^R)^{p2}$ is p-EXT^{gq}, but not p-EXT^{gq,s}, whereas $(Q^R)^{p1}$ is not even p-EXT^{gq}. These observations are instances of the next fact. Let Q as before be of type $\langle\langle ee,t\rangle, t\rangle$.

Fact 13

(a) For $f \in M_{\langle ee,t\rangle}^{\mathrm{TFT}^+}$, $Q_M(f) = Q_M^{p1}(f) = Q_M^{p2}(f)$.

(b) If Q is EXT, then $Q^{p1} = Q^{p2}$.

(c) Q is EXT iff Q^{p1} is p-EXT^{gq} iff Q is p-EXT^{gq,s}.

(d) Q^{p2} is always p-EXT^{gq}.

Proof. Straightforward verification, observing that EXT for Q means that the first argument of $\mathbf{R}_Q$ is irrelevant, and that the second part of (c) is Fact 8. □

(a) says that on total (characteristic functions of) relations, Q coincides with its partial versions, so it makes sense to call these *extensions* of Q.

Two examples of type $\langle\langle ee,t\rangle, t\rangle$ are

$$W_M(f) = \mathrm{T} \iff f^{+M} \text{ is a well-ordering of } M$$
$$W\!f_M(f) = \mathrm{T} \iff f^{+M} \text{ is a well-founded relation}$$

W is not EXT, since it requires the ordering to be total ($\forall x \exists y P(x,y)$ must be true in the model (M, f^{+M})), but $W\!f$, which only says that f^{+M} has no infinite descending chain, is EXT. So there is just one partial version of $W\!f$, but the two partial versions of W are distinct. Using Fact 12 we see that they are:

$$W_M^{p1}(f) = \mathrm{T} \iff f^{+M} \text{ is a well-ordering of } M$$

$$W_M^{p2}(f) = T \Leftrightarrow \exists A \subseteq M[dom(f) = A^2 \;\&\; f^{+M} \text{ is a well-ordering of } A]$$

for $f \in M_{\langle ee,t \rangle}^{PFT^+}$.

There is a general conclusion to be drawn here, not so much about EXT as about this way of quantifying over partial sets and relations. To express it, we do two things. First, we get rid of the existential quantifier in Fact 12. Indeed, the set A there is determined by f, via the usual *dom* function. To be precise, define this function as follows. Let R be any n-ary relation.

$$dom(R) = R, \text{ if } n = 1$$
$$dom(R) = \{a : \exists b_1, \ldots, b_{n-1} R(a, b_1, \ldots, b_{n-1})\}, \text{ if } n > 1$$

For example, if f is a (partial) function from M^2 to M_t, i.e. a (many-one) relation between ordered pairs of individuals and truth values, then $dom(f)$ is a set of ordered pairs, i.e. a binary relation, so $dom(dom(f))$ is the domain of *that* relation.

Second, we recall the notion of *relativization* of (total) quantifiers. Expressed in the RT framework, if for every M, Q_M is a relation between $R_1, \ldots, R_k$, where R_i is an n_i-ary relation over M, then the relativized quantifier Q^{rel} has one extra set argument and is defined by

$$Q_M^{\text{rel}}(A, R_1, \ldots, R_k) \iff Q_A(R_1 \cap A^{n_1}, \ldots, R_k \cap A^{n_k})$$

This is an important notion for natural language quantifiers, since almost all such quantifiers turn out be relativized, which in turn explains significant facts about the way quantification works in natural language (see Peters and Westerståhl 2006, ch. 4). We may also note that relativized quantifiers are automatically EXT.

Now, using the above, together with Facts 11 and 12, one proves the following result.

Proposition 14
If Q is a quantifier of type $\langle\langle e \ldots e, t \rangle, t \rangle$ in TFT$^+$, then, for all $f \in M_{\langle e \ldots e, t \rangle}^{PFT^+}$,

(a) $(Q^R)_M^{p1}(f) = T \iff \pi^{-1}(Q)_M(f^{+M})$
(b) $(Q^R)_M^{p2}(f) = T \iff \pi^{-1}(Q)_M^{\text{rel}}(dom(dom(f)), f^{+M})$

Moreover, the proposition generalizes to (total) quantifiers of arbitrary type; I leave the working out of this as an exercise.

What this result tells us is that, although extending total quantifiers to corresponding partial ones is possible and even natural, what can be expressed by these partial quantifiers can already be expressed by the total ones, or their relativizations. Intuitively, this seems to be exactly what one should expect. Consider again the partial predicate *prime* (section 2.4). Suppose I am talking about a bunch (a finite set M) of mathematical objects: natural numbers, reals, functions, sets, etc., and I say

(9) Most (things) are prime.

The Rescher quantifier Q^R = *most things* doesn't apply directly to partial predicates, but we can use either of its two partial versions. With $(Q^R)^{p1}$ we get, letting *prime*$^{+M}$ be the set of prime numbers in M,

(10) Most things in M are prime^{+M}.

This is expressible by the total Rescher quantifier, but perhaps an unlikely interpretation of my words. It is more plausible that $(Q^R)^{p2}$ was used:

(11) Most numbers in M are prime^{+M}.

By Proposition 14 (b), this is expressible with the (total) *most*, the relativization of Q^R.

5.3. Summing up

We have seen that although total quantifiers themselves aren't very natural from a partial perspective, there are perfectly natural partial versions of them. These partial versions exhibit EXT-like properties in predictable ways (Fact 13); there are more options available for 'constancy' than in the total case. However, if relativization is allowed, interpreting sentences with partial predicates and relations can be done already with the total quantifiers, so there seems to be no real (semantic) *need* for the partial versions.

Of course, there are endless ways of construing partial quantifiers that are *not* versions in any straightforward sense of total ones; hopefully the reader has got a glimpse of the variety of options that partiality allows from the discussion above. It remains to be seen if some of these options are actually 'realized' in natural languages. That is, I am not doubting here that partial predicates and relations are used in language; the issue is what kind of partial quantification, if any, is employed.

As noted, one (the only?) proposal in this direction came from Barwise and Cooper (1981). Seen in the present framework, they considered quantifiers q in PFT$^+$ of type $\langle\langle e,t\rangle,\langle\langle e,t\rangle,t\rangle\rangle$ (or, more simply, $\langle\langle e,t\rangle\langle e,t\rangle,t\rangle$ if we forget about currying) but restricted attention to the special case when each q_M is a partial function from $M_{\langle e,t \rangle}^{\text{TFT}^+}$ to $[M_{\langle e,t \rangle}^{\text{TFT}^+} \longrightarrow \{T,F\}]$, so the only partial object is q_M itself; all the other objects involved are total.[8]

A main intuition behind this sort of partiality is the alleged lack of truth value of a sentence like

(12) The three boys went to see a movie.

when there aren't exactly three boys in the discourse universe (or some suitably chosen salient universe). These intuitions can certainly be debated. Peters and Westerståhl (2006) argue that (disregarding such intuitions) the only crucial use of partial quantifiers in Barwise and Cooper (1981) occurs in their notion of *strong* quantifiers, which is used to explain the distribution of noun phrases in existential-there sentences.[9] They also argue that it is doubtful that partiality is really called for in that explanation.

Apart from what has been said in this section, and in Barwise and Cooper (1981) and Peters and Westerståhl (2006), I know of no principled discussion of partial quantifiers in natural language. It may be a topic worth exploring further.

6. Discussion

6.1. EXT versus PERM

In stark contrast with EXT, it is obvious how to formulate invariance properties like ISOM and PERM for arbitrary types, even in a partial framework. Any bijection h from M to M' lifts straightforwardly to a bijection h_τ from $M_\tau^{\text{TFT}^+}$ to $M_\tau'^{\text{TFT}^+}$, for any type τ, so u of type τ is ISOM if for any such h,

$$u_{h(M)} = h_\tau(u_M)$$

PERM is the weaker condition which only concerns permutations of M:

$$u_M = h_\tau(u_M)$$

Exactly the same goes for PFT^+, since a bijection from M to M' lifts equally straightforwardly to a bijection from $M_\tau^{\text{PFT}^+}$ to $M_\tau'^{\text{PFT}^+}$.

This just re-emphasizes the familiar fact that EXT and PERM (or ISOM) are completely different conditions. Further illustration is afforded by a quick look at which operators have the respective properties in various types. For example, in TFT^+, the only PERM operator of type $\langle e,e \rangle$ is the identity function, whereas there are no PERM operators of type $\langle\langle e,t\rangle,e\rangle$ (cf. van Benthem 1989, section 2.1). Similarly in PFT$^+$: an $\langle e,e\rangle$ type operator u is PERM iff for all M and all $a \in M$, if $u_M(a)$ is defined then $u_M(a) = a$; and there are no PERM operators of type $\langle\langle e,t\rangle,e\rangle$ except the null (everywhere undefined) operator.

By contrast, an operator u of type $\langle e,e\rangle$ in PFT$^+$ is p-EXT iff there exists a fixed global partial function $\mathbf{F}$ (like the successor function S) such that for all M and all $a \in M$, if $u_M(a)$ is defined then $u_M(a) = \mathbf{F}(a)$. And there are lots of p-EXT operators of type $\langle\langle e,t\rangle,e\rangle$ in PFT$^+$.

6.2. EXT as a 'constancy' property

This paper has looked at EXT as a reasonable 'constancy' property, worth spelling out for arbitrary types. Two questions could be asked about this strategy. First, are there other similar properties that should also be studied? Second, is EXT really reasonable?

It has been argued that EXT is not quite reasonable, or at least that it is perhaps sufficient for constancy but not necessary, since some familiar quantifiers are not EXT. Notably, the standard universal quantifier ∀ (type $\langle\langle e,t\rangle,t\rangle$) is not EXT, but doesn't it 'mean the same' on every universe? The matter is discussed at some length in Peters and Westerståhl (2006) (chapters 3.4 and 4.5), with the tentative conclusion that all natural language quantifiers, *except* some which essentially involve a predicate *thing* that always denotes the universe, are EXT. While this may be a significant observation, it still leaves the issue of a necessary condition for constancy somewhat up in the air.

A slightly different take on the matter might be as follows. In contrast with invariance properties like PERM, EXT is *not closed under definability*. The quantifier ∃ is EXT, but not its inner negation (saying of a set that its complement is not empty). Any language with rudimentary means of expression will have the power to refer essentially to the universe, and thereby to define non-EXT operators.[10] In view of this, it would clearly be unreasonable to require that all logical constants are EXT. But a weaker requirement could be that they are all *definable* from (logical and) EXT operators. And this seems indeed to be the case, for all the 'usual' logical constants. Moreover, it seems to be an empirical fact that all natural language quantifiers (all quantifiers required in the analysis of natural language) are definable from EXT quantifiers (see Peters and Westerståhl 2006, ch. 4.5). This would be enough to motivate spelling out EXT for arbitrary types, as we have begun to do here.

One may still feel that an analysis of 'constancy' has not been accomplished. This leads to the first question asked above: Are there alternative analyses? One such analysis, taking constancy in terms of what is variable and what is constant in valid *inferences*, is sketched in Peters and Westerståhl (2006), ch. 9.3. But if we stick to the idea of constancy as independence (somehow) of the *universe*, there is perhaps one other version worth exploring. The idea, which could be called *rigidity*, would be that a universal operator u is constant over universes if there is a fixed global operator $\mathbf{U}$ such that on each M, u_M is the restriction, in some sense, of $\mathbf{U}$ to M. This idea is clearly very similar to EXT, but not exactly the same. It might even avoid some of the problems we ran into with EXT. Its proper formulation, and the exact relation to EXT, must however be left for another occasion.

6.3. Further issues

If the goal of this paper was to find the proper formulation of EXT for arbitrary types, the result so far is at least incomplete, and at worst a failure. But sometimes there is illumination even in failure. For example, it may be a mistake to look for *the* proper formulation of EXT. Perhaps there are several; we have suggested three, preliminarily called p-EXT^{gq,s}, p-EXT^{gq}, and p-EXT, each corresponding in some way to EXT for total (strictly) relational types. We managed to get an idea of what these amount to for partial quantifiers, and we noted that the last two make good sense for arbitrary types.

However, our findings are certainly incomplete. For one thing, one would like to know if there is a good notion of EXT for total operators of types other than the strictly relational ones, and if so, how it correlates with the formulations for the partial case that we found. For another, whereas EXT is unproblematic for all (strictly) relational types in the total case, this is not so for the partial case. The reason is that many of the facts we observed about the various formulations of partial EXT relied on the assumption that we were dealing with first-order quantifiers, or, more generally, with operators of types whose level is at most 2. Are they generalizable, or does something important happen at level 2? Along with the issues mentioned in the previous subsection, these are questions for further study. Their answers, like the preliminary ones found in this paper, would be small pieces of the puzzling question of what characterizes a logical constant.[11]

Notes

1. Another variant has instead *product types* and unary function types; the difference between that system and TFT$^+$ is negligible here.

2. For the record, we should make clear exactly what (set-theoretic) object a partial function is. We identify a (unary) *partial function from A to B* with a many-one relation (set of ordered pairs) whose domain is a subset of A and whose range is a subset of B. It is total iff the domain is equal to A. Similarly for partial functions with several arguments. This has the consequence that a partial function from A to B is automatically a partial function from any superset of A to B.
3. It is common but somewhat misleading to call N and B *truth values*. The labels may seem fine but the question is if our notion of truth can really make sense of truth values other than T and F. As Muskens points out, it is better, and in accordance with the picture that PRT presents, to think of T,F,N,B as *truth combinations* rather than truth values: 'true and not false', 'false and not true', 'neither true nor false', and 'both true and false', respectively (thus preserving the intuitive idea of only two truth values). But the common practice is to talk about 3- and 4-*valued* logics.
4. More exactly, he considers PRT equipped with a formal language and a proof system, calling the resulting relational *type theory* TT_2^4, and similarly for TFT_4, with a (total) functional type theory called TY_2^4. The language for TT_2^4 is a sub-language of the language for TY_2^4 (both *languages* are functional, based on lambda abstraction and application), and he shows that a sentence φ in the TT_2^4-language is a TT_2^4 logical consequence of a set of sentences Γ in that language (with respect to models based on the frames for PRT defined above) if and only if φ is a TY_2^4 logical consequence of Γ.
5. Farmer studies a variant of PFT (i.e. PFT$^+$ with unary functions and currying), letting individual types allow partial functions but not Boolean types, and using a classical (2-valued) logic to describe this system. However, he does not seem to be aware of the problem mentioned earlier with currying partial functions.
6. In general, for quantifier type $\langle \sigma_1 \ldots \sigma_n, t \rangle$ we get the condition:

    If $(f_1, \ldots, f_n) \in dom(q_M)$, $(g_1, \ldots, g_n) \in dom(q_{M'})$, and $f_i^{+M} = g_i^{+M'}$, $1 \leq i \leq n$, then $q_M(f_1, \ldots, f_n) = q_{M'}(g_1, \ldots, g_n)$.

    Similarly for the other versions of EXT below.
7. We really mean $u_{M'} \restriction M_{\langle \sigma, t \rangle}^{PFT^+}$, of course, but since any domain in PFT$^+$ is determined by the set of individuals, the shorter notation $u_{M'} \restriction M$ makes sense. Similarly for the general case of a type $\langle \sigma_1 \ldots \sigma_n, \tau \rangle$. For completeness, we should also stipulate that an operator of type e is never p-EXT, whereas an operator of type t always is.
8. Concerning EXT for such quantifiers, two options seem natural (and nothing in what Barwise and Cooper say indicates which one would be preferable): Whenever $A, B \subseteq M \subseteq M'$ (we simplify matters by using sets rather than characteristic functions as arguments of q):

    (i) If $q_M(A, B)$ and $q_{M'}(A, B)$ are both defined, then $q_M(A, B) = q_{M'}(A, B)$.

    (ii) If $q_M(A, B)$ is defined, then $q_{M'}(A, B)$ is also defined and $q_M(A, B) = q_{M'}(A, B)$.

    Indeed, modulo the trouble of expressing this for characteristic functions instead, (i) is p-EXT^{gq} (cf. footnote 6 and use the formulation (8)), which is equivalent to p-EXT^{gq,s} for these quantifiers, since all arguments are total, and (ii) is p-EXT.
9. Roughly, the problem is to explain why *There are several/at least two/no girls in the garden* is fine, whereas *There are most/the five/all girls in the garden* is not. See Peters and Westerståhl (2006), ch. 6.3, for a detailed overview of this issue.
10. For example, if the language has individual variables (or corresponding expressions) and identity, or 1-place predicates and Boolean connectives, or a predicate *thing*.
11. Work on this paper was supported by a grant from the Swedish Research Council. I would like to thank Reinhard Muskens for some helpful remarks on type systems.

References

Barwise, Jon, and Robin Cooper
    1981   Generalized quantifiers and natural language. *Linguistics and Philosophy* 4: 159–219.
Belnap, Nuel
    1977   A useful four-valued logic,. In *Modern Uses of Multiple-Valued Logic*, J. M. Dunn, and G. Epstein (eds.), 8–37. Dordrecht: Reidel.
Bonnay, Denis
    2006   *Qu'est-ce qu'une Constante Logique?* Paris: Dissertation, IHPST (Université de Paris I).
Farmer, William B.
    1990   A partial functions version of church's simple theory of types. *The Journal of Symbolic Logic* 55: 1269–1291.
Feferman, Solomon
    1999   Logic, logics, and logicism. *Notre Dame Journal of Formal Logic* 40: 31–54.
Gallin, D.
    1975   *Intensional and Higher-Order Modal Logic*. Dordrecht: North-Holland.
Lindström, Per
    1966   First-order predicate logic with generalized quantifiers. *Theoria* 32: 186–195.
Montague, Richard
    1974   *Formal Philosophy* (edited and with an introduction by Richmond Thomason). New Haven: Yale University Press.
Muskens, Reinhard
    1989a   *Meaning and Partiality*. Amsterdam: Dissertation, University of Amsterdam.
    1989b   A relational formulation of the theory of types. *Linguistics and Philosophy* 12: 325–346.
Peters, Stanley, and Dag Westerståhl
    2006   *Quantifiers in Language and Logic*. Oxford: Oxford University Press.
van Benthem, Johan
    1989   Logical constants across varying types. *Notre Dame Journal of Formal Logic* 30: 315–342.
    2002   Logical constants; the variable fortunes of an elusive notion. In *Reflections of the Foundations of Mathematics: Essays in Honor of Solomon Feferman* (Lecture Notes in Logic 15), Wilfrid Sieg et al. (ed.), 420–440. Natick, MA: AK Peters Ltd.
van Benthem, Johan, and Kees Doets
    1983   Higher-order logic. In *Handbook of Philosophical Logic, Vol I*, Dov Gabbay, and Franz Guenthner (eds.), 275–329. Dordrecht: D. Reidel.

Expressive completeness and computational efficiency for underspecified representations[1]

Chris Fox and Shalom Lappin

1. Introduction

(Cooper 1983) pioneered underspecified scope representation in formal and computational semantics through his introduction of quantifier storage into Montague semantics as an alternative to the syntactic operation of quantifying-in. This work established the basis for a fruitful line of research in underspecified semantics over the past twenty-three years. In this paper we address an important issue in the development of an adequate formal theory of underspecified semantics. We are concerned with achieving expressive completeness in a system for underspecified scope representations in a way that maximizes computational efficiency.

In (Fox and Lappin 2005a) we propose Property Theory with Curry Typing (PTCT) as a formal framework for the semantics of natural language. PTCT allows fine-grained distinctions of meaning without recourse to modal notions like (im)possible worlds. It also supports a unified dynamic treatment of pronominal anaphora and VP ellipsis, as well as related phenomena such as gapping and pseudo-gapping.

PTCT consists of three sublanguage components. The first component encodes a property theory within a language of terms (an untyped λ-calculus). The second adds dynamic Curry typing (Curry and Feys 1958) to provide a system for expressing type judgements for terms. The third uses a first-order logic to specify the truth-conditions of the propositional subpart of the term language. Our semantic representation language is first-order in character, rather than higher-order. We achieve the sort of expressive power previously limited to higher-order theories within a formally more constrained system. This provides an effective procedure for modelling inference in natural language.

(Fox and Lappin 2005a; Fox and Lappin 2005b) use product types to generate underspecified semantic representations within PTCT, the representation language, rather than through meta-language devices, which are invoked in most current treatments of underspecification (Reyle 1993; Bos 1995; Blackburn and Bos 2005; Copestake, Flickinger, and Sag 2006). The expressive power of the language permits the formulation of filters on scope readings that cannot be captured in other theories of underspecification which rely on special purpose extra-linguistic operations and a weak system for constraint specification.

In Section 2 we summarise the main features of PTCT and our account of underspecified representations. Section 3 is devoted to showing how filters on underspecified scope terms can solve the problem of expressive incompleteness that (Ebert 2005) raises for other theories of underspecification. In Section 4 we indicate how filters can be used to reduce the complexity involved in computing the set of possible scope readings that an underspecified term generates. Section 5 compares our account to other approaches to scope ambiguity current in the literature. Finally, in Section 6 we state the main conclusions of this work.

2. PTCT

2.1. Syntax

The core language of PTCT consists of the following sub-languages, where x ranges over a set of variables, c ranges over a set of constants, B is a basic type, and Prop characterises the type of propositions.

(1) Terms $t ::= x \mid c \mid l \mid T \mid \lambda x(t) \mid (t)t$
(logical constants) $l ::= \hat{\sim} \mid \hat{\wedge} \mid \hat{\vee} \mid \hat{\rightarrow} \mid \hat{\leftrightarrow} \mid \hat{\forall} \mid \hat{\exists} \mid \hat{=}_T \mid \hat{\cong}_T \mid \varepsilon T$

(2) Types $T ::= B \mid \text{Prop} \mid T_1 \Longrightarrow T_2 \mid X \mid \{x \in T : \varphi'\} \mid \Pi X.T$
where X ranges over types excluding those of the form $\Pi X.T$.

(3) Wff $\varphi ::= \alpha \mid \sim\varphi \mid (\varphi_1 \wedge \varphi_2) \mid (\varphi_1 \vee \varphi_2) \mid (\varphi_1 \rightarrow \varphi_2) \mid (\varphi_1 \leftrightarrow \varphi_2)$
$\mid (\forall x \varphi) \mid (\exists x \varphi) \mid (\forall X \varphi) \mid (\exists X \varphi)$
(atomic wff) $\alpha ::= t =_T s \mid t \in T \mid t \cong_T s \mid {}^T t$

PTCT is a first-order theory in which types and propositions are terms over which we can quantify. This allows rich expressiveness whilst restricting the system to first-order resources (Fox and Lappin 2005a: Chapter 9).

The language of terms is the untyped λ-calculus, enriched with logical constants. It is used to *represent* the interpretations of natural language expressions. It has no internal logic, but when we add a proof theory, the simple language of types together with the language of terms can be combined to produce a Curry-typed λ-calculus.

The syntactic rules of PTCT given here are flexible. They allow the generation of syntactic expressions that have no intuitively meaningful interpretation. This does not undermine the system. The rules give a minimal characterisation of the syntax while our proof theory and our model theory characterise the proper subset of well-formed PTCT terms that constitute meaningful expressions.

In a separation type $\{x \in T : \varphi'\}$, φ' is a term representable fragment of a wff, where term representability can be defined recursively. This restriction on separation types avoids semantic paradoxes of type membership which could otherwise emerge in the specification of these types. The values of bound type variables is limited to non-polymorphic types in order to avoid impredicative type membership statements.

In the first-order language of wffs we formulate type judgements for terms, and truth conditions for those terms judged to be in Prop.

It is important to distinguish between the notion of a proposition itself (in the language of wff), and that of a term that *represents* a proposition (in the language of terms). $^{\mathsf{T}}(t)$ will be a true wff whenever the proposition represented by the term t is true, and a false wff whenever the proposition represented by t is false. The representation of a proposition t ($\in$ Prop) is distinct from its truth conditions ($^{\mathsf{T}}(t)$). The identity criteria for propositions, taken as terms, are those of the λ-calculus with α, β, and η reduction.

We note that if $t \notin$ Prop, then $^{\mathsf{T}}(t)$ will be false. We enforce a strictly bivalent Boolean evaluation in the proof theory and model theory. In principle we could modify this semantics. We might, for example, take the truth value of $^{\mathsf{T}}(t)$ to be undefined when $t \notin$ Prop, whilst preserving Boolean negation (with the "law of excluded middle") for propositions. We will not pursue this issue here.

2.2. Proof theory

The rules and axioms governing the logical behaviour of PTCT can be summarised as follows. The rules for the basic connectives of the wff have standard classical first-order behaviour. The axioms for identity of terms $=_T$ are those of α, β, and η reduction in the untyped λ-calculus. The rules for typing λ-terms are the rules/axioms of the Curry-typed calculus, augmented with rules governing those terms that represent propositions (Prop). Additional rules for the language of wffs govern the truth conditions of terms in Prop, which represent propositions. Finally, the rules for equivalence $\cong_T$ specify it as the relation of extensional equivalence.

We illustrate some of these rules as they apply to conjunction, as it appears in the language of terms ($\hat{\wedge}$), of type judgements, and of wff ($\wedge$).

(4) The basic connectives of the wff

$$\frac{\varphi \quad \psi}{\varphi \wedge \psi} \wedge i \quad \frac{\varphi \wedge \psi}{\varphi} \wedge e \quad \frac{\varphi \wedge \psi}{\psi} \wedge e$$

(5) Typing rules for λ-terms

$$t \in \mathsf{Prop} \wedge t' \in \mathsf{Prop} \to (t \hat{\wedge} t') \in \mathsf{Prop}$$

(6) Truth conditions for Propositions

$$t \in \mathsf{Prop} \wedge t' \in \mathsf{Prop} \to (^\mathsf{T}(t \hat{\wedge} t') \leftrightarrow {}^\mathsf{T}t \wedge {}^\mathsf{T}t')$$

We have encoded the proof theory of PTCT in a tableau system, which we present in (Fox and Lappin 2005a: Chapter 5), together with proofs of soundness and completeness. A slightly earlier version of the proof theory appears in (Fox and Lappin 2004).

2.3. Equivalence and identity

There are two equivalence relations in this theory, intensional identity and extensional equivalence. $t \cong_T s$ states that the terms t, s are extensionally equivalent in type T. In the case where two terms t, s are propositions ($t, s \in \mathsf{Prop}$), then $t \cong_\mathsf{Prop} s$ corresponds to $t \leftrightarrow s$. In the case where two predicates of T ($t, s \in T \Longrightarrow \mathsf{Prop}$) are extensionally equivalent ($t \cong_{(T \Longrightarrow \mathsf{Prop})} s$), t, s each hold of all and only the same elements of T. Therefore $\forall x(x \in T \to ({}^\mathsf{T}t(x) \leftrightarrow {}^\mathsf{T}s(x)))$.

$t =_T s$ states that two terms are intensionally identical in type T. The proof system for PTCT permits us to derive $t =_T s \to t \cong_T s$ for all types inhabited by t, (s), but not $t \cong_T s \to t =_T s$. Therefore, two expressions (terms) can be provably equivalent but intensionally distinct. We have achieved this result without recourse to modal notions.

The fact that we can distinguish between equivalence and intensionality permits us to sustain differences in meaning in natural language that elude other intensional logics. The precise definition of equivalence and identity are given by our proof theory and model theory in (Fox and Lappin 2005a: Chapter 5). See (Fox and Lappin 2004) for a slightly earlier version of these theories.

2.4. Model theory

We construct our set of models for PTCT on the basis of the model theory for the untyped λ-calculus given in (Meyer 1982). $\mathscr{D} = \langle D, [D \to D], \Phi, \Psi \rangle$ where D is isomorphic to $[D \to D]$.

(7) (a) D is a non-empty set,

(b) $[D \to D]$ is some class of functions from D to D,

(c) $\Phi : D \to [D \to D]$,

(d) $\Psi : [D \to D] \to D$,

(e) $\Psi(\Phi(d)) = d$ for all $d \in D$.

We can interpret the calculus using the following.

(8) $[\![x]\!]_g = g(x)$
$[\![\lambda x.t]\!]_g = \Psi(\lambda d.[\![t]\!]_{g[d/x]})$
$[\![ts]\!]_g = \Phi([\![t]\!]_g)[\![s]\!]_g$

where g is an assignment function from variables to elements of D. This interpretation exploits the fact that Φ maps every element of D into a corresponding function from D to D, and Ψ maps functions from D to D into elements of D.

Note that we require functions of the form $\lambda d.[\![t]\!]_{g[d/x]}$ to be in the class $[D \to D]$ to ensure that the interpretation is well defined. Here we are just following (Meyer 1982).

We interpret the types as terms in D that correspond to subsets of D. A model of PTCT is $\mathcal{M} = \langle \mathcal{D}, \mathsf{T}, \mathsf{P}, \mathsf{B}, \mathcal{B}, \mathcal{T}', \mathcal{T} \rangle$, where

(a) $\mathcal{D}$ is a model of the λ-calculus,

(b) $\mathsf{T} : D \to \{0, 1\}$ models the truth predicate $^\mathsf{T}$,

(c) $\mathsf{P} \subset D$ models the class of propositions,

(d) $\mathsf{B} \subset D$ models the class of basic individuals,

(e) $\mathcal{B}(\mathsf{B})$ is a set of sets whose elements partition B into equivalence classes of individuals,

(f) $\mathcal{T}' \subset \mathcal{T}$ models the class of non-polymorphic types

(g) $\mathcal{T} \subset D$ models the term representation of types,

with sufficient structural constraints on T, P, $\mathcal{T}$, and $\mathcal{T}'$ to validate the rules of PTCT.

In (Fox and Lappin 2005a) we prove the soundness and completeness of PTCT with respect to the proof theory and model theory specified there.

2.5. Underspecified representations in PTCT

We extend the type system of PTCT to include product types $S \otimes T$, which have elements of the form $\langle s,t \rangle$. We add the type $S \otimes T$, and a tableau rule corresponding to the following axiom.

(9)   PROD: $\langle x,y \rangle \in (S \otimes T) \leftrightarrow x \in S \land y \in T$

Unlike monomorphic lists, the k-tuples that instantiate product types allow us to express polymorphic relations.

The appropriate notions of pairs and projections required for product types are λ-definable.

(10) $\langle x,y \rangle =_{def} \lambda z(z(x)(y))$

(11) fst $=_{def} \lambda p(p\lambda xy(x))$

(12) snd $=_{def} \lambda p(p\lambda xy(y))$

We write $\langle t_1, t_2, \ldots, t_n \rangle$ for $\langle t_1, \langle t_2, \langle \ldots t_n \rangle \rangle \ldots \rangle$, and $T_1 \otimes T_2 \otimes \ldots \otimes T_n$ for $T_1 \otimes (T_2 \otimes (\ldots \otimes T_n) \ldots)$. We specify that for any k-tuple $\langle t_1, \ldots, t_k \rangle \in T_1 \otimes \ldots \otimes T_k$, the last element of the k-tuple, t_k, is a designated object, like 0 or $\bot$. This condition insures that it is possible to recognise the end of a k-tuple and so compute its arity. The designated element of a k-tuple plays the same role as the empty list does in the tail of every list. It renders the elements of product types equivalent to weak lists with elements of (possibly) distinct types. As in the case of lists, we generally suppress this final designated element when representing a k-tuple.

2.6. Generalised quantifiers

Generalised quantifiers (GQs) represent noun phrases. We follow (Keenan 1992) and (van Eijck 2003) in taking a GQ to be an arity reduction operator that applies to a relation r to yield either a proposition or a relation r' that is produced by effectively saturating one of r's argument with the GQ.[2] On this view, applying the GQ corresponding to "*every student*" (every_student' or $\lambda Q \forall x(\text{student}' \to Q(x))$) to the binary relation $\lambda yx(\text{loves}'(x,y))$ gives the one-place relation $\lambda x(\text{every\_student}'(\lambda y.\text{loves}'(x,y)))$. Through β-reduction this gives $\lambda x(\forall y(\text{student}'(y) \to \text{love}'(x,y)))$, which is the property of loving every student.

GQs are of type $(X \Longrightarrow \text{Prop}) \Longrightarrow \text{Prop}$, which we write Quant^X for clarity (where X is typically B). Core propositional relations, such as verbs, are of type $X_1 \Longrightarrow \ldots \Longrightarrow X_n \Longrightarrow$ Prop. Slightly modifying van Eijck's Haskell-based treatment of GQs (van Eijck 2003), we define an operator R to "lift" quantifiers to the appropriate level to combine with a relation.

(13) $R \in \text{Quant}^X \Longrightarrow ((X \Longrightarrow T) \Longrightarrow T)$

(14) $Q \in \text{Quant}^X \wedge r \in (X \Longrightarrow \text{Prop}) \rightarrow RQr = Qr$

(15) $Q \in \text{Quant}^X \wedge r \in (X \Longrightarrow T) \wedge (T \notin \text{Prop}) \rightarrow RQr = \lambda x RQ(rx)$

We compose representations of n quantifiers with a relation r using

$$RQ_1(RQ_2 \ldots (RQ_n r) \ldots)$$

2.7. Indexed permutations of GQ scope sequences

Natural language is ambiguous with respect to the scoping of quantifiers, modifiers, conjunction, and negation. Many of these scopings are purely semantic in nature. So, for example the following sentence (16) allows two alternative scope readings, given in (17) and (18).

(16) Every man loves a woman

(17) $\forall x(\text{man}'(x) \rightarrow \exists y(\text{woman}'(y) \wedge \text{loves}'(x,y)))$

(18) $\exists y(\text{woman}'(y) \wedge \forall x(\text{man}'(x) \rightarrow \text{loves}'(x,y)))$

We want our theory to produce "*underspecified*" representations that subsume all the various readings, and from which the different readings can be generated. We can express computable functions in PTCT, and so we can incorporate the machinery of underspecified semantics directly into the representation language.

We specify a family of functions *perms_scope$_k$* (where $k > 1$) that generate all $k!$ indexed permutation products of a k-ary indexed product term $\langle t_1, \ldots, t_k \rangle$ as part of the procedure for generating the set of possible scope readings of a sentence. In (Fox and Lappin 2005b) we specify a standard algorithm (Campbell 2004: following) for mapping a k-tuple $\langle 1, \ldots, k \rangle$ into the indexed $k!$-tuple of its permutations as part of the interpretation of *perms_scope$_k$*. In Section 4 we formulate an alternative tree construction algorithm to generate the set of all possible permutations of scope taking elements to which *perms_scope$_k$* applies. We will use the factorial permutation trees that this algorithm generates to demonstrate the complexity reduction that filters on underspecified representations can achieve.

For our treatment of underspecification, *perms_scope$_k$* needs to take a k-ary product of scope taking elements (by default, in the order in which they appear in the surface syntax) and a k-ary relation representing the core proposition as its arguments. The scope taking elements and the core representation can be combined into a single product, e.g. as a pair consisting of the k-tuples of quantifiers as its first element and the core relation as its second. The permutation function $perms\_scope_k$ produces the $k!$-ary product of scoped readings. When a k-tuple of quantifiers is permuted, the λ-operators that bind the quantified argument positions in the core relation are effectively permuted in the same order as the quantifiers in the k-tuple. This correspondence is necessary to preserve the connection between each GQ and its argument position in the core relation across scope permutations.

A scope reading is generated by applying the elements of the k-tuple of quantifiers in sequence to the core proposition, reducing its arity with each such operation until a proposition results. The ith scope reading is identified by projecting the ith element of the indexed product of propositions that is the output by our $perms\_scope_k$ function. The PTCT term consisting of the application of $perms\_scope_k$ to an input pair of a k-tuple of GQs and a core relation therefore provides an underspecified representation of the sentence corresponding to this term. Below we describe a function that projects a fully specified scope reading. In principle we can follow (van Eijck 2003) and give a uniform type to these representations by defining arbitrary arity product types to cover the type of the k-tuple of GQs that is the first element in the pair to which $perms\_scope_k$ applies and the $k!$-tuple which is its value.

Consider example (16) "*Every man loves a woman*". The GQs interpreting the subject NP, the object NP and the core relation are given in (19), (20) and (21), respectively, and the PTCT term expressing the underspecified representation of the sentence is given in (22).

(19) $Q_1 = \lambda P \hat{\forall} x \varepsilon B(\mathsf{man}'(x) \rightarrow P(x))$

(20) $Q_2 = \lambda Q \hat{\exists} y \varepsilon B(\mathsf{woman}'(y) \wedge Q(y))$

(21) $\lambda uv.\mathsf{loves}' uv$

(22) $perms\_scope_2(\langle\langle Q_1, Q_2\rangle, \lambda uv.\mathsf{loves}' uv\rangle)$

The permutations of the quantifiers and the core representation that we produce are

(23) $\langle\langle\langle Q_1, Q_2\rangle, \lambda uv.\mathsf{loves}' uv\rangle \langle\langle Q_2, Q_1\rangle, \lambda vu.\mathsf{loves}' uv\rangle\rangle$

Applying relation reduction to computing the final propositions gives us a product containing the two readings.

(24) $perms\_scope_2(\langle\langle Q_1, Q_2\rangle, \lambda uv.\mathsf{loves}' uv\rangle)) =$
$\langle\hat{\forall} x \varepsilon B(\mathsf{man}'(x) \rightarrow \hat{\exists} y \varepsilon B(\mathsf{woman}'(y) \wedge \mathsf{loves}'(x,y))),$
$\hat{\exists} y \varepsilon B(\mathsf{woman}'(y) \wedge \hat{\forall} x \varepsilon B(\mathsf{man}'(x) \wedge \mathsf{loves}'(x,y))))\rangle$

To obtain resolved scope readings from an underspecified representation, we define a family of functions *project_scope*$_k(i)$ that compute the *i*th permutation of a *k*-ary product of propositions. Specifically, a function of this kind returns the *i*th proposition in the product of scope readings that *perms_scope*$_k$ gives as its value. We extend the type system to include the type Num of natural numbers. We can then define *project_scope*$_k$'s type as

$$\langle \text{Prop}_1, \ldots, \text{Prop}_k \rangle \Rightarrow \text{Num} \Rightarrow \text{Prop}$$

where Num $\leq k$. To ensure that the function is total, we can define *project_scope* $_k(i)$ so that it projects the $(i \mod k)$th term, for example. A detailed proposal for the inclusion of natural numbers into PTCT is provided in (Fox and Lappin 2005a: Chapter 6).

3. Filters and expressive completeness

There are various kinds of constraints that limit the set of possible scope readings for a particular sentence to a proper subset of the set of $k!$ orderings of the k scope taking elements which appear in it. A common condition on relative scope is the strong preference for wide scope assignment to certain quantifiers by virtue of their lexical semantic properties, like "*a certain N'*".

A second kind of condition depends upon the syntactic domain in which a GQ appears. So, for example, a quantified NP within a relative clause cannot take scope over a quantified NP in which the relative clause is embedded.

The following two examples illustrate these constraints.

(25) Every critic reviewed a certain book.

(26) A student who completed every assignment came first in the class.

The strongly preferred reading of (25) is the one on which "*a certain book*" takes wide scope relative to "*every critic*". In (26) "*every assignment*" can only take narrow scope relative to "*a student who completed every assignment*".

Scope constraints of these kinds can be formulated as filters on the $k!$-tuple of permutations $\langle \langle Qtuple_1, Rel_1 \rangle, \ldots, \langle Qtuple_{k!}, Rel_{k!} \rangle \rangle$ that *perms_scope*$_k$ generates for an argument pair $\langle Qtuple_1, Rel_1 \rangle$. Each such filter is a Boolean property function that imposes a condition on the elements of the $k!$-tuple.[3]

Let $\langle Quants, Rel \rangle$ be a variable ranging over pairs in which *Quants* is a k-tuple and *Rel* is a k-ary relation. We take *a_certain* to be a PTCT property that is true of all and only GQs that represent "*a certain N'*", and is false of anything else. As the k-tuples are indexed, there is a one-to-one correspondence between the elements of a k-tuple and their respective indices.

Let $tuple\_element(i, Quants) = Q_i$ if Q_i is the ith member of $Quants$, and the distinguished term ω otherwise.

We can specify the lexical scope constraint illustrated in (25) as the filter in (27), where i and j are variables ranging over integers (type Num).

(27) $\lambda \langle Quants, Rel \rangle [\hat{\sim}(\hat{\exists} i \varepsilon \text{Num} \hat{\exists} j \varepsilon \text{Num}(a\_certain(tuple\_element(i, Quants))) \hat{\wedge}$
$\hat{\sim} a\_certain(tuple\_element(j, Quants)) \hat{\wedge}$
$j \hat{<} i))]$

This condition requires that no element of a $k!$-tuple of scope readings contains a k-tuple of GQs in which the index of a $a\_certain$ GQ is higher than that of a non-$a\_certain$ GQ (and so outscoped by it). Notice that we have only quantified over integers (elements of the type Num) in this filter. We have taken advantage of the isomorphism between k-tuples of integers and k-tuples of indexed GQs to avoid quantifying over GQ expressions. Therefore, we have remained within the first-order expressive resources of PTCT.[4]

In order to formulate the condition illustrated in (26) we must introduce syntactic relations. Let $relcl\_embed(Q_1, Q_2)$ hold iff the NP corresponding to Q_2 appears in a relative clause contained in the NP corresponding to Q_1. We can formulate the constraint as in (28).

(28) $\lambda \langle Quants, Rel \rangle [\hat{\sim}(\hat{\exists} i \varepsilon \text{Num} \hat{\exists} j \varepsilon \text{Num}(relcl\_embed(tuple\_element(i, Quants))$
$tuple\_element(j, Quants))$
$\hat{\wedge} j \hat{<} i))]$

This filter prevents a GQ that interprets an NP in a relative clause from having scope over a GQ that interprets an NP in which the relative clause is embedded.

(27) and (28) achieve partial disambiguation of an underspecified representation to which they apply (non-vacuously) by ruling out a subset of the set of possible scope readings that this representation generates independently of the filters.

Underspecified representations can also be disambiguated by information acquired through subsequent discourse. So, for example, resolving anaphoric expressions like pronouns and definite descriptions in sentences following a statement that exhibits scope ambiguity may eliminate certain readings of the antecedent.

(29) (a) *Speaker 1:* Every student wrote a program for some professor.

(b) *Speaker 2:* Yes, I know the professor. She taught the Haskell course.

(c) *Speaker 3:* I saw the programs, and they were all list-sorting procedures.

Identifying "*some professor*" in (29a) as the antecedent for "*the professor*" and "*she*" in (29b) gives "*some professor*" scope over "*every student*" in (29a).

Interpreting "*a program*" in (29a) as the antecedent for "*the programs*" and "*they*" in (29c) causes "*a program*" to have narrow scope relative to "*every student*" in (29a). Therefore, taken conjointly (29b) and (29c) forces on (29a) the fully resolved scope order

$$\langle \text{"some professor", "every student", "a program"} \rangle$$

Let "*every student*" $= Q_1$, "*a program*" $= Q_2$, and "*some professor*" $= Q_3$. We can formulate the filters contributed by (29b) and (29c) as (30) and (31), respectively (where GQ in $\hat{=}_{GQ}$ abbreviates the appropriate type of Q_i).

(30) $\lambda \langle Quants, Rel \rangle [\hat{\forall} i \varepsilon \text{Num} \hat{\forall} j \varepsilon \text{Num}((tuple\_element(i, Quants) \hat{=}_{GQ} Q_3 \wedge$
$\qquad tuple\_element(j, Quants) \hat{=}_{GQ} Q_1) \hat{\rightarrow}$
$\qquad i \hat{<} j)]$

(31) $\lambda \langle Quants, Rel \rangle [\hat{\forall} i \varepsilon \text{Num} \hat{\forall} j \varepsilon \text{Num}((tuple\_element(i, Quants) \hat{=}_{GQ} Q_1 \wedge$
$\qquad tuple\_element(j, Quants) \hat{=}_{GQ} Q_2) \hat{\rightarrow}$
$\qquad i \hat{<} j)]$

We specify the function *filter_tuple*($\langle F, T \rangle$) which maps a pair consisting of a j-tuple F of filters and a k-tuple T to a k'-tuple (possibly the empty tuple) of all the elements of T that satisfy each filter in F.[5] We construct a PTCT term of the form (32) to represent the k'-tuple obtained by applying the elements of F to the $k!$-tuple that is the value of *perms_scope*$_k$($\langle Quants_k, Rel \rangle$).

(32) *filter_tuple*($\langle F, perms\_scope_k(\langle Quants_k, Rel \rangle) \rangle$)

(Ebert 2005) shows that most current theories of underspecification are expressively incomplete to the extent that they cannot identify the proper subset of possible scope readings specified by Boolean operations other than conjunction, and in particular by negation. He cites the following example to illustrate the problem.

(33) Every market manager showed five sales representatives a sample.

Ebert stipulates that, in his example, real world knowledge allows all scope permutations except the one corresponding to $\langle \exists, 5, \forall \rangle$, where *a sample* takes wide scope, *five sales representatives* intermediary position, and *every market manager* narrow scope. He demonstrates that storage (Cooper 1983; Pereira 1990), hole semantics (Bos 1995; Blackburn and Bos 2005), Minimal Recursion Semantics (Copestake, Flickinger, and Sag 2006), and Normal Dominance Conditions (Koller, Niehren, and Thater 2003) cannot formulate underspecified representations that express the set containing only the five remaining scope readings.

By contrast it is straightforward to formulate a filter in PTCT that rules out the problematic scope sequence in Ebert's case while permitting the five other readings.

(34) $\lambda \langle Quants, Rel \rangle [\hat{\forall} i \varepsilon \text{Num} \hat{\forall} j \varepsilon \text{Num} \hat{\forall} k \varepsilon \text{Num}((tuple\_element(i, Quants) \hat{=}_{GQ} Q_\exists \wedge$
$tuple\_element(j, Quants) \hat{=}_{GQ} Q_5 \wedge$
$tuple\_element(k, Quants) \hat{=}_{GQ} Q_\forall) \rightarrow$
$\sim (i \lesssim j \wedge j \lesssim k))]$

PTCT is, in principle, able to achieve expressive completeness in Ebert's (2005) sense.[6]

4. Efficient computation of possible scope readings

At first glance it might seem that it is, in general, necessary to generate the full $k!$-tuple that is the value of $perms\_scope_k(\langle Quants_k, Rel \rangle)$ before applying the filters of F to the elements of this $k!$-tuple in order to compute the value of (32). If this were true, filters would never reduce the search space of possible scope readings that must be accessed in the course of their application. Fortunately, this is not the case.

In (Fox and Lappin 2005b) we specify an algorithm based on (Campbell 2004) for generating the indexed list of all possible permutations of an input list. This procedure was used to partially characterise the computable function $perms\_scope_k$. It is possible to use an alternative algorithm to implement this function, where the indexed $k!$-tuple of possible permutations of an initial k-tuple is obtained through the construction of a tree.

(35) (a) Given a k-tuple $\langle Q_1, \ldots Q_k \rangle$, a tree is generated breadth first, starting by creating the root of the tree, then producing successive levels, continuing until level k is generated, as follows.

Base Case Take the tuple $\langle Q_1 \rangle$ consisting of the initial element of the k-tuple $\langle Q_1, \ldots, Q_k \rangle$ to be the root of the tree. Let this be level 1 of the tree.

Recursive Case Level $(i+1)$ of the tree is created from level i by considering each node n_m of level i in turn (starting with the left-most node n_1, and continuing to the right-most node), and constructing all the daughters of each node n_m as follows.

Base Case' Construct the left-most daughter d_1 of the current node n_m by adding the $(i+1)$th tuple in which the $(i+1)$th element of $\langle Q_1, \ldots, Q_k \rangle$ is concatenated with the i-tuple at n_m in the right-most position of the $(i+1)$-tuple at d_1.

Underspecified representations 49

Recursive Case' Obtain the daughter d_{j+1} of the current node n_m immediately to the right of d_j by moving the $(i+1)$th element of $\langle Q_1, \ldots, Q_k \rangle$, added at level $(i+1)$, one place to left.
In this way, construct all daughters of n_m until the right-most daughter is generated as the $(i+1)$-tuple in which the $(i+1)$th element of $\langle Q_1, \ldots, Q_k \rangle$ appears in the left-most position.

The tree is finished when the kth level has been generated.

(b) To obtain the $k!$-tuple of all possible permutations of $\langle Q_1, \ldots, Q_k \rangle$ concatenate the k-tuples at the leaves of the tree from left to right into a $k!$-tuple.

(c) Indexing: assign each k-tuple element of the $k!$-tuple an index i, starting with 1, in the the left-to-right order in which they appear as leaves of the finished tree.

If this algorithm takes as its input the triple $\langle Q_1, Q_2, Q_3 \rangle$, then it generates the following tree.

(36)
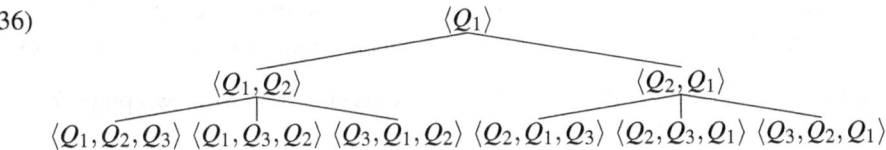

Filters can apply as constraints to nodes in the tree as the algorithm produces them. If a node violates a filter, then it is deleted, and the subtree that it dominates is not generated. In this way filters can reduce the size of the tree, and so limit the search space of possible scope readings explored for a $perms\_scope_k(\langle Quants_k, Rel \rangle)$ term to a proper subset of the elements of the $k!$-tuple that is its value.

So, for example, the filter $Q_1 < Q_2$ prunes the tree in (36) to give the one in (37).

(37)
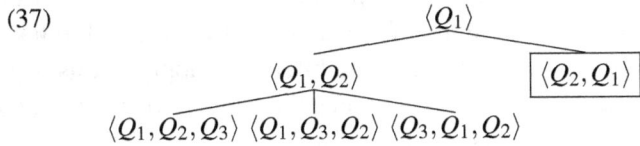

Identifying the size of a tree with the number of its nodes, we can compute the size of a tree T, $|T|$, through the formula

(38) $|T| = \Sigma_{i=1}^{k} i!$, where i is the index of the ith element of the initial k-tuple which the algorithm takes as its input.

Therefore, the size of the tree in (36) is $1! + 2! + 3! = 9$. The size of the tree in (37) is 6, which is a reduction of 30%.

The size of a subtree ST dominated by a node n at level i, but not including n, is given by the formula

(39) $|ST| = \Pi_{j=i+1}^{k} j + \Sigma_{j'=i+1}^{k-1} j'$

Consider the quadruple $\langle Q_1, Q_2, Q_3, Q_4 \rangle$. The algorithm in (35) produces an indexed $k!$-tuple of 24 k-tuples as the leaves of a tree T_4 with 4 levels and 33 nodes. If a filter like $Q_1 < Q_2$ applies at level 2, the first branching node of T_4, it prunes the right-half of T_4 under $\langle Q_2, Q_1 \rangle$, and so it eliminates a subtree of 15 nodes, reducing T_4 by 15/33 = 45.4%. The remaining left side of T_4 has the three nodes $\langle Q_1, Q_2, Q_3 \rangle$, $\langle Q_1, Q_3, Q_2 \rangle$, $\langle Q_3, Q_1, Q_2 \rangle$ at level 3. If the filter $Q_2 < Q_3$ applies at this level, the 8 leaf nodes under $\langle Q_1, Q_3, Q_2 \rangle$ and $\langle Q_3, Q_1, Q_2 \rangle$ are pruned. Therefore, the conjunction of the filters $Q_1 < Q_2$ and $Q_2 < Q_3$ reduces T_4 by 15 + 8 = 23 nodes, which is (approximately) 70% of the full tree.

It is not difficult to construct a plausible case in which the interpretation of a sentence containing four quantified NPs is disambiguated by a conjunction of two filters of this kind through anaphora resolution in subsequent discourse.

(40) (a) *Speaker 1:* It's amazing. A critic recently reviewed two plays for every newspaper in a major city.

(b) *Speaker 2:* Yes, I wonder how he got away with that. He published the same reviews of the current productions of "*A Midsummer Night's Dream*" and "*New-Found-Land*" in every major paper in New York last week.

Clearly, the earlier in the tree construction process (the higher up in the tree) that a filter applies, the greater the reduction in search space of possible scope readings that it achieves. It is also possible to optimise the interaction of filters and the tree construction algorithm by specifying a procedure that reorders the elements of the input k-tuple to permit the filters to apply at the earliest point in the generation of the tree. For example, if the algorithm takes as its input the triple $\langle Q_1, Q_2, Q_3 \rangle$ and one of the filters that apply to this triple is $Q_2 < Q_3$, then the reordering operation will map the triple into $\langle Q_2, Q_3, Q_1 \rangle$. We will leave the formulation of this operation for future work.

(Ebert 2005) proves a theorem that entails that if a theory is expressively complete, then it will, in the worst case, produce a combinatorial explosion equivalent to generating all $k!$ scope readings for a sentence. This result holds for PTCT in the limit case, where no filters have been applied to a *perms_scope*$_k$ ($\langle Quants_k, Rel \rangle$) term, or they do not operate early enough in the tree construction algorithm to restrict the scope permutation tree. However, as we have seen, there is a large class of cases in which filters significantly reduce the search space through tree pruning, and so they offer a mechanism for rendering scope disambiguation computationally efficient.

5. Other treatments of scope ambiguity

5.1. Quantifier storage

Quantifier storage as defined in (Cooper 1983) and (Pereira 1990) is perhaps the first system for generating non-compositional underspecified scope representations. A generalised quantifier (GQ) is stored as the first element of a pair whose second element identifies the variable that is used to mark the GQ's argument position in the syntactic structure of the sentence. The representation produced for the clause consists of the core propositional relation and a set of stored GQ pairs. When a GQ is discharged from storage, it is applied to the core relation, binding the variable in its original position. As the elements of the storage set are unordered, they can be discharged in any sequence, where each sequence yields a possible scope reading.

Storage provides an elegant and straightforward way of generating underspecified scope representations for a sentence. However, there are (at least) three difficulties with this approach. First, storage is an additional mechanism defined outside of the semantic representation language as such. The expressions that it produces are not themselves part of this language (a typed λ-calculus) but stages in the derivation of well-formed terms of the representation language. While storage is easily implemented in a declarative fashion, as in (Pereira 1990) and (Blackburn and Bos 2005), it remains an essentially procedural device that is added to a compositional semantic theory as a means of obtaining scope ambiguity without attaching alternative scope readings to distinct syntactic structures, as in (Montague 1974).

By contrast, on our account underspecified representations are themselves terms of PTCT, the representation language. Therefore, this issue does not arise; the underspecified representation is expressed directly in the representation language.

Second, because storage is a mechanism constructed outside of the representation language, it is necessary to specify an additional constraint language for stating the Boolean conditions required to restrict the set of possible scope readings derived from the storage set.[7]

Again, this problem does not arise on our treatment of underspecification. The filters that express constraints on scope readings are λ-terms of PTCT, and so the resources required for the formulation of these constraints are available within the representation language.

Finally, even if a constraint language is added to storage, it will be necessary to specify an additional mechanism to prevent the generation of the full set of possible scope orderings prior to the application of the filters.

As we have seen in Section 4, when *perms_scope$_k$* is interpreted as a computable function whose application involves the tree generation algorithm in (35), filters can be acquired incrementally in discourse and applied to underspecified representations in PTCT in a straightforward way that can significantly reduce the search space of possible scope readings.

5.2. Hole semantics, minimal recursion semantics, and normal dominance constraints

(Bos 1995), and (Blackburn and Bos 2005) develop a constraint-based system for underspecified representation for first-order logic that they refer to as *Predicate Logic Unplugged* (PLU). This system is a generalisation of the *hole semantics* approach to underspecification which (Reyle 1993) first developed within the framework of Underspecified Discourse Representation Theory. Copestake, Flickinger, and Sag's (2006) Minimal Recursion Semantics is an application of hole semantics within a typed feature structure grammar (HPSG). Koller, Niehren, and Thater's (2003) Normal Dominance Conditions can be seen as a refinement and development of the central ideas of hole semantics. The problems that we identify with the hole semantics model apply to all three theories, and so, in the interests of simplicity, we will summarise (a version of) PLU as the representative of this approach.[8]

An underspecified representation of a quantified first-order formula in PLU is an ordered tripe $\langle LH, F, R \rangle$. LH is a set of labels for formulas and of holes, which are (essentially) metavariables that take formulas as values. F is a set of labelled formulas, which may contain holes for subformulas. R is a set of scope constraints expressed as partial order relations on labels and holes. The PLU representation of (41) is (42).

(41) Every student wrote a program.

(42) $\langle \{l_1, l_2, l_3, h_0, h_1, h_2\},$
$\{l_1 : \forall x(\text{student}'(x) \to h_1), l_2 : \exists y(\text{program}'(y) \land h_2), l_3 : \text{wrote}'(x,y)\},$
$\{l_1 \leq h_0, l_2 \leq h_0, l_3 \leq h_1, l_3 \leq h_2\}\rangle$

The partial ordering constraints in (42) define a bounded lattice with h_0 as $\top$, the propositional core of the formula, l_3 as $\bot$, and l_1 and l_2 as midpoints of the lattice between $\top$ and $\bot$. As l_1 and l_2 are not ordered with respect to each other, either formula can be substituted for the hole in the other formula. l_3 must be substituted last in the remaining hole. If l_1 is taken as the value of h_0, l_2 is substituted for h_1, and then l_3 is substituted for h_2, the result is a wide scope reading of the universal quantifier, as in (43). Alternatively, if l_2 is taken as the value of h_0, l_1 is assigned to h_2, and l_3 to h_1, we obtain (44).

(43) $\forall x(\text{student}'(x) \rightarrow \exists y(\text{program}'(y) \wedge \text{wrote}'(x,y)))$

(44) $\exists y(\text{program}'(y) \wedge \forall x(\text{student}'(x) \rightarrow \text{wrote}'(x,y)))$

These are the only two scope resolutions that satisfy the partial order conditions in (42).

Hole semantics provides a more expressive and flexible system for constructing underspecified representations than storage. It generalises naturally to scope elements other than GQs, like negation and modifiers. It is possible to identify a subset of scope readings that satisfy the constraints of an underspecified hole semantic representation by imposing a particular order of substitution of labels for holes in a schematic formula set. However, it does suffer from the first and second difficulties which we raised against storage. Underspecified representations are constructed out of metavariables, schematic formulas, and partial ordering statements in a metalanguage that is distinct from the semantic representation language. The substitutions of labelled formulas for holes that generate the well-formed formulas of the representation language which correspond to scope readings are also metalinguistic operations added to the representation language.

More seriously, as we have observed, (Ebert 2005) shows that PLU and other hole semantics theories are expressively incomplete because their constraint languages do not permit the formulation of Boolean conditions on scope like those given in (27), (28), and (34). As in the case of storage, it is possible to add a constraint language with sufficient expressive power required to state conditions of this kind.[9] But this requires further enrichment and complication of the theory. As we have seen, these problems do not arise on our account.

5.3. Glue language semantics and packed scope representations

(Dalrymple et al. 1999) and (Crouch and van Genabith 1999) suggest a theory on which representations of GQs and core relations are expressed as premises in an underspecified semantic glue language. These premises are combined by the natural deduction rules of linear logic in order to yield a formula that represents the scope reading of a sentence. The rules can apply to premises in different orders of derivation to generate alternative scope readings. Unlike PLU, the glue language can be higher-order. Although their formal properties differ, glue language semantics is closely related to hole semantics in the general view of underspecification that it adopts. It would seem that in order achieve expressive completeness in the sense of (Ebert 2005), glue language semantics must add a system for stating constraints on the linear logic proof theory which it employs to derive fully specified interpretations.

(Crouch 2005) describes a procedure for using the linear logic derivations of glue language semantics to generate all scoped interpretations for a sentence. These interpretations are encoded as a set of packed clauses in which components of meaning shared by several readings are expressed as a single common clause. Scope readings are distinguished by clauses in the set that encode their distinctive elements. Packing uses the approach that is applied in chart parsing to construct a graph for non-redundant representation of the full set of possible syntactic structures for a parsed phrase. In this system the choice space of Boolean combinations of clauses in a packed representation that are to be tested for satisfiability is optimised using Maxwell and Kaplan's (1995) method for rendering disjunctive constraint satisfaction efficient.

Packing offers an efficient way of representing and reasoning with the full set of possible scope readings for a sentence. However, it requires that this set be computed as part of the parsing and compositional interpretation of a sentence. With underspecified representations it is possible to avoid computing the set of scoped readings until a subsequent point in the processing of a discourse or text. In PTCT filters can be extracted from new discourse information, where some of these filters significantly reduce the search space of interpretations.

5.4. Relation reduction

(van Eijck 2003) develops an approach to underspecified representations, in the functional programming language Haskell, which uses relation reduction and arbitrary arity relations. This inspired our account, which we have developed within a more restrictive formal theory.

We give a fully general treatment of scope and generalise van Eijck's approach in certain respects. In particular, we introduce a function for selecting specific scope readings, and we make explicit the mechanisms for constraining scope readings using filters. Our approach to underspecification is also polymorphic, which leaves open the possibility of dealing with core relations whose arguments are of different types.

We developed PTCT to have a rich system of types, broadly comparable to that of Haskell, but within a language that we have shown to be of more restricted formal power.

6. Conclusion

We have presented a treatment of underspecified scope representation within PTCT which uses product types to represent sequences of scope taking terms. These types permit us to accommodate polymorphism in the core relation arguments.

We have characterised an underspecified representation as a PTCT term in which a function $perms\_scope_k$ applies to a pair containing an initial sequence of scope taking elements and a core relation. It returns as its value an indexed $k!$-product of possible scope readings. $project\_scope(perms\_scope_k(\langle Qs,R\rangle),i)$ projects the ith scope reading in the $k!$-tuple of scope readings $perms\_scope_k(\langle Qs,R\rangle)$.

We have formulated constraints on scope readings as filters on the $k!$-tuples that $perms\_scope_k$ produces. These filters are PTCT property terms which encode Boolean conditions and quantification over the integers of indexed k-tuples. In principle, they permit PTCT to achieve expressive completeness in the sense of (Ebert 2005).

We have also specified a tree generation algorithm to characterise (the permutation part of) the computable function that $perms\_scope_k$ denotes. When filters are applied as constraints on nodes in the tree that the algorithm generates, they can significantly reduce the search space of possible scope readings given by an underspecified representation.

Underspecified representations, the projection of a particular scope interpretation, and constraints on possible scope readings are all specified by appropriately typed λ-terms within the semantic representation language, PTCT, rather than through operations on schematic metalinguistic objects. Our proposed treatment of underspecified representations within PTCT achieves both significant expressive power and and efficient computation of possible scope interpretations.

Notes

1. We are grateful to Christian Ebert for helpful comments on an earlier draft of this paper. His recent Ph.D. dissertation has stimulated and influenced much of the work we report here. We would also like to thank Dick Crouch and Ron Kaplan for useful discussion of

the complexity issues we address.
2. In Keenan's presentation, some generalised quantifiers can bind more that one of r's arguments, and so reduce its arity by more than 1. These GQ are formed from constituent quantifiers that exhibit relations of mutual dependence. Due to these relations, the GQ which they yield cannot be reduced to a simple functional composition of one quantifier with another. An example of such a GQ is $\langle$"*every student*", "*a different book*"$\rangle$ in "*Every student read a different book.*"
3. See (van Eijck 2003) for examples of filters on lists specified as Boolean functions on the elements of a list.
4. In (Fox and Lappin 2005a: Chapter 6) we formulate a version of Num using Presburger arithmetic (Presburger 1929), so avoiding a commitment to the full power of Peano arithmetic.
5. In fact, this will be a family of functions *filter_tuple*$_{j,k}(\langle F_j, T_k \rangle)$. In the interests of simplicity we will suppress the j and k indices on *filter_tuple* in the text.
6. (Ebert 2005) observes that to actually arrive at expressive completeness it is necessary to extend **PTCT** to deal with nested quantificational structures, like the subject NP in "*Two representatives from three companies saw most samples*". He sketches a proposal for doing this.
7. (Keller 1988) defines a type of storage that encodes relations of syntactic nesting within the stored GQ corresponding to an NP that contains another quantified NP. Although these nested stores avoid certain problems of variable binding encountered with Cooper storage, they do not, in themselves, impose constraints on possible scope readings of the sort that we have discussed in the previous section. See (Blackburn and Bos 2005) for a discussion and an implementation of Keller stores.
8. See (Ebert 2005) for detailed discussion and results concerning the formal relations among these theories with respect to their expressive power.
9. We are grateful to Ian Pratt-Hartman for helpful discussion of this point.

References

Blackburn, Patrick, and Johan Bos
    2005   *Representation and Inference for Natural Language*. Stanford: CSLI.

Bos, Johan
    1995   Predicate logic unplugged. *Proceedings of the Tenth Amsterdam Colloquium*. Amsterdam.

Campbell, W. H.
    2004   Indexing permutations. *Journal of Computing in Small Colleges* 19: 296–300.

Cooper, Robin
    1983   *Quantification and Syntactic Theory*. Synthese Language Library. Dordrecht: D. Reidel.

Copestake, Ann, Dan Flickinger, and Ivan A. Sag
    2006   Minimal recursion semantics. *Research on Language and Computation* 3: 281–332.

Crouch, D.
    2005   Packed rewriting for mapping semantics to KR. *Proceedings of the Sixth International Workshop on Computational Semantics*. Tilburg, 103–114.

Crouch, D., and J. van Genabith
1999   Context change, underspecification, and structure of glue language derivations. In *Semantics and Syntax in Lexical Functional Grammar*, Mary Dalrymple (ed.), 117–189. Cambridge, MA: MIT Press.
Curry, H. B., and R. Feys
1958   *Combinatory Logic*. Volume 1 of *Studies in Logic*. Amsterdam: North Holland.
Dalrymple, M., J. Lamping, F. Pereira, and V. Saraswat
1999   Quantification, anaphora, and intensionality. In *Semantics and Syntax in Lexical Functional Grammar*, Mary Dalrymple (ed.), 39–89. Cambridge, MA: MIT Press.
Ebert, C.
2005   Formal investigation of underspecified representations. Ph.D. diss., Department of Computer Science, King's College London.
Fox, Chris, and Shalom Lappin
2004   An expressive first-order logic with flexible typing for natural language semantics. *Logic Journal of the Interest Group in Pure and Applied Logics* 12 (2): 135–168.
2005a   *Formal Foundations of Intensional Semantics*. Oxford: Blackwell.
2005b   Underspecified interpretations in a Curry-typed representation language. *The Journal of Logic and Computation* 15: 131–143.
Keenan, Ed
1992   Beyond the Fregean boundary. *Linguistics and Philosophy* 15: 199–221.
Keller, W.
1988   Nested cooper storage: The proper treatment of quantification in ordinary noun phrases. In *Natural Language Parsing and Linguistic Theories*, U. Reyle, and C. Rohrer (eds.). Dordrecht: Reidel.
Koller, A., J. Niehren, and S. Thater
2003   Bridging the gap between underspecified formalisms: Hole semantics as dominance constraints. *Proceedings of 11th EACL*. Budapest: ACL.
Maxwell, J., and R. Kaplan
1995   A method for disjunctive constraint satisfaction. In *Formal Issues in Lexical Functional Grammar*, M. Dalrymple, R. Kaplan, J. Maxwell, and A. Zaenen (eds.). Stanford: CSLI.
Meyer, A.
1982   What is a model of the lambda calculus? *Information and Control* 52: 87–122.
Montague, R.
1974   *Formal Philosophy: Selected Papers of Richard Montague*. New Haven, CT: Yale University Press. edited with an introduction by R. H. Thomason.
Pereira, Fernando
1990   Categorial semantics and scoping. *Computational Linguistics* 16: 1–10.
Presburger, Mojzesz
1929   Über die Vollständigkeit eines gewissen Systems der Arithmetik ganzer Zahlen, in welchem die Addition als einzige Operation hervortritt. *Comptes Rendus du I congrès de Mathématiciens des Pays Slaves*. 92–101.
Reyle, U.
1993   Dealing with ambiguities by underspecification: Construction, representation and deduction. *Journal of Semantics* 10: 123–179.
van Eijck, J.
2003   Computational semantics and type theory. Unpublished ms., CWI, Amsterdam.

Storage in deterministic dependency parsing

Joakim Nivre

1. Introduction

There are two naive strategies that we can use when faced with the ubiquitous phenomenon of ambiguity in natural language processing: brute-force enumeration and deterministic disambiguation. In brute-force enumeration, we simply enumerate all the fully specified representations that are compatible with a given input, e.g., all the possible parse trees for an input string given some grammar. This often leads to serious efficiency problems with respect to both time and space. In deterministic disambiguation, we find some more or less principled way of resolving each ambiguity as it arises, which means that we only derive a single fully specified representation for each input. While this avoids the efficiency problems associated with brute-force enumeration, it can instead lead to erroneous decisions because of early commitment, a problem that is often aggravated by error propagation.

More sophisticated techniques that have been proposed for dealing with this problem usually have in common that they avoid early commitment by efficiently computing and representing a set of possible interpretations without enumerating them. A typical example of this is the technique known as *storage* in computational semantics, often referred to as *Cooper storage* after the pioneering work of Robin Cooper (Cooper 1975), which is a mechanism for postponing the resolution of scope ambiguities and for efficiently computing and representing the unresolved interpretation. Another example is the use of dynamic programming and packed parse forests in syntactic parsing, which allows the derivation and storage of an exponentially large number of parse trees in polynomial time and space. However, it is worth noting that, although this makes parsing tractable without early commitment, it is much less efficient than deterministic disambiguation, which can often be realized in linear time and space.

In this paper, I discuss how techniques inspired by storage in computational semantics can be used to improve a technique for dependency-based syntactic parsing that is essentially an instance of naive deterministic disambiguation. The ultimate goal is to be able to improve parsing accuracy without compromising efficiency by using storage-like mechanisms to postpone certain disambiguation decisions, e.g., about the syntactic function of topicalized constituents. This paper is limited to a discussion of possible techniques for reaching this goal. The experimental evaluation of different methods is left for future research.

The paper is structured as follows. In section 2, I introduce deterministic dependency parsing, supported by treebank-induced classifiers. In section 3, I exemplify the problems that arise from the early commitment inherent in deterministic disambiguation, using some examples from Swedish syntax. In section 4, I then discuss two different ways of introducing storage techniques into deterministic dependency parsing. In section 5, finally, I conclude with some suggestions for future research.

2. Deterministic dependency parsing

Deterministic dependency parsing has recently emerged as not only one of the most efficient but also one of the most accurate methods for dependency parsing, provided that the deterministic parser is guided by a classifier trained on treebank data. This method was pioneered by Kudo and Matsumoto (2002) for Japanese and Yamada and Matsumoto (2003) for English and has later been developed and applied to a wide range of languages by Nivre, Hall, and Nilsson (2004), Cheng, Asahara, and Matsumoto (2004), and Attardi (2006), among others. In the CoNLL-X shared task on multilingual dependency parsing, the deterministic classifier-based approach was represented by one of the two top performing systems (Nivre et al. 2006). In this section, I begin by defining the representations used in dependency parsing, move on to discuss deterministic parsing algorithms, and finally explain the role of treebank-induced classifiers for accurate deterministic parsing.

2.1. Dependency graphs

In dependency parsing, the syntactic analysis of a sentence is represented by a dependency graph, which we define as a labeled directed graph, the nodes of which are indices corresponding to the tokens of a sentence. Formally:

- Given a set R of dependency types (arc labels), a *dependency graph* for a sentence $x = (w_1, \ldots, w_n)$ is a labeled directed graph $G = (V, E, L)$, where:

  1. $V = \{0, 1, 2, \ldots n\}$
  2. $E \subseteq V \times V$
  3. $L : E \to R$

- A dependency graph G is *well-formed* if and only if:

  1. The node 0 is a root (ROOT).
  2. G is (weakly) connected (CONNECTEDNESS).
  3. Every node has at most one head, i.e., if $i \to j$ then there is no node k such that $k \neq i$ and $k \to j$ (SINGLE-HEAD).

The set V of *nodes* (or *vertices*) is the set of non-negative integers up to and including n. This means that every token index i of the sentence is a node ($1 \leq i \leq n$) and that there is a special node 0, which does not correspond to any token of the sentence and which will always be a root of the dependency graph (the only root in a well-formed dependency graph).

The set E of *arcs* (or *edges*) is a set of ordered pairs (i, j), where i and j are nodes. Since arcs are used to represent dependency relations, we will say that i is the *head* and j is the *dependent* of the arc (i, j). As usual, we will use the notation $i \to j$ to mean that there is an arc connecting i and j (i.e., $(i, j) \in E$) and we will use the notation $i \to^* j$ for the reflexive and transitive closure of the arc relation E (i.e., $i \to^* j$ if and only if $i = j$ or there is a path of arcs connecting i to j).

The function L assigns a dependency type (arc label) $r \in R$ to every arc $e \in E$. We will use the notation $i \xrightarrow{r} j$ to mean that there is an arc labeled r connecting i to j (i.e., $(i, j) \in E$ and $L((i, j)) = r$).

Figure 1 shows a Swedish sentence with a well-formed dependency graph. Since a well-formed dependency graph is always a tree rooted at 0 (Nivre 2006), I will from now on refer to well-formed dependency graphs as *dependency trees*.

2.2. Parsing algorithm

The task for a disambiguating dependency parser is to derive the correct dependency tree G for a given sentence $x = (w_1, \ldots, w_n)$. A deterministic parser

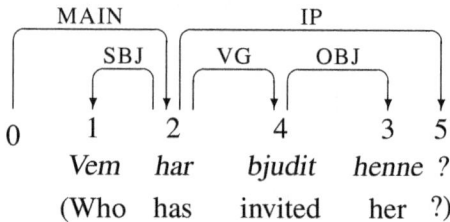

Figure 1. Dependency structure for Swedish sentence (subject interrogative)

solves this problem by deriving a single analysis for each sentence. Most of the algorithms proposed for deterministic dependency parsing have similarities with shift-reduce parsing for constituency-based representations. Thus, the algorithm of Yamada and Matsumoto (2003), which performs unlabeled dependency parsing only, have only three elementary parsing actions, one *shift* action and two *reduce* actions (one for head-initial structures, one for head-final structures). The algorithm of Nivre (2003) can be seen as a variation of this approach, where the *reduce* action for head-initial structures is split into one action for adding the dependency arc and a separate action for popping the dependent from the stack. This allows arc-eager parsing, which reduces the amount of nondeterminism in the parsing process and makes parsing strictly incremental (Nivre 2004). This algorithm can be characterized as follows:

- Given a set R of dependency types (arc labels) and a sentence $x = (w_1, \ldots, w_n)$, a parser configuration for x is a triple $c = (\sigma, \tau, G)$, where:
  1. σ is a stack of nodes i ($0 \leq i \leq j$ for some $j \leq n$).
  2. τ is a sequence of nodes $(k, k+1, k+2, \ldots n)$ ($k > j$).
  3. G is a dependency graph for x.

- The parser is initialized to $((0), (1, 2, \ldots, n), G_0)$, where $G_0 = (\{0, 1, 2, \ldots, n\}, \emptyset, \emptyset)$.

- The parser terminates in any configuration of the form $(\sigma, (), G)$, outputting a dependency graph G', which differs from G only in that, for every root i in G such that $i \neq 0$, there is an arc $0 \rightarrow i$ in G'.

- The following transitions (parser actions) are possible in a non-terminal configuration satisfying the constraints stated for each transition:

1. $(\sigma|i,j|\tau, G) \Longrightarrow (\sigma, j|\tau, G[j \xrightarrow{r} i])$ $\quad \neg \exists k : k \to i \text{ in } G$
2. $(\sigma|i,j|\tau, G) \Longrightarrow (\sigma|i|j, \tau, G[i \xrightarrow{r} j])$ $\quad i \neq 0, \neg \exists k : k \to j \text{ in } G$
3. $(\sigma|i, \tau, G) \Longrightarrow (\sigma, \tau, G)$ $\quad \exists k : k \to i \text{ in } G$
4. $(\sigma, i|\tau, G) \Longrightarrow (\sigma|i, \tau, G)$

where $\sigma|i$ is a stack with top element i, $j|\tau$ is a list with head j and tail τ, and $G[i \to j]$ is the graph that differs from G only by the addition of the arc (i, j).

The idea is that the sequence τ represents the remaining input tokens in a left-to-right pass over the input sentence x; the stack σ contains partially processed nodes that are still candidates for dependency arcs, either as heads or dependents, and the graph G is the partially constructed dependency graph. Provided that every transition can be performed in constant time, the algorithm has time complexity $O(n)$, where n is the number of words in the input sentence (Nivre 2003). Moreover, the algorithm guarantees that the graph G given at termination is acyclic and satisfies ROOT and SINGLE-HEAD, which means that it can be transformed to a dependency tree by adding arcs from the special root 0 to any other roots in the graph (Nivre 2006). One limitation of this parsing algorithm is that it only derives strictly projective dependency trees (i.e., trees where the projection of every head is continuous), whereas dependency parsing in general needs to allow non-projective trees as well. However, this limitation can be overcome by special pre- and post-processing techniques for recovering non-projective dependencies, so-called *pseudo-projective parsing* (Nivre and Nilsson 2005).

2.3. Classifier-based parsing

Deterministic parsing algorithms need an *oracle* for predicting the next parser action at nondeterministic choice points. In *classifier-based* parsing, such oracles are approximated with *classifiers* trained on data derived from treebanks. This is essentially a form of *history-based parsing*, where features of the parsing history are used to predict the next parser action (Black et al. 1992; Magerman 1995; Ratnaparkhi 1997).

Let $\Phi(\sigma, \tau, G)$ be a feature vector representation of a parser configuration with stack σ, input sequence τ and dependency graph G. Training data for the classifier can be generated by running the parser on a sample of treebank data, using the gold standard dependency graph as an oracle to predict the next

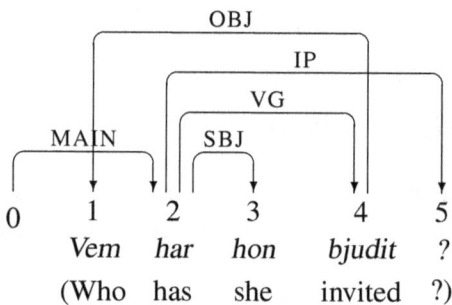

Figure 2. Dependency structure for Swedish sentence (object interrogative)

parser action and constructing one training instance $(\Phi(\sigma, \tau, G), t)$ for each occurrence of a transition t in a parser configuration represented by $\Phi(\sigma, \tau, G)$. The features in $\Phi(\sigma, \tau, G)$ can be arbitrary features of the input x and the partially built graph G but usually consist mainly of linguistic attributes of input tokens, including their dependency types according to G.

The history-based classifier can be trained with any of the available supervised methods for function approximation, such as memory-based learning or decision trees, but the best performance has so far been achieved with support vector machines (Vapnik 1995), which has been used for parsing in a wide range of experiments (Kudo and Matsumoto 2002; Yamada and Matsumoto 2003; Sagae and Lavie 2005; Nivre et al. 2006).

3. The problem

In the previous section I have sketched how it is possible to achieve highly accurate dependency parsing, despite the naive approach of deterministic disambiguation, using history-based classifiers trained on large data sets derived from treebanks. Nevertheless, it is clear that some of the errors performed by deterministic incremental parsers are due to the fact that the parser sometimes has to commit to an analysis before all the relevant evidence can be taken into account.

A typical example is the analysis of topicalized constituents in Swedish (and other verb-second languages), exemplified by *wh*-questions in figure 1 and figure 2. When processing these sentences incrementally, the parser has to make an early decision about whether the topicalized constituent (*Vem*) should be linked to the finite (auxiliary) verb (*har*) by the subject relation (as in figure 1) or not at all (as in figure 2). To some extent, this problem can be alleviated by the lookahead available in the input string, but there is never any guarantee that this will lead to the correct decision, despite the fact that the necessary information is available in the rest of the sentence.[1]

Examples such as these abound in natural language syntax. Let us consider just one more case from Swedish syntax:

(1)   a.   *Kommer han, eller hon?*
           Comes he, or   she?
           'Does he come, or she?'
    b.   *Kommer han, går hon.*
           Comes he, goes she.
           'If he comes, she goes.'

When parsing (1a) with the algorithm described above, the first action should be to add an arc labeled MAIN from the root 0 to the token 1, since the finite verb *Kommer* is the head of the main clause. In (1b), by contrast, no such arc should be added, because the finite verb *Kommer* in this case is the head of a (conditional) subordinate clause and should therefore be a dependent of the main clause verb *går*.

So, the question I want to pose is what we can do to improve the parser's ability to make the correct decision in cases like these, while still maintaining the attractive time and space complexity of deterministic parsing.

4. Two possible solutions

I will now outline two methods for postponing difficult decisions of the kind exemplified in the preceding section, both inspired by the notion of *storage*.

4.1. Multi-pass parsing

The most straightforward application of the storage principle is to simply store the tokens that we do not (yet) know where to attach on the stack. Without any other modification to the parsing algorithm, this would mean that the topicalized constituents in figure 1 and figure 2 would remain unattached throughout the parsing process and would at termination be attached to the special root node 0. So, in order to arrive at the desired analysis for each sentence, we would instead have to do a second pass over the input, where we attach tokens that have been stored on the stack, using all the evidence available in the partial dependency graph. This requires only two minor modifications to the algorithm, namely that we allow the parser to be initialized with an arbitrary (acyclic) dependency graph obeying ROOT and SINGLE-HEAD (rather than G_0), and that we output the graph G given at termination (rather than the graph G' obtained by attaching all roots in $\{1,\ldots,n\}$ to 0).

Given that one and the same sentence may contain several problematic constructions, we can either decide to have a single additional pass, where we deal with all the problematic phenomena together, or we can allow multiple passes, fixing only one type of construction in each pass. In either case, however, we want to train different classifiers for the different passes, in order to exploit the fact that the amount of information available in both input and output increases from earlier to later passes.

More precisely, if we want to divide the parsing problem into m passes, we need a partitioning function f on the arc relation and labeling function of an arbitrary dependency tree, such that if $f(E,L) = ((E_1,L_1)\ldots,(E_m,L_m))$ then $\bigcup_{i=1}^{m} E_i = E$, $E_i \cap E_j = \emptyset$ (for any i, j), L_i is a total function on E_i (for any i), and E_i contains exactly the dependency arcs that should be added in pass m. If we use G_j to denote the graph $(V, \bigcup_{i=1}^{j} E_i, \bigcup_{i=1}^{j} L_i)$, then we train the classifier for pass i using G_{i-1} as input and G_i as output. It is worth noting that the training scheme for the original parsing algorithm is just the special case of this where $m=1$.

The basic idea in multi-pass parsing, i.e., that some decisions should be postponed until others have been made, is also the motivation for the iterative approach used by Kudo and Matsumoto (2002) and Yamada and Matsumoto (2003). However, one difference is that they use the same classifier for all passes and do not impose any upper bound on the number of passes but terminate only when no new arc has been added in the previous iteration. This means that the worst-case time complexity of this algorithm is $O(n^2)$ (even though the worst case seldom occurs in practice). By contrast, if we can define linguistically motivated criteria for the partitioning of dependency arcs, such that the number of passes is always bounded by a constant m, which is independent of the length of the input sentence, then we can preserve the linear time complexity of the original algorithm. Interestingly, a proposal along these lines has already been made by Arnola (1998) (for a different parsing algorithm), who hypothesizes that the partitioning (in our terminology) can be defined in terms of dependency types (arc labels), so that there will be one pass for each distinct dependency type, and that there is an optimal sequence in which dependency types should be processed in order to maximize parsing accuracy while maintaining linear-time parsing.

4.2. Generalized pseudo-projective parsing

Another way of implementing the storage idea is to add temporary arcs with temporary labels for problematic constructions. For example, we may decide to always attach topicalized constituents to the lowest node that dominates all its potential heads. In terms of the previous examples, this would mean that we always attach the topicalized *Vem* to the finite (auxiliary) verb *har*, but with a temporary arc label signifying that the real head of *Vem* is in the subtree dominated by *har*. In a post-processing phase, we can then perform a top-down search for the true head, again using all the information available in the rest of the derived dependency tree.

This approach can be seen as a generalization of the idea behind *pseudo-projective* parsing (Nivre and Nilsson 2005). As a matter of fact, since the dependency tree in figure 2 is non-projective, it can only be derived by first attaching *Vem* to *har*, with a temporary label signifying that the true head is a descendant of *har* with the dependency type VG. In a post-processing phase, we then perform a top-down breadth-first search in order to find out that the true head is the main verb *bjudit*. What I am now proposing is to use the same technique also for the tree in figure 1, which is strictly projective but where the true head and dependency type of *Vem* is difficult to determine before we have derived the rest of the structure.

In order to realize this idea we have to implement an instance of the following scheme:

1. Transform the training data for the parser so that problematic constructions are analyzed with temporary heads and dependency labels.

2. Train the parser on the transformed training data.

3. Parse new sentences into the transformed representation.

4. Perform an inverse transformation to the parser output, guided by the information in temporary dependency labels.

In order to preserve the linear time complexity of parsing, we need to ensure that both pre- and post-processing can be performed in linear time as well. Since the transformation of a single arc can usually be performed in time proportional to the total number of arcs, which is linear in string length, this requires either that all arcs can be processed together or that there is (again) a constant upper bound on the number of arcs that need to be processed for an arbitrary sentence.

The use of pre- and post-processing in deterministic dependency parsing has previously been studied not only in connection with pseudo-projective parsing but also as a general technique for improving accuracy under the heading of *tree transformations* (Nilsson, Nivre, and Hall 2006; Nilsson 2007). The generalized pseudo-projective parsing approach also has affinities with the notion of *temporary landing sites* proposed by Buch-Kromann (2006) in the context of parsing with Discontinuous Grammar.

5. Conclusion

In this paper I have proposed two ways of incorporating a notion of storage into deterministic, classifier-based dependency parsing, with the aim of improving accuracy without sacrificing efficiency. The most pressing need for future research is obviously an experimental evaluation of the proposed techniques. For the multi-pass approach it is also important to try to find linguistically motivated principles for partitioning dependency graphs. For generalized pseudo-projective parsing it is crucial to achieve a harmonious integration with pseudo-projective parsing in the original sense, so that non-projective dependencies can still be recovered. Needless to say, it is much too early to say whether any of these techniques will be as successful in dependency parsing as the original notion of storage has been in computational semantics.

Notes

1. Because of the composite tense form, the word order uniquely identifies the subject and the object in the example sentences.

References

Arnola, Harri
    1998   On parsing binary dependency structure deterministically in linear time. Sylvain Kahane, and Alain Polguère (eds.), *Proceedings of the Workshop on Processing of Dependency-Based Grammars (ACL-COLING)*. 68–77.

Attardi, Giuseppe
    2006   Experiments with a multilanguage non-projective dependency parser. *Proceedings of the Tenth Conference on Computational Natural Language Learning (CoNLL)*. 166–170.

Black, Ezra, Frederick Jelinek, John D. Lafferty, David M. Magerman, Robert L. Mercer, and Salim Roukos
    1992   Towards history-based grammars: Using richer models for probabilistic parsing. *Proceedings of the 5th DARPA Speech and Natural Language Workshop*. 31–37.

Buch-Kromann, Matthias
    2006   Discontinous Grammar. a model of human parsing and language acquisitiion. Ph.D. diss., Copenhagen Business School.

Cheng, Yuchang, Masayuki Asahara, and Yuji Matsumoto
    2004   Deterministic dependency structure analyzer for Chinese. *Proceedings of the First International Joint Conference on Natural Language Processing (IJCNLP)*. 500–508.

Cooper, Robin
    1975   Montague's semantic theory and transformational syntax. Ph.D. diss., University of Massachusetts at Amherst.

Kudo, Taku, and Yuji Matsumoto
    2002   Japanese dependency analysis using cascaded chunking. *Proceedings of the Sixth Workshop on Computational Language Learning (CoNLL)*. 63–69.

Magerman, David M.
    1995   Statistical decision-tree models for parsing. *Proceedings of the 33rd Annual Meeting of the Association for Computational Linguistics (ACL)*. 276–283.

Nilsson, Jens
    2007   Tree Transformations in Inductive Dependency Parsing. Licentiate Thesis, Växjö University.

Nilsson, Jens, Joakim Nivre, and Johan Hall
    2006   Graph transformations in data-driven dependency parsing. *Proceedings of the 21st International Conference on Computational Linguistics and 44th Annual Meeting of the Association for Computational Linguistics (COLING-ACL)*. 257–264.

Nivre, Joakim
    2003   An efficient algorithm for projective dependency parsing. Gertjan Van Noord (ed.), *Proceedings of the 8th International Workshop on Parsing Technologies (IWPT)*. 149–160.

2004 Incrementality in deterministic dependency parsing. Frank Keller, Stephen Clark, Matthew Crocker, and Mark Steedman (eds.), *Proceedings of the Workshop on Incremental Parsing: Bringing Engineering and Cognition Together (ACL)*. 50–57.
2006 *Inductive Dependency Parsing*. Springer.

Nivre, Joakim, Johan Hall, and Jens Nilsson
2004 Memory-based dependency parsing. Hwee Tou Ng, and Ellen Riloff (eds.), *Proceedings of the 8th Conference on Computational Natural Language Learning (CoNLL)*. 49–56.

Nivre, Joakim, Johan Hall, Jens Nilsson, Gülsen Eryiğit, and Svetoslav Marinov
2006 Labeled pseudo-projective dependency parsing with support vector machines. *Proceedings of the Tenth Conference on Computational Natural Language Learning (CoNLL)*. 221–225.

Nivre, Joakim, and Jens Nilsson
2005 Pseudo-projective dependency parsing. *Proceedings of the 43rd Annual Meeting of the Association for Computational Linguistics (ACL)*. 99–106.

Ratnaparkhi, Adwait
1997 A linear observed time statistical parser based on maximum entropy models. *Proceedings of the Second Conference on Empirical Methods in Natural Language Processing (EMNLP)*. 1–10.

Sagae, Kenji, and Alon Lavie
2005 A classifier-based parser with linear run-time complexity. *Proceedings of the 9th International Workshop on Parsing Technologies (IWPT)*. 125–132.

Vapnik, Vladimir N.
1995 *The Nature of Statistical Learning Theory*. Springer.

Yamada, Hiroyasu, and Yuji Matsumoto
2003 Statistical dependency analysis with support vector machines. Gertjan Van Noord (ed.), *Proceedings of the 8th International Workshop on Parsing Technologies (IWPT)*. 195–206.

Licensing by modification: The case of Brazilian Portuguese distributive-universal quantifiers

Esmeralda Vailati Negrão

1. Introduction

It has been noticed that modification, especially by a relative clause, has a surprising role in the licensing of structures that would otherwise be ungrammatical. Dayal (2004) develops an explanation for cases of licensing that differ from the canonical form, inasmuch as the licensor is in the scope of its licensee. Based on facts related to the distribution of bare plurals in Italian, free choice *any* in English and the availability of a generic interpretation for definite plural phrases, also in English, Dayal proposes that, instead of an account that would change the directionality of the licensing, licensing by modification should be explained as resulting from the interaction of the semantics of the individual elements involved in the structure.

This paper aims at understanding the contribution given by modification, more specifically modification by a relative clause, in the licensing of Distributive Quantifier Phrases (DQPs) in Brazilian Portuguese (BP).

Under the generative framework, the interpretations associated with sentences in which Quantifier Phrases (QPs) and/or operators interact, giving rise to the phenomena known as quantifier scope, have been taken to be driven by syntactic structure. The idea behind the syntactic treatment of quantifier scope is that, at some level of representation, QPs move to a higher hierarchical position from which they are able to c-command the domain under their scope. Different proposals have been made in the literature to implement these movement mechanisms (Huang, 1982; May,1985; Aoun and Li, 1993; Hornstein, 1995; Beghelli and Stowell, 1997, among others).

This paper will take the theoretical assumptions of the 'Target Landing Site Theory of Scope'(TLS) proposed by Beghelli (1995) and Beghelli and Stowell (1997), a theory which offers a syntactic treatment to scope relations and distributive construals. It shares with the movement theories of quantifier scope the assumption that relations derived from the syntactic hierarchical structure play a determinant role in the semantics of scope relations. The use of the movement approach is advantageous because the principles explaining the properties of other syntactic constructions can be used to derive the scopal properties of quantifier phrases. On the other hand, TLS departs from other movement theories by rejecting the assumption that Quantifier Raising applies uniformly to all QPs. In order to account for the differences in scope patterns exhibited by DQPs, they assume that the hierarchical structure of the sentences contains two other functional projections, Distributive Phrase (DistP) and Share Phrase (ShareP), where DistP dominates ShareP.

Following the analysis proposed by Dayal, I will claim that relative clauses play an important role in the licensing of DQPs since they offer an event/spatio-temporal variable which is bound by the DQP. In pursuit of its main goal, the paper shows a difference in the kind of relative clauses associated with the two distributive universal quantifiers of BP: *cada* - DQPs are modified by restrictive relative clauses, whereas *todo*-DQPs allow for modification by a maximalizing relative clause. This difference will be shown to be very important to the characterization of the semantic distinction between *todo* and *cada* in BP.

2. The behavior of *todo* and *cada* DQPs

In a series of papers, Negrão (1997, 1999, 2001, 2002) and Negrão and Viotti (2000) investigate some of the properties observed in the distribution and in the interpretation of sentences containing distributive quantifiers phrases introduced by *todo* and *cada* in BP. The intriguing properties of these two quantifier phrases can be summarized in the following sequence of data.

The first generalization deals with distributional properties of DQPs. There is an asymmetry in acceptability between sentences containing these quantifier phrases in subject position in contrast with sentences containing them in object position.

(1) a. Todo   aluno   leu   um   livro
        every   student read   a   book

   b. Cada   aluno   leu   um   livro
        each   student read   a   book

   c. *Um   aluno   leu   todo   livro
        a   student read   every   book

   d. *Um   aluno   leu   cada   livro
        a   student read   each   book

Sentences (1c) and (1d), in which *cada*-DQP and *todo*-DQP are in object position, are ungrammatical, whereas sentences (1a) and (1b), in which the DQPs are in subject position, are fully grammatical. Moreover, sentences (1a) and (1b) are unambiguous, that is, they only allow interpretations in which DQPs have wide scope.

However, the asymmetry seems to be neutralized if a sentence modifier, for example a relative clause, is attached to the restriction of the DQP in object position. Observe the data in (2):

(2) a. Aqueles   alunos   leram   todo   livro   que   encontraram
        these   students read   every   book   that   found

        na   biblioteca   sobre   o   assunto
        in the   library   about   the   subject

   b. Aqueles   alunos   leram   cada   livro   que   encontraram
        these   students read   each   book   that   found

        na   biblioteca   sobre   o   assunto
        in the   library   about   the   subject

The second generalization is made in terms of the distributive properties of these quantifier phrases. Following Beghelli (1997) and Beghelli and Stowell (1997), the authors assume that distributivity is a binary relation requiring a distributor and a distributee, that is, a set whose members could be distributed over the members of another set (in Choe's (1987) terms, *sorting key* and *distributed share*, respectively). The distributor role is played by the set denoted by the DQP restriction, whereas the distributee's (distributed share) role may be played either by another phrase containing indefinites or counting expressions, or by the Davidsonian event argument of the predicate, assumed to be an argument of all kinds of predicates. It turns out that, in BP, the event argument of the predicate has a determinant role in the grammaticality of sentences containing a quantifier phrase introduced by *cada*. Contrary to the position assumed by Beghelli and Stowel, Negrão proposes that the argument event is not present in the argument structure of all predicates. She follows Kratzer (1995) in assuming that the argument structure of *individual level* and *stage level* predicates differ by the fact that the latter contains an extra argument position for the event argument, which is claimed to be a *spatiotemporal location*. The event argument is not part of the argument structure of *individual level* predicates. More than requiring a predicate which includes an event in its argument structure when there is no other phrase offering a set to function as a distributed share, DQPs introduced by *cada* require that this event/spatio-temporal argument brings about a temporal sequence of non-overlapping subevents. Aspect/temporal inflection markers, modifiers and predicates that already have iterativity in its lexical meaning are the elements that elicit the required reading.

(3) a. **Cada homem é inteligente*
     each man is intelligent

   b. **Cada funcionária está grávida*
     each employee is pregnant

(4) a. **Cada homem é inteligente num período do ano*
     each man is intelligent in a period of the year

   b. **Cada funcionária está grávida num período do ano*
     each employee is pregnant in a period of the year

The data in (3) show that sentences in which *cada*-DQPs are either the subject of an *individual level* predicate or the subject of a *stage level* predicate are both unacceptable. However, if the content of the *spatiotemporal location* argument is explicitly modified, the contrast between the two kinds of predicates immediately surfaces, as in (4). The sentences in (5) confirm this observation. They contain a *stage level* predicate in the simple past tense, that is, a predicate with an event argument in its argument structure. Nevertheless, whereas sentence (5a) is unacceptable, sentences (5b) and (5c) are perfect. Both modifiers of the event argument, the vehicle in which each guest will arrive in (5b) and the phrase denoting the temporal location in (5c), function as distributed share for the distributive phrase introduced by *cada*.

(5) a. *Cada convidado chegou
       each guest arrived

   b. Cada convidado chegou num carro
      each guest arrived in one car

   c. Pouco a pouco cada convidado chegou
      little by little each guest arrived

The sentences from (3) to (5) contain DQPs in subject position. Sentences with DQPs in object position also become fully grammatical if the reading of a sequence of temporal subevents is made explicit by iterative aspectual markers, verbs in which iterativity is contained in their lexical meaning, and modifiers of the *spatiotemporal location* argument:

(6) a. Alguns alunos têm lido⁵ cada texto
       some students have read each paper

   b. Os alunos aplaudiram cada conferencista
      the students applauded each speaker

   c. Pouco a pouco alguns alunos leram cada texto
      little by little some students read each paper

Müller et al. (to appear) argue that *todo* in BP is a distributive universal quantifier. The authors offer a unified treatment for *todo*-DQPs. Contrary to *cada*-DQPs, a quantifier phrase built with *cada* + NP, *todo*-DQPs, besides being a quantifier phrase built with *todo* + NP, can also be built with *todo* + a singular definite description and *todo* + a plural definite description. In order to achieve this unified treatment, *todo* is claimed to be a distributive universal quantifier "which operates both over its nominal argument and over its predicate, being able to quantify over partitions of both its restriction and its nuclear scope".

(7) Toda familia construiu uma jangada
    every family built a raft

(8) *Toda familia construiu a jangada
    every family built the raft

Sentence (7) has only a distributive reading in which the families distribute over events of building a raft. This explains the ungrammaticality of sentence (8), in which the definite description in object position enforces a singular event reading incompatible with the distributive requirements of *todo-* DQPs.

3. Relative clauses and their role in the licensing of distributive quantifier phrases

Dayal (2004) aims at explaining the exceptional licensing of phrases introduced by *any* in English and bare plural phrases in Italian, triggered by the addition of post-nominal modifiers such as relative clauses. The crucial difference between pre-nominal and pos-nominal modifiers which are phrasal is the fact that they introduce an independent spatio/temporal variable. Her example of the contrast is:

(9) a. **Mary talked to any angry student.*

   b. *Mary talked to any student who was angry.*

According to Dayal, the contrast is explained by the fact that the relative clause introduces the possibility of having a set of students who are angry at a particular time and place independently of the time and place contained in the predicate of the matrix sentence. On the other hand, sentence (9a) is ungrammatical because "there is a clash between the presupposition that the domain of quantification ranges over possible individuals, and a predication that can only apply to actual individuals"(p.7). Another very important point emphasized by Dayal is the fact that this kind of modification differs radically from the intersective interpretation usually associated with relative clauses, as in:

(10)   The student who is from Japan

to which we can associate the interpretation of denoting the unique individual who has the property of being a student and of being from Japan.

It seems that Dayal´s account for the licensing of phrases introduced by *any* in English can be extended to the BP sentences with DQPs in object position presented in (2), repeated here as (11) for convenience:

(11) a. Aqueles   alunos   leram todo   livro   que   encontraram
       these   students   read   every book   that found

       na   biblioteca sobre o   assunto
       in the   library   about the   subject

    b. Aqueles   alunos   leram cada   livro   que   encontraram
       these   students   read   each   book   that found

       na   biblioteca sobre o   assunto
       in the   library   about the   subject

The relative clause offers the set of books denoted by the restriction of the distributive quantifier, a time/place variable independent from the time and place of the main predicate. In the case of the DQPs of BP, this independent event/spatio-temporal variable opens the possibility for the relative clause to function as a distributed share over which the set denoted by the restriction of the Distributive Quantifier Phrase (a distributor requiring a distributed share) can distribute. It is interesting to notice a difference in the behavior of *todo*-DQPs when compared to *cada*-DQPs.

(12) a. O   João   presenteou a   Maria   com   todo   livro
        the   João   gifted   the   Maria   with   every   book

        que   ele   encontrou   na   FNAC   sobre ese   assunto
        that   he   found   in the FNAC   about this   subject

    b. O   João   presentou   a   Maria   com   cada   livro
        the   João   gifted   the   Maria   with   each   book

        que   ele   encontrou   na   FNAC   sobre ese   assunto
        that   he   found   in the FNAC   about this   subject

Sentence (12b) can have a reading in which books found at FNAC may distribute over events of giving a present to Maria. This reading is not available for sentence (12a). This means that the event/ spatio-temporal variable offered to *cada* opens the possibility for *cada*-DQPs to scope over the event argument of the main clause. The option of taking scope over the event argument of the main clause is not available for *todo*-DQPs.

In order to offer an account of the difference between the role played by modification by relative clauses with *cada*-DQPs in contrast with *todo*-

DQPs, a brief digression seems necessary. The traditional typology of relative clauses pointed to the existence of two types of such a construction, restrictive and appositive relative clauses.

Carlson (1977) argues in favour of the existence of a third type of relative clause, *amount relatives*. Among the properties indicated by Carlson as characteristics of amount relatives in comparison with restrictive relatives, it is worth mentioning the following: they may appear in contexts where There-Insertion has applied, as in (13):

(13)   Every man there was on the life-raft died

The nominal head of an amount relative in English can cooccur with a very limited set of determiners and quantifiers:*all*, *any*, *the*, *that*, *what*, *every*.

Grosu and Landman (1998) and Grosu (2002) offer an account for a third kind of relative clause, which does not conform with the properties of relatives traditionally partitioned in restrictive and appositive relative clauses. In this class they include, among others, degree relatives, Carlson's *amount relatives*, and correlatives (Dayal,1995). The properties characterizing this third kind of relative are: the relative may have a definite or universal force, but never an existential force; in contrast with restrictive relatives, they do not have the stacking property and their interpretation is not captured by the set intersection operation.

An example adapted from Carlson may help to reproduce the argumentation in regard to the differences in interpretation between restrictive relatives and degree relatives (*amount* relatives in Carlson's terms):

(14)   O   ladrão levou   todo   eletrônico que cabia na   Kombi
       the   thief   carried every electronic that fits in the Kombi

This sentence is ambiguous. It can mean that the thief carried everything electronic that had the property of fitting in the Kombi, meaning that he left behind electronic things that were too big. This interpretation corresponds to the interpretation assumed to be associated with restrictive relative clauses. The second interpretation can be understood as the thief having carried a Kombi full of electronic devices. This second interpretation characterizes Carlson's *amount* relatives.

If we build a sentence equivalent to (14) with a *cada*-DQP, we will observe that the sentence is not ambiguous anymore.

(15) O   ladrão levou   cada eletrônico que cabia na   Kombi
      the thief   carried each electronic that fits in the   Kombi

The only possible interpretation for sentence (15) has is that the thief carried each electronic piece that had the property of fitting the Kombi, that is, the relative clause associated with **cada**-DQPs seem to be a restrictive relative clause.

Grosu and Landman (1998) propose that the classification of relative clause types should be redone in terms of sortal-internal vs sortal external relatives. Intuitively, the distinction is based in a criterion according to which the semantic contribution of the common noun or noun phrase heading the relative clause is done internaly or externaly to the relative clause. In the case of restrictive relatives, the contribution of the head noun and the semantic content of the relative is equivalent. This is the author's way of capturing the intersection operation characteristic of the interpretation of restrictive relative clauses. In the case of maximalizers relatives, designation given to the third kind of relatives (Carlson's *amount* relatives), the semantic contribution of the head noun and its cardinality is done internally to the relative clause. I want to claim that the internal semantic composition of the head and its cardinality in maximalizers relatives explain the difference in interpretation observed in the sentences in (16):

(16) a. O   João   carregou todo   carrinho que   conseguiu
         the João   carried   every   cart   that (he) could

         por vinte   reais
         for twenty reais

     b. O   João   carregou cada   carrinho que   conseguiu
         the João   carried   each   cart   that (he) could

         por vinte   reais
         for twenty reais

Sentence (16a) where a *todo*-DQP modified by a relative clause occupies the object position means that João earned twenty reais for all the carrying done, whereas sentence (16b), with a *cada*-DQP in object position means that John received twenty reais for each carrying done. The interpretation associated with sentence (16b) is accounted for if we assume that *cada*-DQP, modified by the relative clause which licenses the

DQP by offering a time/place variable independent from the time and place of the main predicate, is able to scope over events of carrying for twenty reais. The fact that *cart* is construed internally to the relative clause does not allow *todo*-DQP to scope over the event argument of the matrix clause.

4. Conclusion

This paper offers an account for the contribution given by modification by a relative clause in the licensing of *todo*-DQPs and *cada*-DQPs. The claim is that, by offering a time/place variable independent from the time and place especifications of the main predicate, relative clauses offer an event over which the distributive universal quantifiers may satisfy their distributive requirements. Differences in the semantic contribution given by the distributive quantifiers *cada* and *todo* has consequences for the kind of relative clause formed and for the scopal properties associated with DQPs built by them.

Notes

1. This research was supported by CNPq (Proc. No. 303742/2004-6).
2. The perspective of developing a semantic analysis built on the syntactic structure of the natural language under investigation was acquired during the years that I had the privilege of being one of Robin Cooper's PhD students, to whom I want to express my gratitude.
3. It is very hard to find the exact translation for the items *todo* and *cada*, as you will see in the analysis developed in the paper. Just as an approximation, it is possible to say that, in English, *todo* sometimes behaves like 'all', sometimes like 'every', and *cada* behaves sometimes like 'each', sometimes like 'every'. The option taken in this paper for presenting the data discussed is to translate *todo* by 'every' and *cada* by 'each', but the remarks made in this footnote should be kept in mind.
4. Postma (2000) offers a different account for similar facts. It is out of the scope of the present paper to discuss the consequences of his proposal.
5. The verbal form 'have (present) + past participle' has an iterative meaning in BP.

References

Aoun, J. and Li, Y.A.
1993 *Syntax of Scope*. Cambridge, Mass: MIT Press.

Beghelli, F.
1995 The phrase structure of quantifier scope. Ph.D. dissertation, University of California - Los Angeles.

Beghelli, F. and Stowell, T.
1997 Distributivity and negation: the syntax of **EACH** and **EVERY**. In: A. Szabolcsi (ed.) *Ways of Scope Taking*. Dordrecht, Kluwer: 71–109.

Carlson, G.
1977 Amount relatives. *Language* **53** *(3)*: 520–542.

Choe, J.-W.
1987 Anti-quantifiers and a theory of distributivity. Ph.D. dissertation, University of Massachusetts – Amherst.

Dayal, V.
1995 Quantification in correlatives. In: E. Bach, E. Jelinek, A. Kratzer and B. Partee (eds.) *Quantification in Natural Languages*. Dordrecht, Kluwer: 179–205.

Dayal, V.
2004 Licensing by modification. Rutgers University, mimeo.

Grosu, A.
2002 Strange relatives at the interface of two millennia. *Glot International* 6 (6): 145–167.

Grosu, A. and Landman, F.
1998 Strange relatives of the third kind. *Natural Language Semantics* **6**: 125–170.

Hornstein, N.
1995 *Logical Form: From GB to Minimalism*. Cambridge, Mass., Blackwell.

Huang, C-T. J.
1982 Logical relations in Chinese and the theory of grammar. Ph.D. dissertation, Massachusetts Institute of Tecnology, Cambridge.

Kratzer, A.
1995 Stage-level and individual-level predicates. In: G. N.Carlson and F.J. Pelletier (ed.) *The Generic Book*. Chicago and London, The University of Chicago Press: 125–175.

May, R
1985 *Logical Form. Its structure and derivation*. Cambridge, Mass.: MIT Press.

Müller, A. et al.
in press *Todo* in *Brazilian* Portuguese: *All* or *every* or neither?

Negrão, E.V.
1997 The scopal properties of DQPs in BP. University of California – Los Angeles, Mimeo.
1999 O português brasileiro: uma língua voltada para o discurso. Tese de livre docência, USP, São Paulo.
2001 The scopal properties of distributive quantifier phrases in Brazilian Portuguese. In: J-Y. Kim and A. Werle (eds.) *The Proceedings of SULA. The Semantics of Under-Represented Languages in the Americas*. University of Massachusetts Occasional Papers in Linguistics – 25. The Graduate Linguistics Students' Association, University of Massachusetts, Amherst: 81–85.
2002 Distributividade e genericidade nos sintagmas introduzidos por **cada** e **todo**. *Revista do GEL*, no. especial: 187–205.

Negrão, E.V. and Viotti, E.C.
2000 Brazilian Portuguese as a discourse-oriented language. In: M.A. Kato and E.V.Negrão (eds.) *Brazilian Portuguese and the Null Subject Parameter*. Frankfurt, Editorial Vervuert/Iberoamericana: 97–116.

Postma, G.
2000 Distributive universal quantification and aspect in Brazilian Portuguese. In: J. Costa (ed.) *Portuguese Syntax. New Comparative Studies*. Oxford: Oxford University Press. 241–265.

Formal semantics and logic

Quantification, the reprise content hypothesis, and type theory

Jonathan Ginzburg and Matthew Purver

60. Robin H. Cooper (RCH): Quantification and dialogue and type theory and CRification

Robin Cooper has always been interested in quantification (at least since 1972, we hypothesize). He has been interested in dialogue for more than 15 years (ever since he pushed the alphabetically first author to get working on it.), he has been working on Type Theory for slightly less (though it is of course a natural outgrowth of his 20 something year engagement with Situation Semantics), and he has been interested in CRification for almost a decade. We dedicate this piece in thanks to his encouragment over the years and with the wish for many productive years of quantification, dialogue, yoga, and Tippet.

1. Introduction

Generalized quantifiers (GQs) were brought to the attention of linguists by (Montague 1974) and a systematic study of them initiated by (Barwise and Cooper 1981) and (Keenan and Stavi 1986). Montague, who was not on the whole concerned with cognitive issues, was unperturbed by the complex denotations (properties of properties) he was bringing into the grammar. Barwise and Cooper, however, were and in order to explain how a hearer can process a GQ without having to determine the identity of this full set of sets, introduced simple counterparts to each GQ entity (*witness sets*). Somewhat coincidentally, witnesses also play an important role in Type Theory with Records (TTR), a framework Cooper has developed over the past decade (see e.g. (Cooper 2005a; Cooper 2005b)), showing in particular how GQ theory can be advantageously reformulated in TTR (Cooper 2004; see also (Fernando 2001) for a highly insightful synthesis between GQT and type theory.

Nonetheless, in this paper, following on from (Purver and Ginzburg 2004), we will argue against the Montogovian *tactic* of using higher-order properties-of-properties as NP denotations. Our main argument derives from the claim that this tactic[1] is in conflict with the evidence provided by phenomena pertaining to clarification of NP utterances, and in particular with the *reprise content hypothesis* (RCH – on which more below).

(Ginzburg and Cooper 2004) provide an analysis for clarification requests (CRs) which includes a context-dependent account of utterance semantics and the grounding thereof. (Purver and Ginzburg 2004) examine the repercussions of this analysis for NP semantics, showing that considering CRification can provide semanticists with another adequacy criterion in an area full of theories. However, both essentially centre around *referential* semantics; our aim here is to examine how the same general approaches might be generalized to non-referential meaning and anaphora. We consider how to develop a semantics for NPs that fits with Montague's overall *strategy* in assigning a well-defined denotation to NPs, while adhering to the RCH. We proceed to show that TTR provides attractive alternative means with which to analyze NP meaning.

In section 2 we provide some background needed for the remainder of the paper: first introducing the general view of meaning and context in dialogue that we assume, and then outlining (Purver and Ginzburg 2004)'s claims. Section 3 then sets out a new formulation of their (HPSG-based) approach using TTR, which yields a straightforward account of the dynamics of grounding, clarification, and anaphora for discourse involving both referential and non-referential NPs. In section 4, we extend the account to deal with so-called scope ambiguities—we say 'so-called' since we will suggest that CRificational evidence indicates these ambiguities are better analyzed as essentially *lexical*.

2. Grounding, CRification, and the RCH

2.1. Dialogue and the structure of context

Following (Ginzburg 1996; Poesio and Traum 1997; Larsson 2002; Ginzburg fcmg), amongst others, we assume that a suitable model of dialogue context is one in which we assume that each conversational participant is assigned their own gameboard, where they record their version of the public conversational action and relative to which they compute their possible reactions. We characterize this gameboard as a data structure whose primary attributes are the following:

- FACTS: a set of commonly agreed upon facts.

- QUD ('questions under discussion'): a partially ordered set that specifies the currently discussed questions.

- MOVES: a list specifying the form and content of the moves made in the conversation.

Given such a structure, we can model many important dialogue phenomena such as asking and answering questions (introducing elements to QUD and discharging them); acceptance and confirmation (extension of FACTS); and many elliptical phenomena (by analysing context-dependent utterances as having their content further specified by the maximal question in QUD).

2.2. Grounding and CRification

(Ginzburg and Cooper 2004) show how a view of utterances as encoding *meaning* rather than *content* can lead to a explanation of the availability of CRs in dialogue. Various formalizations are possible: in (Ginzburg and Cooper 2004) the architecture used is HPSG with simultaneous abstraction; (Cooper and Ginzburg 2002; Ginzburg fcmg) instead take a type-theoretical approach, but the basic insight is the same. Context-dependent elements are labelled explicitly, and a hearer must be able to find suitable corresponding referents in context before the utterance can be *grounded*. Failure to do so for a particular element may then lead to clarification being sought concerning the phrase which contributed this problematic element to the original utterance; the *move* giving rise to the CR maintained until its grounding in the contextual repository PENDING. Generation and interpretation of CRs themselves, with their often highly elliptical *reprise* nature, can be modelled using a set of general context-update rules which license updating of QUD with CRificational questions in the presence of ungrounded elements.

Using an approach based on dependent record types (see (Cooper 2005a)), (1) shows a simplified version of the representation that might be assigned to type an utterance 'Did Bo leave?' together with that for the NP 'Bo':

(1)
$$\begin{matrix} \text{'Bo'} & \text{'Did Bo leave?'} \\ \begin{bmatrix} \text{c-params}: \begin{bmatrix} x: Ind \\ r: \text{named}(x, \text{"Bo"}) \end{bmatrix} \\ \text{cont} = \text{c-params.x}: Ind \end{bmatrix} & \begin{bmatrix} \text{c-params}: \begin{bmatrix} x: Ind \\ r: \text{named}(x, \text{"Bo"}) \end{bmatrix} \\ \text{cont} = ?\text{leave}(\text{c-params.x}): Question \end{bmatrix} \end{matrix}$$

As (1) shows, utterance types are represented as record types; and the C-PARAMS field specifies a record type representing the context-dependent elements. Utterances are taken to be records—grounding involves linking an utterance with an appropriate type. In particular, a witness for the C-PARAMS record type must be found – i.e. a record which represents the speaker's intended instantiation of C-PARAMS in context. Similarly, the truth conditions for propositions expressed by successfully grounded utterances depend on the existence of witnesses for the record type which constitutes the content of a declarative utterance.[2]

In fact, as certain types of CRs ask for repetition of the actual words and phrases used, rather than asking about their semantic content (these are the questions one asks in noisy cocktail parties, when unable to hear words correctly), we assume (following (Cooper and Ginzburg 2002)) that sub-utterances themselves, inlcuding their non-semantic information, must in fact be members of C-PARAMS – with inability to find witnesses for them resulting in CRs. We will leave this out of our analysis here for the most part, though, and concentrate on CRification of content.

2.3. Reprise questions and the Reprise Content Hypothesis

Note that such an analysis suggests that CRs ask about a part of the antecedent's semantic content – namely, that part which is contextually dependent. If so, examining what a CR actually asks about (and how it is answered) might give us some insights into the nature of that content. (Purver and Ginzburg 2004) note that *reprise questions* (a particular type of CR) seem especially suited to this kind of use as a semantic probe: a reprise question, by echoing an antecedent phrase, makes it clear which phrase is being asked about; and (when reprising sub-sentential phrases, at least) seem unable to ask about pragmatically inferred material but are restricted to semantic content. They propose the *Reprise Content Hypothesis*, phrased in both weak (2a) and strong (2b) versions:

(2) a. *A nominal fragment reprise question queries a part of the standard semantic content of the fragment being reprised.*

b. *A nominal fragment reprise question queries exactly the standard semantic content of the fragment being reprised.*

This provides us with a stronger constraint than sentential compositionality: by examining reprise questions, we can hold individual phrases to account, rather than merely ensuring that the overall sentential content to which they contribute is suitable.

They then apply this constraint to NP semantics, pointing out that NP reprises seem to be able to query individuals (3a), or, for plurals, sets of individuals; that in some cases, where the subconstituent N is focussed, that they can ask about the noun predicate, a property of individuals (3b); but that it is very difficult to imagine them as querying GQs (i.e. properties-of-properties):[3]

(3) a. A: And er they X-rayed me, and took a urine sample, took a blood sample. Er, the doctor
B: Chorlton?   [↝ *By 'the doctor' do you mean Chorlton?*]
A: Chorlton, mhm, he examined me, erm, he, he said now they were on about a slide [unclear] on my heart. Mhm, he couldn't find it.

b. Anon 1: They'd carry the sack on their back?
George: On the back, the bushel, yes
Anon 1: The bushel?   [↝ *What property do you mean by 'bushel'?*]

They apply this to many types of NP, arguing that most uses of proper nouns, demonstratives, pronouns and definite descriptions do seem to refer to individuals; but their evidence is less conclusive for non-referential NPs such as indefinites. (Purver 2004) also shows how this approach can be extended to other phrase types including verbs and verb phrases; however, here we confine ourselves to discussing NPs.

3. Referential vs. non-referential NPs: Wide scoping quantification

3.1. C-PARAMS and Q-PARAMS

Contrast (4a) with (4b) as uttered by Aaron to Belinda: the former is typically uttered with the strong expectation that Belinda can recognize who Jo is, whereas the latter involves use of the indefinite precisely because Aaron himself has at best only a relatively weak idea of the identity of the thief, and presumably does not expect Belinda to be in any more knowledgeable a position:

(4) a. A: Jo arrived yesterday.

b. A: A thief broke in here last night.

These contrasting expectations are reflected in the differing clarificational potentials of the two utterances, as we see when we examine possible clarification requests and responses thereto. In (5a), Belinda's question can only be understood as concerning Jo's identity; while in (5b), the corresponding question is very hard to interpret as asking about the thief's identity, but rather seems to ask about the property predicated of them (that of being a thief):

(5) a. A: Jo arrived yesterday.
   B: Jo?
   A: Yes, that's right. / Oh, you know, my friend Jo from school.

   b. A: A thief broke in here last night.
   B: A thief?
   A: Yes, thief. / Well, burglar then, but certainly someone up to no good.

These differences can be captured by assuming that an utterance of the referential 'Jo' contributes to the C-PARAMS of the utterance (as in (1) above), whereas non-referential NPs such as 'a thief' do not. But, if they do not contribute to C-PARAMS, what do they contribute to semantically? In broad terms the answer is clear: non-referential NPs need to contribute their descriptive conditions to the sentential content, while any associated individuals are existentially quantified within the sentence. We introduce a Q-PARAMS field to indicate this existential quantification, and so the representation of (5b) becomes (roughly) as in (6a). In fact, as we want to account for the fact that the subconstituent common noun 'thief' must be grounded, and can be CRified as in (5b) above, we wish to make the associated noun predicate a member of C-PARAMS, as shown in (6b) – but we will ignore this complication hereafter. Another notational simplification—an abuse to be precise—we adopt here is to factor out Q-PARAMS from the descriptive content, as in (6a). More generally, what is required is as in (6b), but the difference will be immaterial for current purposes:

(6) a. $\begin{bmatrix} \text{c-params} = []: RecType \\ \text{q-params} : \begin{bmatrix} x : Ind \\ r : \text{thief}(x) \end{bmatrix} \\ \text{cont} : \text{break\_in(q-params.x)} : RecType \end{bmatrix}$

b. $\begin{bmatrix} \text{c-params} : \begin{bmatrix} p : Pred \\ r1 : \text{named}(p, \text{"thief"}) \end{bmatrix} \\ \text{cont} : \begin{bmatrix} \text{q-params} : \begin{bmatrix} x : Ind \\ r2 : \text{c-params.p}(x) \end{bmatrix} \\ \text{nucl} : \text{break\_in(q-params.x)} \end{bmatrix} \end{bmatrix}$

Generalized Quantifier Theory (GQT) will allow us to arrive at a denotation like (6a), but only via a somewhat long winded way—the denotation (7a) is posited for the NP 'a thief', which via β-reduction given a V denotation (7b), becomes (7c) (see (Cooper 2004), p. 12). However, we could get to that route rather more directly by postulating (7d) as the NP's contribution to content:

(7) a. $\lambda R : ([x : \mathit{Ind}])\mathit{RecType} \begin{bmatrix} \text{par} : [x: \mathit{Ind}] \\ \text{restr} : \text{thief}(x) \\ \text{scope} : R(\text{par}) \end{bmatrix}$

b. $\lambda r : ([x : \mathit{Ind}])[c0 : \text{break\_in}(r.x)]$

c. $\begin{bmatrix} \text{par} : [x: \mathit{Ind}] \\ \text{restr} : \text{thief}(x) \\ \text{scope} : [c0 : \text{break\_in}(\text{par}.x)] \end{bmatrix}$

d. $\begin{bmatrix} \text{c-params} = [] : \mathit{RecType} \\ \text{q-params} : \begin{bmatrix} x : \mathit{Ind} \\ r : \text{thief}(x) \end{bmatrix} \\ \text{cont} = \text{q-params}.x : \mathit{Ind} \end{bmatrix}$

This allows us not only to arrive at a suitable overall representation, but to directly express the distinction between two types of NP via the distinction between inclusion in C-PARAMS or in Q-PARAMS. 'Referential' NPs (the reason for the scare quotes will become obvious shortly) help build up the contextual C-PARAMS component; 'non-referential' NPs help build the sentential content via Q-PARAMS; while both have contents of the same semantic type (individuals) and fill argument roles of a predicate uniformly.

A combinatory rule we would need to build sentences from NPs and VPs, while amalgamating their C-PARAMS and Q-PARAMS, is given in (8):

(8)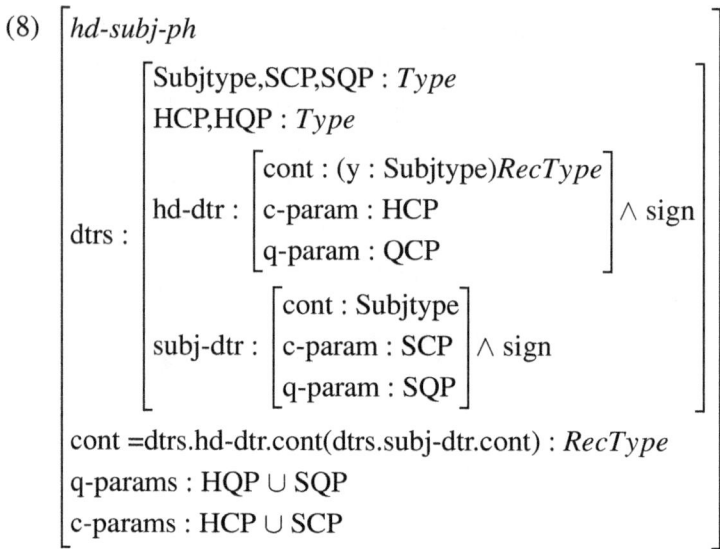

In fact, our set up also allows for a fairly straightforward analysis of intensional verbs such as 'seek'. (Cooper 2005b) proposes to treat sentences such as (9a) as relating an agent with a record type, as in (9b). This is because the witnessing conditions of the record type that fills the object argument role seem to describe well the success conditions of a search, as in Montague's account:

(9) a. Jill seeks a unicorn.

b. $\text{seek}(j, \begin{bmatrix} x : Ind \\ r : \text{unicorn}(x) \end{bmatrix})$

Cooper shows how to implement this analysis via a GQ analysis of NPs. On the current analysis, this would follow straightforwardly by having an intensional verb select for the Q-PARAMS type of its object.[4]

In comparing a GQT–based approach and the non-GQ approach sketched so far simplicity is not a good guide: GQT has, arguably, a somewhat simpler synsem interface, but its denotations are more complex. If we take a dialogical perspective, however, things are not so equal. For a start, the simplicity GQT provides is conditional: it is maintained only in so far as indubitably[5] referential NPs are type raised to the type of GQs, a move that falls foul of the RCH. However, if a GQ–oriented theory buys into distinctness of types among NPs, other problems come up. The first is that the simplicity of the synsem interface is lost—composing NPs and verbs is no longer possible by a single rule.

The second is that reprise questions show no more evidence that GQ-like readings are available from non-referential NPs than they are from referential ones. (Purver and Ginzburg 2004) present reprise data for indefinites and other quantified NPs (see below), but none seem to permit anything other than the NP-referential or subconstituent readings we have already seen:

(10) a. Unknown: What are you making?
Anon 1: Erm, it's a do– it's a log.
Unknown: A log?
Anon 1: Yeah a book, log book.

b. Anon 2: Was it nice there?
Anon 1: Oh yes, lovely.
Anon 2: Mm.
Anon 1: It had twenty rooms in it.
Anon 2: Twenty rooms?
[↝ Is it **twenty** rooms you're saying it had?]
[↝ Is it twenty **rooms** you're saying it had?]
[↝ ??Which twenty rooms are you saying it had?]
Anon 1: Yes.

c. Richard: No I'll commute every day
Anon 6: Every day? [↝ Is it **every** day you'll commute?]
[↝ Is it every **day** you'll commute?]
[↝ ?Which days do you mean by **every day**?]
Richard: as if, er Saturday and Sunday
Anon 6: And all holidays?
Richard: Yeah [pause]

Thirdly, and perhaps most importantly, there are a number of arguments that suggest that the referential/non-referential bifurcation is in fact a rather fragile one. It is to this that we now turn.

3.2. Referential indefinites & accommodation

So far, we follow (Purver and Ginzburg 2004) closely apart from the difference in framework. However, the advantage of the type-theoretic approach developed here becomes clear when considering examples like (11). Here, while Aaron knows that the arriver was Jo, he uses an indefinite because he assumes Belinda might not have a name for Jo:

(11) A: A friend of mine arrived yesterday.
B: A friend of yours?
A: Right – Jo, in fact.

Note that in such cases, it is perfectly easy to understand Belinda's question as asking about the friend being referred to – the reference of the NP 'a friend'. We can also imagine it as querying the appropriateness of the noun property 'friend', of course (in which case Aaron's response might be more along the lines of 'yes, I think I'd count her as a friend - certainly more than an acquaintance'). But while (Purver and Ginzburg 2004) offer an information-structure-based account of how both the NP-query and the noun-property query might be available, they must assume that indefinites are ambiguous (between referential and non-referential versions) to explain the difference between (5b) and (11).

However, we need make no such assumption. (Cooper and Ginzburg 2002) show how a type-theoretic approach lends itself to modelling the process of *accommodation* of a nominal reference – the process by which Belinda can process an example like (4a) even without knowing who Jo is, essentially by existentially quantifying Jo away. In current terms, what is needed is a simple coercion operation which allows (12b) to be produced from (12a):

(12) a. $\begin{bmatrix} \text{c-params} : \begin{bmatrix} \text{x} : Ind \\ \text{r} : \text{named}(x,\text{"Jo"}) \end{bmatrix} \\ \text{q-params} = [] : RecType \\ \text{cont} : \text{arrive}(\text{c-params.x}) \end{bmatrix}$

b. $\begin{bmatrix} \text{c-params} = [] : RecType \\ \text{q-params} : \begin{bmatrix} \text{x} : Ind \\ \text{r} : \text{named}(x,\text{"Jo"}) \end{bmatrix} \\ \text{cont} : \text{arrive}(\text{q-params.x}) \end{bmatrix}$

In the case of example (11), we merely require the opposite move: Belinda and Aaron, inferring or knowing that a particular friend is in fact being referred to, can coerce (12b) to (12a), allowing a referential CR to be asked and successfully interpreted. Note that this move is only available to us because the analysis maintains the same type (individuals) for both referential and non-referential versions. It is very hard to see how such a move would be possible given a GQ approach to NP representation: type-raised NP representations such as (7a) do not seem to lend themselves to this kind of analysis;

and an approach which maintains lower semantic types for referential NPs and higher types for non-referential NPs must of course fare equally badly.

3.3. Anaphora

A related argument can be made from what has always been an important testing ground for any theory of NP meaning, namely anaphora. We consider for now 'discourse anaphora'—anaphora that occur across sentential boundaries—returning to intrasentential anaphora, in particular its 'bound variable' variant in section 4. The vast literature on quantification and anaphora has, with very few if notable exceptions (e.g. (Groenendijk 1998; Asher and Lascarides 2003; Poesio and Traum 1997)), been designed for monologue. Dialogue brings new challenges on this score: querying, disagreement, partial understanding.[6] Both referential and non-referential NPs give rise to discourse anaphora—the challenge is to provide a uniform theory. An account like the one we develop here, where referential and non-referential NPs are of the same semantic type—the level of individuals which directly provide the referents for anaphora— is at an advantage compared to a theory where witnesses need to be 'extracted' independently from GQ denotations.[7]

The main challenge for a theory of meaning for pronouns is of course how to characterize their antecedency conditions. Dialogue takes us away quite quickly from certain received ideas on this score. (13) indicates straight off that antecedents are not going to be located in the contextual repository of shared assumptions, namely FACTS, given the possibility of anaphora out of questions:

(13)   A: Did John phone? B: He's out of contact in Daghestan.

Another reason why FACTS is inappropriate relates to a more general issue: in theories like DRT and DPL (though not SDRT)—once an antecedent (for discourse anaphora), always an antecedent. This strategy of pooling all antecedents together once they become available is problematic in light of the fact, well noted in the AI literature on anaphora resolution (see e.g. (Grosz and Sidner 1986)) that changing the topic of conversation drastically changes anaphoric possibilities. Thus, in (14(5)) 'he' cannot felicitously refer to Jake, despite the fact that the equivalent utterance using a directly referential expression is perfectly coherent:

(14)   A: Jake hit Bill. / B: No, he patted him on the back. / A: Ah. Is Bill going to the party tomorrow? /B: No. / A(5): Is #he/Jake?

This leaves QUD, Moves, or Pending. QUD we can dismiss since its elements lack sufficient structure. So we are left with Moves and/or Pending. (15a) is an example of anaphora from an ungrounded utterance, whereas (15b) (from (Heeman and Allen 1999)) is an example of anaphora from a disfluent utterance:

(15) a. A: Did John phone? B: Is he someone with a booming bass voice?

   b. Peter was, well he was fired .

This suggests, then, that antecedents are to be located in both MOVES and PENDING. Where within the representation of an utterance? The obvious candidate is C-PARAMS, where after grounding reside at the very least entities that serve as values for referential utterances. Moreover, given the fact that C-PARAMS has fields for all sub-utterances, the antecedents of repetition CRs, we have a straightforward account of agreement between antecedent and anaphor, unavailable to standard dynamic theories (including SDRT), where the dynamics is defined on a purely semantic level. This is particularly important in grammatical gender languages (e.g. apparently all EU official languages apart from English), where gender is not well correlated with the intrinsic characteristics of a referent, as illustrated in (16): (16a) shows grammatical gender agreement in German across a number of turns, where crucially the intermediate turn is, on most plausible accounts, lacking in syntactic structure. Similarly, in (16b,c), we see examples from Hebrew, which lacks a neuter gender and correspondingly has no neuter pronouns. There exist two words which correspond to the English 'car', one is masculine, the other feminine. Subsequent pronominal reference must agree with the gender of the antecedent:

(16) a. A: Kommt jetzt ein Zug? B: Ja. Er kommt von Gleis 2.

   b. ledani yesh Oto/mexonit yafe/yafa

   Dany has car(m) /car(f) nice(m/f).

   c. hu kana oto/ota beLod

   he bought him/her in Lod

Nonetheless, there is one important difference between referential NPs and QNPs: the former will have referents/witnesses in place once grounding has taken place. For QNPs, however, this is not the case. Indeed in certain cases no witnesses will get introduced in line with the fact that for non-referential

NPs anaphora is not generally possible from within a query (polar or wh), as originally pointed out in (Groenendijk 1998), or from an assertion that has been rejected:[8]

(17) a. A: Do you have a brother? B: Yes. A: What is he called?

  b. A: Do you have a brother? B: No. A: # What is he called? B: I told you, no brother.

This means, naturally enough that witnesses to QNPs can only emerge in a context where the corresponding assertion has been accepted. A natural move to make in light of this is to postulate a witnessing process as a side effect of assertion acceptance, a consequence of which will be the emergence of referents for QNPs. For uniformity's sake, we can assume that these witnesses get incorporated into the C-PARAMS of that utterance. This means that C-PARAMS serves uniformly as the locus for antecedents of 'discourse anaphora'. The rule of witnessing is actually simply a minor add on to the rule that underwrites assertion acceptance (see (Ginzburg fcmg), Chapter 4)—we view it as providing for a witness for situation/event anaphora since this is what gets directly introduced into c-params. In cases where the witness is a record (essentially when the proposition is positive), NP witnesses will emerge.

(18) Accept move:
$$\begin{bmatrix} \text{preconds} & = & \begin{bmatrix} \text{spkr}: Ind \\ \text{addr}: Ind \\ \text{T1}: RecType \\ \text{LatestMove.cont} = \text{Assert}(\text{spkr,addr,T1}): IllocProp \end{bmatrix} \\ \text{effects} & = & \begin{bmatrix} \text{spkr} = \text{preconds.addr}: Ind \\ \text{addr} = \text{preconds.spkr}: Ind \\ \text{t}: \text{preconds.T1} \\ \text{w} = \text{preconds.LatestMove.c-params} \cup \begin{bmatrix} \text{sit} = \text{t} \end{bmatrix}: Rec \\ \text{Moves} = \langle \text{m1, mo},\ldots \rangle: \text{list}(LocProp) \\ \text{m1.cont} = \text{Accept}(\text{spkr,addr,T1}): IllocProp \\ \text{m0.c-param} = \text{w}: Rec \end{bmatrix} \end{bmatrix}$$

We can now state the meaning of a singular pronoun as follows: C-PARAMS specifies an antecedent located in the C-PARAMS of an *active move*. The pronoun is identical in reference to this antecedent and agrees with it.

(19) $\begin{bmatrix} \text{c-params}: \begin{bmatrix} m: LocProp \\ c1: \text{ActiveMove}(m) \\ m.\text{c-params}: \begin{bmatrix} u2: PsCat \\ u2.\text{cont}: Ind \end{bmatrix} \\ x = m.\text{c-params}.u2.\text{cont}: Ind \end{bmatrix} \\ \text{cat.agr} = m.\text{c-params}.u2.\text{cat.agr}: SynAgrCat \\ c1: \text{gendernumber}^9(\text{cat.agr}) \\ \text{cont} = \text{c-params}.x: Ind \end{bmatrix}$

Here an ActiveMove is a element of Moves such that either (a) *m.cont*.qud-update-contribution is in qud or (b) *m.cont* is max-qud–specific or (c) *m* is in pending

For notational simplicity, we abbreviate the C-PARAMS type in (19) as (20a)—here *m* is the move and *a* the antecedent utterance. We can thereby rewrite (19), omitting the agreement specification, as (20b):

(20) a. $\begin{bmatrix} m: LocProp \\ a: synsem \\ c1: \text{DiscourseAnt}(m,a) \end{bmatrix}$

b. $\begin{bmatrix} \text{c-params}: \begin{bmatrix} m: LocProp \\ a: synsem \\ c1: \text{DiscourseAnt}(m,a) \end{bmatrix} \\ \text{cont} = \text{c-params}.a.\text{cont}: Ind \end{bmatrix}$

How will this meaning aligned with the acceptance move rule enable us to explicate the cases we have seen? Consider (17a): accepting 'yes' will result in augmenting the C-PARAMS of 'yes' with a witness for $\begin{bmatrix} x: Ind \\ c1: \text{brother}(x) \\ c0: \text{have}(b,x) \end{bmatrix}$.
In contrast, for (17b), the witness for T1 is not a record (it is a function mapping T to $\bot$, the witness for a negative type), so no referent for 'a brother' is provided. As far as (13) goes, a referent for 'John' is in c-params once the query is grounded, and this is available as an antecedent since the query is at that point an active move. Finally, in (15) we assume that this is a case where CRification is performed not to *find* a missing contextual value but to *confirm*

it. Hence, PENDING has a value for 'John'. Finally, given their presence in C-PARAMS, we note also an explanation for examples like (21), where a pronoun is CRed and the answers mentioned are the possible antecedents:

(21)   A: A teacher gave a parent a book from the school library. He liked it a lot. B: The teacher or the parent?

This explanation though is incomplete as long as we have not said anything about 'bound variable' anaphora, let alone defended our non-unified account. As we will see in section 4 'bound variable' anaphors are themselves clarifiable, despite their potentially non-referential antecedents.

3.4. Plural NPs

So far, our analyses have all involved singular NPs, both referential and non-referential. How does our approach carry over to plurals? With referential plurals, the transition seems clear: we simply need plural NPs to denote sets of individuals rather than individuals,[10] and this seems perfectly in keeping with the RCH as long as this set is a member of C-PARAMS (see (22a)). Predicating the VP content directly of the set must result in a collective reading, as in (22b) where the set of students left together; distributive readings can equally be handled, as we discuss in section 4.

(22) a. John: they'll be working on the, they'll be working on the kidnapper's instructions though wouldn't they? They would be working on the kidnapper's instructions, the police?
Sid: The police? [↝ Who do you mean by 'the police'?]
[↝ Is it the police who you are saying would be working ...?]
John: Aye
Sid: On
Unknown: [unclear]
Sid: aye the, the senior detectives

b. 'The students met'

$$\begin{bmatrix} \text{c-params} : \begin{bmatrix} s : Set(Ind) \\ r : student'(s) \end{bmatrix} \\ \text{cont} : met(\text{c-params.s}) \end{bmatrix}$$

Turning to non-referential NPs, so far we have concentrated on indefinites, capturing their quantificational force implicitly by the witnessing relation between records and types. It seems clear that the same approach will work here: examples such as (10b) above can be expressed via a suitable set member of Q-PARAMS, and a witness for the record type will require the existence of a suitable set (here, of twenty rooms). And as before, a simple coercion operation between inclusion in C-PARAMS and Q-PARAMS can then account for any shift between truly non-referential and specific uses.

And in fact, we can apply exactly this approach to other quantified plurals. (Barwise and Cooper 1981) provide us with the notion of a *witness set* for a GQ, and show an equivalence (for monotone-increasing quantifiers) between a GQ holding of a verbal predicate and that predicate holding of the witness set. Examples such as (23)a can thus be analyzed—on its collective understanding—by taking the NP to denote its witness set directly (and for this to be a member of Q-PARAMS or C-PARAMS as the (non-)referentiality of its use demands):[11]

(23)

Most students left

$$\begin{bmatrix} \text{q-params} : \begin{bmatrix} x : \text{Set}(\mathit{Ind}) \\ r : \text{most}(x, \text{student})) \end{bmatrix} \\ \text{cont} : \text{left}(\text{q-params.x}) \end{bmatrix}$$

here $\mathit{most}(x, y)$ holds if x contains a majority of the ys

This approach is not sufficient, of course, for monotone-decreasing (e.g. 'few students') or non-monotone ('exactly two students') quantifiers: as (Barwise and Cooper 1981) point out, we must show not only that the verb predicate holds of the witness set, but that it holds of no other members of the restriction set. However, (Purver and Ginzburg 2004) propose an analysis of such QNPs as denoting *pairs* of reference set (the few students who left) and complement set (the students who didn't), noting that this might also help explain the phenomenon of complement set anaphora by providing suitable antecedents – and such an approach could equally be developed in the current approach.

3.5. Interim evaluation

It is worth taking stock at this point: we have so far sketched a non-GQ–based analysis of NPs. At this point we stand to be accused of a number of possible crimes: we seem to have abandoned the Montogovian strategy of assigning NPs a well defined denotation since we break up the contribution of the NP into a C-PARAM,Q-PARAM or CONT contribution. And given this allegedly piecemeal approach how are we fulfilling our obligations to the RCH? With referential NPs, the content is identical to the C-PARAM contribution, apart from potentially certain presuppositional conditions (e.g. naming), which deserve to be factored out of content. With non-referential NPs, the situation is a bit trickier *vis à vis* the RCH—it can guide us less in that respect. Nonetheless, as we observed in section 3.2, given the actual fluidity of the C-PARAM/Q-PARAM divide, in many cases the Q-PARAM contribution can be 'coerced' to become a C-PARAM, in which case reprises give us some guidance. In other cases, we get evidence about the semantic contribution by abstracting away from sentential content (and getting additional evidence in this regard from anaphora and direct sluicing.).

4. Scope ambiguity

Scope ambiguities are among the most studied semantic indeterminacies. GQT provides a particularly simple analysis of these: the ambiguity is explained in terms of the distinct order of application of GQs.

We have already argued against one of the components of this account in section 3, pointing out that there is dialogue evidence against the higher order denotations GQT postulates for QNPs. A significant finding that has emerged from recent corpus studies of CRs in dialogue (see (Purver, Ginzburg, and Healey 2003; Rodríguez and Schlangen 2004; Rieser and Moore 2005)) is the complete absence of CRs that somehow relate to uncertainty regarding scope. One might draw a number of conclusions from this, but perhaps as significant is what emerges when one *constructs* CRs that relate to scopal uncertainty: the ambiguity appears to be localized in an NP:

(24) a. A: The boys kept a cat.
     B: One cat for all the boys or different ones?
     A: They each kept a cat.

   b. A: I'm going to give all you kids a present.
      B: Will we need to share or do we each get something for ourselves?

Note that contrary to what underspecification theories (such as Minimal Recursion Semantics (Copestake et al. 2005) or Hole Semantics (Bos 1995)) would predict, this data indicates that the various scope possibilities *are* computed and can be localized with a single NP.[12] Disambiguation similarly proceeds by using distributive adverbs and adjectives ('each', 'the same/different cat' etc). GQT provides no help here since the meanings of QNPs are constant across distinct readings.

The alternative we sketch here is to distinguish between an independent use of an QNP and a *dependent* use. In the latter case, the NP contributes a function to Q-PARAMS, whose value on an antecedent fills the argument role associated with the NP. The resources of TTR are particularly well placed to explain this kind of ambiguity, as we shall see. We note that such uses have been argued to exist on a number of independent grounds so eliminating scope alternation as a mechanism has added attractions:

- **Functional readings in questions/answers**: ever since Engdahl first pointed out that interrogatives such as (25a) give rise to answers such as (25b) (see (Engdahl 1986)), it has been recognized that questions can specify *dependencies*. More controversially, some have argued that pair-list answers such as (25c) should be analyzed in similar terms (see (Ginzburg and Sag 2000)):

(25) a. Which problem did each scientist solve?
 b. The one his supervisor assigned him.
 c. Dennett solved consciousness, Chomsky solved Plato's problem, Dawkins solved religion ...

- **Dependent adjectives**: certain adjectives are intrinsically relational, requiring either a discourse antecedent or a QNP:

(26) a. # (Requires a context establishing the existence of a prior book) Jo gave the girls a different book.
 b. (OK in neutral context) Each teacher gave the girls a different book.

- **Intrinsically narrow scope QNPs**: Certain QNPs like 'at least N' seem never to take 'wide scope', as exemplified in (27), which lacks a reading asserting that all linguists speak, say, English and German. Steedman (Steedman 1999) observes that this can be captured by assuming that such NPs are obligatorily dependent or at least can never serve as antecedents for dependent uses.

(27)   Every linguist speaks at least two languages.

Let us start with a simple example, as in (28a). We associate with this the content in (28b):

(28) a. The boys each kept a cat.

b.
$$\begin{bmatrix} \text{c-params}: \begin{bmatrix} s: Set(Ind) \\ r: boy'(s) \end{bmatrix} \\ \text{q-params}: \begin{bmatrix} f: ([x: Ind]) \begin{bmatrix} z = f(x): Ind \\ c1: cat(z) \end{bmatrix} \end{bmatrix} \\ \text{cont}: \begin{bmatrix} r: (\begin{bmatrix} x: Ind \\ c1: In(c\text{-}params.s,x) \end{bmatrix}) \begin{bmatrix} c0: kept(r.x, f(r.x)) \end{bmatrix} \end{bmatrix} \end{bmatrix}$$

The content in (28), arises in a straightforward fashion, using rules like those postulated in section 3: 'kept' predicates of the content of 'a cat', 'each' acts as a distributive adverb on the VP, which then predicates of the set-valued subject.[13] The Q-PARAMS values of the two NPs get 'unioned' into a joint record type, which is a constituent of the content.

(29) a. kept a cat $\mapsto$

$$([x: Ind]) \begin{bmatrix} \text{q-params}: \begin{bmatrix} f: ([x: Ind]) \begin{bmatrix} z = f(x): Ind \\ c1: cat(z) \end{bmatrix} \end{bmatrix} \\ \text{nucl}: \begin{bmatrix} c0: kept(x, f(x)) \end{bmatrix} \end{bmatrix}$$

b. each $\mapsto$ (T$_{([x: Ind])RType}$) (z : Set(Ind))(r : ($\begin{bmatrix} x: Ind \\ c1: In(z,x) \end{bmatrix}$))T(r.x)

From this, it becomes clear in all but one respect how to specify the meaning of a dependent use of 'a cat'. The one remaining issue, one which is typically abstracted away from, but which we cannot do so in TTR[14]—is how to specify x, the independent variable which appears in the content of the dependent NP? Cashing this out as a C-PARAM would involve relaying a message to the wrong audience, so to speak, since the antecedent must be resolved *intrasententially* and is constrained grammatically (e.g. by island constraints.). An option used in SDRT (see (Asher and Lascarides 2003) and within TTR (see (Cooper 2004)), which has been used for specification of pronoun antecedents is to use a metavariable for the antecedent and invoke some principle of resolution of DRSs or types. This is a viable possibility, which is combinatorially simple.

We believe though that a preferable solution, on methodological grounds,[15] is to cash this out within the grammar for what it is—an unbounded dependency. One defines an additional field, call it ANT(ECEDENT)S, propagated in standard unbounded dependency fashion and terminating with a binder—a Q-PARAMS contributing NP. The dependency can also be terminated as the grammar requires, e.g. blocked from exiting relative or interrogative clauses.

(30)   Dependent use of 'a cat':

$$\begin{bmatrix} \text{ants} : \begin{bmatrix} \text{q-params} : \begin{bmatrix} x : Ind \end{bmatrix} \end{bmatrix} \\ \text{q-params} : \begin{bmatrix} f : (\begin{bmatrix} x : Ind \end{bmatrix}) \begin{bmatrix} z = f(x): Ind \\ c1 : cat(z) \end{bmatrix} \end{bmatrix} \\ \text{cont} = f(\text{ants.q-param.x}) : Ind \end{bmatrix}$$

A similar analysis will work for (31a): the sole difference is that in such a case the distributive operator is implicit—(31b) suggests we do not want to build it into the NP meaning. A number of ways have been proposed how to incorporate distributivity into the combinatorial process, an issue we cannot resolve here. For discussion and a type logical account see (Winter 2006).

(31)   a. Most villagers owned a cat.

b. Most villagers own a cat and gathered in the square to listen to the visiting ghattologist.

Finally, we return to pronominal anaphora, which we believe can be analyzed by means of the mechanism of dependence sketched above. One cannot evade the fact that pronouns are, in principle, intrinsically context dependent, whatever the intentions of the speaker producing them, as illustrated by the examples in (32):

(32)   a. A: Everybody likes his sister. B: Whose sister? A: Everyone's.

b. A: No woman thinks she is a genius. B: that who is a genius? A: Herself.

In contrast to the cases we discussed earlier, we do not wish anaphors such as these to be treated referentially. On the other hand, we need to make them CRifiable. We adopt a position that is somewhere in the middle between approaches that make a sharp distinction between bound variable and discourse anaphora (e.g. (Reinhart 1983; Chierchia 1995) and approaches in which all anaphora is bound variable (e.g. DRT, DPL, and their descendants.). In order to avoid necessary referentiality of all pronominal anaphora, we need to introduce an alternative meaning to the one introduced in section 3.3. And yet, the only difference that will obtain between the two meanings we propose is that the 'bound variable' meaning has a different contextual specification to the 'discourse anaphora' meaning. This will enable an underspecified entry for (English) pronouns, where the contextual parameter type is disjunctive. This would seem to accord with the intuition that typically pronouns have potentially two kinds of antecedents.

Formulating the bound variable meaning will require one slight modification to he treatment of the field ANTS introduced above: in order to be able to capture the constraint that *agreement* is required to hold with the antecedent, ANTS will be required to be of type *synsem*. This extends to provide a treatment of 'bound variable' anaphora, with the sole extra constraint that *agreement* is required to hold with the antecedent. We propose the following(33) as the meaning of 'bound variable' singular anaphora: here the contextual parameter is the antecedent utterance, restricted nonetheless to be a member of ANTS, hence an intrasentential antecedent:

(33)
$$\begin{bmatrix} \text{c-params}: \begin{bmatrix} a: \begin{bmatrix} \text{q-params}: [x: \mathit{Ind}] \\ \text{cont} = \text{q-params.x}: \mathit{Ind} \\ \text{cat} = \text{NP}: \mathit{SynCat} \end{bmatrix} \\ \text{ants}: \text{set}(\mathit{SynSem}) \\ \text{c1}: \text{Member}(a, \text{ants}) \end{bmatrix} \\ \text{cat.agr} = \text{c-params.a.cat.agr}: \mathit{SynAgrCat} \\ \text{c1}: \text{gendernumber(cat.agr)} \\ \text{cont} = \text{c-params.a.cont}: \mathit{Ind} \end{bmatrix}$$

For notational simplicity, we abbreviate the C-PARAMS type in (33) as (34a). Consequently, we can underspecify a pronoun, again omitting its agreement specification, as (34b):

(34) a. $\begin{bmatrix} a : \text{synsem} \\ c1 : \text{IntrasentAnt}(a) \end{bmatrix}$

b. $\begin{bmatrix} \text{c-params} : \begin{bmatrix} a : \text{synsem} \\ c1 : \text{IntrasentAnt}(a) \end{bmatrix} \vee \begin{bmatrix} m : \text{LocProp} \\ a : \text{synsem} \\ c1 : \text{DiscourseAnt}(m,a) \end{bmatrix} \\ \text{cont} = \text{c-params.a.cont} : \textit{Ind} \end{bmatrix}$

Given this, (35b) is a simplified representation of the meaning of (35a), where we use the underspecified meaning of 'his', which involves a C-PARAMS disjoining the 'discourse' and the 'bound variable' uses. The import of this meaning is to identify the content of 'his' either with 'a thief' (the sole possible member of ANTS in this case) or with a discourse antecedent.

(35) a. A thief abandoned his jemmy.

b. $\begin{bmatrix} \text{q-params} : \begin{bmatrix} x : \textit{Ind} \\ r : \text{thief}(x) \end{bmatrix} \\ \text{c-params} : \begin{bmatrix} a : \text{synsem} \\ c1 : \text{IntrasentAnt}(a) \end{bmatrix} \vee \begin{bmatrix} m : \text{LocProp} \\ a : \text{synsem} \\ c1 : \text{DiscourseAnt}(m,a) \end{bmatrix} \\ \text{cont} : \text{Abandon}(\text{q-params.x}, \text{jemmy-of}(\text{c-params.a.cont})) \end{bmatrix}$

5. Conclusion

Generalized quantifier theory in differing doses is the strategy of choice for analyzing QNPs. Since its inception by Montague, it has been a highly insightful approach but one whose cognitive status is in some doubt. The Reprise Content Hypothesis, which originates in (Purver and Ginzburg 2004), offers a concrete means of establishing this doubt: whereas data from CRification supports the existence of NPs denoting individuals and sets of individuals, of predicate–denoting verbs and common nouns, and even of function denoting NPs, there is no evidence whatever of talk about generalized quantifiers. Although GQ theory provides an elegant solution to the problem of scope ambiguity, once again what evidence dialogue provides for this phenomenon does not support an analysis in terms of scope alternation. In this respect underspecification theories are also unsupported since constructed examples of available CRs concerning scope ambiguities support an approach where ambiguities are resolved and disjoined.

We have sketched an analysis of NP meaning in dialogue using the framework of Type Theory with Records. On this analysis, NPs be they referential or non-referential, denote individuals, but contribute either to the repository of *contextual* or *quantificational* parameters. Scope is handled via dependency. We have shown that this analysis yields a simple picture of grounding and CRification and seems to allow for a theory of intra and intersentential anaphora with minimal additional apparatus, as well as allowing for an account of intensional verbs. We hope to scale up this sketch in future work.

Notes

1. It is quite impertinent on our part to call this a 'tactic' given Montague's brilliant independent motivation for this denotation in terms of intensional verbs like 'seek'. Nonetheless, our account will be able to provide a simple account of such verbs, building on a proposal in (Cooper 2005b). See section 3.1.
2. For simplicity we identify propositions here with record types, as in (Cooper 2005b) rather than with records that include a record type and a situation, as in (Ginzburg fcmg). The latter *Austinian* strategy will, however, receive some support from the role situations play as the 'hosts' of witnesses for anaphora, as discussed in section 3.3.
3. Example (3a,b), and many others following, are taken from the British National Corpus (Aston and Burnard 1998).
4. Ironically, this leaves open the issue of what to do with *referential* arguments of intensional verbs, but we cannot enter into this here.
5. In fact, there *are* reasons for doubt, as we will see shortly, if we take the addressee's perspective.
6. (Groenendijk 1998; Asher and Lascarides 2003) abstract away from metacommunication and, for the most part, disagreement.
7. See e.g. (Cooper 2004), p. 26.
8. The data here are quite subtle. Consider the following clearly felicitous anaphor:

    (i) A: Did a man with a limp pass by here a few minutes ago?
    B: Was he squat with a red beard?

    This would seem to be a *specific* indefinite, whose existence is not at issue, and would constitute a contextual parameter, as discussed in section 3.2.
    Similarly, in (ii), based on examples due to (Dekker 1997), anaphora is possible despite the rejection of the assertion because B has referential access to the fake priest:

    (ii) A: A priest was looking for you. B: He's not a priest just an actor and I doubt he wanted to see me.

    Compare this with the following somewhat similar cases: (iii) seems infelicitous, though (iii') seems acceptable, but involves modal subordination—(iv) is felicitous only to the extent it seems like B has perhaps grudgingly changed his tune after his initial utterance.

(iii) A: Mike, we are getting reports of an attempted escape at Wandsworth prison. Did you see anyone wearing a striped jump suit running near the park around 9:30? Mike: # Was he wearing a hat on as well?

(iii') Would he have been wearing a hat?

(iv) A: A priest was looking for you. B: No way—priests don't come looking for a grubby atheist like me. # What did he want?

9. This ranges over {mascsg,femsg,neutsg }, with potential crosslinguistic differences.
10. Or sums, groups etc, as in the Link–inspired tradition.
11. See, for instance, the possible referential reading given for (10c) above, or examples like:

(i) A: Most folks were upset by the decision.
B: Most folks?
A: Yeah well like Bianca, Amanda, Luigi, and me. That's what? About two thirds of the company?

12. Admittedly, there are only two scopings possible here. But there again, it is reasonable to hypothesize that in spoken language at least, there are rarely more possibilities than this.
13. This treatment of 'each' derives from (Link 1983), via (Winter 2006).
14. There being no tolerance for free variables.
15. For a start, it is preferable to remain on the object level in so far as possible. It is not clear why pronouns should give require such a move, as opposed to various other context dependent elements.

References

Asher, Nicholas, and Alex Lascarides
   2003   *Logics of Conversation*. Cambridge University Press.

Aston, Guy, and Lou Burnard
   1998   *The BNC Handbook: Exploring the British National Corpus with SARA*. Edinburgh University Press.

Barwise, Jon, and Robin Cooper
   1981   Generalized quantifiers in natural language. *Linguistics and Philosophy*, vol. 5.

Bos, Johan
   1995   Predicate logic unplugged. *Proceedings of the 10th Amsterdam Colloquium*. ILLC/Department of Philosophy, University of Amsterdam.

Chierchia, Gennaro
   1995   *Dynamics of Meaning*. Chicago: University of Chicago Press.

Cooper, Robin
   2004   Dynamic generalised quantifiers and hypothetical contexts. In *Ursus Philosophicus, a festschrift for Björn Haglund*.

   2005a   Records and record types in semantic theory. *Journal of Logic and Computation* 15 (2): 99–112.

   2005b   Austinian truth in Martin-Löf type theory. *Research on Language and Computation* 3 (4): 333–362.

Cooper, Robin, and Jonathan Ginzburg
2002 Using dependent record types in clarification ellipsis. J. Bos, M. Foster, and C. Matheson (eds.), *Proceedings of the 6th Workshop on the Semantics and Pragmatics of Dialogue (SEMDIAL)*. Edinburgh, Scotland, 45–52.

Copestake, Ann, Dan Flickinger, Carl Pollard, and Ivan Sag
2005 Minimal recursion semantics: An introduction. *Research on Language and Computation* 3 (2–3): 281–332.

Dekker, Paul
1997 First order information exchange. In *Proceedings of MunDial 97 (Technical Report 97-106)*, Gerhard Jaeger, and Anton Benz (eds.). München: Universität München Centrum für Informations- und Sprachverarbeitung.

Engdahl, Elisabet
1986 *Constituent Questions*. Synthese Language Library. Dordrecht: D. Reidel.

Fernando, Tim
2001 Conservative generalized quantifiers and presupposition. *Proceedings of Semantics and Linguistic Theory*, Volume 11. NYU/Cornell, 172–191.

Ginzburg, Jonathan
1996 Interrogatives: Questions, facts and dialogue. In *The Handbook of Contemporary Semantic Theory*, S. Lappin (ed.), 385–422. Blackwell.

fcmg *Semantics and Interaction in Dialogue*. Stanford, California: CSLI Publications and University of Chicago Press. Draft chapters available from: http://www.dcs.kcl.ac.uk/staff/ginzburg.

Ginzburg, Jonathan, and Robin Cooper
2004 Clarification, ellipsis, and the nature of contextual updates in dialogue. *Linguistics and Philosophy* 27 (3): 297–365.

Ginzburg, Jonathan, and Ivan A. Sag
2000 *Interrogative Investigations: the form, meaning and use of English Interrogatives*. CSLI Lecture Notes no. 123. Stanford: California: CSLI Publications.

Groenendijk, Jeroen
1998 Questions in update semantics. In *Proceedings of TwenDial 98, 13th Twente workshop on Language Technology*, J. Hulstijn, and A. Nijholt (eds.), 125–137. Twente: Twente University.

Grosz, Barbara, and Candace Sidner
1986 Attention, intentions and the structure of discourse. *Computational Linguistics* 12: 175–204.

Heeman, Peter, and James Allen
1999 Speech repairs, intonational phrases and discourse markers: Modeling speakers' utterances in spoken dialogue. *Computational Linguistics* 25: 527–571.

Keenan, Edward, and Jonathan Stavi
1986 A semantic characterization of natural language determiners. *Linguistics and Philosophy* 9: 253–326.

Larsson, Staffan
2002 Issue-based dialogue management. Ph.D. diss., Göteborg University. Also published as Gothenburg Monographs in Linguistics 21.

Link, Godehard
1983 The logical analysis of plurals and mass terms: a lattice-theoretical approach. In *Meaning, Use and Interpretation of Language*, R. Bäuerle, C. Schwarze, and A. von Stechow (eds.). De Gruyter.

Montague, Richard
1974 The proper treatment of quantification in ordinary English. In *Formal Philosophy*, Richmond Thomason (ed.). New Haven: Yale UP.

Poesio, Massimo, and David Traum
1997 Conversational actions and discourse situations. *Computational Intelligence* 13, no. 3.

Purver, Matthew
2004 The theory and use of clarification requests in dialogue. Ph.D. diss., University of London.

Purver, Matthew, and Jonathan Ginzburg
2004 Clarifying noun phrase semantics. *Journal of Semantics* 21 (3): 283–339.

Purver, Matthew, Jonathan Ginzburg, and Patrick Healey
2003 On the means for clarification in dialogue. In *Current and New Directions in Discourse & Dialogue*, R. Smith, and J. van Kuppevelt (eds.), 235–255. Kluwer Academic Publishers.

Reinhart, Tanya
1983 *Anaphora and Semantic Interpretation*. Croom Helm. London.

Rieser, Verena, and Johanna Moore
2005 Implications for generating clarification requests in task-oriented dialogues. *Proceedings of the 43rd Annual Meeting of the Association for Computational Linguistics*. Ann Arbor, 239–246.

Rodríguez, Kepa, and David Schlangen
2004 Form, intonation and function of clarification requests in German task-oriented spoken dialogues. *Proceedings of the 8th Workshop on the Semantics and Pragmatics of Dialogue (SEMDIAL)*. Barcelona, Spain.

Steedman, Mark
1999 Alternating quantifier scope in CCG. *Proceedings of the 37th Annual Meeting of the Association for Computational Linguistics*. University of Maryland, 301–568.

Winter, Yoad
2006 Type shifting with semantic features: A unified perspective. Chris Barker, and Pauline Jacobson (eds.), *Direct Compositionality*. Oxford: Oxford University Press.

What is in a concept? How adjectives might help

Nick Braisby

1. Introduction

Concepts remain as something of a enigma. While much progress has been made in understanding the factors that impinge processes of categorisation (e.g., Nosofsky & Palmeri 1997; Lamberts 2001) and concept formation (e.g., Kaplan & Murphy 2000; Whittlesea 1987) and the possibilities and limitations inherent to similarity (Goodman 1972; Goldstone 1994; Medin, Goldstone and Gentner 1993), a central concern still stands. There are few if any accounts of how to determine the contents of concepts – that is, it is not clear by what criteria we judge something to be contained in a concept or not.

In attempting to throw some light on this problem, this paper draws connections between linguistic analyses of adjectives and psychological approaches to concepts. I have long associated this concern with integrating a diversity of findings, methods and approaches with my former thesis supervisor, Robin Cooper, and I hope that this paper helps pay a fitting tribute to him. I think Robin is unique in his ability to show us how different ideas fit together, and how we may learn and progress from their juxtaposition. He has always combined a demanding standard of intellectual rigour with an interdisciplinary open-mindedness and it is this that makes his approach to the cognitive sciences so refreshing and inspiring. Indeed, it is Robin who led me to see that the specific combination of aspects of linguistics and cognitive psychology is to their mutual advantage. In spite of his achievements, Robin is not simply a researcher – he is an inspiring teacher also, encouraging his students to find their voice and helping them to make their thoughts clearer and more useful to the community. I hope in this paper I can convey my ideas with the same enthusiasm and clarity as Robin, and that in so doing pay tribute to the inspiration he has given me.

2. The content of concepts

There have been a number of competing theories about the content of concepts, ranging from the classical idea that concepts are definitions (cf. Bruner, Goodnow & Austin 1956; Sutcliffe 1993), to the prototype view that they encode properties typically true of the corresponding category, to the approach that they are naïve theories (cf. Murphy & Medin 1985).

However, even when researchers adopt the methodological strategy of focusing on the easier cases, such as relatively well understood, concrete, and observable categories such as natural kinds, a clear picture as to the content of concepts has not emerged. Although the classical view is clear about the criteria to be satisfied by the content of a concept – roughly, it must serve as a definition applicable to all items in the corresponding category – there are reasons to believe there could never be such definitions (cf. Putnam 1975; Wittgenstein 1953).

Prototype accounts contend that the contents of concepts contain attributes and values typical of members of the category. However, what is less clear is what exactly counts as a typical attribute or value. Indeed, equivocation on this point can be seen in two attempts to formalise prototype theory so as to support an account of concept combination, specifically adjective-noun combination.

Cohen & Murphy (1984) describe a model in which concepts are represented as frames with roles or attributes and values. They claim that for each role, there is a list of values, probably ordered by typicality (p. 47). Smith & Osherson (1988) describe a similar frame representation for concepts which contains a set of relevant attributes and, "for each attribute, a set of possible values" (p. 353). The problem is that it would be difficult indeed to list all possible values, no matter how statistically unlikely or atypical they were. Moreover, it would be hard to avoid the consequence that concepts would then also apply to atypical non-members of the corresponding category. For example, if green is a possible colour for lemons, what would then prevent the concept for *lemon* from also applying to limes? The objection that there are other properties which distinguish them, such as shape and size, does not stand up, since the shape and size of limes will presumably also be possible properties for atypical lemons.

Perhaps more problematic for the effort to make precise the information that concepts contain has been the suggestion that concepts should be understood in terms of naïve theories (cf. Murphy & Medin 1985; Rips 1995). Unfortunately, it is simply unclear how to specify theories in the first place, that is, how to determine what information about a category or concept is excluded from the corresponding theory. The difficulty, as Fodor (1983) has pointed out, is that theories are subject to holism – in particular, they are Quinean and isotropic. In short, there appear to be no principled grounds for drawing a boundary between the information contained in one theory and that contained in another.

There are of course numerous other proposals for the contents of concepts, including the exemplar approach (Nosofsky 1984; Medin & Shaffer 1978). One germane to this paper is an account I have developed over a number of years, first starting with my thesis, under the encouragement and watchful supervision of Robin. According to this account (Braisby 1990; 1998; 2005), concepts encode only prototypical attributes and values. While we will not explore this account in any detail, this proposal for the contents of concepts (bearing in mind we are still focusing on easy cases) is one to which we shall refer throughout the remainder of this paper.

2.1. Compositionality and complex concepts

This paper proposes a new method for identifying what is and what is not in a concept, one that relies on a technique that has been used extensively in the psychological literature on noun-noun concept combination.

It has become part of orthodoxy that apparent non-compositionality of complex nominals is reflected in relational interpretations. For example, *glass pan* might be interpreted as a "pan made out of glass" (Wisniewski 1996, p. 439) – the successful interpretation depends on inferring a relation (made of) that links the head and modifier nouns. In the psychological literature these have become known as relation linking interpretations. They are often contrasted with property mapping interpretations, in which a modifier is taken to stand for a property that is then mapped to the head noun. For example, a *fish frog* might be interpreted as a frog that swims – the modifier fish is taken to stand for the property of swimming which is then predicated of the head. Whereas property mapping interpretations are arguably strictly compositional, involving combining information that derives solely from modifier and head nouns, relation linking interpretations appear non-compositional. To derive a relation linking interpretation, a new relation must be inferred, one that is not entailed by either modifier or head.

The non-compositionality of relation linking interpretations is reflected in their varying treatments proposed in the literature. Murphy (1988), for instance, argued that people's understanding of complex concepts necessarily involved world knowledge with this elaborating the information deriving from the constituent concepts.

For present purposes, what is of interest is not the debate concerning the proper treatment of noun-noun combinations, but two general presumptions that are associated with this literature. The first is that a relation linking interpretation of a complex concept signals the inference of a relation that is not contained within either constituent concept. The second is that, unlike noun-noun combinations, the analysis of (predicating) adjective-noun combinations is thought to be unproblematic. As Murphy (1988) says, "Adjective-noun concepts like *red apple* are the simplest forms of complex concepts.... No world knowledge or complicated processing is required.... If these adjective-noun concepts were the only kind of complex concept, one could plausibly argue that the knowledge-dependent processes...are unnecessary." Likewise, Costello & Keane (2000) defend their focus on noun-noun phrases on the grounds that they are semantically more complex and challenging than (intersective) adjective-noun phrases. Murphy, in fact, went on to argue that many examples of adjective-noun combinations are interpreted in ways that go beyond the information contained in the constituent concepts. In this paper, I hope to show that even predicating adjectives, like Murphy's *red apple*, can require relation linking interpretations. To the extent that they do, and to the extent that relation linking interpretations imply information not entailed by either constituent, such interpretations signal that information is outside of the constituent concepts and hence tell us something of what is, and what is not, in a concept.

It is worth clarifying this argument. Consider the approach to concept combination developed by Smith & Osherson (1988). Smith & Osherson proposed an essentially frame-like representation for prototype concepts. The representation of the concept for *apple*, for example, contained weighted attributes such as colour, shape and texture. Each attribute possesses a set of possible values, such as red and brown for colour, with the most likely value being marked. Intersective adjective-noun combinations, such as *red apple*, are then explained as follows. The adjective first picks out the relevant attribute in the head noun, it then dictates the value which is to be marked as most likely, and it increases the weighting for that attribute. Smith & Osherson offer similar explanations for other predicating adjectives.

In effect, this kind of account treats intersective adjectives as involving a very simple property mapping interpretation – the property specified by the modifier concept *red* is mapped onto the head noun concept *apple*. The account is unable to offer any explanation of combinations that require a relational interpretation (a problem readily acknowledged by Smith & Osherson; see also Osherson & Smith 1997).

2.2. Conceptual versus semantic intersectivity

Thus far, we have focused on intersective adjective-noun combinations. It may seem perverse to focus on cases for which there is already largely a consensus in the literature, reflected in the apparent success of frame-like prototype models of concept combination, such as Smith & Osherson's, to account for these particular combinations. However, it is precisely because of this consensus that possible complexities with intersective combinations may have been gone unnoticed.

Intersective adjective-noun combinations are ones that can be understood semantically in terms of the set intersection of the constituent extensions. For example, the category of *red car* contains all those things that are both cars and red, i.e., all those things that lie in the intersection of the sets of cars and red things. For this reason, there are standard patterns of entailment that characterise intersective combinations such as this.

For example,

(1)   *X is a red car*

entails

(2)   *X is red*

as well as

(3)   *X is a car*

As we have seen, generally speaking the attention of the psychological literature has been focused on noun-noun combinations and on some of the more obviously non-compositional adjective-noun combinations such as privatives. Typically, intersective combinations have been the focus of enquiry in developing models of concept combination, whose application has then generally been acknowledged to be limited to those intersective combinations. However, it is not clear that the semantics of intersective combinations is mirrored conceptually. Indeed, there are reasons to believe they may not be.

Prototype models clearly distinguish prototypical attributes from atypical ones. In Smith & Osherson's (1984) model described earlier, the most likely attributes – the prototypical ones – are marked. Indeed, in spite of much disagreement concerning how concepts should be understood, there is a considerable consensus on the robust and widespread manifestation of typicality effects. So much so that it would almost be a surprise if adjective-noun combinations did not differ in some important respects depending on whether they reflected attributes of the prototype. For example, lemons are typically yellow and, let us suppose, only (very) atypically blue. Given the prevalence of typicality effects, it would be unsurprising if the interpretations of *yellow lemon* and *blue lemon* differed in some important respects. Yet, both psychological models of prototype concept combination, and linguistic analyses of adjectives, suggest these two combinations are interpreted in essentially the same way.

These two combinations exemplify different classes of adjective-noun combination. The former is what we might call prototype affirming, while the latter is prototype denying – because it contradicts the prototypical attribute(s). It is possible to imagine a further class – prototype neutral – in which the adjective attributes a property which is not prototypical, but that does not contradict a prototypical attribute either. For example, if the concept of lemon does not indicate whether the lemon is waxed or not, then *waxed lemon* would be an example of a prototype neutral combination.

It is important to be clear about the claim being made about these three types of adjective-noun combination. All three types are semantically intersective. After all, a similar pattern of entailments to (1) to (3) above holds in all cases. Nevertheless, it seems plausible that people may not interpret them all in the same way. Whereas prototype affirming combinations appear to lend themselves most readily to property mapping interpretations – a *yellow lemon* is a lemon that is yellow – prototype denying combinations could involve relational interpretations – for example, a *blue lemon* is a lemon that in some way has been transformed to make it blue. Indeed, this is an argument I have made elsewhere in developing an account of concepts I have called the relational view (Braisby 1990, 1998, 2005).

On the basis of this view, it is possible to outline three different hypotheses concerning the interpretation of intersective adjective-noun combinations.
- prototype affirming: the adjective attributes a property already specified as part of the prototype
- prototype denying – the adjective contradicts a property already specified as part of the prototype
- prototype neutral – the adjective attributes a property not specified as part of the prototype, but is consistent with prototype information

It is these hypotheses that I wish to explore, reporting the results of a preliminary study examining people's interpretations of adjective noun combinations of these three types. Before turning to the study, it is worth pointing out a difficulty inherent in tapping potential relational interpretations for intersective combinations. It is quite plausible that people are implicitly aware of the schema of entailments (1) to (3) above that characterise intersective adjectives. That is, people may be predisposed to consider that an adequate and true response to the question *What is a A N?* is that *it is a N that is A*. To the extent that this schema has been implicitly acquired, tapping potential relational interpretations may be made more difficult. In fact, Murphy (1988), and others since, provided explicit instructions to deter participants from producing such paraphrases (even for non-predicating adjective-noun and noun-noun combinations where such a paraphrase is not available).

Nevertheless, this is exactly what the following experiment set out to examine. The precise experimental hypotheses were that

- Prototype Affirming combinations will tend to elicit property mapping interpretations
- Prototype Denying combinations will tend to elicit relational interpretations
- Prototype Neutral combinations will be intermediate between these two, tending to elicit both property mapping and relational interpretations

3. Method

3.1. Design

Combination Type (prototype affirming, prototype denying, and prototype neutral) was a within-participants factor.

3.2. Participants

Thirty two attendees at an Open University undergraduate summer school in Psychology volunteered to participate.

3.3. Materials

A complete set of stimulus materials is provided in Appendix 1. Stimuli were chosen to represent natural kinds on the grounds that these would possess stronger prototype concepts, and also be more circumscribed in terms of permissible transformations. Nine natural kind nouns were chosen from previous work and, for each, three adjectives were selected to express prototype affirming, denying and neutral combinations, as explained above. Thus, there were 27 natural kind adjective-noun combinations. Five further combinations involving artefact concepts, and one noun-noun combination (*wood oven*) were included as filler items. Results for the artefact concepts are not reported here.

3.4. Procedure

Half of the participants were presented with adjective-noun combinations in a random order, with the other half experiencing the reverse random order. Participants were instructed to read each phrase and then attempt to write down what they thought the phrase meant. They were told that they need not explain the meanings of the individual component words (e.g., *rugby* or *shoe* in *rugby shoe*), but that they may need to state the relationship between them. They were also advised that there might be times when such a relationship could not easily be stated (e.g., that they may feel that *green grass* is simply *grass that is green*).

4. Results

Explanations of the meaning of each phrase were then coded according to whether they provided an attributive interpretation, a transformational interpretation, or a (non-transformational) relational interpretation. Example interpretations and their coding are given in Appendix 1. Data from six participants were discarded because of missing responses and failure to respond in an appropriate manner (e.g., describing a *hungry* sheep as *waiting to eat grass*).

Table 1 shows the mean number of attributive interpretations of the stimulus phrases by Combination Type for the remaining twenty six participants. Numbers of attributive interpretations were subjected to a one-way, repeated-measures ANOVA with Combination Type as the within-participants factor. There was a significant effect of Combination Type ($F(2,40)=23.43$, $p < 0.0005$, $\eta^2=0.54$, and Bonferroni-adjusted post hoc t-tests confirmed that prototype affirming combinations received more attributive interpretations than did prototype neutral combinations ($t(23)=2.49$, $p < 0.05$) and prototype denying combinations ($t(22)=5.77$, $p < 0.001$), and prototype neutral combinations received more attributive interpretations than did prototype denying combinations ($t(21)=4.38$, $p < 0.01$).

Table 1. Interpretations of adjective-noun phrases according to Combination Type (maximum= 9)

	Attributive interpretations	Transformational interpretations
Prototype affirming	8.3	0.7
Prototype neutral	7.3	1.4
Prototype denying	5.5	3.5

The data were also coded according to transformational interpretations, where a participant might spontaneously offer an explanation of the meaning of the phrase that involved a transformation of the head noun so as to explain the attribution provided by the modifier. The numbers of such explanations are also shown in Table 1. As is evident, nearly all explanations were classified as either attributive or transformational.

The numbers of transformational interpretations was also analysed by a one-way, repeated-measures ANOVA with Combination Type as the within-participants factor. There was a significant effect of Combination

Type ($F(2,40)=23.95$, $p < 0.0005$, $\eta^2=0.55$, and Bonferroni-adjusted post hoc t-tests confirmed that prototype affirming combinations received fewer transformational interpretations than did prototype denying combinations ($t(22)=5.77$, $p < 0.001$), and prototype neutral combinations received fewer transformational interpretations than did prototype denying combinations ($t(21)=4.77$, $p < 0.01$). The difference between prototype affirming and prototype neutral conditions just failed to reach significance ($p = 0.11$).

These means belie variety in the extent to which individual adjective-noun combinations elicited transformational interpretations. As shown in Table 2, the proportion of explanations that adverted to transformations of the head noun ranged from 13% (*green sky*) to 77% (*brown banana*) in the case of prototype denying combinations. However, even some prototype neutral and prototype affirming combinations elicited reference to transformations (e.g., *waxed lemon* was described as a lemon covered with a wax coating, and *yellow banana* elicited reference to ripening).

Table 2   Proportions of transformational interpretations of individual adjective-noun phrases according to Combination Type

Natural Kind	Prototype Affirming	Prototype Neutral	Prototype Denying
Apple	0.12	0.40	0.27
Banana	0.35	0.15	0.77
Beetroot	0.04	0.15	0.42
Carrot	0.04	0.08	0.42
Corn	0.15	0.12	0.39
Dog	0.00	0.00	0.20
Lemon	0.12	0.62	0.52
Sheep	0.00	0.00	0.50
Sky	0.00	0.00	0.13

5. Discussion

Surprisingly, given the semantic simplicity of intersective adjective-noun combinations, the data here suggest high levels of relational interpretations of certain classes of combination. In general, prototype-denying combinations produce the highest proportions of relational interpretations, prototype-affirming the least, with prototype neutral combinations intermediate.

There are, of course, variations according to the specific combination considered. For some head nouns, *beetroot* and *carrot* for example, the combinations exemplify this trend. For *banana*, the prototype neutral combination produces the fewest relational interpretations, while for *lemon* it is this type of combination that produces the highest proportion of relational interpretations.

One possible reason for this variation is that notions such as prototype neutral need much more precise operationalisation. Perhaps these data imply that *waxed lemon* is more like a prototype denying combination, with the prototype for *lemon* including the attribute *unwaxed*. In some cases, it may be hard for participants to imagine any relation or transformation that could make the combination sensible. For example, it is hard to state what transformation could render a *green sky*, and only 13% of participants' responses clearly implied a transformation. Compare this with the 77% of responses that implied a transformation for a *brown banana* – the transformation of ripening is evidently much more familiar to participants.

In spite of these item differences however, there is also a clear trend, and the differences in general between the three combination types is large. These data *suggest* therefore that, from the point of view of people's interpretations, intersective adjectives do not form a uniform class. Moreover, as we have seen, the literature takes interpretation to be suggestive of the conceptual processes involved, and so we can tentatively draw the conclusion that these different types of intersective combination differ conceptually. Prototype affirming combinations are typically understood in terms of property mapping, consistent with the idea inherent in prototype models of concept combination that the property expressed by the modifier is already represented as a possibility in the head concept. By contrast, prototype denying combinations show much higher levels of relational interpretations, which imply that the combination is sometimes to be understood non-compositionally via inferring a linking relation. Finally, prototype neutral combinations suggest a mixture of property mapping and relational interpretations, leaving it unclear whether these modifiers are represented in the head concept.

It is worth carefully noting the proportions of relational interpretations. Even for prototype denying combinations these are in the minority. However, as we have already argued, participants may possess a schema for adjectives according to which a combination of *A N* can be paraphrased as *N that is A*. Indeed, despite instructing participants to avoid such paraphrases, many participants produced them. It is therefore possible that the present study underestimates the proportion of relational interpretations. A comprehension study, in which participants choose between relational and property mapping interpretations might yield a more accurate estimate of the extent to which participants adopt relational interpretations for these combinations. In the absence of such data, the conclusions to be drawn from the present study must necessarily be tentative.

What might these results mean for our understanding of concepts and concept combination? In studies of noun-noun combinations, the presence of relational interpretations is usually taken as confirmation that the modifier concept cannot simply be predicated of the head concept. For example, in *stone lion*, a relational interpretation confirms the unacceptability of paraphrasing the combination as a *lion that is stone*. The interpretation confirms the intuitive understanding that the property *stone* cannot simply be mapped to the concept *lion*, unlike the case of *stone statue*. Extending the reasoning in this kind of case to the present results implies that for some intersective adjective-noun combinations the properties expressed by the modifier (e.g. *blue*) cannot simply be mapped to the head concept (e.g., *lemon*). Pursuing the reasoning to its logical conclusion, we can identify a constraint on the nature of the head concept – namely the property expressed by the modifier cannot be represented as a possibility in the head concept (otherwise it would straightforwardly allow property mapping interpretations). This, of course, runs counter to suggestions from Cohen & Murphy (1984), Smith & Osherson (1988), and others, that prototype concepts express a set of possible attributes and values for concepts, with modifiers merely picking out and dictating the appropriate one. So, unlike the case of prototypical attributes and values (*red* and *green* for *apple*, for example), these data suggest that attributes that result from a transformation (e.g., *blue* in the case of *lemon*) are not expressed within the head concept as possible values. Contrary to suggestions emanating from the literature on prototype models of concept combination, it may be that concepts do not express all possible values, but only all typical or prototypical values. Thus, these results pertaining to how adjective noun combinations are interpreted point to a constraint on what is or is not in a concept.

These data raise the prospect that different kinds of variation among a category's exemplars are reflected differently in an account of concepts.

That is, natural variation might be encoded within a concept as different possibilities. Thus, the concept for *apple* might encode both *green* and *red* as possible values. Other, non-natural variants are accommodated differently. For example, *blue lemon* could be interpreted in at least three different ways.

- a blue lemon could be understood as a previously undiscovered type of lemon. If this interpretation is adopted, the concept of lemon changes to encode blue as an additional possible value
- a blue lemon could be understood as a conventional lemon that has been transformed in some way
- a blue lemon could be understood as just another possible variant of lemons

According to these data, the last reading, based on models of prototype concept combination, appears not to be preferred. Indeed, one can easily see why. On this reading, it would be entirely unsurprising that a lemon would be blue – it might be rare, but not cognitively surprising. Likewise, the first option appears cognitively expensive, suggesting a fluid, changing understanding of basic categories, in which previously acquired knowledge may always need revision. Consequently, it would not be surprising that the second reading might be cognitively preferential.

6. Conclusions

Overall, these results and arguments suggest a number of conclusions. First, it appears that from a conceptual point of view, taking as prime evidence the interpretations that people make of adjective-noun combinations, intersective combinations fall into different classes: prototype affirming, prototype denying and prototype neutral. Note, however, that this is not to suggest that adjectives fall into different classes. Rather the classes are defined in terms of the relationship between the adjective and the prototype of the noun concept.

Prototype denying combinations, in particular, elicit significant proportions of relational interpretations, suggesting that property mapping interpretations are not available, contra the suggestions of prototype models of concept combination. It is important to be clear about this argument. Many participants do, in fact, produce property mapping interpretations of these combinations. However, that there are so many relational interpretations needs explanation. Given that some transformations will be unknown (or at least unfamiliar), and the ease with which people can paraphrase *A N* combinations as a *N that is A*, it is perhaps surprising that so many relational interpretations are found. Thus, though relational interpretations are not universal for prototype denying combinations, at least for some items, they seem to be the predominant interpretation.

Given this, we can conclude that prototype models of concept combination, which are associated with apparent success in modelling intersective adjective-noun combinations, are not able to explain interpretations of many prototype denying combinations. Of course, it might be argued that the prototype models only seek to explain property mapping interpretations. The difficulty with this response is that, at least for some of these combinations, relational interpretations predominate. Indeed, given how easy it would be in principle to produce a property mapping interpretation (*a N that is A*) that relational interpretations sometimes predominate strongly suggests (though does not entail) that property mapping interpretations are not available for some prototype denying combinations. And this in turn implies that the attribute expressed by the adjective is not represented as a possible value for the head noun concept.

With regard to the question of what is or is not in a concept, these results then imply that the limits to the information contained in noun concepts are different from those proposed by some prototype theorists. Whereas all possible variants for attributes have been claimed to be explicitly encoded in prototype concepts, these data imply that (noun) concepts only encode prototypical attributes. Adjectives that deny these must combine with the head concept via a relation, consistent with the RVC account I have proposed elsewhere (Braisby 1990, 1998, 2005).

In conclusion, what seems true of the literature on concepts is perhaps true of cognitive science generally. Putting literatures into juxtaposition throws up new questions, and potentially new solutions. I hope that in this paper, consideration of the psychological literature on concepts together with linguistic analyses of adjectives has suggested some new and productive possibilities for further investigation. And in this respect I hope this paper pays appropriate tribute to my mentor Robin's remarkable facility for interdispliinary work.

Appendix 1

Natural Kind	Prototype Affirming	Prototype Neutral	Prototype Denying
Lemon	Yellow Lemon	Waxed Lemon	Blue Lemon
Sky	Blue Sky	Cloudy Sky	Green Sky
Banana	Yellow Banana	Shiny Banana	Brown Banana
Dog	Furry Dog	Sleepy Dog	Furless Dog
Apple	Green Apple	Striped Apple	Purple Apple
Sheep	White Sheep	Hungry Sheep	Green Sheep
Carrot	Orange Carrot	Rough Carrot	Purple Carrot
Beetroot	Red Beetroot	Smooth Beetroot	Blue Beetroot
Corn	Yellow Corn	Juicy Corn	Black Corn

Notes

1. Note that by conceptual content, I am referring to the descriptive or intensional content of concepts – sometimes called narrow content – not their reference or broad content.
2. In fact, this somewhat simplifies the discussion in the psychological literature. Gagne (2001, p. 247) argues that relations are represented within the modifier concept. However, Estes & Jones (2006) present both arguments and empirical evidence to suggest that, on the contrary, relations are represented independently of both modifier and head.
3. This was further developed by Smith, Osheron, Rips & Keane (1988), but this does not alter the argument developed here.
4. A consequence of this is that where adjective-noun combinations are used as comparators as they are in some studies of noun-noun combinations, the choice of adjective must be made carefully.

References

Braisby, Nick
    1990   Situating word meaning. In R. Cooper, K. Mukai & J. Perry (Eds.), *Situation Theory and its Applications, I*. CSLI: Stanford.
    1998   Compositionality and the modelling of complex concepts. *Minds and Machines*, 8, 479–508.

2005 Perspectives, compositionality and complex concepts. In, E. Machery, M. Werning, & G. Schurz (Eds.), *The compositionality of meaning and content (Vol. II: Applications to Linguistics, Psychology and Neuroscience)*. Frankfurt: Ontos Verlag. (pp. 179-202).

Bruner Jerome, Goodnow, Jacqueline and George Austin
1956 A Study of Thinking. New York: John Wiley.

Cohen, Benjamin and Gregory Murphy
1984 Models of Concepts. Cognitive Science, 8, pp. 27–58.

Costello, Fintan and Mark Keane
2000 Efficient creativity: Constraint guided conceptual combination. Cognitive Science, 24(2), 299-349.

Estes, Zachary and Lara Jones
2006 Priming via relational similarity: A copper horse is faster when seen through a glass eye. *Journal of Memory and Language*, 55, 89-101.

Fodor, Jerry
1983 *The Modularity of Mind: an essay on faculty psychology*. Cambridge, MA: MIT Press/Bradford Books.

Gagne, Christina
2001 Relation and lexical priming during the interpretation of noun-noun combinations. *Journal of Experimental Psychology: Learning, Memory, and Cognition*, 27, 236–254.

Goldstone, Robert
1994 The role of *similarity* in categorization: Providing a groundwork. *Cognition*, 52, 125-157.

Goodman, Nelson
1972 Seven strictures on similarity. In N. Goodman (Ed.), *Problems and Projects*. Indianapolis, IN: Bobbs-Merrill.

Kamp, Hans and Barbara Partee
1995 Prototype theory and compositionality. *Cognition*, 57:129-191.

Kaplan, Audrey and Gregory Murphy
2000 Category learning with minimal prior knowledge. *Journal of Experimental Psychology: Learning, Memory, and Cognition*, 26, 829-846.

Lamberts, Koen
2000 Information-accumulation *theory* of speeded categorization. *Psychological Review*, 107, 227–260.

Medin, Douglas and Marguerite Schaffer
1978 A context theory of classification learning. *Psychological Review*, 85, 207-238.

Medin, Douglas, Goldstone, Robert and Dedre Gentner
1993 Respects for similarity. *Psychological Review*, 100, 254-278.

Murphy, Gregory
   1988   Comprehending complex concepts. *Cognitive Science*, 12, 529-562.
Murphy, Gregory and Douglas Medin
   1985   The role of theories in conceptual coherence. *Psychological Review*, 92, 289-316.
Nosofsky, Robert
   1984   Choice, similarity, and the context theory of classification. *Journal of Experimental Psychology: Learning, Memory, and Cognition*, 10(1), 104-114.
Nosofsky, Robert and Thomas Palmeri
   1997   An exemplar-based random walk model of speeded classification. *Psychological Review*, 104, 266-300.
Daniel Osherson and Edward Smith
   1997   On typicality and vagueness. *Cognition*, 64:189 – 206.
Partee, Barbara
   2001   Privative adjectives: subsective plus coercion. To appear in T.E. Zimmermann, ed., *Studies in presupposition*.
Putnam, Hilary
   1975   The meaning of "meaning." In *Mind, language and reality, volume 2: Philosophical papers*. Cambridge: CUP.
Rips, Lance
   1995   The current status of research on concept combination. *Mind and Language*, 10(1-2), pp. 72–104.
Smith, Edward and Daniel Osherson
   1988   Conceptual combination with prototype concepts. in A. Collins. & E. Smith (eds.), *Readings in Cognitive Science: Perspectives from Psychology and Artificial Intelligence*, Morgan Kaufmann.
Smith, Edward, Osherson, Daniel, Rips, Lance, and Margaret Keane
   1988   Combining prototypes: A selective modification model. *Cognitive Science*, 12, 485-527.
Sutcliffe, John
   1993   Concept, class, and category in the tradition of Aristotle. In van Mechelen J., Hampton J. A., Michalski R. & Theuns P. (eds.), *Categories and Concepts: theoretical views and inductive data analysis*. London: Academic Press.
Whittlesea, Bruce
   1987   Preservation of specific experiences in the representation of general knowledge. *Journal of Experimental Psychology: Learning, Memory, and Cognition*, 13, 3-17.
Wisniewski, Edward
   1996   Construal and similarity in conceptual combination *Journal of Memory and Language*, 35, 434–453.

Wittgenstein Ludwig
   1953   *Philosophical Investigations*. Oxford: Basil Blackwell. Translated by G. E. M. Anscombe.

Situation types subatomically

Tim Fernando

1. Introduction

What follows concerns two papers by Robin Cooper on natural language semantics. Cooper 2005 equates a proposition with a type of situations, encoding situations from Austin and *situation semantics* (Barwise and Perry 1983) as records forming a type in the sense of *intuitionistic type theory* (Martin-Löf 1984). Cooper 1998 examines temporal and mereological aspects of situations on which records and types are arguably neutral. That neutrality is traced below to notions distinct from propositions in type theory (or for that matter, in ordinary predicate logic). To be sure, propositions are not unrelated to these notions. But the temporal and mereological structure of situations relevant to event semantics is, I claim, best understood as occupying a level below that of propositions — a level Terry Parsons has dubbed *subatomic semantics* and described as

> the study of those "formulas of English" that are treated as atomic formulas in most investigations of English. The main hypothesis to be investigated is that simple sentences of English contain subatomic quantification over events. (Parsons 1990, page ix)

Rather than taking events as atomic, the approach pursued below treats events and more generally, situations as structured objects, built from temporal formulas. Following terminological practice in AI since McCarthy and Hayes 1969, we shall refer to temporal formulas as *fluents*. Finite sets of fluents enclosed in a box (rather than the usual curly braces) are arranged in temporal sequence (like snapshots in a film strip) to form a situation. For example, using the three fluents *rain*, *dawn* and *dusk*, we can formulate a situation of "rain from dawn to dusk" as a string

$$\boxed{rain, dawn} \boxed{rain}^n \boxed{rain, dusk} \qquad (1)$$

of length $n+2$ (for $n \geq 0$), describing $n+2$ successive moments of time, each with rain, the first at dawn and the last at dusk. Different values of n correspond to different levels of temporal granularity: the larger the n, the finer the grain. For instance, n must be ≥ 1 to satisfy the constraint

(†) any interval from dawn to dusk contains noon (inside it).

Under the semantics for $\Rightarrow$ specified below, the constraint (†) can be expressed as the set

$$\boxed{dawn}\,\square^*\,\boxed{dusk} \;\Rightarrow\; \square^+\,\boxed{noon}\,\square^+ \tag{2}$$

of strings (where $\cdot^*$ is Kleene star, $L^+ \stackrel{\text{def}}{=} L^*L$ and $\square$ is the empty set *qua* symbol/snapshot). We will see that together, (1) and (2) yield a situation

$$\boxed{rain,\ noon}$$

of "rain at noon," whose ontological status is similar to that of (1) but differs from that of a string in (2). This difference is the basis of our analysis below of the ontological commitments made by approaches to negation discussed in Cooper 1998.

The difference at issue here comes down to two different interpretations of the situation-theoretic assertion that a situation s *supports* an *infon* σ, often written $s \models \sigma$. Under one interpretation, an infon σ is construed as an event-type, and

$$s \models \sigma \quad \text{is read:} \quad \text{a } \sigma\text{-event } occurs \text{ in } s\,. \tag{3}$$

Under the other, an infon σ is a constraint (such as (2) above), and

$$s \models \sigma \quad \text{is read:} \quad s \text{ satisfies the constraint } \sigma\,. \tag{4}$$

In both cases, s is a string and σ is a set of strings, i.e. a (formal) language. In (4), $\models$ is $\in$, and a string in σ is viewed as a circumstance of evaluation. In (3), $\models$ is something else, defined in section 2 below where it is written $\blacktriangleright$, and a string in σ is viewed as an object (albeit structured).

The opposition between (3) and (4) mimics a distinction drawn in van Lambalgen and Hamm 2005 between a formula $Happens(e,t)$ relating an event-type e to a time t and a formula $HoldsAt(\varphi,t)$ relating a fluent φ to a time t. The match-up between *Happens*/*HoldsAt* and (3)/(4) is not exact[1] but can be sharpened provided we can associate

(i) a time t with a situation/string s, and

(ii) a fluent φ with a language σ.

Section 3 below is all about (i), and considers both internal and external notions of time discussed in Cooper 1998. Section 4 turns to (ii), examining negative event descriptions through logical connectives on fluents. Section 5 relates the account presented in sections 3 and 4 to the type-theoretic proposal in Cooper 2005, and in particular, describes how relative to a set C of circumstances, an entailment from a language L to a language L' transforms a string (proof) of L into one of L'.

2. Subsumption and constraints

Fix a set Φ of fluents, and let 2^Φ be the family of subsets of Φ. To compare the information contained in strings $s, s' \in (2^\Phi)^*$ over the alphabet 2^Φ, we say that s *subsumes* s', and write $s \trianglerighteq s'$, if s and s' have the same length and s componentwise contains s' — that is,

$$a_1 \cdots a_n \trianglerighteq b_1 \cdots b_m \stackrel{\text{def}}{\iff} n = m \text{ and } b_i \subseteq a_i \text{ for } 1 \leq i \leq n$$

for all $a_1, \ldots, a_n, b_1, \ldots, b_m \subseteq \Phi$. For example,

| rain,dawn | rain,noon | rain,dusk | $\trianglerighteq$ | $\square$ | rain,noon | $\square$ |

We shall regard a language $L \subseteq (2^\Phi)^*$ as a set of possibilities (much as a proposition, in possible worlds semantics, is a set of possible worlds), and lift $\trianglerighteq$ to languages L, L' according to

$$L \trianglerighteq L' \stackrel{\text{def}}{\iff} (\forall s \in L)(\exists s' \in L')\ s \trianglerighteq s'$$

so that $L \subseteq L'$ implies $L \trianglerighteq L'$. As

$$s \trianglerighteq s' \quad \text{iff} \quad \{s\} \trianglerighteq \{s'\},$$

we can conflate a string s with the language $\{s\}$, and write for instance, $s \trianglerighteq L$ for $\{s\} \trianglerighteq L$. Next, we let $L_\square$ consist of all strings s in L with any number of $\square$'s added or deleted at either end of s

$$L_\square \stackrel{\text{def}}{=} \{s \in (2^\Phi)^* : \square^* L \square^* \text{ intersects with } \square^* s \square^*\}.$$

Relaxing the equal length requirement in $\trianglerighteq$, we say L *weakly subsumes* L' and write $L \blacktriangleright L'$ if $L_\square$ subsumes $L'_\square$

$$L \blacktriangleright L' \stackrel{\text{def}}{\iff} L_\square \trianglerighteq L'_\square$$
$$\text{iff} \quad L \trianglerighteq L'_\square.$$

Continuing to conflate a string s with the language $\{s\}$, it follows that

$$L \blacktriangleright L' \quad \text{iff} \quad (\forall s \in L)(\exists s' \in L') \; s \blacktriangleright s'$$

and assuming s' neither begins nor ends with $\Box$,

$$s \blacktriangleright s' \quad \text{iff} \quad s \trianglerighteq \Box^* s' \Box^* .$$

For example,

$$\boxed{rain,dawn \mid rain,noon \mid rain,dusk} \;\blacktriangleright\; \boxed{rain,noon} .$$

Over strings with a position marked by a fixed fluent $p \in \Phi$, weak subsumption $\blacktriangleright$ reduces to inclusion $\supseteq$. More precisely, define a string s to be *p-pointed* if p occurs in exactly one position in s

$$a_1 \cdots a_n \text{ is } p\text{-pointed} \quad \overset{\text{def}}{\Longleftrightarrow} \quad p \in a_i \text{ for exactly one } i \text{ between 1 and } n.$$

Thus, $\boxed{rain,dawn \mid rain \mid rain,dusk}$ is *dawn*-pointed but neither *rain*-pointed nor *noon*-pointed. For *p*-pointed s, let $R_{p,s}$ be the relation between the set $\mathbb{Z} \overset{\text{def}}{=} \{0, 1, -1, 2, -2, \ldots\}$ of integers and the set Φ of fluents, where p marks position 0 as follows

$$\begin{aligned}
R_{p,s}(i, \varphi) \quad \overset{\text{def}}{\Longleftrightarrow} \quad & (i = 0 \text{ and } s \blacktriangleright \boxed{p, \varphi}) \text{ or} \\
& (i > 0 \text{ and } s \blacktriangleright \boxed{p \mid \Box^{i-1} \mid \varphi}) \text{ or} \\
& (i < 0 \text{ and } s \blacktriangleright \boxed{\varphi \mid \Box^{-i-1} \mid p}) .
\end{aligned}$$

For example, for s equal to $\boxed{rain \mid rain, p \mid dry}$,

$$R_{p,s} \;=\; \{(-1, rain), (0, rain), (0, p), (1, dry)\} .$$

In general, $R_{p,s}$ turns s into a Kripke model over the frame $\langle \mathbb{Z}, < \rangle$, valuation $\varphi \mapsto \{i \in \mathbb{Z} : R_{p,s}(i, \varphi)\}$ and point 0 of evaluation (with the usual ordering $<$ on integers, and fluents in Φ regarded as atomic). It is not difficult to see that

$$s \blacktriangleright s' \quad \text{iff} \quad R_{p,s} \supseteq R_{p,s'}$$

for all p-pointed s, s'.

Note that a string s is p-pointed precisely if $s \blacktriangleright \boxed{p}$ and not $s \blacktriangleright \boxed{p \mid \Box^* \mid p}$. In general, given languages L and C over 2^Φ, let

$$C[L] \overset{\text{def}}{=} \{s \in C \;:\; s \blacktriangleright L\} .$$

Thus, the set of p-pointed strings is $C[L]$ for L equal to $\boxed{p}$ and C equal to

$$U_p \stackrel{\text{def}}{=} \{s \in (2^\Phi)^* : \text{not } s \blacktriangleright \boxed{p}\boxed{\square}^*\boxed{p}\}.$$

We will define many languages below as $C[L]$ for appropriate choices of C and L. That said, we can always trivialize L to $\square^*$, as

$$C[L] = C'[\square^*]$$

for C' equal to the intersection $C \cap L^{\blacktriangleright}$ of C with the set $L^{\blacktriangleright}$ of strings that weakly subsume L

$$L^{\blacktriangleright} \stackrel{\text{def}}{=} \{s \in (2^\Phi)^* : s \blacktriangleright L\}.$$

Nevertheless, decompositions $C[L]$ with $L \neq \square^*$ will prove interesting insofar as L can be deemed an ontological commitment of $C[L]$. We will say more about ontological commitment in section 5. In the meantime, let us ask: can we always trivialize C in $C[L]$ to $(2^\Phi)^*$, setting

$$C[L] = (2^\Phi)^*[L']$$

for a suitable L'? No. As $(2^\Phi)^*[L] = L^{\blacktriangleright}$, it suffices to observe that whereas

$$s \in L^{\blacktriangleright} \text{ and } s' \blacktriangleright s \quad \text{implies} \quad s' \in L^{\blacktriangleright}$$

we have $\boxed{p}\boxed{p}\blacktriangleright\boxed{\square}\boxed{p}$ where $\boxed{\square}\boxed{p}$ is p-pointed but $\boxed{p}\boxed{p}$ is not ($\notin U_p$). That is, the requirement U_p that a p-pointed string *not* weakly subsume $\boxed{p}\boxed{\square}^*\boxed{p}$ is *not* an ontological commitment (in the same way that weakly subsuming $\boxed{p}$ can be). So then what is it?

U_p is a constraint which we can write as

$$\boxed{p}\boxed{\square}^*\boxed{p} \Rightarrow \emptyset$$

as we shall now explain. A *factor of* a string s is a string s' such that $s = us'v$ for some (possibly null) strings u and v. Given languages L and L' over 2^Φ, let $L \Rightarrow L'$ be the set of strings over 2^Φ whose factors subsume L only if they subsume L'

$$s \in L \Rightarrow L' \stackrel{\text{def}}{\iff} \text{every factor of } s \text{ subsuming } L \text{ subsumes } L'.$$

Writing $\overline{L}$ for the set-theoretic complement $(2^\Phi)^* - L$, and $L^{\trianglerighteq}$ for the set of strings that subsume L

$$L^{\trianglerighteq} \stackrel{\text{def}}{=} \{s \in (2^\Phi)^* : s \trianglerighteq L\},$$

note that

$$L \Rightarrow \emptyset \;=\; \overline{(\square^* L \square^*)^{\trianglerighteq}}$$

as no string subsumes $\emptyset$. Moreover, as

$s \in L \Rightarrow L'$ iff no factor of s subsumes L without also subsuming L',

it follows that

$$L \Rightarrow L' \;=\; \overline{(2^\Phi)^*(L^{\trianglerighteq} \cap \overline{L'^{\trianglerighteq}})(2^\Phi)^*}\;.$$

Hence, assuming Φ is finite, $L \Rightarrow L'$ is a regular language (i.e. acceptable by finite automata) whenever L and L' are. (Similarly, if C and L are regular, so is $C[L]$.)

In the next section, we relax U_p to the larger language

$$I_p \;\overset{\text{def}}{=}\; \boxed{p}\square^+\boxed{p} \;\Rightarrow\; \square\boxed{p}\square^+$$

consisting of strings s where the occurrences of p form an interval in that p appears (in s) at all positions between n and m whenever p appears at n and m. To exclude the empty interval, we form $I_p\boxed{p}$.

3. Time strung out and constrained

For all fluents $p, p' \in \Phi$, we can restrict $I_p\boxed{p} \cap I_{p'}\boxed{p'}$ to strings where p temporally overlaps p'

$$L(p \bigcirc p') \;\overset{\text{def}}{=}\; \{s \in I_p \cap I_{p'} \;:\; s \blacktriangleright \boxed{p,p'}\}$$
$$= (I_p \cap I_{p'})\boxed{p,p'}$$

or to strings where p temporally precedes p'

$$L(p \prec p') \;\overset{\text{def}}{=}\; \{s \in I_p \cap I_{p'} \;:\; s \blacktriangleright \boxed{p}\square^*\boxed{p'} \text{ and not } s \blacktriangleright \boxed{p,p'}\}$$
$$= C\boxed{p}\square^*\boxed{p'} \text{ for } C = I_p \cap I_{p'} \cap (\boxed{p,p'} \Rightarrow \emptyset)\;.$$

A string $s \in (2^\Phi)^+$ induces an event structure $\langle E_s, \prec_s, \bigcirc_s \rangle$ in the sense of Kamp and Reyle 1993, where

$$E_s \;\overset{\text{def}}{=}\; \{p \in \Phi \;:\; s \in I_p\boxed{p}\}$$
$$\prec_s \;\overset{\text{def}}{=}\; \{(p, p') \in \Phi \times \Phi \;:\; s \in L(p \prec p')\}$$
$$\bigcirc_s \;\overset{\text{def}}{=}\; \{(p, p') \in \Phi \times \Phi \;:\; s \in L(p \bigcirc p')\}\;.$$

For example, if we set

$$\hat{s} \stackrel{\text{def}}{=} \boxed{p_0 \mid p_0 \mid p_1 \mid p_1, p_2}$$

then

$$\begin{aligned}
\mathsf{E}_{\hat{s}} &= \{p_0, p_1, p_2\} \\
\prec_{\hat{s}} &= \{(p_0, p_1), (p_0, p_2)\} \\
\bigcirc_{\hat{s}} &= \{(p_0, p_0), (p_1, p_1), (p_1, p_2), (p_2, p_1), (p_2, p_2)\}\,.
\end{aligned}$$

Given an event structure $\langle \mathsf{E}, \prec, \bigcirc \rangle$, Kamp derives a linear order $\prec^O$ on a set $I(\bigcirc)$ of *temporal instants* as follows. He defines a temporal instant to be a $\subseteq$-maximal set of pairwise overlapping events, setting

$$I(\bigcirc) \stackrel{\text{def}}{=} \{i \in O(\bigcirc) : (\forall i' \in O(\bigcirc))\, i \subseteq i' \text{ implies } i = i'\}$$

where $O(\bigcirc)$ consists of sets of pairwise overlapping events

$$O(\bigcirc) \stackrel{\text{def}}{=} \{i \subseteq \mathsf{E} : (\forall e, e' \in i)\, e \bigcirc e'\}\,.$$

He lifts $\prec$ existentially to $I(\bigcirc)$, defining

$$i \prec^O i' \stackrel{\text{def}}{\iff} (\exists e \in i)(\exists e' \in i')\, e \prec e'$$

for all $i, i' \in I(\bigcirc)$. It turns out that not only does $\prec^O$ linearly order $I(\bigcirc)$, but each event $e \in \mathsf{E}$ defines an $I(\bigcirc)$-interval in that for all $i, j, k \in I(\bigcirc)$,

$$e \in i \quad \text{whenever} \quad e \in j,\, e \in k \text{ and } j \prec^O i \prec^O k\,.$$

Returning to our example of $\hat{s}$ above, we get two instants $\{p_0\}$ and $\{p_1, p_2\}$

$$I(\bigcirc^{\hat{s}}) = \{\{p_0\}, \{p_1, p_2\}\}$$

and lose $\{p_1\}$ as it is a proper subset of $\{p_1, p_2\}$. To recover such points, let us introduce for each fluent p, fresh fluents $\mathsf{lt}(p)$ and $\mathsf{rt}(p)$ to mark the left and right of p respectively. This turns $\hat{s}$ to

$$\tilde{s} \stackrel{\text{def}}{=} \boxed{p_0, \mathsf{lt}(p_1), \mathsf{lt}(p_2) \mid p_0, \mathsf{lt}(p_1), \mathsf{lt}(p_2) \mid \mathsf{rt}(p_0), p_1, \mathsf{lt}(p_2) \mid \mathsf{rt}(p_0), p_1, p_2}$$

with three Kamp instants

$$I(\bigcirc^{\tilde{s}}) = \{\{p_0, \mathsf{lt}(p_1), \mathsf{lt}(p_2)\}, \{\mathsf{rt}(p_0), p_1, \mathsf{lt}(p_2)\}, \{\mathsf{rt}(p_0), p_1, p_2\}\}$$

136 *Tim Fernando*

reducing the length 4 of $\tilde{s}$ (and $\hat{s}$) to 3, in accordance with the dictum "no time without change" (Kamp and Reyle 1993, page 674).

The introduction of fluents $\mathsf{rt}(p)$ and $\mathsf{lt}(p)$ calls for additional constraints. Neither $\mathsf{rt}(p)$ nor $\mathsf{lt}(p)$ overlaps with p

$$\boxed{p,\mathsf{rt}(p)} \;\Rightarrow\; \emptyset \tag{5}$$

$$\boxed{p,\mathsf{lt}(p)} \;\Rightarrow\; \emptyset \tag{6}$$

and both define intervals, stretching indefinitely to the right

$$\boxed{\mathsf{rt}(p)}\boxed{} \;\Rightarrow\; \boxed{}\boxed{\mathsf{rt}(p)} \tag{7}$$

and left

$$\boxed{}\boxed{\mathsf{lt}(p)} \;\Rightarrow\; \boxed{\mathsf{lt}(p)}\boxed{} \tag{8}$$

respectively. Similarly, p is followed by p or $\mathsf{rt}(p)$

$$\boxed{p}\boxed{} \;\Rightarrow\; \boxed{}\boxed{p} \;\big|\; \boxed{}\boxed{\mathsf{rt}(p)} \tag{9}$$

(where $|$ is non-deterministic choice) and preceded by p or $\mathsf{lt}(p)$

$$\boxed{}\boxed{p} \;\Rightarrow\; \boxed{p}\boxed{} \;\big|\; \boxed{\mathsf{lt}(p)}\boxed{} \,. \tag{10}$$

Finally, we require that $\mathsf{rt}(p)$ be preceded by p

$$\boxed{\mathsf{rt}(p)} \;\overset{\mathsf{b}}{\Rightarrow}\; \boxed{p}\boxed{}^{*} \tag{11}$$

and $\mathsf{lt}(p)$ be followed by p

$$\boxed{\mathsf{lt}(p)} \;\overset{\mathsf{a}}{\Rightarrow}\; \boxed{}^{*}\boxed{p} \,, \tag{12}$$

writing $L \overset{\mathsf{b}}{\Rightarrow} L'$ for "L' before every L"

$$s \in L \overset{\mathsf{b}}{\Rightarrow} L' \;\overset{\mathrm{def}}{\Longleftrightarrow}\; \text{every factor of } s \text{ that subsumes } L$$
$$\text{is preceded by a substring that subsumes } L'$$

and $L \overset{\mathsf{a}}{\Rightarrow} L'$ for "L' after every L"

$$s \in L \overset{\mathsf{a}}{\Rightarrow} L' \;\overset{\mathrm{def}}{\Longleftrightarrow}\; \text{every factor of } s \text{ that subsumes } L$$
$$\text{is followed by a substring that subsumes } L' \,.$$

The connectives $\stackrel{b}{\Rightarrow}$ and $\stackrel{a}{\Rightarrow}$ are essentially Koskenniemi's restrictions (Beesley and Karttunen 2003), preserving regularity as

$$L \stackrel{b}{\Rightarrow} L' \;=\; \overline{(\Box^*L')^{\unrhd}(L\Box^*)^{\unrhd}}$$

since

$$s \in L \stackrel{b}{\Rightarrow} L' \quad \text{iff} \quad \text{no factor of } s \text{ subsumes } L \text{ unless} \\ \text{preceded by a substring that subsumes } L'$$

and similarly,

$$L \stackrel{a}{\Rightarrow} L' \;=\; \overline{(\Box^*L)^{\unrhd}\overline{(L'\Box^*)^{\unrhd}}}.$$

For the record, we strengthen I_p by the intersection, denoted $\mathsf{Interval}_p$, of the languages (5) – (12)

$$\mathsf{Interval}_p \;\stackrel{\text{def}}{=}\; (5) \cap (6) \cap \cdots \cap (12).$$

As for $p \bigcirc p'$ and $p \prec p'$, let

$$\mathsf{I}_{p,p'} \;\stackrel{\text{def}}{=}\; \mathsf{Interval}_p \cap \mathsf{Interval}_{p'}$$

and

$$\mathscr{L}(p \bigcirc p') \;\stackrel{\text{def}}{=}\; \mathsf{I}_{p,p'}\left[\,\boxed{p,p'}\,\right]$$
$$\mathscr{L}(p \prec p') \;\stackrel{\text{def}}{=}\; \mathsf{I}_{p,p'}\left[\,\boxed{\mathsf{lt}(p')}\,\boxed{\mathsf{rt}(p)}\,\right]$$

avoiding the hidden constraint $\boxed{p,p'} \Rightarrow \emptyset$ in $L(p \prec p')$.

Turning next to a string s representing an event or situation, we can associate a time $\tau(s) \in \Phi$ with s by intersecting $\mathsf{Interval}_{\tau(s)}$ with the constraint

$$s \;\Rightarrow\; \boxed{\tau(s)}^+$$

requiring that $\tau(s)$ spans s, as well as

$$\Box s \;\Rightarrow\; \boxed{\mathsf{lt}(\tau(s))}\,\Box^+$$
$$s\Box \;\Rightarrow\; \Box^+\,\boxed{\mathsf{lt}(\tau(s))}$$

for an exact fit. We can then reduce the languages where $s \prec s'$ and $s \bigcirc s'$ to $\mathscr{L}(\tau(s) \prec \tau(s'))$ and $\mathscr{L}(\tau(s) \bigcirc \tau(s'))$, respectively.[2] The time $\tau(s)$ is called "external" in Cooper 1998, as opposed to "internal" times mentioned within s, such as *dawn* and *dusk* within $\boxed{dawn, rain}\,\square\,\boxed{dusk, rain}$.

Note that $\boxed{dawn, rain}\,\square\,\boxed{dusk, rain}$ is weakly subsumed by perfectly reasonable strings s' where $\mathsf{E}_{s'}$ contains neither *dawn* nor *dusk*. (Let s' span a week.) In general, we may wish to form a string s from fluents outside E_s; in addition to regularly recurring fluents like *dawn* and *dusk*, the disjunction $\mathsf{rt}(p) \vee \mathsf{lt}(p)$ representing the negation of an interval p does not form an interval (in strings $\in \mathsf{Interval}_p\boxed{\boxed{p}}$).

4. Fluents, languages and witnesses

The notion that $\mathsf{rt}(p) \vee \mathsf{lt}(p)$ represents the negation of an interval p can be understood through constraints of the form

$$\boxed{\varphi \vee \psi} \Rightarrow \boxed{\varphi}\,||\,\boxed{\psi} \qquad (13)$$

$$\boxed{\varphi, \neg\varphi} \Rightarrow \emptyset \qquad (14)$$

$$\boxed{} \Rightarrow \boxed{\varphi}\,||\,\boxed{\neg\varphi} \qquad (15)$$

naturally associated with fluent disjunction $\vee$ and negation $\neg$. This section argues that while we may always assume (13) and (14), we should be more careful with (15), in view of the partiality of events and situations.

First, observe that the soundness of a constraint $L_1 \Rightarrow L_2$ can be tested against Kripke models over the frame $\langle \mathbb{Z}, < \rangle$ by mapping

(i) a string $a_1 \cdots a_n$ to the fluent

$$\varphi_{a_1 \cdots a_n} \stackrel{\text{def}}{=} \bigwedge \{\mathsf{next}^{i-1}(\varphi) : \varphi \in a_i\}$$

with $\mathsf{next}^0(\varphi) \stackrel{\text{def}}{=} \varphi$ and $\mathsf{next}^{i+1}(\varphi) \stackrel{\text{def}}{=} \mathsf{next}(\mathsf{next}^i(\varphi))$, and

(ii) a language L to the fluent

$$\varphi^L \stackrel{\text{def}}{=} \bigvee \{\varphi_s : s \in L\}.$$

Clearly, for $L_1 \Rightarrow L_2$ of the form (13), (14) or (15), the implication $\varphi^{L_1} \supset \varphi^{L_2}$ (i.e. $\neg \varphi^{L_1} \vee \varphi^{L_2}$) is true in all Kripke models over $\langle \mathbb{Z}, < \rangle$.

Beyond soundness, we may ask when a string can be said to establish the truth of a fluent φ. To be precise, let us fix an atomic fluent now, and say a string s *witnesses* φ if s is now-pointed and φ is true in all Kripke models M over $\langle \mathbb{Z}, < \rangle$ that contain $R_{now,s}$ (as defined in section 2 above) in that

$$(\forall \psi \in \Phi)(\forall i \in \mathbb{Z}) \quad R_{now,s}(i, \psi) \text{ implies } M \models \psi^i$$

where

$$\psi^i \stackrel{def}{=} \begin{cases} \psi & \text{if } i = 0 \\ \text{next}^i(\psi) & \text{if } i > 0 \\ \text{prev}^{-i}(\psi) & \text{if } i < 0. \end{cases}$$

For example, both $\boxed{\text{now}, \varphi}$ and $\boxed{\text{now}, \psi}$ witness $\varphi \lor \psi$. Neither witnesses $\varphi \land \psi$, although $\boxed{\text{now}, \varphi, \psi}$ does, suggesting the constraint

$$\boxed{\varphi \land \psi} \Rightarrow \boxed{\varphi, \psi} \tag{16}$$

that cashes conjunction $\land$ out as a comma. The fluent now is useful for strings of length > 1; depending on where we put now in $\boxed{\varphi \mid \psi}$, we can get a witness

$$\boxed{\text{now}, \varphi \mid \psi} \quad \text{of} \quad \varphi \land \text{next}(\psi)$$

or

$$\boxed{\varphi \mid \text{now}, \psi} \quad \text{of} \quad \text{prev}(\varphi) \land \psi .$$

Although every fluent φ is witnessed by $\boxed{\text{now}, \varphi}$, the intent behind constraints such as (13) and (16) is to eliminate connectives. Indeed, the pair $\lor$ and $\land$ suggest defining negation $\neg$ as a map on fluents, with

$$\begin{aligned} \neg(\varphi \lor \psi) &= \neg \varphi \land \neg \psi \\ \neg(\varphi \land \psi) &= \neg \varphi \lor \neg \psi . \end{aligned}$$

More generally, the idea would be to map each n-ary connective θ to an n-ary connective $\overline{\theta}$ such that $\overline{\overline{\theta}} = \theta$ and for all $\varphi_1, \ldots, \varphi_n$,

$$\neg \theta(\varphi_1, \ldots, \varphi_n) = \overline{\theta}(\neg \varphi_1, \ldots, \neg \varphi_n) .$$

For example, let $\overline{\land} = \lor$ and $\overline{\theta} = \theta$ for $\theta \in \{\text{next}, \text{prev}\}$. Adding the constraints

$$\boxed{\text{next}(\varphi)} \stackrel{a}{\Rightarrow} \boxed{\varphi} \tag{17}$$

$$\boxed{\text{prev}(\varphi)} \stackrel{b}{\Rightarrow} \boxed{\varphi} \tag{18}$$

140 Tim Fernando

to (13) and (16), we can for instance, build the witnesses

$$\boxed{p\,|\,\text{now}\,|\,p} \quad \text{and} \quad \boxed{p\,|\,\text{now}\,|\,\neg q} \quad \text{of} \quad \hat{\varphi} \stackrel{\text{def}}{=} \text{prev}(p) \wedge \text{next}(p \vee \neg q)$$

as follows.

Step 1. Form $C[\![\,\text{now},\hat{\varphi}\,]\!]$ where C is the intersection of instances of (13), (14), (16), (17) and (18) given by subformulas of $\hat{\varphi}$.

Step 2. Restrict the fluents in strings in $C[\![\,\text{now},\hat{\varphi}\,]\!]$ to now and the atomic and negated atomic subformulas of $\hat{\varphi}$ (i.e. $p, \neg p, q$ and $\neg q$), defining for every subset Ψ of Φ and every string $a_1 \cdots a_n \in (2^\Phi)^*$,

$$\cap_\Psi(a_1 a_2 \cdots a_n) \stackrel{\text{def}}{=} (a_1 \cap \Psi)(a_2 \cap \Psi) \cdots (a_n \cap \Psi)$$

(e.g. $\cap_{\{\text{now},p,\neg p,\neg q,q\}}(\boxed{p,r,p \vee \neg q\,|\,\text{now},\hat{\varphi}\,|\,p,\neg q}) = \boxed{p\,|\,\text{now}\,|\,p,\neg q}$).

Step 3. Pick out the $\trianglerighteq$-minimal strings of the language obtained from Step 2, where a $\trianglerighteq$-*minimal string* of a language L is a string $s \in L$ such that not $s \trianglerighteq L - \{s\}$.

Step 4. Delete strings that begin or end with $\square$, leaving the witnesses

$$\boxed{p\,|\,\text{now}\,|\,p} \quad | \quad \boxed{p\,|\,\text{now}\,|\,\neg q}$$

of $\hat{\varphi}$, neither of which satisfies (15) for $\varphi \in \{p,q\}$. (Indeed, bivalence (15) arguably runs counter to the idea of $\trianglerighteq$-minimization in Step 3.)

Generalizing from $\hat{\varphi}$ to a fluent φ subject to constraints C_φ, Steps 1-4 specify the language

$$\mathcal{L}_{\text{now}}^\varphi(C_\varphi) \stackrel{\text{def}}{=} \underbrace{\trianglerighteq\text{-min}(}_{\text{Step 3}}\underbrace{\{\cap_{\Phi(\varphi)}(s)}_{\text{Step 2}} : s \in \underbrace{C_\varphi[\![\,\text{now},\varphi\,]\!]\})}_{\text{Step 1}} - \underbrace{(\square(2^\Phi)^* \mid (2^\Phi)^*\square)}_{\text{Step 4}}$$

where $\trianglerighteq$-min(L) consists of the $\trianglerighteq$-minimal strings of L, and $\Phi(\varphi)$ consists of now and all atomic and negated atomic subformulas of φ. Whenever C_φ is regular, $\mathcal{L}_{\text{now}}^\varphi(C_\varphi)$ is regular (Fernando 2006a). But can we always choose C_φ so that $\mathcal{L}_{\text{now}}^\varphi(C_\varphi)$ yields witnesses of φ?

Sometimes but not always. Consider the Priorean future operator F with existential force in that for a Kripke model M over $\langle \mathbb{Z}, < \rangle$,

$$M \models \mathsf{F}\varphi \stackrel{\text{def}}{\iff} (\exists n \geq 1)\, M_{+n} \models \varphi$$

where M_{+n} is M with its point of evaluation shifted n positions to the right. The instance of the constraint

$$\boxed{F\varphi} \stackrel{a}{\Rightarrow} \boxed{\Box^* \boxed{\varphi}}$$

given by an atomic fluent $\varphi = p$ yields the language $\boxed{\text{now}}\boxed{\Box^*\boxed{p}}$ of witnesses of Fp. But the dual operator G with

$$M \models G\varphi \stackrel{\text{def}}{\iff} (\forall n \geq 1)\, M_{+n} \models \varphi$$

is another matter. No string in the language $\boxed{\text{now}}\boxed{p}^+$ from the constraint

$$\boxed{G\varphi}\boxed{\Box} \Rightarrow \boxed{\Box\boxed{\varphi, G\varphi}}$$

can witness Gp. Indeed, no finite string built from atomic and negated atomic fluents can, the obvious candidate being the infinite string

$$\lim_{n \to \infty} \boxed{\text{now}}\boxed{p}^n .$$

The contrast between Fp and Gp brings out a difficulty for negation insofar as $\neg Fp$ can be equated with $G\neg p$ (and the problem above with Gp applies to $G\neg p$). The existence of witnesses over atomic and negated atomic formulas for φ does *not* guarantee the same for $\neg \varphi$.

Short of forming the witness $\boxed{\text{now}, \neg\varphi}$ for $\neg\varphi$, we can pick out strings that do *not* weakly subsume $\boxed{\text{now}, \varphi}$ via the constraint

$$\boxed{\text{now}, \varphi} \Rightarrow \emptyset . \tag{19}$$

But whereas the constraints $L_1 \Rightarrow L_2$ constituting C_φ above are universally true (in that $\varphi^{L_1} \supset \varphi^{L_2}$ is true in every Kripke model over $\langle \mathbb{Z}, < \rangle$), we can hardly make that claim for (19). That said, we spell out in the next section the sense in which $\boxed{\text{now}, \neg\varphi}$ follows from (19), a weaker form

$$\boxed{\text{now}} \Rightarrow \boxed{\varphi} \mid\mid \boxed{\neg\varphi} \tag{20}$$

of bivalence (15), and (not to forget) $\boxed{\text{now}}$.

5. Entailment, circumstance and object

Given languages L, L' and C over 2^Φ, let us say L entails L' relative to C and write $L \vdash_C L'$ if $C[L]$ weakly subsumes L'

$$L \vdash_C L' \stackrel{\text{def}}{\iff} C[L] \blacktriangleright L' .$$

From the example

$$L = \boxed{\text{now}},\ L' = \boxed{\text{now}, \neg \varphi}\ \text{and}\ C = (19) \cap (20),$$

it is clear that $L \vdash_C L'$ goes beyond $L \blacktriangleright L'$ in invoking a string s from C as a circumstance for evaluating L' provided s weakly subsumes L

$$L \vdash_C L' \quad \text{iff} \quad (\forall s \in C)\ s \blacktriangleright L'\ \text{whenever}\ s \blacktriangleright L\ .$$

But why split the single argument $C[L]$ for $\blacktriangleright$ into two arguments for $\vdash$?

There is, for starters, the matter of emphasis. As a subscript in $\vdash$, C is consigned to the background, leaving the limelight for L (and L'). Perhaps more significantly, the force of C is (typically) universal, whereas that of L is existential.

C	L
circumstances	objects
background	foreground
universal	existential

The universal/existential dichotomy here can be understood in two different ways. Firstly, the semantics of $\Rightarrow, \stackrel{a}{\Rightarrow}$ and $\stackrel{b}{\Rightarrow}$ above are given in terms of *all* factors of a string, whereas $L^{\blacktriangleright}$ consists of strings that weakly subsume *some* string in L. Secondly, all constraints in the previous section, save (19), are true in *all* Kripke models over $\langle \mathbb{Z}, < \rangle$. The synthetic (non-analytic) component of $C[L]$ is L, which carries ontological weight. This is *not* to say that the ontological commitments of $C[L]$ rest entirely in L. Some ontological commitments can be inferred with the use of $\vdash$, as in

$$\boxed{p \wedge \neg q} \vdash_{\hat{C}} \boxed{p, \neg q} \quad \text{for} \quad \hat{C} = \boxed{p \wedge \neg q} \Rightarrow \boxed{p, \neg q}\ .$$

In fact, the similarity between witnesses and proofs, coupled with the idea of proofs-as-objects (supporting *propositions-as-types* in proof-theoretic semantics), suggests that $\boxed{p, \neg q}$ is a canonical ontological commitment (i.e., object) of $p \wedge \neg q$. Construing $\blacktriangleright$ as a part-of relation, it is a small step to say that $p \wedge \neg q$ ontologically commits us not only to $\boxed{p, \neg q}$ but to all strings weakly subsumed by $\boxed{p, \neg q}$, such as $\boxed{p}$. One reason for being uncomfortable with bivalence (15) is that $\boxed{\text{now}, \neg \varphi}$ can be smuggled through $L = \boxed{\text{now}}$ and $C = (19) \cap (15)$.

Lastly, for every string s and language L, let us define the finite language L_s to consist of strings in L that s weakly subsumes

$$L_s \stackrel{\text{def}}{=} \{s' \in L\ :\ s \blacktriangleright s'\}\ .$$

We close by observing that the equivalence

$$L \vdash_C L' \quad \text{iff} \quad (\forall \hat{s} \in C)(\forall s \in L_{\hat{s}})(\exists s')\ s' \in L'_{\hat{s}}$$

reduces $L \vdash_C L'$ to the claim

$$x \in C, y \in L_x \longmapsto t_{L'}(x,y) \in L'_x$$

that a certain program is guaranteed to succeed, given $x \in C$ and $y \in L_x$. That program $t_{L'}(x,y)$ searches through the finitely many strings weakly subsumed by x for one in L' (spurred on by y in L_x).

Notes

1. Some differences between van Lambalgen and Hamm 2005 and the string approach here are noted in Fernando 2006b.
2. We can, of course, also capture say, $s \prec s'$ directly as $U_{s,s'}[s\square^* s']$ where the constraint $U_{s,s'}$ asserts s and s' each occur at most once.

References

Barwise, J., and J. Perry
    1983   *Situations and Attitudes*. MIT Press, Cambridge, MA.
Beesley, K.R., and L. Karttunen
    2003   *Finite State Morphology*. CSLI Publications, Stanford.
Cooper, R.
    1998   Austinian propositions, Davidsonian events and perception complements. In *The Tbilisi Symposium on Logic, Language and Computation: Selected Papers*, J. Ginzburg, Z. Khasidashvili, C. Vogel, J.-J. Lévy, and E. Vallduví (eds.), 19–34. CSLI Publications, Stanford.
    2005   Austinian truth, attitudes and type theory. *Research on Language and Computation* 3 (4): 333–362.
Fernando, T.
    2006a   Finite-state temporal projection. *Proc. 11th International Conference on Implementation and Application of Automata*, Lecture Notes in Computer Science 4094. Springer-Verlag, 230–241.
    2006b   Representing events and discourse: comments on Hamm, Kamp and van Lambalgen. *Theoretical Linguistics* 32 (1): 57–64.
Kamp, H., and U. Reyle
    1993   *From Discourse to Logic*. Kluwer Academic Publishers, Dordrecht.
van Lambalgen, M., and F. Hamm
    2005   *The Proper Treatment of Events*. Blackwell.
Martin-Löf, P.
    1984   *Intuitionistic Type Theory*. Bibliopolis, Napoli. Notes by Giovanni Sambin of a series of lectures given in Padua, June 1980.
McCarthy, J., and P. Hayes
    1969   Some philosophical problems from the standpoint of artificial intelligence. In *Machine Intelligence 4*, M. Meltzer, and D. Michie (eds.), 463–502. Edinburgh University Press.

Parsons, T.
1990   *Events in the Semantics of English: A Study in Subatomic Semantics*. MIT Press, Cambridge, MA.

Robust VP ellipsis resolution in DR theory

Johan Bos

1. Introduction

The phenomenon of Verb Phrase Ellipsis (henceforth VPE[1]) that manifests itself in the English language has been a popular topic of research in formal semantics and computational linguistics. In fact, it has been studied in great detail regarding various issues: whether the level of resolution should take place on the syntactic or semantic level; how VPE interacts with quantifier scope; and, especially, how to account for ambiguities resulting from the so called sloppy and strict interpretations that occur when VP ellipsis interacts with anaphoric pronouns.

Empirical approaches to VPE, that is, studying or automatically processing VPE on the basis of occurrences in corpora, have almost been completely ignored, with two notable exceptions: Hardt 1997, and Nielsen 2005. Hardt (1997) studied several hundred examples of VPE automatically found in the Penn Treebank, and implemented and evaluated a system for finding antecedents. Similar work was carried out by Nielsen (2005), but in addition he also discussed various ways to identify VPE in open-domain texts, and manually annotated occurrences of VPE in a corpus. Both Hardt and Nielsen provide algorithms for resolving VPE on the surface level, i.e., by expanding the elided verb phrases into its full form.

The goal of this article is to investigate how an existing implementation of a wide coverage NLP system for the semantic analysis of open-domain natural language texts can be extended to deal with the detection and resolution of VPE. In contrast to Hardt 1997 and Nielsen 2005, ellipsis resolution will proceed on the semantic level. As Nielsen (2005) does, we will also deal with the problem of VPE detection in open-domain texts.

The framework proposed in this article for processing VPE is robust, in the sense that it achieves high coverage on open-domain texts. Yet, it is based on formal linguistic theory. The syntactic analysis is carried out in the context of Combinatorial Categorial Grammar (Steedman 2001). The semantic analysis follows Discourse Representation Theory (Kamp 1981). Resolution of anaphoric expressions is inspired by the binding and accommodation theory of presupposition (Van der Sandt 1992).

The article is organised as follows. We will first introduce VPE for those not familiar with it, sketch the basic approach, present the computational formalism that we employ, and describe the corpus that we use. Then we focus on the task of VPE detection and the task of VPE antecedent location, report our results on both tasks, and list various problematic cases encountered. This is followed by a description of a new algorithm for VPE resolution in Discourse Representation Theory.

2. Preliminaries

2.1. VP ellipsis

For those readers unfamiliar with the phenomenon of VPE and the terminology used in the literature I will provide a brief introduction on the topic.

VPE manifests itself in English when verb phrases are abbreviated to an auxiliary verb (do, have, be, will) or deleted in an infinite clause, where the interpretation of the elided VP depends on an earlier introduced verb phrase in the discourse, usually the previous one. Consider the following examples of VPE, where the auxiliary escorting the elided VP is typeset in boldface, and the intended antecedent is underlined:

(1) Carlo <u>lives in San Lorenzo</u> and so **does** Marco.

(2) Carlo <u>hates his boss</u> and Marco **does** too.

The first sentence is interpreted as meaning that both Marco and Carlo live in San Lorenzo. Using the terminology used in (Dalrymple, Shieber, and Pereira 1991), we distinguish between the **source clause** (*Carlo lives in San Lorenzo*) and the **target clause** (*so does Marco*), with *Carlo* and *Marco* being **parallel elements**.

Example (2) introduces a source of ambiguity. It has a strict interpretation, where Marco and Carlo both hate Carlo's boss; and a sloppy interpretation, where Carlo hates Carlo's boss and Marco hates Marco's boss. Although this is an interesting problem, and many theoretical approaches to VPE have been devoted to it, the sloppy-strict ambiguity triggered by VPE seems to occur only sporadically in real data (see Section 5.3).

2.2. Basic approach

VPE resolution is a complex task and involves various aspects of processing. In order to quantify the performance of a VPE resolution algorithm with respect to the various stages of processing involved, I will follow Nielsen 2005 and divide the problem of VPE resolution into three tasks:

1. VPE detection;
2. VPE antecedent location;
3. VPE resolution.

The first problem is the task of determining whether a sentence of English contains an elliptical verb phrase. Given an elliptical verb phrase, the second problem is concerned with finding the correct antecedent in the text. The third problem constitutes the resolution of the elliptical verb phrase: whether the right material (not too much, not too little) of the source clause is abstracted and applied correctly to the target.

For practical reasons, within the scope of this article, we will only consider cases of VPE generated using forms of the auxiliary verb *do*. We have no reason to believe that the analysis put forward in this article does not extend to other forms of VPE, but demonstrating so will be left for future work. Following Nielsen 2005, we will exclude cases of *do-it* and *do-so* anaphora from our analysis, arguing that these are principally different from VPE.

2.3. Syntactic and semantic formalism

As computational framework we use the C&C wide-coverage parser (Clark and Curran 2004) and Boxer (Bos 2005) to produce semantic representations for open-domain English texts. The C&C parser implements Combinatory Categorial Grammar (CCG, following Steedman 2001) using a statistical model trained on CCGbank, an annotated treebank for derivations of CCG (Hockenmaier and Steedman 2002). As CCG is not central to this article, we assume some familiarity with type-logical grammars and won't go into details of CCG theory. Instead, in Figure 1 we illustrate CCG with a simple example derivation as output by the C&C parser.

The example derivation in Figure 1 shows the lexical categories for each word (for instance, NP/N for the determiner *a*, (S[dcl]\NP)/NP for the transitive verb *has*). It further demonstrates how combinatory rules combine the categories (for instance, forward application, fapp, combines a determiner with a

```
bapp('S[dcl]',
  lex('N','NP',
    leaf('John', 'John', 'NNP', 'I-PERSON', 'N')),
  fapp('S[dcl]\NP',
    leaf('has', 'have', 'VBZ', 'O', '(S[dcl]\NP)/NP'),
    fapp('NP[nb]',
      leaf('a', 'a', 'DT', 'O', 'NP[nb]/N'),
      leaf('car', 'car', 'NN', 'O', 'N')))).
```

Figure 1. CCG derivation for *John has a car* as output by the C&C parser.

noun, resulting in a category NP for the phrase *a car*, and backward application, bapp, combines the noun phrase with a verb phrase). The complete analysis receives the category S[dcl], a declarative sentence.

The output of the parser is used to construct Discourse Representation Structures (DRSs), as proposed in Discourse Representation Theory (Kamp and Reyle 1993). In fact, we follow DRT closely, but nevertheless deviate on four points:

1. We restrict ourselves to a first-order fragment of the DRS language;

2. We use a Neo-Davidsonian analysis of events and thematic roles;[2]

3. We extend standard DRT with Van der Sandt's theory of presupposition projection (Van der Sandt 1992);

4. We employ an explicit sentence merge-operator "+" to combine smaller DRSs into larger ones.[3]

Boxer implements DRT on top of the CCG derivations output by the C&C parser. A DRS generated by Boxer is the one below in Figure 2, when given as input the sample derivation shown in Figure 1. This DRS exemplifies the use of discourse referents of type event, and the use of two-place relations to represent thematic roles.

2.4. Analysis of VP ellipsis in CCGbank

In CCGbank, the relation of a VPE sentence to its antecedent is assumed to be anaphoric in nature, and is analysed by giving the auxiliary of an elided VP clause the category S\NP (Hockenmaier 2003, p. 61). Put differently, sentences infected with VPE are considered complete sentences, rather than sentences with a VP missing, in which one would expect a category of the type

```
 _____
|  x3 x2 x1          |
|_____|
|  named(x3,john)    |
|  car(x2)           |
|  sell(x1)          |
|  event(x1)         |
|  agent(x1,x3)      |
|  patient(x1,x2)    |
|_____|
```

Figure 2. DRS for *John sold a car* as output by Boxer.

(S\NP)/(S\NP) for the auxilary. In cases of elliptical inversion, Hockenmaier assigns the category S[inv]/NP to the auxiliary to analyse phrases such as *and so does John*. In either case, the DRS generated for a sentence with an elided VP, without applying any form of ellipsis resolution, is basically of the form illustrated in Figure 3.

```
 _____      _____
|  x3 x2 x1          |    |  x5 x4             |
|_____|    |_____|
(| named(x3,john)    | +| named(x5,bill)      |)
|  car(x2)           |  |  do(x4)             |
|  like(x1)          |  |  too(x4)            |
|  event(x1)         |  |  event(x4)          |
|  agent(x1,x3)      |  |  agent(x4,x5)       |
|  patient(x1,x2)    |  |_____|
|_____|
```

Figure 3. DRS for *John likes a car. Bill does, too*, as output by Boxer, without performing VPE resolution.

2.5. Data

The data that we considered for our corpus study and system development comprises most of the Wall Street Journal sections found in the Penn Treebank. All occurrences of VPE constructed with the auxiliary verb *do* were manually annotated.[4] The data was arbitrarily divided into development data[5] and test data[6]. The development data (in total 89 cases of VPE with the auxiliary "to do") was used to develop and tune the system. The test data (50 examples of

VPE) wasn't uncovered until the system was in a stable state, and then used for evaluation of VPE detection and VPE antecedent location.

3. VPE detection

3.1. Method

As the DRS in Figure 3 suggests, a simple baseline for VPE detection on the level of logical form (here: DRS) is traversing information in DRSs for events symbolised by do that only have one argument role: that of agent. This baseline should have a rather good coverage, but it will also wrongly identify cases as VPE, namely those where the parser identifies forms of *to do* as an intransitive verb when it is part of fixed expressions such as *having to do something*, *doing good/well/better/best* and variations thereof, such as *doing little/much*. Our improved system is a simple extension of the baseline where such cases are filtered out. In addition, it also checks whether the auxiliary "do" is part of a wh-question, in which case it is not considered to be an instance of VPE.[7]

3.2. Evaluation and results

Evaluation of VPE detection is conducted by measuring precision (P, the number of correctly identified VPE divided by the number of identified VPE) and recall (R, the number of correctly identified VPE divided by the total number of VPE in the data set). As usual, in empirical approaches to natural language processing, we also compute the F-score, the harmonic mean of precision and recall. For completeness we show the results for both the development data and the (unseen) test data (Table 1).

Table 1. Results (precision, recall and F-score) of VPE detection on Development and Test Data comparing the baseline and improved system.

Development	P	R	F	Test	P	R	F
Baseline	0.62	0.82	0.71	Baseline	0.54	0.87	0.67
Improved	0.77	0.81	0.79	Improved	0.74	0.87	0.80

As Table 1 shows, recall of both the baseline and improved system is similar, but the improved system excels in precision. Note that the performances of the systems on the development and test data do not deviate strongly—this is an indication that we did not overtune the improved system on the development data.

Comparing these results to other work on VPE detection gives us the following figures. Hardt (1997) reports a recall of 44% and precision of 53% for VPE detection (achieving an F-score of 48%), including all types of VPE, for a small part of the Penn Treebank dataset (in total 48 cases of VPE). Nielsen (2005) outperforms these numbers using a method based on part-of-speech tags and other syntactic features: his system obtains an F-score of 82% on (a part of the gold standard) the Penn Treebank dataset, and 71% on re-parsed data.

A straight comparison of our results with that of Nielsen is not straightforward. Even though the overall corpus is the same (Penn Treebank), the subsets of studied data and types of VPE differ: this study take more data into account, but Nielsen covers a wider variety of VPE cases. However, we many tentavily conclude that our system, with its performance on re-parsed data, shows promising results (F-score of 80%) compared to that of Nielsen's (F-score of 71%) in the task of VPE detection.

3.3. Problematic cases

Even though our system can be said to perform well in the task of VPE detection, it still fails to recognise instances of VPE in certain cases. It also wrongly detects VPE, roughly every fourth case it considers one. A basic error analysis could reveal the causes of these mistakes and perhaps suggests a way to improve the system.

Let's consider first the false positives. These are mainly due to parsing mistakes, where the parser tries to deal with difficult cases such as long-distance dependencies or relatively complex modifier verb interactions. For instance, in (3) the main verb in the embedded question is mistaken for an intransitive rather than a transitive verb. Similarly, in (4) and (5) the auxiliary verb is wrongly analysed as an intransitive verb.

(3) *Index traders [...] don't even know what the companies they own actually **do**, complains Andrew Sigler, chairman of Champion International Corp.* [WSJ section 01]

(4) *But Mr. Smith said [...] the oral agreement **did** in fact exist, and that even [...] at another studio.* [WSJ section 04]

(5) *Makoto Utsumi [...] said the ministry **didn't** in any way suggest to Japanese banks that they stay out of the UAL Corp. leveraged buy-out.* [WSJ section 14]

In many of the 'missed' cases it is the other way around — in those the auxiliary was analysed by the parser as a transitive, instead of an intransitive verb. Because the parser that we use is a stochastic parser, the obvious way to improve the analyses is to provide more training data by extending CCGbank.

4. VPE antecedent location

4.1. Method

The baseline algorithm for finding proper antecedents we will start to work with is straightforward: consider the closest VP that occurs before the elided VP as antecedent. The distance between source and target is measured using the token position of the VPE and that of the head of the verb phrases considered as antecedent. Token positions are represented by natural numbers.

Technically, this is implemented as follows. Once we detect a case of VPE, we record the token position P_E of the auxiliary verb that forms the elided VP. Then we search through the DRS representing the entire context provided, and attempt to locate an event with at least an agent role, with corresponding token position P_A, such that $P_A < P_E$ and there is no P_i corresponding to an event such that $P_A < P_i \wedge P_i < P_E$.

Even though source and target clauses of VPE are normally in close proximity to each other, for simplicity, the search is carried out at the entire previous context, rather than, say, within a two-sentence window. In our implementation, the context is defined by the complete newspaper article as defined in the PennTreebank corpus. For each newspaper article, one DRS spanning all its sentences is constructed. Obviously, this is not an efficient method, but once we know more about proximity of antecedent VPs we can restrict the search space in future versions of our algorithm.

4.2. Evaluation and results

We evaluated VPE antecedent location by checking whether the main verb of the selected event overlaps with that of the annotated antecedent VP. This is the method that Hardt (1997) defines as "Head Match: the system choice and coder choice have the same head." Using this measure, the system achieves an accuracy of 73% on the development data, and 72% on the test data. These figures are in the same ballpark as those reported by Hardt, who reports a success rate of 62% for a baseline system based on recency only, and an accuracy of

84% for an improved system taking recency, clausal relations, parallelism, and quotation into account.

4.3. Problematic cases

Choosing the closest VP is a strategy that will work in a lot of cases, but obviously not in all. Here we list some examples that our system got wrong, with the wrongly selected antecedents underlined. To start, examples illustrating that selecting the most recent antecedent event as antecedent for an elided VP is not always a good strategy, are (6)–(8).

(6) *You either believe Seymour can do it again or you **don't**.* [WSJ section 00]

(7) *They say insurance companies use policies aimed at excluding bad risks because their competitors **do**.* [WSJ section 05]

(8) *Wells Rich declined to comment on the status of the account, as **did** the other agencies.* [WSJ section 05]

It seems that, at least for these cases, selecting a VP as antecedent which is itself part of a larger VP, is not always a good idea, and choosing the outermost VP would have yielded the correct antecedent. In DRS terms, this rule could be implemented by disregarding events which are themselves arguments of thematic roles of other events.

As Asher (1993) argues, for choosing a correct antecedent VP one often needs to take discourse structure into account. A case in point is (9), which our system got wrong by selecting the closest antecedent.

(9) *The arbs may recoup some of their paper losses if the UAL deal gets patched up again, as they **did** in 1982 when Occidental Petroleum Co. rescued them with a $4 billion takeover of Cities Service.* [WSJ section 14]

Although in most cases the antecedent of an elided VP is found in the preceding text, it sometimes is found in the text following the ellipsis. Parallel to the usage of the term VP-anaphora for VPE, one could call such cases instances of VP-cataphora. We found only two cases of VP-cataphora in the corpus:

(10) *As they **did** when the Philippines was a colony of the U.S., teachers for the most part teach in English, even though it is a foreign language for most Phillipine children.* [WSJ section 08]

(11) As she has **done** in the past, she stated her support for Mr. Lawson but insisted on keeping on an advisor who opposed and disparaged his policies. [WSJ section 08]

Even though cases of VP-cataphora are rare, closer inspection might reveal whether there are certain syntactic constructions that license VP-cataphora: it is striking that both examples (10) and (11) start with the adverbial "as". Perhaps there are clear syntactic clues signalling VP-cataphora which are easy to integrate into the VPE antecedent location algorithm.

Finally, we consider a linguistically interesting example of VPE found in the corpus, repeated here as (12).

(12) *If Brazil devises an economic strategy allowing it to resume growth and service debt, this could lead it to open up and deregulate its sheltered economy, analysts say, just as Argentinian President Carlos Saul Menem has been **doing** even though he was elected on a populist platform.* [WSJ section 04]

It is perhaps not crystal clear what the correct antecedent is, but it certainly not the one found by the system. It seems to me that the antecedent is *allowing it to resume growth and service debt*. If this is so, this would be also an instance of a sloppy reading, but a special one, as the sloppy interpretation of the pronoun refers to Argentina, a concept only mentioned indirectly in the text by the noun phrase *Argentinian President*.

5. VP ellipsis resolution

5.1. Resolving strategies

With the computational framework we have at our disposal, we can choose to resolve VPE either on the syntactic level (i.e., the level of CCG derivation) or on the semantic level (i.e., the level of DRS). While a comparison of these two possibilities would be an interesting topic of study, in the scope of this article, we choose to restrict ourselves to the latter option—that is, resolving elliptical VPs by reconstruction on the level of discourse representation structure.

This choice immediately raises another question: will resolution take place before or after resolution of anaphoric expressions, such as proper names, pronouns, and definite descriptions. We will argue that it is at least technically simpler to perform VPE resolution after resolving anaphoric expressions.

Various ways of reconstruction have been proposed in the literature: by predication or abstraction over the subject in the antecedent verb phrase (Sag 1976; Klein 1987), by employing higher-order resolution (Dalrymple, Shieber, and Pereira 1991), or by semantic abstraction over constituents (Asher 1993). We implement a novel copying and renaming approach, which is inspired by a method first proposed by Bäuerle (1988) within the framework of DRT.

5.2. A copying and renaming algorithm

In order to explain our resolution method, we will need to introduce some new terminology. We will call the DRS associated with the source clause the **source DRS**, and the DRS in which the VPE is detected the **target DRS**. (For simplicity we assume that each clause corresponds to exactly one DRS.) The discourse referent of type event corresponding to the antecedent VP in the source DRS is called **source event**, and the discourse referent of the elided VP **target event**. Finally, the semantic material to be copied in the process of VPE resolution is called the **antecedent DRS**.

Basically, the way our resolution algorithm works is by constructing an antecedent DRS based on the source DRS, abstract over the source event, and applying the result to the target event. What enters the antecedent DRS depends on the parallel relations between source and target DRS. The parallel relations denote a non-empty set of two-place relations, the **P-set**. The elements of the P-set are determined by the thematic roles in the target DRS, as well as by relations introduced by additional modifiers of the elided VP. For example, in Figure 3, the P-set is the singleton $\{agent\}$. But for an elided phrase with a temporal modifier such as *Bill did yesterday* the P-set would be $\{agent, temploc\}$.

The semantic material that enters the antecedent DRS are those relations which have the source event as internal argument but are not members of the P-set. In addition, discourse referents and properties belonging to external arguments could be copied to the antecedent DRS. We distinguish three cases for each external argument:

1. If it is declared in the domain of the source DRS: copy the discourse referent and associated conditions;

2. If it is declared in the global DRS: don't copy the discourse referent;

3. If it is part of a conditional DRS: copy the antecedent of the conditional.

Case 1 is triggered by anaphoric expression in the source clause such as proper names and definite descriptions that are accommodated or bound to the global DRS (see Figure 4). Case 2 applies to indefinite noun phrases in the source clause (Figure 5), and the third case to universally quantified noun phrases (Figure 6).

```
 ------------------     ------------------     ------------------
| x2 x1            |   | x4 x3            |   | x6 x5            |
|_____|   |_____|   |_____|
(| named(x2,john)  |+(| car(x4)          |+| car(x5)          |))
 | named(x1,bill)  |   | sell(x3)         |   | too(x6)          |
 |_____|  | event(x3)        |   | event(x6)        |
                       | agent(x3,x2)     |   | agent(x6,x1)     |
                       | patient(x3,x4)   |   | sell(x6)         |
                       |_____|   | patient(x6,x5)   |
                                              |_____|
```

Figure 4. DRS for *John sold a car. Bill did, too* as output by Boxer, performing VPE resolution. Note that both proper names are accommodated in the global DRS, and that the semantic material for *a car* has been copied to the target DRS.

```
 ------------------     ------------------     ------------------
| x3 x2 x1         |   | x4               |   | x5               |
|_____|   |_____|   |_____|
(| named(x3,john)  |+(| see(x4)          |+| see(x5)          |))
 | car(x2)          |   | event(x4)        |   | too(x5)          |
 | named(x1,bill)  |   | agent(x4,x3)     |   | event(x5)        |
 |_____|  | patient(x4,x2)   |   | agent(x5,x1)     |
                       |_____|   | patient(x5,x2)   |
                                              |_____|
```

Figure 5. DRS for *John saw the car. Bill did, too* as output by Boxer, performing VPE resolution. Note that both proper names are accommodated in the global DRS. Note that the semantic material for *the car* has not been copied to the target DRS.

Note that renaming of variables is done using standard tools of α-conversion and β-reduction, that are also used during semantic construction. This means that there is no need to rename any discourse referents when they are copied from the source DRS to the antecedent DRS; instead, renaming will be carried out as a side-effect of β-reduction after applying the antecedent DRS to the target DRS.

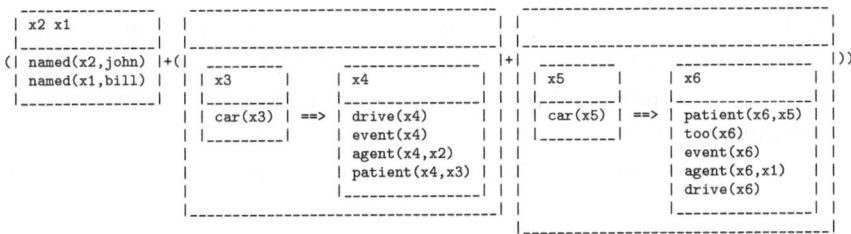

Figure 6. DRS for *John drove every car. Bill did, too* as output by Boxer, performing VPE resolution.

5.3. Sloppy interpretations

Our algorithm always produces a strict reading for a pronoun appearing in the antecedent verb phrase. As sloppiness in VPE interpretation appears to be a true rarity in real data, this is hardly a concern for a system aiming for wide-coverage rather than theoretically accurate analyses. Indeed, in the corpus (financial newspaper articles) used for this study, we only found two examples in the development data (89 cases of VPE) that allow for sloppy interpretation:

(13) IBM, though long a leader in the Japanese mainframe business, didn't introduce its first PC in Japan until five years after NEC **did**, and that wasn't compatible even with the U.S. IBM standard. [WSJ section 04]

(14) Neil Kinnock, Labor Paryy leader, dubbed the 46-year-old Mr. Major a lap dog unlikely to veer from his boss's strongly held views, as Mr. Lawson sometimes **did**. [WSJ section 08]

6. Conclusion

We presented a wide-coverage NLP system for a deep semantic analysis of text and in particular its coverage and performance on analysing VP ellipsis. We conducted an evaluation of the system on examples of VPE annotated in the Wall Street Journal part of the Penn Treebank. The system detects VP ellipsis and resolves them on the level of logical form using a copying-and-renaming approach. It achieves high precision and recall on detecting elided VPs, and a reasonable accuracy on locating correct antecedents.

Nonetheless, clearly more research is required for improving the algorithm for VPE antecedent location, especially in dealing with VP-cataphora, and antecedents that are part of nested verb phrases. In addition, taking discourse structure into account to constrain possible antecedents for VPE, as suggested by Asher (1993), could improve the performance of the algorithm further.

The success of the resolution algorithm for VPE proposed in this paper depends mainly on the ability to determine parallel elements between source and target clause. We have claimed that this can be done on the basis of thematic roles. As detecting parallelism is a non-trivial job, a quantified assessment of our resolution algorithm is left as a topic for future work.

Notes

1. Sometimes referred to as VP-deletion or VP-anaphora, especially in the earlier literature on VP ellipsis.
2. We limit ourselves to a small inventory of thematic roles, namely *agent*, *patient* and *theme*.
3. More formally, if B_1 and B_2 are DRS, then so is (B_1+B_2). The merge is dynamic, in the way that discourse referents in B_1 bind free occurrences in B_2.
4. A large portion of this annotated data was kindly provided to me by Leif Nielsen, who used it in his thesis (Nielsen 2005).
5. Sections 00, 01, 02, 03, 04, 05, 06, 07, 08, 10, 12, and 14 were used as development data.
6. Sections 09, 11, 13 and 15 were used as test data.
7. The standard model used by the C&C parser is not trained on questions, and therefore often gets an unwanted analysis in wh-questions with do-support. A way to solve this problem is to select a different model, indeed a model trained on questions, when a question is given to the parser, but this idea will be left for future work.

References

Asher, Nicholas
    1993   *Reference to Abstract Objects in Discourse*. Dordrecht: Kluwer Academic Publishers.

Bäuerle, Rainer
    1988   Ereignisse und Repräsentationen. Technical Report LILOG Report 43, IBM Deutschland GmbH.

Bos, Johan
    2005   Towards wide-coverage semantic interpretation. *Proceedings of Sixth International Workshop on Computational Semantics IWCS-6*. 42–53.

Clark, S., and J.R. Curran
    2004   Parsing the WSJ using CCG and Log-Linear Models. *Proceedings of the 42nd Annual Meeting of the Association for Computational Linguistics (ACL '04)*. Barcelona, Spain.

Dalrymple, Mary, Stuart M. Shieber, and Fernando C.N. Pereira
    1991   Ellipsis and Higher-Order Unification. *Linguistics and Philosophy* 14: 399–452.

Hardt, Daniel
    1997   An Empirical Approach to VP Ellipsis. *Computational Linguistics* 23 (4): 525–541.

Hockenmaier, J., and M. Steedman
2002   Generative Models for Statistical Parsing with Combinatory Categorial Grammar. *Proceedings of 40th Annual Meeting of the Association for Computational Linguistics.* Philadelphia, PA.
Hockenmaier, Julia
2003   Data and Models for Statistical Parsing with Combinatory Categorial Grammar. Ph.D. diss., University of Edinburgh.
Kamp, H., and U. Reyle
1993   *From Discourse to Logic; An Introduction to Modeltheoretic Semantics of Natural Language, Formal Logic and DRT.* Dordrecht: Kluwer.
Kamp, Hans
1981   A Theory of Truth and Semantic Representation. In *Formal Methods in the Study of Language*, Jeroen Groenendijk, Theo M.V. Janssen, and Martin Stokhof (eds.), 277–322. Mathematical Centre, Amsterdam.
Klein, Ewan
1987   VP Ellipsis in DR Theory. *Studies in Discourse Representation Theory and the Theory of Generalised Quantifiers.*
Nielsen, Leif Arda
2005   A corpus-based study of Verb Phrase Ellipsis Identification and Resolution. Ph.D. diss., King's College London.
Sag, Ivan
1976   Deletion and logical form. Ph.D. diss., MIT.
Steedman, M.
2001   *The Syntactic Process.* The MIT Press.
Van der Sandt, R.A.
1992   Presupposition Projection as Anaphora Resolution. *Journal of Semantics* 9: 333–377.

The symbiosis between computational linguistics, logic and computer science

Bengt Nordström

1. Computer science was born by logic

It is not an exaggeration to say that logic gave birth to computer science. It is a strange historical fact that logicians were theoretically studying how to mechanically compute something without having any goal of doing this in practice. Around 1930 many logicians were trying to characterize the mathematical functions which could be computed by a machine. Turing invented his Turing-machine which was very influential in the design of the first computers (in fact, Turing himself was deeply involved in the design of the first English computers). The first American computers were designed by von Neumann, a mathematician who was involved in the discussions on computability.

Why were logicians interested in computability? The interest in computers before the existence of them had to do with deep problems in the foundations of Mathematics. Gottlob Frege spent a large part of his life trying to give the mathematical language a strict basis in the late 19:th century. Bertrand Russell discovered that Frege's system was inconsistent and it became clear that the informal mathematical language was resting on a shaky foundation. Hilbert suggested that this could be solved if we were able to construct a method which could decide if a mathematical statement is true or not. Such a method should require no intelligence to perform and it then became necessary to exactly define what we mean by such a method.

2. The need for logic in computational linguistics

Much work in computational linguistics is using methods from logic. Logic is after all the first field where language was studied as a mathematical object. Montague's work on semantics (Montague 1974) of natural language is of deep significance. He was taking up methods from logic and applied them to linguistics. Most logicians at that time thought that natural language would not be suitable for formalization and linguists were also sceptical of using logical methods.

3. The need for logic in computer science

The software crisis was discovered around 30 years ago and is getting more and more serious. Programs are used in safety-critical systems and there are numerous examples of serious errors. It is clear that a better understanding of the logic of programming is necessary. Modern programming languages like Java are inherently complicated (a description of the syntax and semantics of the language (Gosling et al. 2005) is 649 pages, only the description of a simple version of the assignment statement requires more than 20 pages). On the other hand, theoretical work in programming logic describes syntax and semantics of programming languages in only one page. So there is hope for simpler programming languages. But the bridge between theory and practice can only be built from both sides.

4. Parallel developments

Many parallel developments are taking place in the three subjects. I will here briefly mention two: rules and abstract syntax.

4.1. Rules and computation

There are two different kinds of rules in logic. A deduction rule explains how to form a true conclusion from true premises. This kind of rule can be read (executed) in two directions, from conclusions to premises (top-down) or from premises to conclusions (bottom-up). In the first case, you start with a goal (the conclusion) to be proven and you split it into subgoals to be proven. You reduce one problem into a number of subproblems. In the second case, you combine the solutions of the subproblems to the solution of the given problem.

There are also computation rules on proofs (contraction rules), which in some sense explains how we can simplify proofs. Given a proof which contains a detour, we can simplify it by removing the detour. As an example, if we have used modus ponens to prove B from $A \supset B$ and A, we can remove this proof step, since a proof of $A \supset B$ consists of a method which takes a proof of A to a proof of B. Instead, we can just apply this method to the proof of A. This kind of computation rule is the same as conversion in lambda-calculus and the expansion of definitions in languages with abbreviations.

The two kinds of computation rules correspond to two different programming paradigms in computer science: Logic Programming and Functional Programming. In Logic Programming computation is (top-down) deduction and in Functional Programming a computation step is to simplify an expression. In the latter case, if e computes to v, then $e = v$. This is not the case in logic programming, where a computation starts with a theorem to be proven and ends with a proof of it.

In linguistics we have grammar rules which explain how to generate (or analyze) a grammatically well-formed string from its parts (which are also well-formed strings). These rules are closely related to deduction rules in logic (just change the word wellformed to the word true). It is therefore not a coincidence that Logic Programming is popular in linguistics (we interpret rules for correctness as computation rules).

After a short period of popularity in the beginning of the 1970's, the programming logic paradigm has relatively few followers within computer science research. The lack of control over the steps of computation makes it difficult to estimate the computational behaviour of the program, and the ways to control this are ad hoc and destroys the nice properties of the language.

The first (and practically most important) paradigm for programming is imperative programming (with its descendant object oriented programming). The inspiration for this comes from the machine languages of the computers, and it is not clear if there is (or should be) a correspondence of this in logic.

4.2. The notion of abstract syntax

In computer science we make a distinction between the concrete and abstract syntax of a language. The concrete syntax is a text string representing a phrase in the language. The abstract syntax is a mathematical object (usually an inductively defined object) which contains the essential syntactic information of a phrase. It describes the syntactical parts of the phrase and how these parts are put together. The abstract syntax is used as an intermediate structure when programs are manipulating other programs. Interpreters, compilers, static analysers and type checkers are defined by induction over this structure.

We can see the abstract syntax as a mathematical object representing the essential syntactic structure of a formal language. To parse the concrete syntax is to translate it to the abstract syntax. This is an important way of modularizing languages processors. Linearization is the reverse process, it takes an abstract syntax tree to a string in concrete syntax. As a simple example, the concrete syntax of the phrase

while i do j := j+1 end

is the string

```
"while i do j := j+1 end"
```

while the abstract syntax is the mathematical object

$$while\ (v(i),\\ cons(\ assign(\ v(j),\\ plus(v(j),1)),\\ empty)$$

This describes that the while-statement consists of two parts, an expression and a statement list. In this case, the expression is the variable i, while the statement list consists of one element, an assigment statement, etc.

The notion of abstract syntax was probably first introduced by McCarthy (McCarthy 1962) in computer science. In linguistics it was introduced by Curry (Curry 1961) , who called it the tectogrammatical structure.

Logicians are not interested in parsing, and this explains their lack of interest in abstract syntax. Induction over the abstract syntax is expressed by induction over the concrete syntax, letting the reader do the parsing while reading the formulae.

By concentrating on the abstract syntax it is possible to simplify the formal description of languages drastically, it is a way to modularize the description. For a formal language you first describe the abstract syntax (and its structure) and then describe the relation between abstract and concrete syntax. It is possible to express more details about the language by expressing the mathematical structure of the abstract syntax using a powerful type system. As a simple example, the phrase "colourless green ideas sleep furiously" can be parsed to abstract syntax, but a powerful type system can be used to reject it. The type system can be defined so that only meaningful phrases are correct.

These ideas are used by Aarne Ranta in his GF system (Ranta 2004) , which uses Martin-Löf's type theory to express the structure of abstract syntax.

5. How to express the structure of abstract syntax

We can use ideas from type theory (Martin-Löf 1984; Nordström, Petersson, and Smith 1990) to express the structure of abstract syntax. Before we describe a type system with dependent types, we will describe a simple system with no types dependent on objects.

6. A simple type system

We define the type system by induction over the types. Assume that $A_1, \ldots, A_n$ are given types.

6.1. Functions

The type
$$A \to B$$
contains objects which are functions from A to B. The knowledge which we express when we say that $f \in A \to B$ is that the application $f\, a$ is well-defined and is an object in B for all $a \in A$.

6.2. Cartesian product

An object may consist of a finite number of objects, each of different types.
The *cartesian product*
$$A_1 * \ldots * A_n$$
is a type for $n \geq 0$. The elements of this type are tuples of the form $(a_1, \ldots a_n)$, where $a_i \in A_i$. For the case that $n = 0$, we use the underscore notation for both the element and the type: $\_ \in \_$.

6.3. Labelled disjoint union

An object of this type is constructed from an object of one of a finite number of types. The *labelled disjoint union*
$$c_1 A_1 \mid c_2 A_2 \mid \ldots \mid c_n A_n$$
is a type if the constructors $c_1, \ldots, c_n$ are distinct, $n \geq 1$. The elements of the type are of the form $c_i\, a$, for $a \in A_i$.

This type forming operation is used to express inductively defined sets, For instance the type of natural numbers can be given by the recursive definition
$$Nat =_{def} 0 \_ \mid s\, Nat$$

6.4. Record types

A record is an object which like a tuple has a finite set of components, the difference is that the components in records have names. These names can be used to project the component from the record, the expression $c_i\ e$ projects the component with the name c_i from the record e.

The *record type* (or labelled cartesian product)

$$\{c_1 = A_1, c_2 = A_2, \ldots, c_n = A_n\}$$

is a type. The knowledge which we express when we say that we have an element e of this type is that then the application $c_i\ e$ is wellformed and has the type A_i, and also that

$$e = \{c_1 = c_1\ e, c_2 = c_2\ e, \ldots c_n = c_n\} \in \{c_1 = A_1, c_2 = A_2, \ldots, c_n = A_n\}$$

Two elements d and e in $\{c_1 = A_1, c_2 = A_2, \ldots, c_n = A_n\}$ are equal if $c_i\ d = c_i\ e \in A_i$ for $0 \leq i \leq n$.

So, each record type has its own equality relation defined, and if the expressions d and e are of a record type, then $d = e \in \{\}$. There is an inherent notion of subtyping here, if

$$e \in \{c_1 = A_1, c_2 = A_2, \ldots, c_n = A_n\}$$

then

$$e \in \{c_1 = A_1, c_2 = A_2, \ldots, c_j = A_j\}$$

if $j \leq n$.

We can compare a record type with a labelled union. In the same way as a labelled union is defined by its constructors mapping elements from other types *to* the labelled union, a record type is defined by its projectors mapping *from* the record type to other types.

7. Dependent types

If we have a system of types where a type can depend on an object in another type, then we open the possibilities for dependent function types and dependent records. One way of introducing such a type is to have a type of small types U, whose objects are types. Then, if $a \in U$, we can form the type $El\ a$, whose objects are objects in the type which a represent. In this case, it is clear that the type $El\ a$ depends on the object a. We usually write the type $El\ a$ simply as a, since it is always clear from the context whether a stands for the object a in U or the type of elements in a. The language with dependent types is just a small modification of the earlier presented language.

7.1. Dependent functions

The type
$$x \in A \to B$$
is a type. In this case the type B may depend on the variable $x \in A$. The knowledge which we express when we say that $f \in (x \in A \to B)$ is that the application $f\ a \in B[x \leftarrow a]$, where $B[x \leftarrow a]$ stands for the expression obtained by substituting a for all free occurrences of x in B.

7.2. Dependent records

The type
$$\{c_1 = A_1, c_2 = A_2, \ldots, c_n = A_n\}$$
is a type. Each type expression A_i may depend on previous projections c_j, $j < i$, so for instance A_4 may depend on c_1, c_2 and c_3.

Here, the knowledge we express when e is of the type is that
$c_i\ e \in A_i$, and we know that
$$e = \{c_1 = a_1, c_2 = a_2, \ldots c_n = a_n\}$$
where $a_i = c_i\ e$.

7.2.0.1. *Example from Mathematics.*

The type $\sum_{n \in N} A^n$ is the type of pairs, the first being a natural number n and the second a vector $(a_1, \ldots, a_n)$ of length n.

7.2.0.2. *Example from logic*

The quantifier $\forall x \in A.B$ can be expressed as the corresponding dependent function type and the quantifier $\exists x \in A.B$ can be expressed as the corresponding dependent record type. These are examples of the Brouwer - Heyting - Kolmogorov interpretation of constructive mathematics.

7.2.0.3. *Example from semiformal language.*

Forms are important examples of expressions in semiformal language. It is often the case that a form contains a part whose structure is dependent on the value of a previous part. For instance, when you fill in a form for your address, the structure of the address depends on the country you live in. The syntax of a telephone number depends on the area code of the number (for instance in Göteborg we can only have 6 or 7 digits after the area code).

7.2.0.4. Example from linguistics

In a dialogue, the structure of the dialogue depends on earlier expressions in the dialogue. If you have said that you live in Göteborg, then you cannot afterward say that you live at Bigatan, this is simply erroneous since there is no street with that name in Göteborg.

The usage of records in linguistics has been pioneered by Robin Cooper (Cooper and Ginzburg 2002).

8. Applied logic

A formal language, like other human constructions (houses, cars, tools) can be studied in three different ways. We can reason about it theoretically (by making a mathematical model of it), we can implement (make, construct) it and make practical experiments with it. The main tradition in logic is to study it theoretically. But computer science has given us ways of implementing it and both computer science and linguistics have a strong need to use these implementations. The need for correct programs makes it necessary to use computers to formally verify programs and the need for natural language processors (machine-translation, dialogue systems etc) will give rise to new applications of logic.

9. Formal, informal and semiformal language.

We can view a formal language as a set of strings which can be recognized by a computer, i.e. there is a program which can output "yes" if the string belongs to the language and output "no" otherwise. In that sense, the set of meaningful propositions in predicate logic or some other nontrivial logic is a formal language, while the set of true propositions is not. A computer cannot decide the truth of a proposition.

A natural language is a set of strings which can be recognized by a human. So this is formally a vague concept, different humans recognize different strings as well-formed. Hence, if we want to see English as a formal language, the only way to do this is to only look at well-agreed fragments of it. The whole language can never be a formal language.

References

Cooper, Robin, and Jonathan Ginzburg
    2002   Using dependent record types in clarification ellipsis. Johan Bos, Mary Ellen Foster, and Colin Matheson (eds.), *Proceedings of the sixth workshop on the semantics and pragmatics of dialogue,*. Edinburgh University, 45–52.

Curry, Haskell B.
    1961   Some logical aspects of grammatical structure. Roman O. Jakobson (ed.), *Structure of Language in its Mathematical Aspects. Proceedings of the 12th Symposium in Applied Mathematics.* 56–68.

Gosling, James, Bill Joy, Guy Steele, and Gilad Bracha
    2005   *Java Language Specification, The (3rd Edition) (Java Series)*. Addison-Wesley Professional.

Martin-Löf, P.
    1984   *Intuitionistic Type Theory*. Napoli: Bibliopolis.

McCarthy, John
    1962   Towards a mathematical science of computation. *Proceedings of the Information Processing Cong. 62.* Munich, West Germany: North-Holland, 21–28.

Montague, Richard
    1974   English as a formal language. In *Formal Philosophy: Selected Papers of Richard Montague*, Richmond Thomason (ed.), 188–221. New Haven: Yale University Press.

Nordström, B., K. Petersson, and J. M. Smith
    1990   *Programming in Martin-Löf's Type Theory. An Introduction.* Oxford University Press.

Ranta, Aarne
    2004   Grammatical framework: A type-theoretical grammar formalism. *Journal of Functional Programming* 14 (2): 145–189.

Language Technology

Example-based grammar writing

Aarne Ranta

1. Introduction

Writing programs that implement grammars of natural languages is almost as old as computer programming itself, starting from Bar-Hillel's work in the early 1950's (Bar-Hillel 1953). Another branch of programming that started in those years is numerical algorithms. Today, very few programmers have to write numerical algorithms by hand, since they are well supported by libraries and even by hardware. With grammars, the situation is different. Grammars for natural languages are being written over and over again, and writing a grammar implementation today is almost as demanding as it was, say, 30 year ago.

One reason why grammar implementations have not become a commodity like numerical algorithms is, undoubtedly, that they are still seen as a research problem. There is no universally accepted implementation of even the English grammar, because there is no universally accepted formal description of the English language. The disagreement concerns both the form and the content of the grammar: should the grammar be context-free or TAG or HPSG? how to deal with auxiliary verbs and with topicalization?

However, there is a constantly growing need of grammars that do not necessitate the solution of hard research problems. One example area, on which we will concentrate here, is *dialogue systems*. A dialogue system is a computer program with which the user can talk. The system uses speech recognition to receive its input, and speech synthesis to render its output. In between, the system performs more general natural language processing steps: parsing, semantic interpretation, dialogue management, answer generation.

The performance bottleneck of most dialogue systems is speech recognition. With today's technology, it is not easy to tell the difference between, say, *how to recognize speech* and *how to wreck a nice beach*. But how do we humans tell the difference? Very often not by more accurate phonetic analysis, but by ruling out irrelevant alternatives. This is also the way most dialogue systems solve the problem of speech ambiguity. They use a *language model*, a program component that defines what utterances are relevant for the task at hand. There are two principal ways to build language models: statistically and by grammars.

A statistical language model is based on a corpus of utterances that potential users have made. From this corpus, a Markov model can be extracted showing the probability of (even unseen) combinations of words. A grammar-based language model may also be built on top of a corpus, but the model itself uses a small set of grammar rules to define what is possible, optionally with a probability. What kind of a language model to build depends on the application, available resources, and the taste of the designers. Also combinations of these methods are possible. But we will in the following focus on purely grammar-based language models, which are widely used. They have created a growing need of *grammar engineering*.

A dialogue system is a complex piece of software, of which the grammar is only a small part. The other parts may require specialized knowledge other than grammar writing. Therefore, a programming project developing a dialogue system cannot necessarily hire a linguist to write grammars, but uses engineers from some other domain of expertise to do this.

2. Three kinds of knowledge

Writing a grammar without knowing linguistics should be a task as natural as writing computer animations without knowing pixel geometry algorithms – but it is far from this. Roughly three kinds of linguistic knowledge are needed:

- domain-specific: what are the correct terms and idioms in this domain?

- practical: how do you express things in correct English/French/...?

- theoretical: what are the rules for building correct expressions in English/French/...?

The domain-specific knowledge is something that the programmer may be assumed to have. To take an example, let us consider a dialogue system for operating an MP3 player. The domain-specific knowledge is needed to specify that the system is about *songs* or *tracks*, *artists*, *playlists*, etc. This terminology is not obvious to outsiders, even if they are native speakers of the target language.

The practical linguistic knowledge is the general native speaker's knowledge of her language. The speaker can recognize if a sentence is well formed, if a word is properly inflected, etc. A person can be quite proficient in domain terminology without having this kind of practical language knowledge. For instance, sportsmen who participate in international competitions may know the terminology of their own sports in another language much better than average native speakers of that language.

Theoretical linguistic knowledge is the most special of the three kinds we distinguished. It includes explicit knowledge of grammatical concepts and rules, but also practical skills in expressing these concepts in an often very special format, a grammar formalism. Most native speakers lack this kind of knowledge of their language; on the other hand, one does not need to be a native or even a fluent speaker to have it, because the language-specific facts can be looked up in grammar books and dictionaries.

In order to produce a good dialogue system grammar, all three kinds of knowledge are needed. A domain expert is needed to pick up the correct expressions for each concept; a native (or close-to-native) speaker is needed to assess the general soundness of the expressions covered by the grammar; a theoretical linguist is needed to implement the rules taking care of intricacies such as inflection, agreement, and word order variations.

In some rare cases, the three skills are found in one and the same person. What is more common is that the domain expert is also a native speaker but not a theoretical linguist. Would it be possible for such a person, or for a domain expert and a native speaker together, to build a system without the need of a linguist?

Software localization is a process in which a program is adapted to a new language. Some dialogue systems, for instance, those used in cars, may have to be localized to dozens of languages. All the production may take place in just one country, and it is conceivable that a programmer only knows the special terminology of the domain (or looks it up from a database) but has no fluency in the target language. Could it still be possible for her to build a baseline dialogue system for that language, so that it could be handed over to native speaker for testing, without the need to involve native speakers in the development?

3. Grammars as libraries

In many areas of programming, problems arising from the need for different kinds of knowledge are solved by using *libraries*. A library is written by an expert who knows exactly how the things work in a special field. She designs and implements sophisticated datastructures and algorithms, using the best knowledge from a long tradition in that field. Very few other programmers could really understand, let alone modify, her code. But very many others will be able to use it in their programs, because the complexity is hidden behind a high-level *API (Application Programmer's Interface)*.

In the domain of grammars, libraries are a rare phenomenon. Even reuse of software is rare - formats are often incompatible, and programs are protected by prohibitive licences. When components are reused, the usual form of reuse is pipelines where string data is sent from one component to another. For instance, in a dialogue system, the output of speech recognition is a textual string that is sent to a parser, which in turn sends a query string to a dialogue management component. These components do not match each other exactly. For instance, the speech recognizer may be much more or much less general than the capacities of the parser, which in turn does not match the capacity of the dialogue manager. The components are often acquired from third-party providers and cannot easily be modified.

Component-based reuse is not enough for providing an accurate language model for speech recognition. The more precisely the model matches the application domain, the more ambiguity can be eliminated and the better is the quality of speech recognition. Focusing on grammar based models, we conclude that the speech recognition grammar cannot be a standard component but must be written specifically for each application. The grammar writer needs many skills - of which we identified three kinds. Can some of these skills be eliminated, by using a library that takes care of them?

Terminology databases are a good example of library-like reuse of resources in localization. A programmer with practical and theoretical linguistic skills can look up the domain vocabulary in the database. If she is lucky, the database does not only give the dictionary forms of the words, but also enough information to use them properly in different functions, e.g. in correct inflectional forms.

But can we eliminate the need for theoretical linguistic skills in grammar writing? Even more importantly: can we eliminate the need to write the same grammatical rules over and over again, with slight variations for different applications. To give an example, almost any system will need some kind of adjectival modification. MP3 systems will need to understand *German song*, flight-booking systems *cheap flight*, etc. The structure will moreover be very much the same in all languages: a common noun modified by an adjective. But its concrete realization varies a lot. In many languages, unlike English, the adjective agrees with the gender of the noun: *chanson allemande, artiste allemand* (French "German song, German artist"). In many languages, both parts moreover undergo variation in number and case.

German, in addition to gender, number, and case, has a distinction between strong and weak adjective declensions, the choice of which depends on the foregoing determiner. Since there are 3 genders, 2 numbers, and 4 cases, we end up with 2 * 3 * 2 * 4 = 48 combinations. Since the gender only matters in the plural, the number can be reduced to 32 - but there is still a frightening number of rules that need to be written, if the pure context-free format provided by the common speech recognition grammar formats is used.

A satisfactory solution to the adjectival modification problem would be a syntactic structure library whose API provides the grammatical categories Noun and Adjective, as well as a function for combining a Noun with and Adjective to yield a (complex) noun. This API would be implemented for a great number of languages. To localize a dialogue system to a new language, say German, would then involve using two libraries:

- the term database taking care of expressing "song", "artist", "German", etc

- the syntactic structure library taking care of adjectival modification, determination, etc.

In this way, the knowledge requirements for grammar writers would be strongly reduced, and productivity - but also quality - would improve.

4. The GF Grammar Formalism: a first example

GF (Grammatical Framework, Ranta 2004) is a grammar formalism based on a distinction between *abstract syntax* and *concrete syntax*. An abstract syntax is a system of *categories* and *constructor functions*, defining a set of *(abstract) syntax trees*. In many applications, an abstract syntax is used for defining a *semantic structure*, which could also be called a *domain ontology*.

Here is an example abstract syntax for a tiny MP3 dialogue system.

```
abstract Music = {
cat
  Action ;
  Object ;
  Kind ;
  Property ;
fun
  play : Object -> Action ;
  previous : Kind -> Object ;
  Modif : Property -> Kind -> Kind ;
  song : Kind ;
```

```
    artist : Kind ;
    german : Property ;
}
```

The four categories (`cat`) correspond to objects and concepts of the domain. The six constructor functions (`fun`) define how these objects can be combined. For instance, the constructor `Modif` tells that a `Property` can be combined with a `Kind` to form yet another `Kind`.

A concrete syntax tells how abstract syntax trees are *linearized* (`lin`) into strings of a language. In general, the value of linearization is not just a string but a *record* that can contain other information than just strings. The following example shows an English concrete syntax of the previous abstract syntax, with each record containing just a string s:

```
concrete MusicEng0 of Music = {
lin
  play o = {s = "play" ++ o.s} ;
  previous k = {s = "the" ++ "previous" ++ k.s} ;
  Modif p k = {s = p.s ++ k.s} ;
  song = {s = "song"} ;
  artist = {s = "artist"} ;
  german = {s = "german"} ;
}
```

The symbol `++` is used for the *concatenation* of strings, and the *projection* `r.f` yields the field `f` of a record `r`.

In good dialogue system design, most components do not manipulate strings of the dialogue language, but abstract, language-independent semantic representations. The abstract syntax trees are very convenient as such representations. For instance, the above grammar produces the tree

```
play (previous (Modif german artist))
```

of type `Action`, which via the linearization relation is the semantic representation of the string

```
play the previous german artist
```

When a system is localized to a new language, the only thing that has to be written is a new concrete syntax for the same abstract syntax as before. So here is a German version of our tiny system:

```
concrete MusicGer0 of Music = {
lin
  play o = {s = "spiele" ++ o.s} ;
  previous k = {s = "den" ++ "vorigen" ++ k.s} ;
  Modif p k = {s = p.s ++ k.s} ;
  song = {s = "song"} ;
  artist = {s = "künstler"} ;
  german = {s = "deutschen"} ;
}
```

The tree shown above is linearized to the German sentence

```
spiele den vorigen deutschen künstler
```

5. Low-level linguistic problems

The German grammar of the previous section works correctly, but just because of the lucky coincidence that the two nouns *künstler* and *song* are both masculine, and that the only position in which they enter requires the accusative case. If we add a neuter noun, e.g.

```
fun album : Kind ;
lin album = {s = "album"} ;
```

we get a grammatically incorrect Action *spiele den vorigen album*. Likewise, if we add a construct where the noun appears in the subject position,

```
fun name : Object -> Action ;
lin name o = {s = "wie" ++ "heißt" ++ o.s} ;
```

all instances of it become incorrect: *wie heißt den vorigen künstler*, etc.

The German grammar therefore has to be redesigned to make it work. The abstract syntax, fortunately, needs no change: it is enough to change the *linearization types* (lincat) of the categories so that they admit of certain *parameters* (param). In the present grammar, we need two parameter types,

```
param
  Case = Nom | Acc ;
  Gender = Masc | Fem | Neutr ;
```

and we set the linearization types deviating from pure strings as follows:

```
lincat
  Object   = {s : Case => Str} ;
  Kind     = {s : Case => Str ; g : Gender} ;
  Property = {s : Gender => Case => Str} ;
```

Now it is possible to express the agreement rules by passing around parameters. For instance, the adjectival modification rule becomes

```
lin Modif prop kind = {
    s = \\c => prop.s ! kind.g ! c ++ kind.s ! c ;
    g = kind.g
  } ;
```

In words, both the property and the kind are inflected in the case required by the context in which the noun is used. The property is inflected in agreement to the gender of the kind. The gender of the modified kind is the same as the one of the kind modified.

All these rules are possible to write without changing the abstract syntax. The resulting grammars can moreover be translated into standard speech formats with tools provided by GF (Bringert 2007). Moreover, the grammar writing process can be helped by using GF's abstraction techniques. For instance, it is not necessary to write the inflection table of each property separately, but one can define a regular adjective operation (oper), which from a string produces all required forms:

```
oper regAdj : Str -> Property ;
```

But the grammar writing process is on a slippery slope now. What exactly are the parameters and linearization types that will scale up to any application? In the above example, we only needed two of the four cases of German, no plurals, and no weak-strong distinction for adjectives. But even now, if we complete the conversion of the grammar to the new type system, we end up with three times as much code as the string-only grammar. This shows that the theoretical linguistic knowledge dominates in what is needed to write the grammar. Surely much more theoretical knowledge will be needed if a full system of cases and other parameters is introduced, while the domain knowledge would remain constant. Thus the programmer has to be proficient in German grammar, and she must moreover know the GF grammar formalism well.

6. The GF Resource Grammar Library

The GF Resource Grammar Library is an attempt to collect domain independent theoretical linguistic knowledge into a reusable library. It covers at the moment of writing ten languages, and five more languages are being implemented. The linguistic facts implemented for all these languages fall into three categories:

- a complete inflectional morphology, presented as a set of inflection paradigms

- a lexicon of structural and irregular words

- a comprehensive fragment of syntax, presented as a set of abstract syntax categories and functions

The morphology and lexicon components are separate for each language. While some languages do have a large lexicon in the library, the inflection paradigms are considered more important than a static lexicon, because new applications often need special vocabulary that is unlikely to be included in a lexicon. Fortunately, for such new words the paradigms are often regular. Thus for all languages, the API has regular patterns for nouns, adjectives, and verbs,

```
regN : Str -> N ;
regA : Str -> A ;
regV : Str -> V ;
```

which cover a vast majority of words by using heuristic string matching. For instance, the English `regN` operation recognizes nouns of types *dog-dogs*, *fly-flies*, *boy-boys*, *bus-buses*, and *hero-heroes*. For words that do not inflect regularly, operations with more arguments are provided. For instance, English irregular verbs like *write-wrote-written* can be defined using the three-argument paradigm

```
irregV : Str -> Str -> Str -> V ;
```

For most languages, irregular words can also be accessed via a prebuilt lexicon, whose size is typically a few hundred lemmas.

The syntax component is largely the same for all languages. It contains categories such as

```
Utt ;     -- utterance
S ;       -- sentence (with fixed tense)
Cl ;      -- clause (with variable tense)
Imp ;     -- imperative
VP ;      -- verb phrase
NP ;      -- noun phrase
V ;       -- one-place verb
V2 ;      -- two-place verb
```

In the current version, there are 44 categories. Trees of these categories are formed by 190 constructor functions, such as

```
UttS      : S -> Utt ;
UttImpSg  : Imp -> Utt ;
UseCl     : Cl -> Tense -> Anter -> Pol -> S ;
PredVP    : NP -> VP -> Cl ;
UseV      : V -> VP ;
ComplV2   : V2 -> VP -> VP ;
```

The application grammarian can use these functions and categories instead of hand-written strings, records, and tables. The German grammar can then be written as follows:

```
concrete MusicGer of Music =
          open GrammarGer, ParadigmsGer, IrregGer in {
  lincat
    Action = Utt ;
    Object = NP ;
    Kind = CN ;
    Property = AP ;
  lin
    name o = UttQS (UseQCl TPres ASimul PPos
      (QuestIAdv how_IAdv (PredVP o (UseV heißen_V)))) ;
    play o = UttImpSg PPos
      (ImpVP (ComplV2 (dirV2 (regV "spielen")) o)) ;
    previous k = DetCN (DetSg (SgQuant DefArt) NoOrd)
                  (AdjCN (PositA (regA "vorig")) k) ;
    Modif = AdjCN ;
    song = UseN (reg2N "Lied" "Lieder" neuter) ;
    album = UseN (reg2N "Album" "Alben" neuter) ;
    artist = UseN (reg2N "Artist" "Artisten" masculine) ;
```

```
    german = PositA (regA "Deutsch") ;
}
```

The English grammar is very similar, due to the language-independent syntax API. A fast way to adapt the grammar into English would be to copy the code and change all lexical parts, i.e. applications of inflection paradigms to lemmas. In addition, the question asking for the name of something would have to be rephrased to the form *what is the name of x*.

However, GF provides a method that is better than copy-and-change: *parametrized modules*. A parametrized module is a concrete syntax that is *incomplete* in the sense that it depends on a set of parameters. For the Music grammar, we can write a parametrized module depending on two sets of parameters: the resource grammar API defined in the abstract syntax module Grammar, and a music-specific lexicon whose API is defined in an *interface* module LexMusic:

```
interface LexMusic = open Grammar in {
  oper
    album_N : N ;
    song_N : N ;
    artist_N : N ;
    german_A : A ;
    previous_A : A ;
    play_V2 : V2 ;
    what_name : NP -> Utt ;
}
```

The parametrized module itself is MusicI:

```
incomplete concrete MusicI of Music =
            open Grammar, LexMusic in {
  lincat
    Action = Utt ;
    Object = NP ;
    Kind = CN ;
    Property = AP ;
  lin
    name = what_name ;
    play o = UttImpSg PPos (ImpVP (ComplV2 play_V2 o)) ;
    previous k = DetCN (DetSg (SgQuant DefArt) NoOrd)
                       (AdjCN (PositA previous_A) k) ;
```

```
    Modif = AdjCN ;
    song = UseN song_N ;
    album = UseN album_N ;
    artist = UseN artist_N ;
    german = PositA german_A ;
}
```

To instantiate it in a new language, we just need to give instances of Grammar and LexMusic. Instances of Grammar are provided by the resource library, whereas instances of LexMusic have to be provided by the application grammarian. Here are the English and German instances of LexMusic:

```
instance LexMusicEng of LexMusic =
            open GrammarEng, ParadigmsEng in {
  oper
    album_N = regN "album" ;
    song_N = regN "song" ;
    artist_N = regN "artist" ;
    german_A = regA "German" ;
    previous_A = regA "previous" ;
    play_V2 = dirV2 (regV "play") ;
    what_name o =
      UttQS (UseQCl TPres ASimul PPos (QuestVP whatSg_IP
        (UseComp (CompNP (DetCN (DetSg (SgQuant DefArt)
          NoOrd) (ComplN2 (regN2 "name") o)))))) ;
}

instance LexMusicGer of LexMusic =
          open GrammarGer, ParadigmsGer, IrregGer in {
  oper
    album_N = reg2N "Album" "Alben" neuter ;
    song_N = reg2N "Lied" "Lieder" neuter ;
    artist_N = reg2N "Artist" "Artisten" masculine ;
    german_A = regA "Deutsch" ;
    previous_A = regA "vorig" ;
    play_V2 = dirV2 (regV "spielen") ;
    what_name o = UttQS (UseQCl TPres ASimul PPos
      (QuestIAdv how_IAdv (PredVP o (UseV heißen_V)))) ;
}
```

The final top-level grammars are obtained from MusicI by specifying how the interfaces are instantiated. The code that has to be written is otherwise similar for the different languages;

```
concrete MusicEng of Music = MusicI with
  (Grammar = GrammarEng),
  (LexMusic = LexMusicEng) ;

concrete MusicGer of Music = MusicI with
  (Grammar = GrammarGer),
  (LexMusic = LexMusicGer) ;
```

When parametrized modules are used, the localization task for a grammar thus boils down to writing an instance of the domain-specific interface (and the completely mechanical top-level instantiation module). The Music grammar is ready to be ported to Finnish, by providing

```
instance LexMusicFin of LexMusic =
                open GrammarFin, ParadigmsFin in {
  oper
    album_N = regN "albumi" ;
    song_N = regN "laulu" ;
    artist_N = regN "esittäjä" ;
    german_A = regA "saksalainen" ;
    previous_A = regA "edellinen" ;
    play_V2 = dirV2 (regV "soittaa") ;
    what_name o =
      UttQS (UseQCl TPres ASimul PPos (QuestVP whatSg_IP
        (UseComp (CompNP (DetCN (DetSg (SgQuant DefArt) NoOrd)
          (ComplN2 (genN2 (reg2N "nimi" "nimiä")) o)))))) ;
}

concrete MusicFin of Music = MusicI with
  (Grammar = GrammarFin),
  (LexMusic = LexMusicFin) ;
```

7. Example-based grammar writing

Turning back to the question of what skills are required of a grammar writer, it is clear that the resource grammar library relieves some of the requirements.

The grammarian no more needs to know the low-level linguistic facts about parameters, inflection, agreement, and word order. But she does need to know some high-level linguistic concepts, such as noun phrase, verb phrase, predication, and modification. These concepts are the key to the names of the library categories and functions. However, even for those understanding the names, learning to navigate in the library is a nontrivial effort.

Thus there is an element of theoretical linguistic knowledge left in the requirements for an application grammarian. In addition to this, a practical knowledge of the target language in the intended domain is of course necessary: it is needed to pick the proper constructs among the many possible ones in the library.

The easiest way to find functions in the resource grammar library is by using a parser. For any rule the grammarian wants to implement, she picks an example, parses it in the resource grammar, and uses the resulting tree. For instance, suppose you want to write a new linearization rule for

```
fun play : Object -> Action
```

with the phrasing *I want to play X*. You can find the proper combination of library functions by parsing the string *I want to play this* in the category Utt, which is the linearization type of the category Action. The following GF interaction shows what happens.

```
> p -cat=Utt "I want to play this"

UttS (UseCl TPres ASimul PPos (PredVP (UsePron i_Pron)
  (ComplVV want_VV (ComplV2 play_V2 this_NP))))
```

The constant this_NP can be seen as a variable in this construct, and the linearization rule can be written by just pasting the tree in the code.

```
lin play this_NP =
  UttS (UseCl TPres ASimul PPos (PredVP (UsePron i_Pron)
    (ComplVV want_VV (ComplV2 play_V2 this_NP)))) ;
```

Notice that, although this_NP is a constant in the resource grammar library, it is in this rule treated as a bound variable. This is a consequence of the normal binding rules of programming languages, where bindings in a narrow scope overshadow those in a broader scope.

Parsing strings and pasting them in the code one by one is not the most efficient working method. It would be much simpler to write those strings directly in a file. In order to enable this, GF has been extended with a new expression form for parsing a string in a certain category and a certain grammar. The previous example is written as follows using this expression form:

```
lin play this_NP = in Utt "I want to play this" ;
```

How does this exactly work? Compiling modules with in examples is performed as a preprocessing phase. The module looks as follows:

```
--# -resource=present/LangEng.gfc
incomplete concrete MusicI of Music =
              open Grammar, LexMusic in {
  lincat
    Action = Utt ;
    -- other lincat rules as usual
  lin
    play this_NP = in Utt "I want to play this" ;
    -- other lin rules as usual, or with examples
}
```

This module resides in a file called MusicI.gfe, which is preprocessed into a file called MusicI.gf. The resource flag on the first line tells what resource grammar is used for parsing the in examples. The preprocessing can be performed separately, but also as a part of the normal grammar compilation by using the flag -ex when invoking the grammar compiler. The result of preprocessing is an ordinary GF source file, where the in expressions are replaced by expressions for the obtained parse trees.

8. Generalizing from examples

The implementation of example-based grammar writing is simple to explain with a few lines, but its pragmatics are more complex. First, let us reflect on what it *means* to give an example as a grammar rule or as a part of one. This resembles some very familiar ways of asking a human speaker about the translation of some phrase. Suppose you ask me,

How do you say 'I remove Waterloo from Cool Hits' in German?

If I answer *ich streiche Waterloo aus Cool Hits*, you learn that the string *I remove Waterloo from Cool Hits* in English can be translated by the string *I remove Waterloo from Cool Hits* in German. However, depending on your general knowledge of German, you may be able to learn much more, by generalizing from the single string. If you don't do any such generalization, the question is formalized as follows in GF's example-based grammar writing:

```
fun i_remove_waterloo_from_coolhits : Action ;
lin i_remove_waterloo_from_coolhits =
    in Utt "ich streiche Waterloo aus Cool Hits" ;
```

In the first generalization, you learn that you can replace *Waterloo* with other song names and *Cool Hits* with other playlist names and get correct German phrases. This corresponds to treating the constants *Waterloo* and *Cool Hits* as variables for song names:

```
fun i_remove : Name -> Name -> Action ;
lin i_remove waterloo coolhits =
    in Utt "ich streiche Waterloo aus Cool Hits" ;
-- the resource must have waterloo, coolhits : Name ;
```

The second generalization is to give these variables a stronger type: not just string, but any noun phrase. Thus, when performing the substitution of *dieser Song* for *Waterloo* and *diese Wiedergabeliste* for *Cool Hits*, you know that the new arguments must be turned into accusative and dative cases, respectively: *ich streiche diesen Song aus dieser Wiedergabeliste*.

```
fun i_remove : NP -> NP -> Action ;
lin i_remove waterloo coolhits =
    in Utt "ich streiche Waterloo aus Cool Hits" ;
-- the resource must have waterloo, coolhits : NP ;
```

The third generalization is, obviously, to be able to vary the subject of the sentence, i.e. treat *I* as a noun phrase variable:

```
fun remove : NP -> NP -> NP -> Action ;
lin remove i_NP waterloo coolhits =
    in Utt "ich streiche Waterloo aus Cool Hits" ;
-- the resource must have i_NP, waterloo, coolhits : NP ;
```

A very powerful generalization is obtained by changing the type of the values. Actions are just fixed-tense utterances, but the example would also cover sentences with all variations in tense, polarity, and word order. You can for instance learn from the same example that *wenn ich Waterloo aus Cool Hits nich gestrichen hätte* is the correct translation of *if I hadn't removed Waterloo from Cool hits*. You don't need any further examples to infer this, if you know your German grammar and we just missing the word idiomatically used for "remove from a playlist". The example-based rule achieves this by using the resource category Cl for clauses with variable tense, polarity, and word order:

```
fun remove : NP -> NP -> NP -> Cl ;
lin remove i_NP waterloo coolhits =
    in Utt "ich streiche Waterloo aus Cool Hits" ;
```

The resource grammar thus models a general linguistic competence of a speaker who just does not know the correct wordings in a domain. A single example has the potential to generate a large body of utterances resulting from the combination of the new information with old competence.

The general linguistic competence of a speaker of many languages includes the ability to map structures from one language to another. This is illustrated by the use of example-based rules in parametrized grammar modules. When we include the rule

```
lin play this_NP = in Utt "I want to play this" ;
```

in an incomplete concrete module, we in fact say that, in any language covered by this grammar, the phrase corresponding to *I want to play X* is used for expressing the construction play. The English example thus generates German and Finnish at the same time - and in this case, the result is correct in all these languages.

But we can go even farther in mapping structures between languages. Suppose we want to phrase the question "Who made Waterloo?" in German. Any German speaker, at least from the Southern dialects, would claim that the correct phrase is something corresponding to "Who has made Waterloo?", i.e. uses the perfect instead of the imperfect past tense. Now, this sentence is not in German, and it is not correct English either - yet it tells an appropriately bilingual person that the German phrase to use is *Wer hat Waterloo gemacht?*. Thus we can formulate a German grammar implementation as follows:

```
--# -resource=present/LangEng.gfc
concrete MusicGer of Music =
         open GrammarGer, LexMusicGer in {
  lin who_made this_NP = in Utt "who has made this" ;
  -- other lin rules as usual, or with English examples
}
```

9. Lexical substitution

The Resource Grammar Library does not come with a large lexicon. It has complete sets of inflection paradigms but only some hundred of lexical items, to cover the irregular cases and to give some material to test the library. How can we parse all examples we need in grammar writing?

The readily available solution is *lexical substitution*. We use the small test lexicon included in the resource library to parse the examples, but redefine the lexical items by using the inflection paradigms. This is again done by overshadowing the lexical constants with local definitions:

```
lin previous_artist = (in NP "the old car") where {
    old_A = previous_A ;
    car_N = artist_N
    } ;
```

The syntax tree returned by parsing *the old car* is

```
DetCN (DetSg (SgQuant DefArt) NoOrd)
  (AdjCN (PositA old_A) (UseN car_N))
```

which after the substitutions in the where clause and the instantiations of LexMusic constants gives

```
lin previous_artist =
  DetCN (DetSg (SgQuant DefArt) NoOrd)
    (AdjCN (PositA (regA "previous")) (UseN (regN "artist")))
```

in English, and corresponding variants in the other languages. Notice that the lexicon substitutions need not belong to the same language as the parsed example. For instance, one can define the German linearization of name as follows:

```
lin name this_NP = (in Utt "how does this sleep") where {
    sleep_V = heißen_V
    } ;
```

resulting in *wie heißt dies*. This is, again, a common way to explain a language intuitively:

> In English you say "I am hungry". You can say the equivalent in French (je suis affamé), but people just don't. It is a grammatically correct statement that is never used. It is not a French idiom. Instead in French you say "j'ai faim", which means "I have

hunger", which in English is a grammatically correct phrase that nobody uses. "I have hunger" is not an English idiom.[1]

The explanation of how to say "I am hungry" in French can be implemented as follows:

```
lin hungry i_NP = (in Utt "I have beer") where {
    beer_N = regGenN "faim" feminine
    } ;
```

10. The ambiguity problem

Example-based grammar writing inherits the problem of ambiguity of natural language parsing. If we write the rule

```
lin play this_NP = in Utt "play this" ;
```

we get three alternative solutions:

```
UttImpPl  PPos (ImpVP (ComplV2 play_V2 this_NP))
UttImpPol PPos (ImpVP (ComplV2 play_V2 this_NP))
UttImpSg  PPos (ImpVP (ComplV2 play_V2 this_NP))
```

The language-independent resource API makes a distinction between singular, plural, and polite imperatives, because it is a real distinction in many of the languages covered. (Actually, Italian and Spanish have four variants: singular or plural, polite or familiar.) The resulting German grammar now depends on which of the variants is chosen. It says *spielt* for the first alternative, *spielen Sie* for the second, and *spiele* for the third.

The GF grammar compiler returns the first parse alternative whatever it is, warns about the ambiguity, and shows the other alternatives in a comment. Thus the grammar writer can manually choose some other alternative than the first one. Having to inspect and modify generated code is not desirable in general. This technique moreover requires that the grammarian knows the library API well, which we wanted to avoid. But given that the API has to be used, it is better used in a partial control of the parse result in the source file, so that post-editing of generated files is avoided:

```
lin play this_NP = UttImpSg PPos (in Imp "play this") ;
```

11. Related work

The idea of using wide-coverage resource grammars as a basis of small-coverage application grammars was introduced in the Core Language Engine (CLE, Rayner & al. 1992). The technique used for specialization is not library-based compilation as in GF, but *explanation-based learning*, which bears some similarity with example-based grammar writing. In explanation-based learning, a list of examples is used for carving out a fragment of the resource grammar. However, these examples are translated into context-free rules, and they don't hence imply the parametric variations of the explicitly given examples. This means that larger example sets are needed than in example-based grammar writing. Another difference is semantics. In GF, examples appear in the linearization rules of semantically motivated functions. The resulting application grammar is therefore automatically equipped with a semantics. In explanation-based learning, semantics must be given afterwards to the specialized grammar.

References

Bar-Hillel, Y.
    1953   A quasi-arithmetical notation for syntactic description. *Language* 29: 27–58.

Bringert, Björn
    2007   Speech recognition grammar compilation in grammatical framework. Submitted for publication.

Ranta, A.
    2004   Grammatical Framework: A Type-theoretical Grammar Formalism. *The Journal of Functional Programming* 14(2): 145–189.

Rayner, M., D. Carter, P. Bouillon, V. Digalakis, and M. Wirén
    2000   *The Spoken Language Translator*. Cambridge: Cambridge University Press.

Some general problems in machine translation of Swedish noun phrases to English

Anna Sågvall Hein and Eva Pettersson

This study aims at enlightening some general problems in machine translation of Swedish noun phrases to English and to demonstrate how they can be handled in a rule-based translation system. The study is based on a translation corpus of automotive service literature. Focus is set on definite noun phrases with a lexical head. It is assumed that definiteness is invariant, and this assumption is, largely, confirmed. Shifts of definiteness are, mainly, found in the translation of headings and other sentence fragments. However, also in full sentences, shifts of definiteness are observed. A few of them need special transfer rules while the majority may be regarded as free variation and handled by the standard invariance rule. The rules are expressed in the MULTRA transfer formalism and their effect on the translation quality is measured by running them in the MULTRA machine translation system. Translation quality is estimated by measuring the formal similarity between the machine translated text and a reference translation, in terms of a modified version (NEVA) of the BLEU measure. The results show that one of the rules has a negative effect, when applied to all segments in the text. However, restricting this rule to apply to headings only leads to an improvement in evaluation scores. All other applicable rules have a positive effect on the scores, and the best results are achieved when combining them all. The conclusion drawn is that an improvement in translation quality may be achieved by adding transfer rules for shifting from definite to indefinite form in certain contexts.

1. Introduction

In research on machine translation focus is set on core issues of language. The primary challenge is not to explore the most problematic translation cases, as in research on human translation theory, but to formalise more or less well-known translation problems in a way that the computer can handle. In a rule-based approach, this requires a detailed knowledge of various constructions. Typically, a machine-translated text will be more consistent and less varied than a text translated by a human.

In our on-going work in machine translation from Swedish to English we observed that even though definiteness to a large extent is invariant there are also cases where this is not so. The study aims at enlightening these cases and to demonstrate how they can be handled in a rule-based machine translation system. It is based on a corpus of automotive service literature.

We will start the presentation by an outline of the corpus. Definite Swedish NPs and their English translations in the corpus will be examined with a focus on shift of definiteness and structure. Informal transfer rules will be formulated and formalised in the MULTRA transfer formalism (Beskow 1993). The rules will be tested in the MULTRA machine translation system (Så gvall Hein 1994) and the results will be discussed. We will conclude by summarising the contributions of the rules as well as pointing at some problems in reflecting translation variation in a rule-based system.

2. The corpus

The corpus was established in the MATS[1] project. It comprises 25 Swedish documents with English translations from the automotive service domain. It was provided by Scania CV AB. The corpus is representative of the different document types and text types of the company, including the Workshop manual, Technical information, etc. The selection was made by Scania CV AB. The documents are encoded in a Scania specific version of sgml. The encoding makes it possible to identify headings and other kinds of structured text segments (table cells etc.). The corpus was split in two parts, a training corpus and an evaluation corpus. The training corpus comprises 19 documents, and the test corpus holds the other 6 documents. The corpus studies will be based on the training corpus, and in testing the rules we will use the evaluation corpus. Quantitative data about the corpus are presented in Table 1.

	Documents	Text segments	Text words	Bytes	Word types
Swedish Training	19	7259	45301	273504	6820
Swedish Test	6	1699	11741	66818	2393
Swedish Total	**25**	**8958**	**57042**	**340322**	**9213**
English Training	19	7263	57863	296336	4340
English Test	6	1699	14832	74178	1929
English Total	**25**	**8962**	**72695**	**370514**	**6269**

Table 1. The Mats corpus

The preparation of the corpus includes the alignment of text segments and words (Tiedemann 2003). It has been uploaded on the web and can be searched via a graphical interface (Tiedemann 2003). It is possible to search for Swedish text units (strings of characters) and have them displayed in their text segment contexts together with their English counterparts, and vice versa. Using these options, we can easily extract cases where an SL word has a certain translation as well as the full variation of translations in any language direction.

The documents are highly structured into cover text, headings at different levels, tables, figures, listings etc. These segments and their constituent parts such as figure text, table cells, list element etc. have a fairly independent status in the text and will be treated as text segments in their own right. They are marked by SGML tags by which they may be identified. They will be referred to as *structured text segments* as opposed to *unstructured text segments*, by which we refer to the sentences (and sentence fragment) in the plain text. The distribution of the text segments into these two basic categories is displayed in Table 2.

	Unstructured text segments	Structured text segments
Swedish Training	2973	4286
Swedish Test	758	941
Swedish Total	**3731**	**5227**

Table 2. The distribution of unstructured and structured text segments in the Swedish part of the MATS corpus

The English version of the corpus contains more word tokens and fewer word types than the Swedish one: 72,695 versus 57,042 and 6,269 versus 9,213. This is due to the fact, that Swedish morphology is richer than English, both as regards inflection, derivation and compounding. For instance, the definite form of Swedish nouns is expressed by means of endings, whereas in English the definite form has an analytical expression, e.g. *motorn* and *the engine*. Further, Swedish compounds appear as word tokens, whereas in English they are split, e.g. *torkarmotor* and *wiper motor*.

Frequency data on the word types including signs of punctuation were calculated and uploaded on the web. Among the Swedish 50 top word types we find only four content words, i.e. *sätt* [set, put; way] 249, *motorn* [the engine, the motor] 171, *styrenheten* [the control unit] 161, and *kortslutning* [short circuit] 146. As expected, the frequency distribution in English is more dense, and there are 17 content words among the 50 top word types: *control* 545, *fault* 435, *unit* 421, *engine* 371, *pressure* 342, *system* 293, *fuel* 280, *speed* 260, *sensor* 245, *remove* 209, *circuit* 204, *air* 201, *housing* 194, *position* 192, *valve* 191, *switch* 191, and *cable* 190.

3. Definiteness in the corpus – the general picture

We start our investigation by comparing the total number of definite nouns in the two language versions of the bilingual corpus. A total of 1,724 definite noun forms (1,375 lemmas) and 7,195 occurrences were found in the Swedish part of the training corpus. In the English part, 7,063 occurrences of the definite article were found. Thus definiteness appears to be invariant in roughly 98 % of the cases. Consequently, the general strategy to adopt in a Swedish-English machine translation system for technical text is to transfer the definiteness feature without any change.

Informal rule 1: *A Swedish definite NP translates into an English definite NP; a Swedish indefinite NP translates into an English indefinite NP*

Still the definite form is somewhat more frequent in Swedish than in English and according to our estimates there are some 130 cases where a shift from definite to indefinite takes place. We will now concentrate on identifying the contexts in which these shifts take place to see how they can be handled by specific rules overriding the general rule.

3.1. Structured text segments

All in all, there are 708 headings at various levels in the training corpus. The great majority, i.e. 661 (93 %), are nominal expressions. In addition, there are some instances of adjectives, prepositional phrases, imperative clauses, and How-to-clauses. Here, only the nominal expressions will be examined. Headings are not referential; they are used to introduce a thematic sub-domain of the document. Thus, as may be expected, indefinite singular forms without quantifiers, sometimes referred to as "naked NPs" are, typically, used. The translation of these text segments is unproblematic with regard to definiteness; they confirm the basic assumption.

However, in 41 Swedish headings, a definite form is used instead. Generally, the definite form refers back to an object that has been explicitly introduced earlier in the text, typically in the same paragraph. This is not the case here, where the heading signals the beginning of a new part of the document. However, 39 of the definite headings refer to parts of the vehicle such as *givaren* [the sensor]; 2 refer to processes in automotive maintenance, i.e. *arbetsbeskrivningen* [the work description] and in the operation of the engine, i.e. *bränslets väg* [the path of the fuel].

The parts of the vehicle as well as the processes involved may be considered given, known, in the general context of automotive maintenance and as it is specified by the title of the individual documents. Using the definite form in the headings may be seen as a means of concretising the description by bringing an individual generic entity into focus. This strategy, however, is not an option in English. The translation into English always implies a shift to the indefinite form. So we formulate a rule:

Informal rule 2: *A Swedish definite NP translates into an indefinite English NP, if the NP constitutes a heading*

This rule is more specific than the previous one since it applies to headings only. In the Multra translation system, all applicable rules are applied. However, a more specific rule is preferred to a more general one. Thus, when both Informal rule 1 and Informal rule 2 are applied, the result of Informal rule 2 will be chosen in the first place.

The shift from definite to indefinite in headings is sometimes accompanied by a shift of structure. Below we present examples of two types of NPs, where the first translates with invariant structure, and the second with a structural shift.

1. **definite ⇒ indefinite; no structural shift**
   singular or plural, no pre-modifier, co-ordinated or not, with or without post-modifier(s)

   - *Retardern* ⇒ *Retarder*
   - *Felkoderna* ⇒ *Fault codes*
   - *Bränslemängden och insprutningstidpunkten* ⇒ *Fuel quantity and injection timing*
   - *EDC-styrenheten E44* ⇒ *EDC control unit E44*
   - *Bränsletryckgivarna, T92 och T93* ⇒ *Fuel pressure sensors, T92 and T93*
   - *Kontrollampan för EDC, W27* ⇒ *Warning lamp for EDC, W27*

2. **definite ⇒ indefinite; structural shift**
   singular head with a pre-modifier in the genitive case

   a) shift to compound
      Bränslets väg [the path of the fuel] ⇒ *Fuel path*

b) shift to NP with a post-modifier introduced by *of*
    EDC-styrenhetens function [the function of the EDC control unit]
    ⇒ *Function of the EDC control unit*

c) shift to NP with a parallel/appositional post-modifier preceded by comma
    EDC-styrenhetens anslutningar [the connections of the EDC control unit] ⇒ *EDC control unit, connections*

As regards 2, the use of the genitive attribute in Swedish enforces the definite form of the attributive noun. An indefinite form **växellådas typskylt* [type plate of gearbox] is not well-formed in itself; it calls for an indefinite article to make it complete. The indefinite article, on the other hand, signals the introduction of an object and is not appropriate for expressing the generic sense that is called for in a heading. Consequently, in these cases there are, basically, two options in Swedish, either to use the definite form, as in the examples above, or to paraphrase the expression into a head with a post-modifier: *Typskylt för växellådan* [type plate of/for the gearbox]. A third, but clumsy alternative would be *Växellådstypskylt* [gearbox type plate]. In the training corpus, these two options are not used.

In the training corpus of structured segments we find three alternative types of shifts in the translation of these constructions, as illustrated in a), b), and c) above. The compound construction is substantially more frequent than the of-construction, while the parallel construction is rare. The shifts have to be taken care of in the transfer grammar of the MT system. In doing so, we may choose one alternative as the default translation, disregarding the variation, or try to find structural evidence for making a distinction between a), b) and c). Our first choice will be based on frequency, and we will treat the compound alternative as the default case. The impact of this choice and the need for making more fine-grained rules will be explored in the experiment that will be set up. Below we formulate the default rule in an informal way:

Informal rule 3: *A definite Swedish NP consisting of a genitive attribute N1 and a head N2 translates into an indefinite English compound with N1 as the modifier and N2 as its head if the NP constitutes a heading.*

3.2. Unstructured text segments

According to our estimates, there are at least 132 definite Swedish noun phrases in the training corpus that translate into indefinite English NPs. Some types were spotted and examined in the investigation of the headings. However, at least 94 cases remain to be found in the unstructured part of the corpus. It is outside the scope of this study to make a full investigation of all of them. Rather, we use the definite forms of the most frequent noun in the corpus, *motor* [engine, motor], as a handle for bringing out the crucial cases.

3.2.1. The case of the motor

motor appears in the following definite forms in the corpus: *motorn* (definite singular basic case, 171 occurrences), *motorns* (definite singular genitive case, 39 occurrences), *motorerna* (definite plural basic case, 8 occurrences).

In Table 3 we present types of transfer in the translations of *motorn*. Definiteness is maintained in 165 cases (of 171), i.e. 96.5 %. This is slightly less than our estimate of all the nouns in the corpus, cf. 98 %. We distinguish 5 different types of transfer with regard to definiteness and structure, and below we comment on the different types.

Type of transfer	Transfer	Instances
1	def ⇒ def	163
2	def ⇒ def shift of structure	2
3	def ⇒ indef	3
4	def ⇒ indef shift of structure incl VP	2
5	Omission	1
		Total: 171

Table 3. Definiteness and structure in the translation of *motorn* (singular, basic case)

Type 1: Definiteness is maintained and no shift of structure; the default rule applies

Type 2: Definiteness is maintained and there is a shift of structure

We found two instances of a shift of structure from a definite np with a modifier, to a definite compound e.g. *anslutningsdonet till motorn* [the connector of/to the motor] ⇒ *the motor connector*. The head of the PP modifier turns into the first modifying component of the compound and the head of the NP remains the head of the compound. The change was observed only for two heads, i.e. *anslutningsdon* [connector] and *elanslutning* [electrical connection] followed by the preposition *till*. The change may be informally expressed by the following rule.

Informal rule 4: *A definite Swedish NP consisting of a head noun 'anslutning' or 'anslutningsdon', N1, and a post-modifier with the preposition 'till', N2, translates into an English compound in the definite form with N2 as the modifier and N1 as its head.*

We constrain the rule with regard to the lexical units involved since we have no data how systematic this type of shift is. Constructions of this kind involving other lexical units will be translated in an isomorphic way by means of default rules.

Type 3: Definite to indefinite and no shift of structure

We found two types of shift from definite to indefinite without a shift of structure, as illustrated below:

a) ***Motorn** stannar.* ⇒ ***Engine** stops.* (2)

b) *Gaspådragsgivare **på motorn*** ⇒ *Throttle actuation sensor **on engine*** (1)

As regards both a) and b) there are analogous examples in the corpus where definiteness is maintained, such as **The engine** *is switched off* and *components on **the engine***. Thus the shift of definiteness is regarded as a case of free variation and the default rule will be applied.

Type 4: Definite to indefinite and a shift of NP structure including a VP

There are two cases of this type as illustrated below:

a) *För att inte **motorn** ska **överbelastas*** [*In order not to overload the motor] ⇒ *To prevent **motor overload***

b) *hur hårt **motorn** är **belastad*** [*how heavily the engine is loaded] ⇒ *the degree of **engine load***

Shift involving the VP are outside the scope of this study and no action will be taken.

Type 5: Translation omitted

There is only one example of an omission, i.e. *insprutningspumpen påmotorn* [the injection pump of the engine] ⇒ *the injection pump*; there is no trace of the PP *påmotorn* in the English translation. Either the PP was found to be superfluous by the translator and left out consciously, or it is an accidental omission. The case will be left without action.

Below we examine types of transfer in the translations of the singular genitive form *motorns*:

Type	Transfer	Instances
1	def ⇒ def	1
2	def ⇒ def shift of structure	28
3	def ⇒ indef	-
4	def ⇒ indef shift of structure incl VP	10
		Total: 39

Table 4. Translation of *motorns* (genitive case, singular)

In Table 4 there is only one example of transfer with definiteness and structure maintained, i.e. *motorns kylvätsketemperatr* ⇒ *the engine's coolant temperature*, the English synthetic genitive being rare.

Type 2 dominates. The most frequent structural shift results in an English compound (10 types) such as *motorns hastighet* ⇒ *the engine speed*; after that comes the PP *of* translation alternative (8 types), e.g. *motorns framsida* ⇒ *the front of the engine*. There is also a shift into a PP with *in* occurring only, however, with the NP head *temperatur*, i.e. *motorns temperatur* ⇒ *the temperature in the engine*.

Even though there is no problem with definiteness, there is a translation choice between the compound and the NP PP construction. Since the compound alternative dominates it will be chosen as the default case. A further question is whether it should be lexically constrained, or not. Initially, we formulate the rule in a general way:

Informal rule 5: *A definite Swedish NP consisting of a genitive attribute N1 and a head N2 translates into a definite English compound with N1 as the modifier and N2 as its head.*

There is no instance of Type 3 in Table 4, but 10 of Type 4 (4 types). Type 4 occurs only with the head nouns: *varvtal* [speed], *vridmoment* [torque], *effekt* [output], and *acceleration* [acceleration]. However, in parallel we find translation alternatives where definiteness is maintained. This is regarded as a case of free variation and the default rule will apply.

However, there are exceptions to this strategy as illustrated below:

Beroende på faktorer som begärt gaspådrag, **motorns** *varvtal,* **motorns** *acceleration och laddlufttemperatur*

Depending on factors such as throttle actuation, **engine** *speed,* **engine** *acceleration and charge air temperature*

In the co-ordinated Swedish NP there is a mixture of indefinite nominals such as *begärt gaspådrag* [throttle actuation] and definite NPs such as *motorns varvtal* [the speed of the engine]. In the English translation, the indefinite form is required for all the members of the co-ordinated NP. It is difficult to capture this analogy in all its variations in the transfer formalism, and no attempt will be made. Thus the English translation produced by the MT system will maintain the Swedish variation between indefinite and definite.

In the translation of the definite plural form *motorerna*, two contexts need to be distinguished: the noun with a post-modifier denoting type such as *Motorerna M9 och M10* which translates into an indefinite English NP: *Motors M9 and M10* (2 types, 2 occurrences), and cases without an apposition which translate in a straightforward manner without any shift of definiteness (6 types, 6 occurrences) or structure. A transfer rule for the apposition will be formulated.

Motorerna *M9 och M10* ⇒ **Motors** *M9 and M10*

Informal rule 6: *A definite Swedish NP consisting of a head and an apposition denoting type translates into an indefinite English NP consisting of a head and an apposition denoting type.*

3.2.2. Summarising the findings of motor in the definite forms

The invariance assumption is confirmed in 200 cases (of 218), i.e. 91.7 %. Among them, however, we also find structural shifts for which transfer rules are formulated. As regards Type 3, rules for shifting definiteness are formu-

Type	Transfer	Instances
1	def ⇒ def	170
2	def ⇒ def shift of structure	30
3	def ⇒ indef	5
4	def ⇒ indef shift of structure incl VP	12
5	Omission	1
		Total: 218

Table 5. Types of transfer of *motor*, definite forms

lated for two types of constructions. As regards type 4, all cases of shift of definiteness may be regarded as free variation and the default rule will apply. However, there are also 2 types of structural shifts that are disregarded; either the shifts involve VPs, or they are based on analogy, for which the rule formalism is not well suited. Finally, there is one case where a translation segment has been omitted, and it is also disregarded.

To what extent can we generalise the findings made in the case study? With this question in mind, we extended the study to the second most frequent definite form in the corpus, *styrenheten* [the control unit]. It has a frequency of 161, and in 154 of these cases definiteness is maintained. A shift of definiteness that has to be handled by means of special rules takes place in two contexts. One occurs, quite regularly, in a structured text segment, i.e. *EDC-styrenheten E44* [the EDC control unit E44] ⇒ *EDC control unit E44*. The other one is an example of a co-ordination context, where Swedish allows the combination of definite and indefinite while English does not, e.g. *Styrenheten avstängd, inget gaspådrag* [The control unit shut off, no throttle actuarion]. ⇒ *Control unit shut-off, no throttle actuation*. As noted above, the rule formalism is not well suited for handling analogy and no rule will be formulated. No new types of shifts of definiteness or structure were found.

The third most frequent noun form *givaren* [the sensor] with 73 occurrences in the training corpus was also inspected. Its translations can be modelled by means of the rules that were defined, so far. A somewhat different version of the coordination context was found, i.e. *Givaren [the sensor] feljusterad eller felaktig* ⇒ *Sensor incorrectly adjusted or faulty*. The omission of the copula *är* [is] seems to be the motivation for the shift from definite to indefinite. Before this shift is modelled in a systematic way more evidence is needed.

We conclude, so far, that the rules for handling definiteness and structural shifts of NPs motivated by the motor case study have a fairly broad coverage. The assumption will be tested below.

4. Formalising the rules

In order to try out the effect of the informal rules that were defined, we have to formalise them in the MULTRA transfer formalism (Beskow 1993) and include them in the transfer grammar of the Multra machine translation system (Så gvall Hein 1997).

MULTRA is a prototype of a transfer-based machine translation system. The translation process includes three basic steps: analysis, transfer, and generation. The output of the analysis is a feature structure representing the grammatical structure of the input segment. It is the input to the transfer step in which the Swedish grammatical structure is transferred into an English grammatical structure. The transfer step represents the fundamental translation step. It handles the substitution of lexical units and the application of structural translation rules. In the generation step, finally, the English grammatical structure is turned into an English text segment.

Transfer rules are formulated in the MULTRA transfer formalism.

The rules have a source part and a target part. Each source part covers a portion of the grammatical feature structure to be transferred and the target part of the same rule specifies the corresponding part of the target structure.

Transfer rules are composed of transfer equations and transfer relations. A transfer rule consists of at least one source equation and one target equation. Transfer equations as well as transfer relations are based on unification. Transfer equations are used for testing and assigning features. Transfer relations define translation correspondences between feature structures.

In particular, transfer equations may be used to:

- copy a feature from the source to the target

- eliminate a source feature

- assign a new feature to the target

Typically, a transfer rule combines a number of transfer equations and transfer relations. There is no restriction on the number of transfer operations that a rule may comprise and the rule writer is free to specify the appropriate portion of the input structure that is needed for an idiomatic translation. The rules are applied in a recursive manner. For the transfer process to succeed the application of the rules will have to cover the complete source structure and all feature attributes in the source structure need to be mentioned.

For an illustration, we present MULTRA formalisations of the three first informal rules that were defined above. The formalisation of the remaining rules is made in an analogous way.

Informal rule 1: *A Swedish definite NP translates into an English definite NP; a Swedish indefinite NP translates into an English indefinite NP*

```
LABEL
    DEF_Rule_1
SOURCE
    <* DEF>=?X
TARGET
    <* DEF>=?X
TRANSFER
```

The rule consists of a transfer equation: The value of the definiteness feature (DEF) is assigned to the variable ?X in both the source and the target; i.e. the DEF value is copied from the source to the target.

Informal rule 2: *A Swedish definite NP translates into an indefinite English NP, if it constitutes a heading*

```
LABEL
    DEF_Rule_2
SOURCE
    <* TEXT.SEGMENT>=HEADING
    <* PHR.CAT>=NP
    <* DEF>=DEF
    <* CASE>=BASIC
    <* NUMB> =?X
TARGET
    <* TEXT.SEGMENT>=HEADING
    <* PHR.CAT>=NP
    <* DEF>=INDEF
    <* CASE>=BASIC
    <* NUMB> =?X
TRANSFER
```

The rule consists of 5 transfer equations. The text segment is a heading. Its phrasal category is NP. The value of the definiteness feature is DEF. Case is BASIC and the value of the number feature is assigned to the ?X variable.

In the target, all feature values remain the same as in the source apart from the definiteness feature that is set to INDEF. Here we make use of the possibility of assigning a feature in the target regardless of the source structure.

The rule is applicable only to text segments that are headings. However, due to the non-deterministic and recursive nature of the transfer process, also Rule 1 will be applied, implying that no shift of definiteness takes place. Thus two transfer alternatives will be produced. However, MULTRA provides a general strategy for systematically ordering competing transfer alternatives according to rule specificity (Beskow 1993). Rule 2 is more specific than Rule 1 in that it includes more transfer equations. This means, that a translation based on Rule 2 is preferred to one generated by Rule 1.

Informal rule 3: *A definite Swedish NP consisting of a head and an NP premodifier in the genitive case translates into an indefinite English compound, if it constitutes a heading*

```
LABEL
    DEF_RULE_3
SOURCE
    <* TEXT.SEGMENT>= HEADING
    <* PHR.CAT>= NP
    <* DEF>=DEF
    <* CASE>=BASIC
    <* NUMB> =?X1
    <* MOD PHR.CAT>= NP
    <* MOD DEF>=DEF
    <* MOD CASE >=GEN
    <* MOD HEAD>=?X2
    <* HEAD>=?X3
TARGET
    <* TEXT.SEGMENT>= HEADING
    <* PHR.CAT>= NP
    <* DEF>= INDEF
    <* NUMB>=?X1
    <* NP TYPE>=COMPOUND
    <* MOD>=?X4
    <* HEAD>=?X5
```

```
TRANSFER
    ?X2 <=> ?X3
    ?X4 <=> ?X5
```

The rule consists of 10 transfer equations in the source part, 7 transfer equations in the target part, and two transfer relations: The feature structure representing the HEAD of the modifier in the source is assigned to the variable ?X2, and the feature structure representing the HEAD of the NP in the source is assigned to the variable ?X3. A transfer (translation) relation is defined between ?X2 and ?X3, and between ?X4 and X5, respectively. Further, ?X4 is assigned as the value of the modifying constituent of the English compound, and ?X5 as the value of the compound head. An example of the application of this rule is *Bränslets väg* ⇒ *Fuel path*.

5. Evaluating the new rules

The system comes with standard versions of grammars for analysis, transfer and generation. In addition, there is a general dictionary and domain specific dictionaries. Here we will use a dictionary for the automotive domain, combined with the general dictionary.

We will start by running the system with the standard version of the grammars, the base-line grammar, where the default alternative is to maintain the definiteness feature. Similarity between the machine translated text and the reference translation will be calculated in terms of string comparison measures.

The above suggested transfer rules are then added gradually to the base-line grammar, one at a time. The evaluation scores are compared to the base-line scores, and a decision is made whether to keep the rule in the next run or not.

5.1. Evaluation method

The effect of including the above formulated transfer rules, will be evaluated automatically by means of the string comparison measure NEVA (Forsbom 2003). NEVA is a modified version of the widely used BLEU measure (Papineni et al. 2002). NEVA differs from BLEU in that BLEU gives a zero score for all segments shorter than 4 words, while NEVA handles all segments, regardless of length (Forsbom 2003). Since the MATS corpus holds a considerable amount of structured text segments, that are usually rather short, the NEVA measure is better suited than BLEU for our evaluation task.

Experiments show that BLEU values correspond fairly well to human judgements (Papineni et al. 2002). Being a variant of BLEU, the NEVA measure should hence correspond equally well to human estimates.

Due to the high variety in translation, the more reference translations used in the evaluation, the more reliable results are achieved. Most often, there is however only one reference translation available, as is the case in our study. Even though somewhat other scores would be given if several reference translations were used, the results of our evaluation are assumed to indicate whether the rules improve the translation quality or not.

5.2. Evaluation results

In testing the rules, different settings were evaluated:

1. base-line grammar only (includes rule 1)
2. base-line grammar combined with rule 4
3. base-line grammar combined with rule 5
4. base-line grammar combined with rule 6
5. base-line grammar combined with rule 6 and rule 2
6. base-line grammar combined with rule 6, rule 2 and rule 3

The settings were explored for the test corpus as a whole, and for the structured segments of the corpus only. The results are illustrated in table 6.

	All segments	Structured segments only
base-line grammar	0.4555	0.4572
base-line grammar + rule 4	0.4555	0.4572
base-line grammar + rule 5	0.4501	0.4513
base-line grammar + rule 6	0.4561	0.4579
base-line grammar + rule 6 and 2	0.4564	0.4582
base-line grammar + rule 6, 2 and 3	0.4571	0.4589

Table 6. Evaluation results in terms of NEVA scores

The results indicate that a higher translation quality may be achieved by means of transfer rules for shifting from definite to indefinite form in certain contexts.

Rule 6, 2 and 3 all show an improvement in NEVA scores. The best results are achieved when combining them all.

Rule 4 is not applicable to any segments in the test corpus, and no conclusion may be drawn as for the benefit of including this rule.

As for rule 5, it has a negative effect on the scores. An examination of the reference corpus shows quite some variation in the translation of Swedish noun phrases with a genitive attribute; all in all, there are 106 types (145 instances) of this kind. Roughly a third of them (36 types) are translated into definite compounds as proposed by the rule (e.g. *släpets styrenhet Rightarrow the trailer control unit*). In most of the remaining cases, English genitive constructions using the preposition *of* (e.g. *avluftningsverktygets lock Rightarrow the cap of the bleeding tool* (28 types), as in the base-line grammar, or the apostrophe (e.g. *vattenvärmarens drift Rightarrow the heater's operation*) (11 types) are used. There are also a few cases where other prepositions (*on, in, for*) are used or where there has been a shift to an indefinite compound.

The *of*-alternative is the default in the base-line grammar. Making rule 5 the default rule for translating noun phrases in the genitive form, regardless of context, is thus no solution; a deeper investigation of when the different alternatives should be used is called for. The most viable approach may well turn out to be a combination of rules and phrasal dictionary entries covering the deviant types.

In general, the NEVA scores of the structured segments are somewhat higher than for the corpus as a whole, as could be expected in view of the more restricted language used in these contexts. Surprisingly, however, the improvement in NEVA scores is not higher than for the corpus as a whole.

6. Summary with conclusions

In this study we investigated some cases of definiteness in a corpus of Swedish technical text and its translation into English. The study was based on a sentence-aligned parallel corpus of automative service literature. An outline of the corpus in quantitative terms was given.

The focus on the study was set on definite NPs with a lexical head. Definiteness was assumed to be invariant to a high degree. A total of 7,195 Swedish definite NPs were found in the corpus and 7,063 definite English NPs. With provision for the fact that Swedish indefinite NPs may be translated into English definite NPs, we conclude that definiteness is invariant in roughly 98 % of the cases. Still, there are at least 132 cases in the corpus of shifts from definite to indefinite.

As a first step towards the identification and exploration of the counter examples, a sub corpus of structured text segments (headings, figure texts, cover text etc.) was isolated and examined. It comprises more than half (5,227) of the total number of text segments (8,958). In the majority of the cases, structured text segments are uninflected (indefinite) nominal expressions. However, in the Swedish version of the strutured corpus, 41 cases of definite NPs were observed. This is never the case in English. It represents a systematic shift of definiteness to be modelled by the machine translation system.

In order to find out more details about the distribution and contexts of the deviant cases in the plain, unstructured text, we made a close examination of the three most frequent nouns in the corpus: *motor*, *styrenhet*, and *givare*. The examination supported the invariance hypothesis. In 91.74 % of the 218 occurrences of *motor* in the definite form (see Table 5), definiteness was maintained. Ten cases represented a free variation between definite and indefinite English NPs (subject position, prepositional object). Two types of contexts were observed, in which a shift of definiteness was found to be mandatory. The first one appears to be text type specific. It concerns nouns with appositions such as type designators (e.g. *Motorerna M5 och M6*). The second one is more general and seems to be valid for other types of text as well. It concerns definiteness in co-ordinated NPs. In the Swedish corpus we find examples of co-ordinated NPs including definite as well as indefinite NPs, whereas the English translations are consistent in this respect. The phenomenon has to be modelled in the translation system, as well as the more specific case with the apposition.

In the close examination of headings and the most frequent nouns in the corpus, systematic, frequent cases of structural shifts were also observed. In specific, the shift from Swedish NPs with genitive pre-modifiers or prepositional post-modifiers to English compounds will have to be modelled. In several cases there are competing alternatives that need to be further explored.

Most of the phenomena that were discussed, so far, can be modelled by transfer rules in the MULTRA system. The basic operation of MULTRA was outlined and the transfer formalism was briefly introduced. Further, it was demonstrated how transfer rules can be formulated in the MULTRA formalism.

To test our hypothesis that an improvement in translation quality may be achieved by adding transfer rules for the phenomena introduced above, we gradually added these transfer rules to the system, one at a time. The evaluation scores were compared to the base-line scores, to decide whether to keep the rule in the next run or not.

The results show that a systematic shift from a Swedish NP with genitive pre-modifier to an English compound, has a negative effect on the scores, due to a high degree of variation in the reference corpus in how to express genitive constructions. Restricting this rule to only apply to headings (including a shift from definite to indefinite form) was however successful.

All other applicable rules showed an improvement in evaluation scores, and the best results were achieved by combining them all.

The results thus indicate an improvement in translation quality, when adding transfer rules for shifting from definite to indefinite form in certain contexts.

Notes

1. MATS is short for Methodology and Application of a Translation System, a co-operative project between Uppsala University, Scania CV AB and Translator Teknikinformation AB. The basic aim of the project was scaling up the Multra machine translation prototype for large-scale use. It was carried out 2000-09-01–2001-05-31 with support from VINNOVA (Swedish Governmental Agency for Innovation Systems), Scania CV AB, Translator Teknikinformation AB, and Uppsala University.

References

Beskow, Björn
   1993   Unification based transfer in machine translation. In *RUUL 23*. Uppsala University, Department of Linguistics.

Forsbom, Eva
   2003   Training a super model look-alike: Featuring edit distance, n-gram occurrence, and one reference translation. In *Proceedings of the Workshop on Machine Translation Evaluation: Towards Systemizing MT Evaluation, held in conjunction with MT SUMMIT IX*, 29–36. New Orleans, Louisiana, USA.

Papineni, K., S. Roukos, T. Ward, and W.-J. Zhu
   2002   Bleu: a method for automatic evaluation of machine translation. In *Proceedings of the 40th Annual Meeting of the Association for Computational Linguistics (ACL)*, 311–318. Philadelphia.

Sågvall Hein, Anna
   1994   Preferences and linguistic choices in the multra machine translation system. In *Proceedings of 9:e Nordiska Datalingvistikdagarna*, R. Eklund (ed.). Stockholm.
   1997   Language control and machine translation. In *Proceedings of the 7th International Conference on Theoretical and Methodological Issues in Machine Translation*. St. Johns College, Santa Fe, New Mexico.

Tiedemann, Jörg
   2003   Recycling translations - extraction of lexical data from parallel corpora and their application in natural language processing. Ph.D. diss., Uppsala University.

Computing word similarities for ontologies

Martin Volk, Hans Hjelm and Henrik Oxhammar

1. Introduction

Ontologies are "resources representing the conceptual model underlying a certain domain" (Cimiano 2006). They are useful in a variety of applications, such as Query Expansion, Cross-language Information Retrieval (CLIR), and automatic dictionary construction. (Staab and Studer 2003) gives an overview of a great variety of uses. Ontologies will become increasingly prevalent with the growth and acceptance of the Semantic Web. However, as for many other knowledge representation resources, their construction, when performed manually, is both time consuming and prone to inconsistencies. This problem is sometimes referred to as the knowledge acquisition bottleneck.

The process of inducing a (partial) ontology structure from natural language text goes under the name *Ontology Learning* (see e.g. (Maedche 2002)). The goal of Ontology Learning is to facilitate the work of the ontology engineer as much as possible, by presenting her or him with a suggestion for an ontology over the domain at hand. Obviously, the less reordering and fleshing out the ontology engineer has to perform manually, the better the Ontology Learning system has done its job.

One should note that the primary objects of study in an ontology are *concepts* (and relations between these), rather than terms or words. The concepts in the ontology can be said to form the top of the semiotic triangle, connecting *symbols* (words or terms) with *referents* (real life objects). One important task in Ontology Learning therefore becomes to identify which words or terms are used to refer to the same concept in a particular domain. And in order to automatically classify textual information against an ontology, all concepts should have a rich set of terms that are closely related to their descriptors.

We describe automatic approaches for identifying such words or terms, looking at both mono- and cross-language texts. We present our results when evaluating ontology learning and enrichment against Eurovoc (a multilingual thesaurus covering various fields of the European Communities) and against the Common Procurement Vocabulary (a multilingual ontology with more than 8,000 product classes). We work in the context of CLIR and Automatic Product Classification and show how these applications profit from large ontologies.

2. Ontologies for cross-language information retrieval

Cross-Language Information Retrieval (CLIR) refers to a scenario where the query on the one hand and the documents on the other are in different languages. Imagine a researcher who has reading skills in French but does not know exactly how to phrase her information need in that language. In a CLIR system she can enter her query in English and still find documents in French (and in English).

Methods of CLIR are typically divided into: approaches based on bilingual dictionary look-up or Machine Translation (MT); corpus-based approaches utilizing a range of IR-specific statistical measures; and concept-driven approaches, which exploit semantic information (multilingual ontologies) to bridge the gap between surface linguistic forms in the various languages. The ontology-driven approaches presuppose extensive, multilingual, semantic resources.

There are few CLIR systems in operation to date. One is the Madiera portal[1] which provides access to European social sciences data archives. When the user enters a query and clicks the box [Translate], the system will look up the term in a special-purpose multilingual thesaurus. If the term is found, the search will be performed in all languages supported. The multilingual social science thesaurus is available in German, Danish, Greek, English, Spanish, Finnish, French, Norwegian and Swedish. It currently includes more than 3000 terms.

Our group at Stockholm University has prototyped a similar system for Swedish-English cross-language information retrieval over the web pages of the university. The system is called SUiS (Stockholm University Information System)(Nilsson, Hjelm, and Oxhammar 2005) and is implemented as a front end to a web search engine. SUiS supports four question types (Who? What? When? Where?), expands the query with the corresponding term in the other language, and highlights the relevant passage in the found documents. The query expansion is based on an ontology which describes concepts in the university domain (e.g. "lecturer is a subclass of teacher"). One of SUiS' special features is that it answers what-questions directly based on the ontology information (e.g. "What is a lecturer?"). This ontology was hand-coded by a group of students at Stockholm University which explains its limited scope of around 300 concept classes with terms in both Swedish and English.

In contrast, the MUCHMORE project evaluated the use of a very large ontology, the UMLS (Unified Medical Language System) in CLIR experiments between English and German (Volk 2003).

UMLS is organized in three parts. The Specialist Lexicon provides lexical information, such as a listing of word forms and their lemmas, part-of-speech and morphological information. The Metathesaurus is the core vocabulary component, which unites several medical thesauri and classifications into a complex database of concepts covering terms from 9 languages. Each term is mapped to a unique concept identifier. An entry for *HIV pneumonia* in the Metathesaurus main termbank (MRCON) looks like this:

C0744975|ENG|P|L1392183|PF|S1657928|HIV pneumonia|3|

In addition to the mapping of terms to concepts, the Metathesaurus organizes concepts into a hierarchy by specifying relations between concepts. These are thesaurus-type generic relations like *broader_than, part_of, sibling* etc. The UMLS Metathesaurus includes several million terms mapped to hundred thousands of concepts.[2] The majority of the terms are in English, but UMLS also includes large numbers of terms in about a dozen other languages.

The usefulness of UMLS for CLIR was evaluated over a parallel corpus of English-German scientific medical abstracts obtained from the web site of Springer Verlag. The MUCHMORE corpus consisted of approximately 9000 documents with a total of around one million tokens for each language. Abstracts were taken from 41 medical journals (e.g. *Der Nervenarzt, Der Radiologe* etc.) each of which constitutes a medical sub-domain (e.g. Neurology, Radiology, etc.). This corpus constituted the document collection. In addition, 25 queries were collected by a team of medical experts who also provided the set of relevant documents per query.

The evaluation showed that mapping the German queries to UMLS terms and in the same way mapping the English queries to UMLS terms resulted in retrieval precision about as good as using a commercial machine translation system on the queries. But even more interesting, the evaluation showed that retrieval precision was clearly better when a bilingual similarity thesaurus was automatically derived from the parallel corpus.

This proved the usefulness of computing word similarities for information retrieval purposes and lead to the experiments on ontology enrichment and ontology learning described in this paper.

3. Ontology enrichment for text classification

Accessing business information about competitors is central when a company wants to launch a new product or enter a new market. In collaboration with Bonnier's Affärsinformation AB we have investigated the automatic classification of company profiles (short texts describing the activities of a particular company). The goal was to classify them according to a European Union standard for public procurement, the Common Procurement Vocabulary (CPV)[3]. The CPV is a multilingual controlled vocabulary with over 8,000 product and service classes that are structured in a strict taxonomic (is-a) relationship structure, seven levels deep.

At first, we tried an information retrieval approach for the classification. We regarded the company profile texts as queries and the 8,000 product classes as documents. But the results were far from satisfactory.

Our experiments (Oxhammar 2005) showed that often the few terms which describe each CPV concept do not occur in the company profile text (even when manual inspection revealed that the profile text did indeed specify a product class). For example, according to our gold standard, the following company profile should be classified as CPV concept 2211000 Journals.

> Array Publications was founded in 1990 and has grown to become a leading publisher of computer and software related magazines in The Netherlands. Array Publications publishes twelve magazines for the IT market: [...] All titles have accomplished market leadership in the Dutch marketplace.

We observe that there is no mention of the concept descriptor Journals in this profile, which means that this profile cannot be correctly classified.

We tried several automatic techniques for enlarging the concept descriptions by computing similar terms to the ones given. For example we developed a method to exploit WordNet for this purpose (Warin, Oxhammar, and Volk 2005). This looked promising at first sight, but the automatically added terms were general language terms and therefore did not lead to a substantial improvement of the classification accuracy. Obviously, these methods had their limitations and other means for improving the classification results were necessary. It became evident that the concept descriptions needed to be broadened with additional terms which were common in the company profiles.

Therefore we investigated a (semi-) unsupervised method with the specific purpose of bridging the gap between the vocabulary describing the concepts in the CPV and the terminology used in company profiles, by adding terms from this domain to the terms which describe the CPV concepts. Our method draws upon ideas from previous work on automatic construction of semantic lexicons (Riloff and Shepherd 1997; Phillips and Riloff 2002; Roark and Charniak 1998). The methods (often referred to as bootstrappers) use manually selected concepts (e.g. Harvesting Machinery), from which an initial set of *seeds* (e.g. Mowers) are selected and queried against a text collection (in our case company profiles). When relevant terms are identified (e.g. 'cotton', 'plough', 'wheat') that are not yet part of the concept descriptors, they are added to the concept description.

In later iterations these added terms are themselves used as seeds so that the method dynamically creates larger and larger concept descriptions. We experimented in particular with different feature selection techniques, which are known to be useful in identifying discriminative terms in the area of text categorization.

3.1. Feature selection techniques

Feature selection is being addressed in many areas, including text learning tasks such as text categorization and clustering. In these areas, feature selection techniques are mainly adopted for selecting relevant and informative features (words or phrases) in order to reduce the dimensionality of the large feature space, thereby shortening computational cost and learning time(Sebastiani 2002).

In our experiments we considered four such techniques, each technique having its own rationale for estimating the association strength between seeds and co-occurring terms. The techniques (see Table 1) were: the *Expected mutual information* measure (EMI), the *Odds ratio* (ODDS) and the *GSS coefficient* (GSS). To compare these techniques with a simple word associations metric, we adopted the scoring function suggested by (Riloff and Shepherd 1997) and called it AD (for ADopted scoring function).

Feature Selection Techniques
$AD(t_k, c_i) = \frac{freq(t_k, c_i)}{freq(t_k, T)}$
$EMI(t_k, c_i) = \sum_{c \in (c_i, \bar{c}_i)} \sum_{t \in (t_k, \bar{t}_k)} P(t, c) \cdot \log \frac{P(t,c)}{P(t) \cdot P(c)}$
$ODDS(t_k, c_i) = \frac{P(t_k \mid c_i) \cdot (1 - P(t_k \mid \bar{c}_i))}{(1 - P(t_k \mid c_i)) \cdot P(t_k \mid \bar{c}_i)}$
$GSS(t_k, c_i) = P(t_k, c_i) \cdot P(\bar{t}_k, \bar{c}_i) - P(t_k, \bar{c}_i) \cdot P(\bar{t}_k, c_i)$

Table 1. Definitions of the chosen feature selection techniques.

In the formulae above, t_k denotes a candidate term, c_i a seed and T denotes the complete text collection. The scoring function AD computes the fraction of the number of times a term co-occurred with a seed, divided by the term's document frequency, which results in promoting terms that occur in few documents but frequently together with the seed. We adopted the mathematical definitions of the three additional techniques from (Sebastiani 2002). The idea behind all three of these functions is to promote those terms that are distributed most differently among the positive examples c_i and the negative examples $\overline{c}_i$ of a seed. Each technique ranks candidate terms, based on their score, in descending order.

3.2. Bootstrapping concept descriptions using word similarities

One straightforward approach for generating semantic lexicons is described by (Riloff and Shepherd 1997). Their algorithm takes five initial seeds for the selected concepts and enlarges those concepts by identifying the two closest nouns in a sentence which contains a seed. It assigns a score to each noun according to a function similar to AD. We adopted (Riloff and Shepherd 1997)'s approach but simplified it further. Our method regards any term located anywhere in a text as a candidate. Therefore, in contrast to (Riloff and Shepherd 1997), our method regards not only nouns as candidates, but words of any word class anywhere in the document. Additionally, we combined this bootstrapping algorithm with the sophisticated feature selection techniques mentioned in section 3.1. We ran the bootstrapper for eight iterations, and whenever possible, added five new terms at each stage.

Our training collection consisted of 7415 documents, which had been crawled from various corporate web sites throughout Europe. Only those textual parts which we identified as English were indexed. We experimented with 17 concepts located in various parts of the CPV.

The initial seed set for each concept was automatically created by selecting a small number of terms that describe their descendants. For example if we are to expand Harvesting Machinery, then 'mowers' and 'landmowers' will be members of our initial seed set, since these are the descriptors of the two children of the concept Harvesting Machinery in our ontology.

Note that the task was not to *populate* the CPV with instances (e.g. 'Mower XVL-50'), nor to *enrich* the CPV with new *concepts* (e.g. Electrically-powered Mowers). The purpose was to *broaden* existing concepts with terms from a collection of company profiles in order to improve the accuracy of our classifier. For example Harvesting Machinery would probably be broadened with terms such as 'grass', 'hay', 'forresting' etc.

3.3. Results of the comparison

To measure the quality of the enlarged concepts, we classified 15 company profiles against the original (non-enlarged) CPV, which we regard as our *baseline* (BL). Next, we queried the same profiles against each of the four enlarged versions of the CPV, that our bootstrapper, in combination with the different feature selection techniques, had generated. The output from each query was a list of concepts, ranked according to their relevance for a given profile. We measured the classification accuracy using the retrieval effectiveness measure *Mean Average Precision* and compared the results.

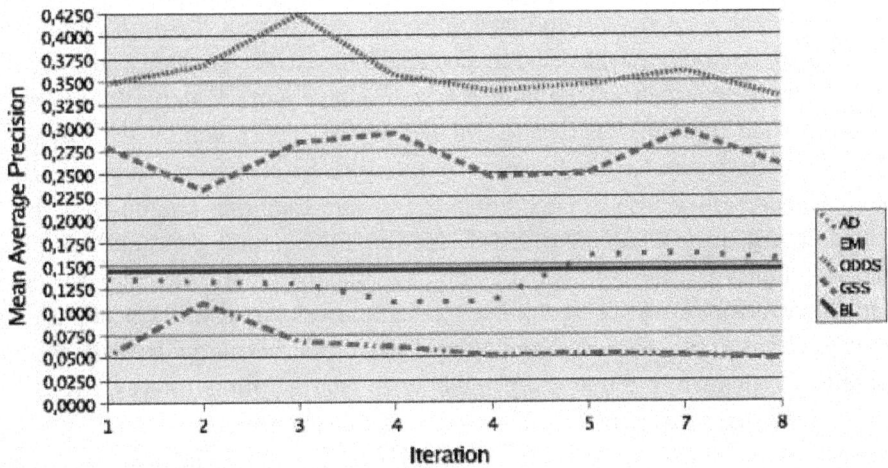

Figure 1. Evaluation results combining bootstrapper and various feature selection techniques. Values given are the mean average precision at various iterations over 15 queries.

Figure 1 depicts the mean average precision scores at each iteration after querying 15 test documents against each version of the CPV. Out of the four enlarged versions of the CPV, the one generated using (Riloff and Shepherd 1997)'s AD scoring function resulted in a classification performance well below our baseline. Combining our bootstrapper with this function clearly polluted the concept descriptions with non-relevant terms, and the bootstrapper suffered from it. This was to be expected, as this scoring technique has almost no power to discriminate between relevant and non-relevant terms. Combining the bootstrapper with the EMI technique results in a very small increase in classification performance (compared to the baseline).

But the GSS coefficient and the Odds ratio are clearly two feature selection techniques that found many relevant terms, and which therefore resulted in the highest classification performance. These techniques best recognized the associations (and non-associations) between candidates and the seeds. They were therefore better capable of separating good concept terms from bad ones. These results show that feature selection techniques can identify similar terms for enlarging concept descriptions in ontologies.

4. Learning ontology relations from parallel texts

The above sections have demonstrated the advantages of having an elaborate ontology. But what if such an ontology does not exist for the domain in question? Various methods have been proposed to extract ontology information from textual documents (Biemann 2005). We have worked in particular on extracting such information from parallel corpora. The potential gain of using parallel texts for ontology learning is twofold. First, we are able to extract lexical representations for each concept in more than one language, which is valuable e.g. in a CLIR setting (cf. section 2). Second, we stand to gain a higher quality of the conceptual, language independent, ontology structure. One straightforward way to achieve the latter works as follows: Let's assume that we want to place the concept "garlic" in a food ontology. By processing a parallel corpus we find that the English term "garlic" most likely corresponds to the Swedish term "vitlök". This term contains the root "lök" which means "onion". In this way we can conclude that "garlic" is a special type of "onion".

The obvious question then becomes: how do we, via the parallel texts, establish the equivalence links between the terms in the different languages, and how accurate are the results? Many researchers have proposed various kinds of distributional association methods for this task, see e.g. (Church and Gale 1991) and (Fung and Church 1994). In the following we present a systematic comparison of two approaches on a variety of language pairs, using the JRC-Acquis parallel corpus (Steinberger et al. 2006) to train the models, and Eurovoc V4.2[4] to evaluate the results.

(Sahlgren 2006) discusses how different distributional models can be used to identify words that stand in either a *syntagmatic* or a *paradigmatic* relation to one another. Words that stand in a syntagmatic relation are words like *cradle – baby*; there is a thematic connection, but the two words do not necessarily share many semantic features. Conversely, the words *cradle – bed* are paradigmatically related; many more semantic features are shared. (Lund and Burgess 1996) refer to these relations as *associative* and *semantic*, respectively.

In (Sahlgren 2006: p. 61), the *refined distributional hypothesis* is put forth:

> A word-space model accumulated from co-occurrence information contains syntagmatic relations between words, while a word-space model accumulated from information about shared neighbors contains paradigmatic relations between words.

The refined distributional hypothesis is, at least partly, confirmed by experiments also presented in (Sahlgren 2006). But what about the cross-language case, working with parallel texts – which type of relations do the two models capture there? The focus of this study is to investigate whether a matrix containing information about co-occurrence (a *co-occurrence model* from here on) or shared neighbors (a *shared neighbors model* from here on) is more effective for the task at hand. Especially, we want to answer the following question: which of the two models has the most direct correspondence with the translational equivalence relation?

4.1. Data and gold standard

We used the JRC-Acquis parallel corpus for training both types of models. The corpus consists mainly of legal texts concerning matters involving the EU, thus the texts are technical and use a consistent terminology. We have used all pairwise combinations of the following languages in our experiments: German, English, French and Swedish. This means that six language pairs have been evaluated and thus twelve translation directions. The corpus contains about seven million words per language.

The JRC-Acquis parallel texts are distributed in a format where they have been aligned automatically on a paragraph level, but the paragraphs are very short and usually only contain one sentence or even one part of a sentence. There are two alignment versions available for download;[5] we used the version produced by the Vanilla aligner[6] in our experiments.

As a gold standard, against which to check the translations proposed by the system, we use Eurovoc V4.2, a freely available thesaurus existing in more than 20 languages and covering topics where the EU is active. The thesaurus contains 6,645 concepts, each of which is given a *descriptor*, or recommended term, in each language. For example we find entries like "economical development" or "overpopulation".

These descriptors constitute the gold standard; when the system translates the descriptor for a concept in the source language with the descriptor for the same concept in the target language, the translation is counted as correct, otherwise as incorrect.

The expressions included in an ontology can consist of a single word or they can be multi-word units. When we are looking at a particular domain, these expressions are assumed to correspond to the *terms* in that domain. A lot of research has been carried out in the field of *Term Extraction* towards automating the extraction of terms (see e.g. (Castellví, Bagot, and Palatresi 2001; Jacquemin 2001)). In our experiments, we assume that the term extraction process has already been carried out correctly and that the relevant terms correspond to the descriptors in Eurovoc.

We lemmatize the data, including the descriptors in the gold standard, using Intrafind's[7] LiSa system for morphological analysis (Hjelm and Schwarz 2006).[8] We also apply a very simple term spotting technique (for more on term spotting, see (Jacquemin 2001)): Going through each text from left to right, we simply mark the longest matching string of complete words, that also is a descriptor for the language in question, as a term. We mark the terms so that they are recognizable and so that the system is able to treat them as single textual units. For example:

```
A new accounting system was installed. ⇒
a new ACTERM_accounting_system#4362 be install .
```

Note that, due to the "longest match" rule, the term spotter here selects "accounting system", even though "accounting" is also a descriptor for English. The concept identifier is added at the end of the term in order to simplify the evaluation process.

4.2. Experimental setup and results

Throughout all experiments, we use cosine as our similarity measure and we use the log_2 of the frequencies in the models rather than raw frequencies. The intuition behind this is that a word co-occurring twice with another word should be weighted higher than a word that co-occurs only once – but probably not *twice* as high.

When building a *co-occurrence* model, rows in the matrix represent terms and columns represent documents, or in this case paragraphs. This is the typical situation in Information Retrieval systems.

A *shared neighbors* model, on the other hand, usually makes use of a fixed-size sliding window to determine which words are to be considered neighbors of the focus word. This means that, when building the shared neighbors model for a language, we use all parallel corpora where the language in question constitutes one part. Different parts of the co-occurrence vector are reserved for the different languages, and we also use the monolingual corpora to model the shared neighbors in the monolingual case. This is illustrated in figure 2.

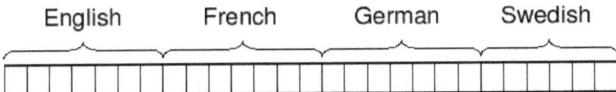

Figure 2. A co-occurrence vector for the shared neighbors model with information from several languages.

In these experiments, we use the entire target language part of the alignment unit as the window, as illustrated in figure 3. There is no inherent reason for choosing the *target* language words as features when building a cross-language shared neighbors model. In fact, since four languages were involved in these experiments, we implemented a model where words from all four languages were used. This brought a very moderate increase in accuracy (0.2% points on average), which hardly justifies the extra effort.

We make no weight adjustment for the proximity of the words, since we do not wish to make any assumptions about the similarity of word order between the languages involved.

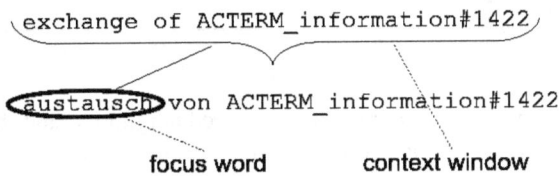

Figure 3. Constructing the shared neighbors model for translating from German to English.

For each model, we evaluate each of the twelve translation directions. As translation candidates, we only consider the descriptors of the target language; the assumption being that the term extraction process has been carried out correctly for each language and that a *term* in the source language should be translated with a *term* in the target language. As input to the system, we use all source language descriptors that occur at least once in the source language text of the parallel corpus at hand. We also split the descriptors arbitrarily into eleven frequency classes: 1, 2-5, 6-10, 11-50, 51-100, 101-500, 501-1000,

	Percent correct
Shared neighbors model	56.0
Co-occurrence model	61.4

Table 2. Percent correct over all frequency classes, totally 37,316 translations evaluated.

1001-5000, 5001-10000, 10001-50000 and 50001<=. We wanted to check whether there is a correlation between frequency and translation accuracy.

We calculate the average accuracy for all twelve translation directions, for each frequency class as well as the overall accuracy, regardless of frequency (displayed in table 2). Figure 4 shows a comparison between the shared neighbors model and the co-occurrence model over these frequency ranges.

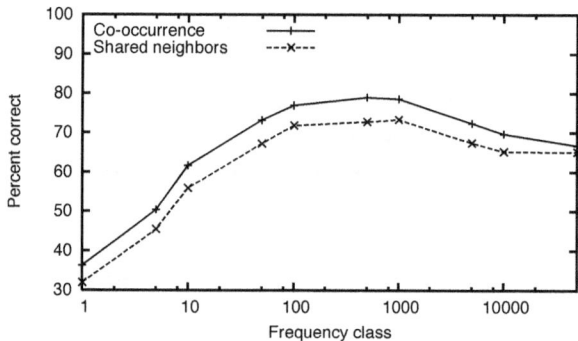

Figure 4. Comparison of the accuracy of the shared neighbors- and the co-occurrence models over different frequency ranges.

The co-occurrence model consistently outperforms the shared neighbors model in these experiments. This is true, regardless of frequency class and language pair (though we do not list the results for each language pair here). Since the number of translations that were evaluated is high and the difference in accuracy is over 5% on average, the co-occurrence model is to be preferred. The correspondence between the different models and the syntagmatic and paradigmatic relations have previously been investigated for the monolingual case. We hope to have made a contribution to clarifying the correspondence between the two models and the translational equivalence relation in the cross-language case through this study.

5. Conclusions

Ontologies are most useful when they come with dense term descriptions of the concepts (rather than brief term listings). We have demonstrated that these descriptions can be automatically inferred from a large text collection in the respective domain. The precise impact of this enlargement on recall and precision in text classification needs further investigation.

We believe that parallel corpora provide a better basis to ontology learning than monolingual corpora. But the learning methods that have recently begun to emerge rely crucially on precise term alignment across languages. We have compared two alignment methods by evaluating their output to the Eurovoc thesaurus. We found that the Co-occurrence model outperformed the Shared neighbors model.

These are just two examples of how automatically computed word similarities are the basis for innovative methods and applications in Natural Language Processing. We believe that computing word similarities is a central building block towards automatically grasping the semantics of textual documents.

Biemann, Chris
    2005   Ontology learning from texts. A survey of methods. *LDV-Forum* 20 (2): 75–93.

Castellví, M. Teresa Cabré, Rosa Estopà Bagot, and Jordi Vivaldi Palatresi
    2001   Automatic term detection: A review of current systems. Chapter 3 of *Recent Advances in Computational Terminology*, Didier Bourigault (ed.), 53–87. Philadelphia, PA: John Benjamins Publishing Company.

Church, Kenneth, and William Gale
    1991   Concordances for parallel text. *Proceedings of the Seventh Annual Conference of the UW Centre for the New OED and Text Research.* 40–62.

Cimiano, Philipp
    2006   *Ontology Learning and Population from Text: Algorithms, Evaluation and Applications.* New York, NY: Springer-Verlag.

Fung, Pascale, and Kenneth Church
    1994   K-Vec: A new approach for aligning parallel texts. *Proceedings of COLING 94.* COLING, 1096–1102.

Hjelm, Hans, and Christoph Schwarz
    2006   LiSa - morphological analysis for information retrieval. Stefan Werner (ed.), *Proceedings of the 15th NODALIDA Conference*, Volume 1 of *University of Joensuu electronic publications in linguistics and language technology.* NoDaLiDa, Joensuu: Ling@JoY.

Jacquemin, Christian
    2001   *Spotting and Discovering Terms through Natural Language Processing.* Cambridge, MA: The MIT Press.

Lund, Kevin, and Curt Burgess
    1996   Producing high-dimensional semantic spaces from lexical co-occurrence. *Behavior Research Methods, Instruments, and Computers* 28 (2): 203–208.

Maedche, Alexander
2002 *Ontology Learning for the Semantic Web.* Norwell, MA: Kluwer Academic Publishers.

Nilsson, Kristina, Hans Hjelm, and Henrik Oxhammar
2005 SUiS - cross-language ontology-driven information retrieval in a restricted domain. Stefan Werner (ed.), *Proceedings of the 15th NODALIDA Conference.* Joensuu: Ling@JoY : University of Joensuu electronic publications in linguistics and language technology 1.

Oxhammar, Henrik
2005 Mapping product descriptions to an ontology. *Proceedings of the 15th NODALIDA conference, Joensuu 2005.*

Phillips, W., and E. Riloff
2002 Exploiting strong syntactic heuristics and co-training to learn semantic lexicons. *Proceedings of the 2002 Conference on Empirical Methods in Natural Language Processing (EMNLP 2002).*

Riloff, Ellen, and Jessica Shepherd
1997 A corpus-based approach for building semantic lexicons. *Proceedings of the Second Conference on Empirical Methods in Natural Language Processing*, pp. 117–124.

Roark, Brian, and Eugene Charniak
1998 Noun-phrase co-occurence statistics for semi-automatic semantic lexicon construction. *COLING-ACL*, pp. 1110–1116.

Sahlgren, Magnus
2006 The word-space model: Using distributional analysis to represent syntagmatic and paradigmatic relations between words in high-dimensional vector spaces. Ph.D. diss., Stockholm University, Stockholm.

Sebastiani, Fabrizio
2002 Machine learning in automated text categorization. *ACM Computing Surveys* 34 (1): 1–47.

Staab, Steffen, and Rudi Studer
(eds.)2003 *Handbook on Ontologies.* Berlin: Springer Verlag.

Steinberger, Ralf, Bruno Pouliquen, Anna Widiger, Camelia Ignat, Tomaz Erjavec, Dan Tufis, and Dániel Varga
2006 The JRC-Acquis: A multilingual aligned parallel corpus with 20+ languages. *Proceedings of LREC.* Genoa.

Volk, Martin
2003 Ontologies in cross-language information retrieval. *WM 2003: Professionelles Wissensmanagement - Erfahrungen und Visionen.* Luzern, 43–50.

Warin, Martin, Henrik Oxhammar, and Martin Volk
2005 Enriching an ontology with WordNet based on similarity measures. *Proc. of the MEANING-2005 Workshop.* Trento.

Objects and relations in the world of microbiology: Information extraction from biological texts

Barbara Gawrońska

1. Introduction and background

An increasing problem for the community of molecular biologists is the need to navigate the huge amounts of current knowledge that has been generated over the last decades (Narayanan 2002, Olsson, Gawronska, and Erlendsson 2006). A large part of this knowledge is represented in the form of natural language texts: articles and abstracts. Since keeping up with the vast number of scientific articles being published, the usefulness of Natural Language Processing and Language Technology has been recognized by researchers in biology and bioinformatics. Text mining and NLP for the purpose of bioinformatics have been listed as topics of interest by programming committees of most international conferences in bioinformatics during the last four years, such as European Conference on Computational Biology (ECCB), Data Integration in the Life Sciences (DILS), Integrated Bioinformatics, and International Conference on Bioinformatics Research and Development (BIRD).

Most of the early text mining efforts in bioinformatics have been based on using only statistics regarding co-occurrence of terms (Becker et al. 2003; Chaussabel and Sher 2002; Darasiela et al. 2004; Jellier et al. 2005; Jenssen et al. 2001; Stapley and Benoit 2000; Tanabe et. al. 1999; Wren et al. 2004). As pointed out by Jellier et al. (2005), this frequent use of simple co-occurrence measures owes its popularity to being easy to implement. The method is also robust and allows efficient processing of huge amounts of texts. Such text retrieval and text mining devices can inform the researcher that there seems to be some relation between e.g. a gene and a protein, or that two genes are often mentioned in similar contexts, but in most cases the type of the relation is not specified, and information about the modality of the relation (true, hypothetical, false) is not present.

In recent years, there has been a shift of focus towards methods which make use of rules, templates/patterns and grammars as well a tendency to combine statistical and rule-based methods. Examples can be found both in bioinformatics (Darasiela et al. 2004; Novitchkova, Egorov, and Darasiela 2003) and biomedical information extraction (McDonald et al. 2004), as well as in other domains. Ono et al. (2001) used a protein name dictionary together with surface clues on word patterns and simple part-of-speech rules to predict protein interactions. In a similar effort, Ng and Wong (1999) developed a method (BioNLP) based on pattern-matching, which searches for sentences matching a set of rules describing selected functions carried out by proteins. The work by Rindflesch et. al. (2000) represents a hybrid approach (a stochastic word tagger is combined with rule-based semantic and syntactic analysis).

As pointed out by McDonald et al. (2004), a restriction common to most relation extraction models is the lack of ability of extracting more than one relation per sentence. Another shortcoming is that relations not expressed by verbs but by, e.g. nouns or participles, are normally omitted.

Among the on-line available Information Extraction tools, MedScan (Novichkova, Egorov, and Darasiela 2003) includes an ambitious attempt to extract positive and negative regulation relations from texts. The developers of the system point out the importance of modality and subordinated clause analysis. However, MedScan seems to suffer from a very low recall rate. In a pilot investigation performed by Olsson, Gawronska, and Erlendsson (2006) the system did not find any relations among biological objects in 80% of the abstracts that have been tested. More than 50% of the extracted relations were incorrect. Errors were due mainly to insufficient grammatical analysis, but also to the fact that the system seemed to identify only those names of biological objects that were represented in a specialized ontology.

The work presented here aims at overcoming – or, at least, reducing – the shortcomings we have observed in available systems for analysis of biological texts. The approach we employ is generally rule-based, but it utilizes the results of statistical analysis of domain-specific corpora. The ultimate goal of the project is to achieve an output that would be compatible with representations in biological databases, and thus would enable partly automated comparison between experimental data, standard databases, and information from current scientific literature. In other words, we aim at an Information Fusion system (www.infofusion.se), i.e. a system for synergistic integration of information from different sources.

In previously published work (Gawronska, Torstensson, and Erlendsson 2004, Gawronska and Erlendsson 2005, Gawronska, Erlendsson, and Olsson 2005, Olsson, Gawronska, and Erlendsson 2006), we presented an experimental system for extraction of relations between biological objects from biomedical texts, and reported the first results. The early results were quite encouraging: the system prototype performed considerably better than MedScan. Still, the recall was not satisfactory (depending on the test corpus, between 63 and 70% of sentences were parsed).

An analysis of the early parsing results revealed that the main reasons for low recall were lexical gaps and insufficient recognition of mathematical symbols and formulae. Another problem was the lack of patterns for Latin names of plants in the system, which sometimes led to wrong sentence delimitation during the normalization procedure. Given a sequence like *Capsicum annuum L. cv. Pukang*, the normalization procedure interpreted the dot after *cv* as a sentence delimiter. Errors in parsing and semantic analysis were mainly due to the following phenomena (Olsson and al. 2006):

- long ambiguous coordinations with multiple instances of *and, or* and *as well* as, e.g.:
    *a higher incidence of axillary lymph node metastasis ($p = 0.05$), poorly differentiated (grade III) tumors ($p = 0.03$), negative ER **and** PR status ($p = 0.02$ and 0.001, respectively), **as well as** p53 protein expression ($p = 0.05$) **and** a higher Ki67 labelling index ($p = 0.004$)*
- coordinations involving different word or phrase classes (prepositional phrase and infinitive clause, adjective and noun), e.g.
    *... morphological and expression patterns, **and** proteome images*
- coordinations involving participle clauses and prepositional phrases attached to the coordinated constituents, like:
    *In parallel with these changes, increases in photosynthetic efficiency **and** capacity, pigment pool sizes, increased capacities of the Calvin cycle enzymes, **and** enzymes of starch and sucrose biosynthesis, **as well as** glycolysis and oxaloacetate/malate exchange are seen, suggesting that BNCBF overexpression has partially mimicked cold-induced photosynthetic acclimation constitutively*
- sentence coordination by comma and "content-empty" adverbials, like *however*, e.g.:
    *The correlation between DNA ploidy and chromosomal aberrations revealed a significant association between aneuploidy and aneusomy for both chromosomes 1 ($p = 0.002$) and 7 ($p = 0.00001$), **however,** a number of diploid tumors were found to be aneusomic, especially for chromosome 1*
- long appositional constructions without indicators of their beginnings and ends:

> *serratamolide (AT514), a cyclodepsipeptide from Serratia marcescens 2170 that induces cell cycle arrest and apoptosis in various cancer cell lines*

Several of such constructions are difficult to disambiguate even for a human reader who does not have sufficient domain knowledge. It seems thus unrealistic to aim at automatic disambiguation of all coordinated phrases and appositional constructions. A more relevant goal would be to make the system to identify highly ambiguous constructions and present them to the user in their original form. On the other hand, the system should not refrain from analysing all sentences with coordinated phrases or appositional constructions, since many of them are possible to resolve automatically.

In the following, we will present certain refinements and modifications recently introduced to the system and aimed at coming closer to the above formulated goal. In section 2, we give an overview of the architecture of the current system, and point out the differences between the present implementation and the early prototype. Section 3 is devoted to the question of identification of phrases referring to biological objects, with focus on Named Entity Recognition, delimitation of appositional construction, and interpretation of coordinated phrases. In section 4, we address the problem of selecting and representing relevant relations between biological objects. Section 5 is devoted to a preliminary evaluation of the system and to a discussion of possible directions for further work.

2. The architecture of the system

The main stages in the information extraction process, and the textual and lexical resources supporting this process are shown in Figure 1. Although there are no big principal differences between the diagram in Figure 1 and the earlier versions of the system architecture (Gawronska and Erlendsson 2005, Olsson, Gawronska, and Erlendsson 2006), the current implementation is, from the technical point of view, considerably more efficient than the prototype. The most important innovation is the fact that all text processing components are now implemented in the same programming language, C# (version 2.0; <www.microsoft.com/net>) in the environment Visual Studio (version 8.; <www.microsoft.com/visualstudio>). This eliminates the need of developing and maintaining interfaces between different programming languages (Delphi, C and Prolog were the languages of the prototype). Another innovation worth mentioning is represented by the top node in the diagram in Figure 1. The Document Retrieval component takes care of communication between our system and the search engines available in connection to the large text database PubMed. Instead of downloading the texts manually, and sending them manually to the Information Extraction procedure, the user can now use one graphical interface for the different functions: downloading full text, selecting text passages, performing Named Entity Recognition, tagging, parsing, and semantic analysis.

The main lexical resource used by the prototype was WordNet (version 1.6; Miller 1995). However, since searching this large database was very time-consuming, and since the majority of lexical items stored in WordNet did not occur in the biological texts, we decided to utilize only a limited part of the noun hierarchy and to replace WordNet be two more limited lexicons: a lexicon of general English, developed in connection to previous language technology projects and enriched by domain-specific vocabulary extracted from PubMed (totally around 106 000 entries, general and domain specific), and a small domain-specific lexicon, containing verbs that are frequent in biological literature (approximately 300 entries). The lexicons are provided with a developer interface, which makes it easy to introduce new items and modify the existing items. Both lexicons allow storage of multiword entries. These entries (lexical phrases) are identified in the text before the Named Entity Recognition and the tagging procedure are applied (this is represented by the component "Phrase identification") in Figure 1.

The resource called "Tag Memory" (on the left in Figure 1) represents a small dynamic database of tagged items. It is filled by successfully tagged phrases and words during processing of a single text. New word sequences are matched against the Tag Memory. If a word form or a sequence of word forms in a given text has already been classified, there is no need of searching the lexicon or applying NER, or morphological analysis anymore – the tag is simply copied from the memory database.

The above mentioned modifications had a considerable impact on the speed of text processing, especially the speed of parsing. Parsing one sentence with the Prolog grammar took between 1 and 5 seconds. Now, with the same grammar rules implemented in C#, approximately 800 sentences are parsed within 1 second.

Figures 2-5 show the outputs from the different system components. After normalization, the abstract from PubMed are divided into a background part (describing previous research), which is not sent for further processing, and a foreground part, concerning the experiment described in the abstract (an example is presented in Figure 3). The algorithm for dividing the text is described in Olsson, Gawronska, and Erlendsson (2006). After Named Entity Recognition and tagging (Figure 3), the text is analyzed syntactically (Figure 4 shows a sample output tree). The semantic component includes certain disambiguation of preposition phrase attachment and coordinated constructions, and attempts to decide whether the sentence is too ambiguous to be interpreted. If the sentence, or at least its parts, is judged as unambiguous, the tree should be converted to a simple graphical representation. For the time being, the conversion to graphs is not implemented, and the real output from the semantic component are logical structures. A possible graphical representation is shown in Figure 5. The decision concerning the exact format of the output will be made after more consultations with biologists.

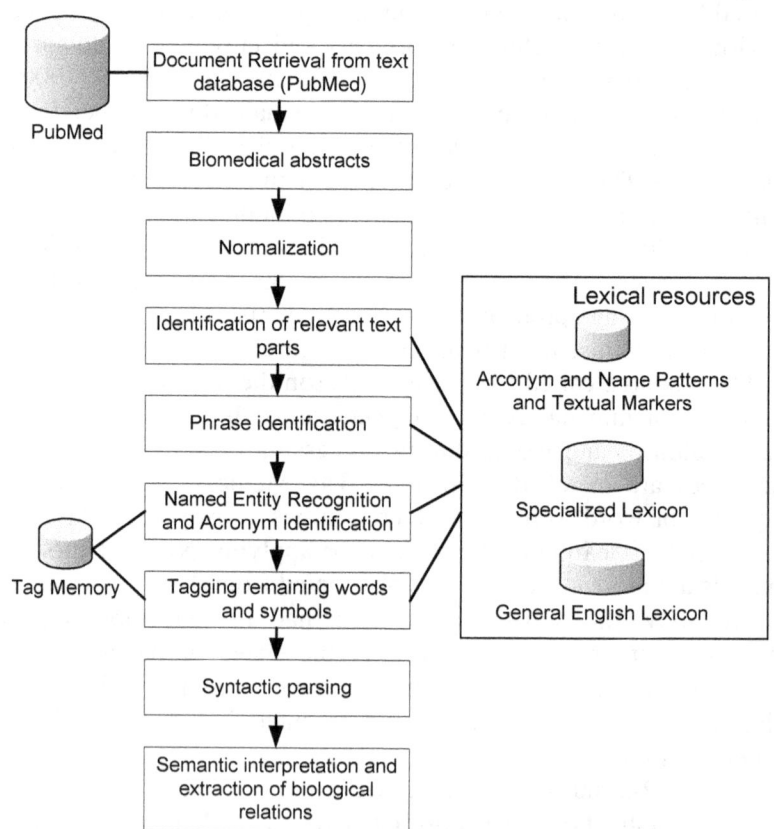

Figure 1. The architecture of the Information Extraction system

---

~~10 - ID: 15711025.~~
~~Although favorable effects of estrogen replacement therapy on atherosclerosis have been recognized, the benefit versus risk of estrogen replacement on overall cardio- vascular health remains controversial. The main adverse effect jeopardizing the clinical usage of estrogen is the increased risk of breast and endometrial cancer. Zearalenone (ZEN) is a universal endogenous hormone possessing estrogen-like effects and facilitating plant growth. alpha-Zearalanol (alpha-ZAL), a new phytoestrogen, is a reductive product of ZEN. Our preliminary evidence suggested that alpha-ZAL is anti-atherosclerotic.~~
The aim of this study was to examine the effect of alpha-ZAL on atherosclerotic formation and serum lipid profile. Adult female nulliparous rabbits were ovariectomized or sham-operated and fed a high-cholesterol diet with different doses of alpha-ZAL or 17beta-estradiol for 12 wk. The aortic intimal atherosclerotic plaque was significantly larger in the cholesterol-fed group compared to control and sham groups. alpha-ZAL and 17beta-estradiol treatments significantly reduced plaque formation and improved serum profile of lipid (TC, TG, HDL-C and LDL-C) and lipoprotein (ApoAI and ApoB). Both alpha-ZAL

Figure 2. A sample abstract, automatically divided into a background and a foreground part. In this case, the division has been made on the basis of the phrase *The aim of the study*.

Both<both> alpha-ZAL<namedentity> and<conjunction> 17beta-estradiol<namedentity> reconciled<pprt,cut_result,state_change> uterine<noun> atrophy<namedentity,default> ,<punctuation> although<subjunction> alpha-ZAL<namedentity> was<verb,aux> significantly<adverb> less<adjective> > potent<adjective> than<preposition> 17beta-estradiol<namedentity> in<preposition> stimulating< aprt> uterine<noun> growth<noun>

Figure 3. A fragment of the output from the NER and tagging procedures.

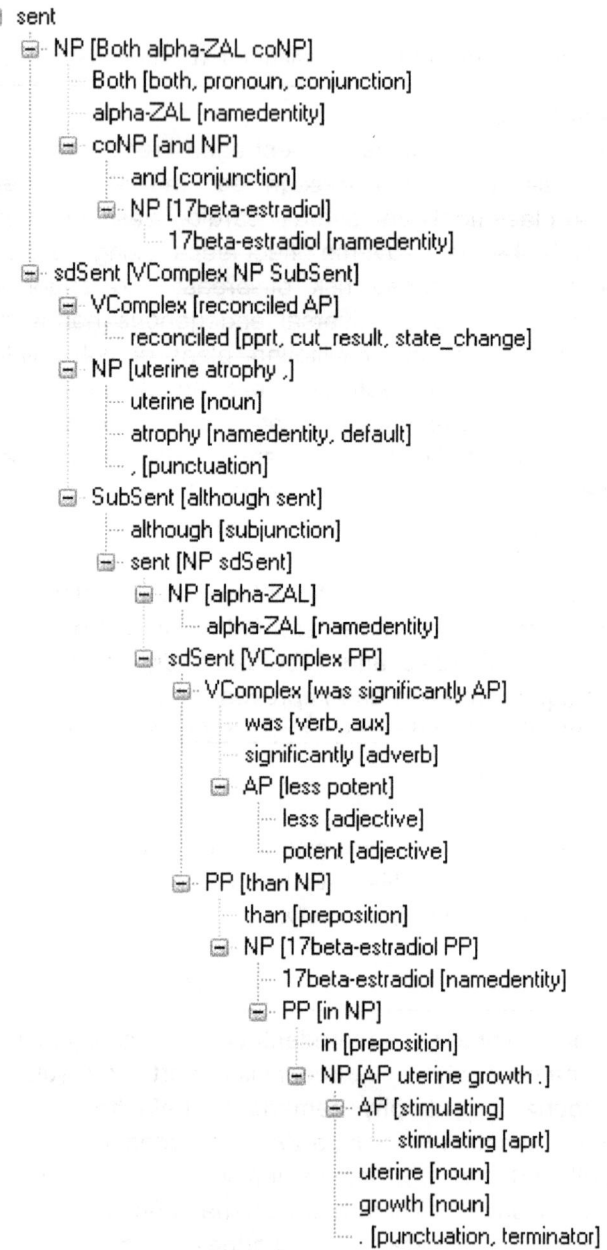

Figure 4. A parse tree corresponding to the tagged sentence in Figure 3.

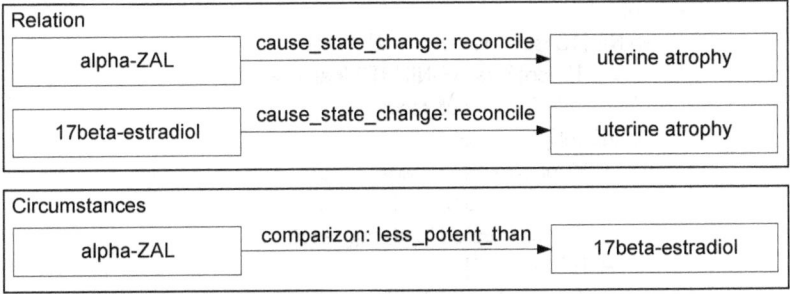

Figure 5. A graphical representation corresponding to the sentence in Figures 3 and 4.

3. Identification of phrases referring to biological objects

3.1. Named Entity Recognition

A system for analysis of biological texts requires a domain-specific Named Entity Recognition (NER) procedure, since no lexicon provides access to all possible names of genes and proteins: new biological objects are continuously discovered and named by the researchers. In the prototype version of our system, the following main patterns for name formation were implemented:

Pattern 1: lower case + integer (>=2) + X (e.g. p16. p70S6K, p16INK4a)
Pattern 2: lower case (>=1) + upper case (>=1) + int (>=0) (e.g. hTERT)
Pattern 3: integer + lower case + integer x 2 (e.g. 9p21)

The NER algorithm was enriched by adding rules for handling hyphenation: between two or more named entities (*TAM-DNA* or *alpha-(N(2)-deoxyguanosinyl)-N-desmethylTAM*) as well as between named entities and nouns and/or adjectives, such as *dG-desmethyl-TAM, N-desmethyltamoxifen, TAM-exposed*. Furthermore, rules taking care of mathematical symbols were added, so that strings of the format: *TAM/kg* and *CGT-->CAGT* are now correctly recognized and delimited. Figure 6 shows the result of syntactic analysis of a sentence containing several complex names of biological objects.

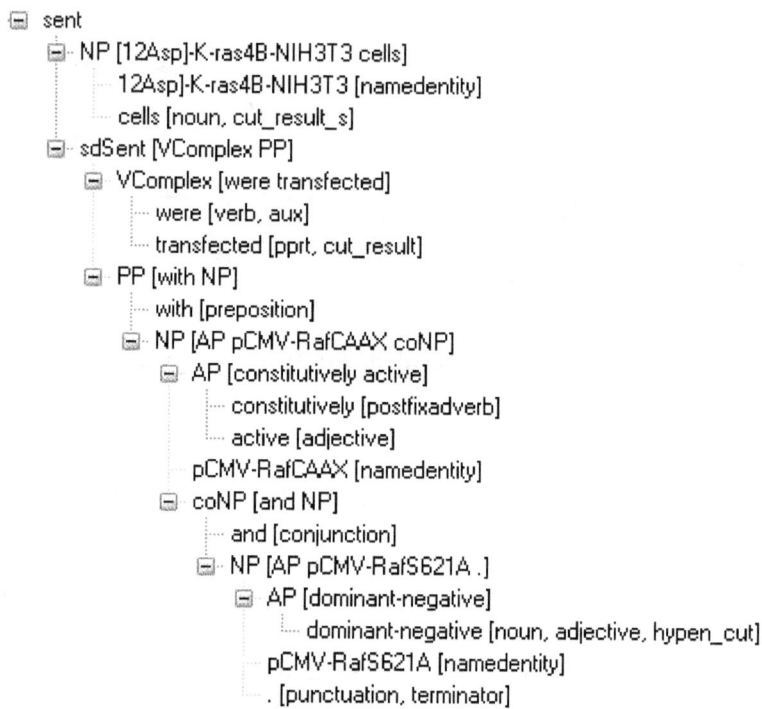

Figure 6. An example of long hyphen-connected names of biological objects. The parse tree corresponds to the sentence: *[12Asp]-K-ras4B-NIH3T3 cells were transfected with constitutively active pCMV-RafCAAX and dominant-negative pCMV-RafS621A*

3.2 Recognition of appositional constructions

Appositional constructions are very frequent in biological texts, and their identification plays an important role for sentence understanding. The most common pattern: a full name of an object followed by an acronym within parentheses, for instance *the hepatic stellate cell (HSC)* is relatively easy to process automatically. Already the prototype version of the system utilized a procedure for linking acronyms with full names of biological objects (Olsson, Gawronska, and Erlendsson 2006). In a sentence like *During fibrosis the hepatic stellate cell (HSC) undergoes a complex activation process*, where the acronym appears in parentheses, the algorithm linked the acronym *HSC* with the phrase *hepatic stellate cell* by going three steps backwards from the left parenthesis, marking the word with initial 'h' (*hepatic*) and linking this word and the words between hepatic and the parenthesis (*stellate cell*) to the acronym. In cases where the full name, rather than the acronym, appeared within parentheses, the algorithm checked the acronym against the initial letters of the words within parentheses as in the example sentence *This protein belongs to a cell cycle regulator group called CDKI (cyclin-dependent kinase inhibitors)*. In the current version, the following types of appositional constructions are successfully identified:

- coordinated sequences of names within parentheses or after semicolon, like
    nuclear receptor co-regulators (SRC1, p300, CARM1, GRIP1, SPA, REA and Uba3)
- most cases of appositions with Latin names, like
    Six adult female rhesus monkeys (***Macaca mulatta***)
- appositions with abbreviations containing both characters and integers, as in *Fischer 344 **(F344)** and Sprague Dawley **(SD)** rats*
- formulae, e.g. *nucleotide insertion (**CGT-->CAGT**) was detected at codon 273...., four groups: **ENNG + ChL, ENNG + TAM , ENNG + E(2) and ENNG + TAM + E(2)***
- appositional constructions on adjective phrase level: ***Immature (21-23 day; 6/group)**, ovariectomized F344 and SD rats..., Ovariectomized (**OVX**) animals...*

Figures 7-10 show fragments of parse trees that correspond to some of the appositional constructions mentioned above.

```
NP [Six AP rhesus monkeys App]
    Six [numeral]
    AP [adult female]
        adult [noun, adjective]
        female [noun, adjective]
    rhesus [noun]
    monkeys [noun, cut_result]
    App [( Macaca mulatta )]
```

Figure 7. A Latin name in an appositional construction

```
NP [A nucleotide insertion App]
   A [determiner, marker]
   nucleotide [namedentity, default]
   insertion [noun]
   App [( CGT-->CAGT )]
      ( [punctuation]
      CGT-->CAGT [namedentity]
      ) [punctuation]
```

Figure 8. Apposition involving a formula

```
NP [Fischer 344 App coNP]
   Fischer [namedentity]
   344 [integer, number]
   App [( F344 )]
      ( [punctuation]
      F344 [namedentity, [Fischer 344]]
      ) [punctuation]
   coNP [and NP]
      and [conjunction]
      NP [Sprague Dawley App rats .]
         Sprague Dawley [namedentity]
         App [( SD )]
            ( [punctuation]
            SD [namedentity, acronym, [Sprague Dawley]]
            ) [punctuation]
         rats [noun, cut_result]
```

Figure 9. Appositions containing integers and names of researchers

```
NP [AP receptor co-regulators App]
    AP [nuclear]
        nuclear [noun, adjective]
        receptor [noun]
        co-regulators [noun, pprt, cut_result, cut_result, hypen_cut]
    App [( SRC1 , p300 , CARM1 , GRIP1 , SPA , REA and Uba3 ) .]
        ( [punctuation]
        SRC1 [namedentity]
        , [punctuation]
        p300 [namedentity]
        , [punctuation]
        CARM1 [namedentity]
        , [punctuation]
        GRIP1 [namedentity]
        , [punctuation]
        SPA [namedentity]
        , [punctuation]
        REA [namedentity]
        and [conjunction]
        Uba3 [namedentity]
        ) [punctuation]
        . [punctuation, terminator]
```

Figure 10. A long coordination of names of biological objects with appositional acronyms

A special case is constituted by appositions that include the whole coordinated phrase, as in *Akt1 deficiency had a profound effect on endometrium and prostate neoplasi*a, **two types of human cancer...** Here, quantifiers are utilized as cues, so the current example can be resolved in a correct way. Still, these constructions cause problems, if a quantifier is not present.

3.3. Coordination

As stated in section 1, complicated coordinated constructions constitute a notorious problem in the text domain under investigation. We decided to approach this challenge in the following way:

– very frequent coordinated phrases have been extracted from a large (35

millions words) corpus (Dura et al. 2006) and stored as multiword entries in the lexicon. Some examples are: *before and after, with and without, treatment and prevention, studied and compared, examined and compared*
- Very frequent PPs that normally function as adverbials on sentence level, for example *at a high frequency, during the experiment, under these conditions*, were stored in the lexicon as adverbs in order to reduce the ambiguity in preposition phrase attachment to coordinated constructions.
- the number of possible constituents in a coordinated phrase is reduced using multiword entries in the lexicon, and by recognition of appositional constructions;
- in the syntactic parser, default rules are used, and the disambiguation problem is left to the semantic component. This means that a preposition phrase or a relative clause that follows a sequence of coordinated nouns is always attached to the last noun. The input to the semantic component is thus consequently formatted, and the decisions concerning the degree of ambiguity are easier to make. For example, if there are more than two embedded preposition phrases after a coordinated construction, the sentence can quite safely be judged as too ambiguous.
- the semantic interpreter employs certain semantic patterns, based on domain knowledge and/or corpus analysis, to the parse trees that have been recognized as ambiguous;
- if the tree cannot be disambiguated by existing semantic patterns, to present the default (syntax-based) solution to the user together with the original sentence and an information about the possible ambiguity.

The syntactic rules handling coordination are relatively straightforward. Coordination both with and without overt conjunctions is allowed between adverbs and adjective phrases. In coordination between noun phrases and preposition phrases, at least one overt coordination marker (before the last constituent) is required. On sentence level, a conjunction, or another overt coordination marker (semicolon, or a comma followed by an adverb, like *however, nevertheless* etc.) is always required. These constraints have of course a certain negative impact on the recall rate, but too few restrictions on coordination led to many cases of wrong phrase delimitation. On the sentence level, constructions with and without subject ellipsis are allowed, although constructions without ellipsis are rather rare.

The semantic interpreter tries to resolve ambiguity in attribute attachment using information stored in the specialized verb lexicon (see

Information extraction from biological texts 241

the example in section 3.3.1 below), and a set of heuristic rules. The main rules are the following:

- given a noun phrase tree containing Noun/Adj$_i$ Noun$i$/Adj$_{i+1}$ ....Conj Noun/Adj$_{n-1}$ Noun$_n$, check if the following combinations are present in the lexicon as multiword units: Noun/Adj$_i$ Noun$_n$, Noun/Adj$_{i+1}$ Noun$_n$...Noun/Adj$_{n-1}$ Noun$_n$. If yes, interpret the sequence as a sequence of compounds, where Noun$_n$ is the head of each compound. This means that a sequence like: *breast, endometrial and thyroid cancer* is interpreted correctly, as "breast cancer **and** endometrial cancer **and** "thyroid cancer", since the names of the different cancer types are stored in the lexicon.
- given a noun phrase tree containing NamedEntity (App)$_i$, NamedEntity (App)$_{i+1}$...Conj Named Entity(App)$_n$ Noun,interpret it as a sequence of compounds where Noun is the head of each compound. This rule results in correct interpretation of phrases like *Ishikawa and ECC-1 cells* (="Ishikawa cells and ECC1 cells") or *Fisher344 (F344) and Sprague Dawley (SD) rats* (="Fisher344 (F344) rats and Sprague Dawley (SD) rats").
- Given a coordinated noun phrase containing both *as well as* and other conjunctions, interpret first the coordinations on both sides of *as well as*
- If there is a preposition phrase attached to a constituent before the conjunction, and a preposition phrase after the last constituent in the coordinated phrase, treat the last preposition phrase as an attribute of the last constituent only. This rule takes care of constructions like ***ADM is a survival factor for certain cancer cells and an indirect suppressor of the immune response.***
- Treat relative clauses introduced by a relative pronoun by default as correlating with the whole coordinated sequence, and postnominal particle constructions as correlating with the last coordinated constituent. Generate a warning for ambiguity.
- If the phrase could be handled by the previous rules, or if there are no attributive phrases, and if all constituents are nouns or named entities, keep the parsing tree unchanged and proceed with further analysis. Otherwise, show the sentence and the parsing tree for the user and generate a warning for ambiguity.

3.3.1. Reducing ambiguity in coordinated constructions – an example

Let us illustrate the strategy for handling coordination using an example. The sentence E2 up-regulated progesterone receptor (PR), glyceraldehyde

3-phosphate dehydrogenase (GAPDH), and transforming growth factor-alpha (TGF-alpha) in both Ishikawa and ECC-1 cells is ambiguous in many ways. The main constituents of the object noun phrase progesterone receptor (PR), glyceraldehyde 3-phosphate dehydrogenase (GAPDH), and transforming growth factor-alpha (TGF-alpha) are correctly identified as 1) progesterone receptor (PR), 2) glyceraldehyde 3-phosphate dehydrogenase (GAPDH), and 3) transforming growth factor-alpha (TGF-alpha) by means of the apposition recognition procedure. The default syntax rule attaches the preposition phrase in both Ishikawa and ECC-1 cells to the last constituent, which is semantically not correct, but which cannot be resolved by syntactic means. Furthermore, the noun phrase both Ishikawa and ECC-1 cells is parsed as a coordination consisting of the named entity Ishikawa and the noun phrase ECC-1 cells. Again, the correct interpretation requires semantic knowledge. The parse tree is shown in Figure 11.

The syntactic tree is searched for biological relations. The main predicate is classified as "bioverb". Thus, the information is regarded as relevant, and the verb up-regulate is extracted. The first argument of the verb is unambiguous and extracted as a whole: E2. The object noun phrase, however, contains both coordinated constituents and a preposition phrase. Such constructions are treated as potentially ambiguous. The coordination preceding noun phrase is extracted, and the output at this point is:

up-regulate(E2, [progesterone receptor (PR)])
up-regulate(E2, [glyceraldehyde 3-phosphate dehydrogenase (GAPDH)]
up-regulate(E2, [transforming growth factor-alpha (TGF-alpha)])

The relation "up-regulate" is classified in the specialized verb lexicon as a subtype of regulation relations. The lexicon contains some additional information about the main biological relations, such as default participants and default place for the interaction. Since the default place for regulation is a cell, the preposition phrase *in both Ishikawa and ECC-1 cells* is interpreted as concerning the whole relation, and since the coordination patterns *NamedEntity1 and NamedEntity2 Noun* normally get the compound interpretation *NamedEntity1 Noun and NamedEntity2 Noun*, the reading *Ishikawa cells and ECC-1 cells* is generated. However, preposition phrase attachment disambiguated on the basis of default lexical information is marked as possibly ambiguous.

Information extraction from biological texts 243

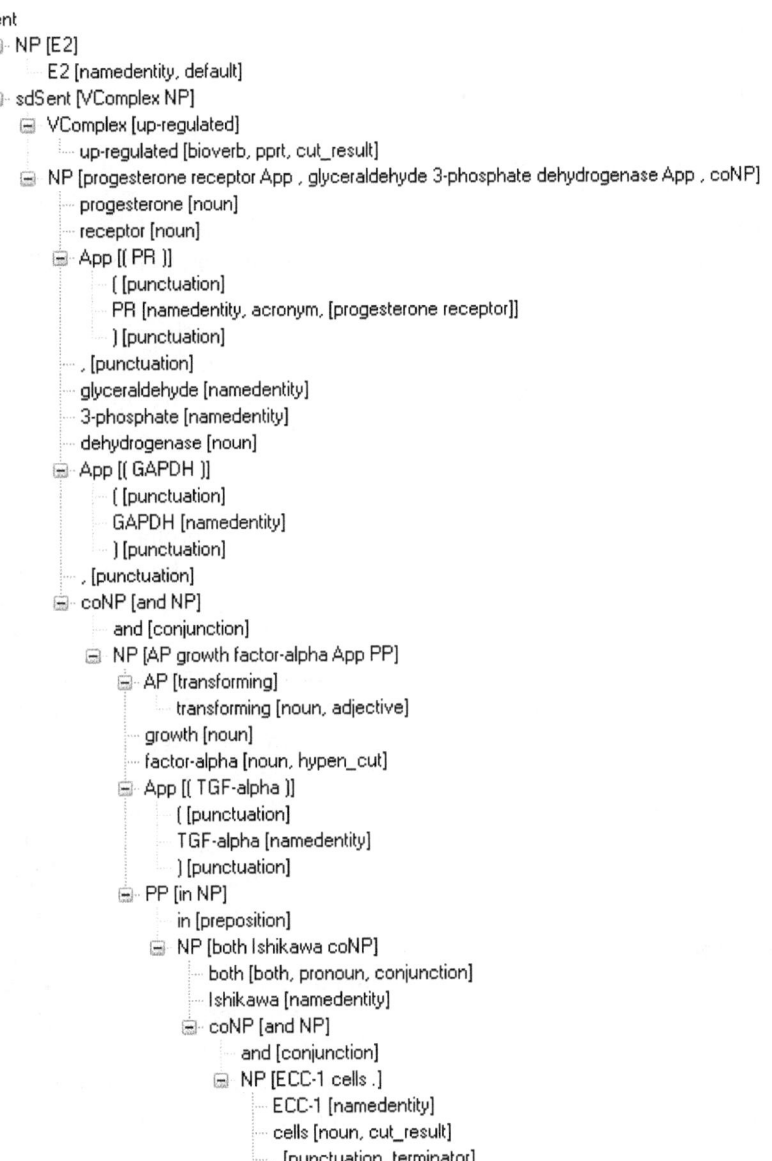

Figure 11. The parse tree corresponding to the sentence *E2 up-regulated progesterone receptor (PR), glyceraldehyde 3-phosphate dehydrogenase (GAPDH), and transforming growth factor-alpha (TGF-alpha) in both Ishikawa and ECC-1 cells*

4. Relations between biological objects – identification and interpretation

The procedure for extraction of biological relations is verb-centred and inspired by Situation Semantics and Cognitive Linguistics (Barwise and Perry 1981a, 1981b, 1983, Cooper 1992, Perry 1988). The goal of the extraction can be formulated as matching situations expressed in the text against a standarized set of "situation types" which is constituted by notions used in the Kyoto Encyclopedia of Genes and Genomes (KEGG; Kanehisa et al. 2004).

In our corpus investigation, we found that nearly all content verbs could be divided into those describing situations in the world of the researchers and those describing situations in the world of biological objects and biological processes.

Events in the world of biological objects and processes were described using cause/effect verbs, participation or resemblance verbs, and verbs denoting the location, existence, appearance or state change of an object or a process. The affect/cause group of verbs was by far the largest in the corpus (~30% of all verb occurrences), and is also the most relevant for the purpose of relation extraction. Verbs in this group often have a direct correspondence with KEGG relations. Commonly occurring examples are verbs such as *affect, activate, control, encode, inactivate, inhibit, induce, regulate, mediate, methylate*. Table 1. shows a fragment of the verb lexicon which functions as the central resource for extraction of relations. Most verbs are directly connected to KEGG relations (methylation, activation, inhibition, indirect effect). Other relations are "state change", "co-occurrence", "aspectual relation" and "causative relation". The last two types are of importance for the parsing and extraction procedure, since they indicate that the relevant biological relation is with a high probability degree encoded by the syntactic direct object of the verb (e.g. ...*cause methylation*). Noun derived from verbs, like *methylation, activation*, are linked to the verbs during the tagging procedure. The lexicon contains also certain syntactic and semantic information, e.g. the form of valence-bound preposition, and the default place of the relation.

Table 1. A fragment of the verb lexicon (simplified)

Verb	Prep	Default place	Relation type
activate		cell	activation
begin			aspectual_relation
bind		gene, chromosome	binding
block		cell	inhibition
cause			causative_relation
coincide	with		co-occurrence
contribute	to		indirect_effect
correlate	with		indirect_effect
decrease			state_change_minus
inhibit		cell	inhibition
methylate		cell	methylation

Most of the events in the world of the researchers were described using verbs of cognition and communication in constructs such as 'Researcher Verb Object/Process' (e.g. *analyze, examine, investigate, study, deduce, detect, find*), 'Researcher V Study/Result' (*present, restrict, extend, carry out*), or 'Object/Process is Past Participle' (e.g. *know, understand, consider*) Another group referring to the world of the researcher are verbs of manipulation in constructs such as 'Researcher Verb Object' (e.g. *add, expose, extract, generate, infect, screen, cultivate, rearrange*) or 'Researcher V Tool to/for Process' (e.g. *use, employ*). The manipulation events are not of interest for the current purpose: the potential users are primarily interested in the results of the experiments, not in the design. While sentences with manipulation verbs should be disregarded, the verbs of cognition and communication may play a role for the extraction results. These verbs express either intentional (*we hypothesise that..., we claim...*) or factual (*our results show that... our results indicate that...*) aspects of the situation that is of interest (Perry 1988) and some of them shall be represented in the output (for the time being, we represent three values: hypothesis, negation and neutral claim).

The extraction algorithm is based on a recursive search in the disambiguated parse tree, starting with the highest predicate (VComplex) node. The details are presented in Olsson, Gawronska, and Erlendsson (2006).

4. Conclusions and future work

The technical modifications and the improvement of rules handling named entities, appositions, and coordination, were tested on a corpus of previously unseen medical abstracts, selected from PubMed using the keywords "endometrial cancer" and "rat" (in conjunction). The corpus consisted of 264 abstracts, i.e. approximately 2640 sentences. We could state that the system was considerably more robust than the prototype: 78% of sentences were parsed (the recall rate of the prototype was slightly above 60%), and the speed was 100 times higher. The precision rate was slightly lower: out of the parsed sentences, 25% were parsed partially (the main difference between the Prolog Definite Clause Grammar parser and the C# parser is the fact that the latter allows partially parsed trees). An analysis of the partially parsed sentences revealed that the problems were due to the uneven quality of the general English lexicon. The search in the lexicon is less time-consuming than searching WordNet; however, we noticed cases of wrong word classification. Given the quite repetitive vocabulary of the biomedical abstracts, it is understandable that some cases of wrong lexical classification may generate a considerable number of parsing errors.

There was definitely an improvement in parsing coordinated constructions and appositional constructions.

The semantic part of the system is still under development, so a proper evaluation was not possible. However, our informants (biologists) regarded the modified format of the output (relations between single objects instead of relations between whole coordinated noun phrases) as a clear advantage.

The conclusion to be drawn from the current results is that a rule-based information extraction system relying on syntactic and semantic knowledge can in fact be quite fast and robust. General linguistic knowledge should, however, be combined with corpus studies during the development of the system. It is important to gain knowledge about the language of a particular domain and gather most frequent collocational and syntactic patterns from a domain-specific corpus.

The goals for further work include, of course, lexicon improvement. Furthermore, the semantic interpreter must be fully developed and properly evaluated. The next important question will be to evaluate the user interface and to gather information about the relevance of the extracted relations, using competent biologists as informants.

Acknowledgements

This work has been supported by the Knowledge Foundation (KK-stiftelsen) within the Information Fusion Research Profile at the University College of Skövde.
Many thanks to my colleague Björn Erlendsson for all programming and technical support.

References

Barwise, Jon and John Perry
    1981a   Shifting Situations and Shaken Attitudes. Linguistics and Philosophy vol. 8: 105 - 161.
    1981b   Situations and Attitudes. *Journal of Philosophy* vol. 77: 668–91.
    1983   *Situations and Attitudes*. Cambridge: MIT-Bradford.
Becker, K.G., Hosack, D.A., Dennis Jr, G., Lempicki, R.A., Bright, T.J., Cheadle, C. and Engel, J.
    2003   PubMatrix: a tool for multiplex literature mining. *BMC Bioinformatics* 4:61.
Chaussabel, D. and Sher, A.
    2002   Mining microarray expression data by literature profiling. *Genome Biol.* 3 (10): research0055.1–research0055.16.
Cooper, Robin
    1992   A Working Person's Guide to Situation Theory, in S. Hansen and F. Sorensen, eds., *Semantic Representation and Interpretation* Fredericksberg: Samfundslitteratur.
Darasiela, Nikolai, Anton Yuryev, Sergei Egorov, Svetalana Novichkova, Alexander Nikitin,. and Ilya Mazo
    2004   Extracting human protein interactions from MEDLINE using a full-*sentence* parser. *Bioinformatics* 20 (5): 604-611.
Dura, Elzbieta, Björn Erlendsson, Barbara Gawronska, and Björn Olsson
    2006   Towards Information Fusion in Pathway Evaluation: Encoding of Relations in Biomedical Texts. *Proceedings of the 9th International Conference on Information Fusion*, Florence, 10-13 July 2006. 240-247.
Gawronska, Barbara, and Björn Erlendsson
    2005   Syntactic, Semantic and Referential Patterns in Biomedical Texts: towards in-depth text comprehension for the purpose of bioinformatics. In Sharp, B. (ed.): *Natural Language Understanding and Cognitive Science. Proceedings of the 2nd International Workshop on Natural Language Understanding and*

Cognitive Science NLUCS 2005, Miami, USA, May 2005. 68-77

Gawronska, Barbara, Björn Erlendsson, and Björn Olsson
2005   Tracking Biological Relations in Text: A Referent Grammar Approach. Biomedical Ontologies and Text Processing *Proceedings of Workshop held in conjunction with the European Conference on Computational Biology, ECCB 2005*, Madrid, Spain, Sept 28, 2005.

Gawronska, Barbara, Niklas Torstensson, and Björn Erlendsson
2004   Defining and Classifying Space Builders for Information Extraction. In Sharp, B. (ed.): *Proceedings of NLUCS- (Natural Language Understanding and Cognitive Science)*, Porto, Portugal, April 2004. 15-27

Jelier, R., Jenster, G., Dorssers, L.C.J., van der Eijk, C.C., van Mulligen, E.M., Mons, B. and Kors, J.A.
2005   Co-occurrence based meta-analysis of scientific texts: retrieving biological relationships between genes. *Bioinformatics* 21 (9): 2049–2058.

Jenssen, Tor-Kristian., Astrid Laegreid,. Jan Komorowski, and Eivind Hovig
2001   A literature network of human genes for high-throughput analysis of gene expression. *Nature Genetics* 28: 21-28..

Kanehisa, M., Goto, S., Kawashima, S., Okuno, Y., and Hattori, M.
2004   The KEGG resources for deciphering the genome. *Nucleic Acids Res.* 32, D277-D280.

McDonald, Daniel M., Hsinchun Chen, Gondy Leroy, and Hua Su
2004   Combining Ontologies and Grammatical Relations to Yield Diverse Semantic Relations from Biomedical Texts, *Proceedings of Pacific Symposium on Biocomputing*. January 2004

Miller, George A.
1995   WordNet: An on-line lexical database of English. In *Communications of ACM*, Vol. 38, Nr. 11: 39 – 41.

Narayanan, Ajit, Ed Keedwell., and Björn Olsson
2002   Artificial Intelligence techniques for bioinformatics. *Applied Bioinformatics* Vol. 1 Nr. 4: 191-222.

Ng, S.-K. and Wong, M.
1999   Toward Routine Automatic Pathway Discovery from On-Line Scientific Text Abstracts, *Genome Informatics* 10:104-112.

Novichkova, Svetalana, Sergei Egorov, and Nikolai Daraselia
2003   MedScan, a natural language processing engine for MEDLINE abstracts. In *Bioinformatics* vol. 19:13: 1699-1706.

Olsson, Björn, Barbara Gawronska, and Björn Erlendsson
2006   Deriving pathway maps from text analysis using a grammar-based approach. Journal of *Bioinformatics and Computational Biology* 4(2): 483-502.

Ono, T., Hishigaki, H., Tanigami, A. and Takagi, T.
  2001   Automated extraction of information on protein-protein interactions from the biological literature. *Bioinformatics* 17: 155-161
Perry, John
  1998   Situation Semantics. *Routledge Encyclopedia of Philosophy*. London: Routledge
Pustejovsky, James, and J. Castano
  2002   Robust relational parsing over biomedical literature: Extracting inhibit relations, *Proceedings of PSB* 2002, Hawaii, USA, 362-373.
Rindflesch, T., Tanabe, L., Weinstein, J., Hunter, L.
  2000   EDGAR: Extraction of drugs, genes, and relations from biomedical literature. In *Proceedings of PSB* 2000, Hawaii, USA, 517-528.
Stapley, Benjamin and Gerald Benoit
  2000   Biobibliometrics: Information retrieval and visualization from co-occurrences of gene names in Medline abstracts. In *Proceedings of PSB* 2000, Hawaii, USA, 529-540.
Tanabe, L., Scherf, U., Smith, L.H., Lee, J.K., Hunter, L. and Weinstein, J.N.
  1999   MedMiner: an Internet text-mining tool for biomedical information, with application to gene expression profiling. *Biotechniques*. 27(6):1210-1214.
Wren, J.D., Bekeredjian, R., Stewart, J.A., Shohet, R.V., and Garner H.R.
  2004   Knowledge discovery by automated identification and ranking of implicit relationships. *Bioinformatics* 20: 389–398.

Conversation

Dialogue for one

Rodger Kibble

1. Introduction

A celebrated contribution to the literature on dialogue (Cohen and Levesque 1990) bears the title "Rational interaction as the basis for communication". In this paper I do not propose to engage with the details of that proposal, but will instead explore some implications of adopting the opposite slogan: *communication as the basis for rational interaction*. The line of argument will be as follows:

1. Only communicating agents can be said to have a proper grasp of concepts and propositions;

2. The ability to participate in dialogue is a prerequisite for the ability to construct a reasoned argument or explanation;

3. Extended argumentative or explanatory monologue can be reconstructed as the outcome of an "inner dialogue" with the contributions of the virtual interlocutor partly or wholly suppressed;

4. Coherence relations in text, such as those described by Mann and Thompson (1987), Taboada and Mann (2006) can be analysed as by-products of sequences of implicit dialogue moves rather than as primitive operators.

The first three points are not novel in themselves, though it may be unusual to bring them together in this way. For instance, van Kuppevelt (1995) argues in some detail that the topic-comment structure of texts can be analysed in terms of implicit questions and sub-questions, but does not link this analysis to the topic of linguistic rationalism. On the other hand, philosophers of language who have supported point 1, such as Davidson and Brandom, are generally content to illustrate their arguments with rather brief fragments of constructed dialogue, rather than embarking on close textual analysis. The specific proposal in point (4) was previously advanced by Kibble (2006a).

2. Linguistic rationalism

Philosophers have often claimed that language is a pre- or co-requisite for rationality. Indeed, Deligiorgi (2002: 144) finds in Kant the notion that

> rational autonomy cannot be exercised by a solitary thinker

but depends on the communication of publicly criticizeable judgments. Among late 20th century philosophers, Hamblin (1970) holds that a rational agent may entertain inconsistent beliefs but the hallmark of rationality is the ability to appreciate and remedy inconsistenties *when they are pointed out* by another agent. Davidson (2001) claims that rational creatures are those that hold propositional attitudes, and it is only possible to determine whether an agent has these attitudes by communicating with it.

> One belief requires many beliefs, and beliefs demand other basic attitudes such as intentions, desires and, if I am tight, the gift of tongues.
>
> (Davidson 2001: 96)

For instance: to believe that a cat has run up a particular tree involves many beliefs about cats and trees in general, and it is unsafe to attribute such an unverifiable complex mental state to a dog. For Brandom (1994: Brandom (2000) rationality consists in being able to articulate reasons for one's actions and propositional claims in response to challenges from other agents, and to acknowledge consequential commitments arising from those actions and claims.

> The rationality that qualifies us as *sapients* ... can be identified with being a player in the social, implicitly normative game of offering and assessing, producing and consumint, reasons.
>
> (Brandom 1994: 81)

Brandom's claim is that both *formal*, logical reasoning as exhibited in (4) below and prudential or *instrumental* reasoning are secondary to content-based material inference:

> For the propositional contents of the intentional states appealed to in practical reasoning presuppose assertional-inferential proprieties, and hence linguistic social practice.
>
> (Brandom 1994: 231)

2.1. Expressive role of logical vocabulary

A key component of Brandom's linguistic rationalism is *logical expressivism*: the claim that the ability to reason logically is parasitic on the mastery of *material* content-based inference. So for example, an agent who assents to the claim (1-a) is thereby committed to the claim (1-b):

(1)   a.   Brighton is to the east of Worthing.
       b.   Worthing is to the west of Brighton.

To endorse this kind of inferential move is simply to demonstrate an understanding of the terms *east* and *west*, or to conform to the conventional uses of these terms within a speech community. Example (2) illustrates inference involving *incompatibility* between concepts:

(2)   a.   John either lives in Worthing or Eastbourne.
       b.   Worthing is to the west of Brighton.
       c.   John lives east of Brighton.
       d.   John lives in Eastbourne.

In this case, anyone committed to (2-a) - (2-c) is thereby committed to (2-d) as a consequence of the incompatibility between *X is east of Y* and *X is west of Y* (discounting circumnavigation).

The function of logical constructs such as negation and the conditional is to *make explicit* these tacit inferences which make up our understanding of concepts. That is, an agent needs to be proficient in producing and recognising inferences like the above before it can proceed to deductions like (3) and (4):

(3)   If Worthing is to the west of Brighton, then Brighton is to the east of Worthing.

(4)   If John lives in Brighton or Worthing, and he does not live in Worthing, then he lives in Brighton.

Example (3) is an instance of materially correct reasoning, using the conditional to make explicit the semantic relation between *east* and *west*. Example (4) illustrates a special case of material, content-based reasoning which is also logically valid, since it will remain valid under any uniform substitution of non-logical vocabulary.

2.2. Expressive role of discourse connectives

We can generalise Brandom's expressivism to cover so-called discourse connectives. Sentential or phrasal connectives associated with coherence relations can often be seen as expressing a weak form of material inference. For instance if speaker A observes that (5-a) is the case, the likelihood that a hearer B will adopt the commitment (5-b) is increased:

(5)   a.   A: It's raining.
        b.   B: I shall wear my waterproof coat.

B can also act on this inference without expressing it, in the following way for example: B is about to go shopping, notices dark clouds on the horizon, and so takes care to stow a waterproof in their rucksack. This inference can be expressed, made explicit, with a suitable discourse connective:

(6)   It's raining, *so* I shall wear my waterproof coat.

Discourse connectives (including logical operators) may operate across utterances/speakers:

(7)   a.   A. The president is going to veto the environmental bill.
        b.   B Why would he do that?
        c.   A. *Because* he supports big business.

(8)   a.   A. The president's going to sign the environmental bill.
        b.   B. *Even though* he supports big business?
        c.   A. Yes, *because* he's convinced by the scientific evidence of climate change.

(9)   a.   A. The president tends to support big business.
        b.   B. *Nevertheless*, he's going to sign the environmental bill
        c.   B. *because* he's convinced by the scientific evidence of climate change.

(10)   a.   A. *Suppose* John either lives in Worthing or Brighton, only he doesn't live in Worthing?
        b.   B. *Then* he lives in Brighton.

Note that the above examples would still be intelligible and acceptable with the italicised content removed (with slight changes in wording in some cases). The connectives do not contribute to the substantive content of the text but are a kind of meta-operator, signalling how the interlocutor is supposed to process the content of the utterance. Thus B's contribution to (8) signals an apparent incompatibility between his utterance and A's preceding statement; B's utterance is thus to be construed as a *challenge* and A's following utterance as a *response* to B's challenge.

2.3. Pre-emptive role of discourse connectives

The picture of linguistic practice that has been somewhat hastily sketched distinguishes the following modes of communication:

1. The simplest mode consists of an exchange of atomic speech acts such as assertions, questions and challenges, with no explicit signalling of the relations between successive acts. Although formally simple, this mode requires interlocutors to carry out some reasoning to assess the relevance of successive utterances to the presumed discourse goals.
2. as above, but additionally using discourse markers to signal inferential moves as in examples (7) and (8).
3. The final stage involves sentences of arbitrary complexity, constructed using logical and other discourse connectives.

   (11)   The president is going to veto the environmental bill
          because he supports big business.

   (12)   The president's going to sign the environmental bill
          even though he supports big business,
          because he's convinced by the scientific evidence of climate change.

The link between these styles of practice is *pre-emption*: a speaker who constructs complex utterances like (11) and (12) is able to anticipate likely objections or questions and so short-cut the need for dialogues such as (7) or (8). Further examples can be seen in the comparison between the (a) and (b) sequences below:

(13)   a.   A: It's going to rain. B: So? A: You should take an umbrella.

       b.   A: It's going to rain, *so* you should take an umbrella.

(14)   a.   A: You should take an umbrella. B: Why? A: It's going to rain.

       b.   A: You should take an umbrella, *because* it's going to rain.

3. Extended monologue as implicit dialogue

The previous sections have argued that certain types of persuasive monologue can be reconstructed as the outcome of an implicit dialogue and has sketched a route from simple dialogues to complex monologue. This by no means implies that such a route has actually been followed either in the historic development of language or in the acquisition of communicative competence by human infants, though this is a plausible conjecture. The claim put forward in this paper is less ambitious: we can exploit these connections between dialogue and monologue in the interests of methodological parsimony, in that certain discourse relations do not need to be specified explicitly but can be analysed as a by-product of specific dialogue moves.

Some fundamental questions that arise are:

- can every monologue be analysed as an implicit dialogue; or alternatively, can all coherence relations be modelled in terms of dialogue moves?

- can every dialogue be transformed into a monologue?

The first question will remain open; in this paper I concentrate on *presentaional* relations which seem to have a natural connection with dialogue moves, such as MOTIVATE, EVIDENCE, JUSTIFY. The answer to the second question is almost certainly negative. I will argue in particular that a key requirement is *nuclearity*: this assumes that the interlocutors have some joint purpose, which may be to see to it that some task is carried out, or to arrive at the truth (or reasonable consensus) on some matter of fact or judgment.

3.1. Nuclearity in dialogue and monologue

One of the central claims of RST is that a coherent text can be recursively decomposed into spans called *Nucleus* and *Satellite*, where the Nucleus is more central to the author's purpose and material in the Satellite is ancillary. In dialogue terms, the Nucleus would be the proponent's central claim or instruction, while any challenges or queries from the hearer would make up satellites. Both nuclear and satellite components can themselves contain sub-nuclei and satellites; for instance a proponent's response to a hearer's challenge could be classed as a satellite. For example if we compare (8) and (12) above: the former can be analysed as

Cause

Nucleus

    Concession

    Nucleus (8-a) A. The president's going to sign the environmental bill.

    Satellite (8-b) B. *Even though* he supports big business?

Satellite (8-c) A. Yes, *because* he's convinced by the scientific evidence of climate change.

This analysis can be carried over into (12), repeated and marked up as (15):

(15) $<Nuc><Nuc>$ The president's going to sign the environmental bill, $</Nuc>$
$<Sat>$ even though he supports big business, $</Sat></Nuc>$
$<Sat>$ because he's convinced by the scientific evidence of climate change. $</Sat>$

3.2. Presentational relations

This section briefly outlines the presentational relations as defined by (Mann and Taboada 2006), where N is *Nucleus*, S is *Satellite*, W is *Writer/Speaker/Author...* and R is *Reader/Hearer/Recipient....*

Antithesis

"N and S are in contrast ... comprehending S and the incompatibility between the situations increases R's positive regard for N"

Background

"S increases the ability of R to comprehend an element in N"

Concession

"W acknowledges a potential or apparent incompatibility between N and S; recognizing the compatibility between N and S increases R's positive regard for N"

Enablement

"R comprehending S increases R's potential ability to perform the action in N"

Evidence

"R's comprehending S increases R's belief of N"

Justify

"R's comprehending S increases R's readiness to accept W's right to present N"

Motivate

"Comprehending S increases R's desire to perform action in N"

Preparation

"S precedes N in the text; S tends to make R more ready, interested or oriented for reading N"

Restatement

"S restates N, where S and N are of comparable bulk; N is more central to W's purposes than S is."

Summary

"S presents a restatement of the content of N, that is shorter in bulk"

3.3. Selected dialogue moves

I will assume an Information State model of dialogue, specified as simply as possible for the purposes of this paper, in the spirit of e.g., Larsson and Cooper (2000) though differing in technical details. The IS consists of a record of utterances in a dialogue and a triple of public *commitment stores* for each interlocutor:

CStore contains *acknowledged* propositional or practical commitments

PCStore contains *pending* commitments which the agent has not explicitly or implicitly accepted.

DCStore is a *stack* containing *disputed* commitments

I will further assume there are only two participants in a dialogue. Subscripts identify the commitment stores of Speaker and Hearer, .g. $CStore_S$, $PCStore_H$. In the following definitions, lower-case Greek letters $\phi, \psi \ldots$ are proposiitonal variables while upper-case letters $\Phi, \Psi \ldots$ stand for speech acts or non-communicative actions. I further assume a cooperative dialogue protocol such that agents will always answer a question whenever they are able.

assert(S, H, ϕ)

- $CStore_S = CStore_S \cup \{\phi\}$
- $PCStore_H = PCStore_H \cup \{\phi\}$

challenge$(S, H, \phi/\Phi, (\psi))$

S challenges either the proposition ϕ, or the appropriateness of the speech act Φ. S optionally asserts ψ which is incompatible with ϕ. Condition: $\phi \in CStore_H$

- $PCStore_S = PCStore_S - \{\phi\}$
- $DCStore_S = [\phi \mid DCStore_S]$
- ($CStore_S = CStore_S \cup \{\psi\}$)
- ($PCStore_H = PCStore_H \cup \{\psi\}$)

endorse(S, H, ϕ)

S agrees to a commitment resulting from H's previous assertion or instruction.

- $PCStore_S = PCStore_S - \{\phi\}$
- $CStore_S = CStore_S \cup \{\phi\}$

If $DCStore_S \neq \emptyset$:

- $DCStore'_S = \texttt{tail}(DCStore_S)$
- $\psi = \texttt{head}(DCStore_S)$
- $PCStore_S = PCStore_S \cup \{\psi\}$

instruct(S, H, α)

S attempts to bestow a *practical* commitment on H.

- $CStore_S = CStore_S \cup \{willdo(H, \alpha)\}$
- $PCStore_H = PCStore_H \cup \{willdo(H, \alpha)\}$

query$((S, H, \phi/\Phi)$

This encompasses clarification questions as well as *wh-* and *yes/no* questions directed at H's most recent utterance. As with **challenge**, a query may be directed at a speech act itself or the propositional content.

- $PCStore_S = PCStore_S - \{\phi\}$
- $DCStore_S = [\phi \mid DCStore_S]$

retract(S, H, ϕ)

S informs H that S is withdrawing commitment to ϕ.

- $CStore_S = CStore_S - \{\phi\}$

ϕ is removed from $PCStore_H$ and $DCStore_H$ if present.

Dialogue protocol

1. An assertion or instruction adds a commitment to H's PCStore. H should respond with an action that clears the PCStore:
   - **endorse** the commitment, moving it from PCStore to CStore;
   - **query** or **challenge** the commitment, deleting it from PCStore.

2. A query or challenge moves a commitment from PCStore to DCStore.

- H should respond by either retracting the commitment or providing a supporting assertion.
- If *S* endorses H's subsequent utterance, this commitment is moved back to *PCStore* and *S* must once again either endorse or challenge it.
- If *S* queries or challenges H's subsequent utterance, the original commitment will remain on the stack "beneath" the newly disputed commitment.

3. No dialogue can properly terminate until *PCStore* and *DCStore* are empty.

In contrast with Kibble (2006b: Kibble (2006a), we do not emply a specific **respond** act: the protocol and update operations are intended to allow assertions and other acts to also function as responses.

3.4. Reconstructing rhetorical relations

The general strategy for reconstructing rhetorical relations on the basis of dialogue moves is to analyse certain kinds of monologue as the edited and possibly re-ordered outcome of a dialogue between two virtual agents, the Planner *Pl* and the Critic *Cr*. The Critic incorporates a "user model" representing the state of knowledge of a specific or typical interlocutor. In terms of the update operations outlined above, a trace of the stacking operations on $DCStore_{Cr}$ provides the basic flow of the argument. The following examples illustrate the use of various presentational relations (with one instance of CAUSE along with the putative underlying dialogues. Generated text may also include the content of *Cr*'s challenges or queries as can be seen in example (19) below. Further details of text planning algorithms can be found in (Kibble 2006a; Kibble 2006c).

(16) You should take an umbrella. It's going to rain. (MOTIVATE)
   a. **assert**(*Pl, Cr, umbrella*)
   b. **challenge**(*Cr, Pl, umbrella, -*)
   c. **assert**(*Pl, Cr, rain*)
   d. **endorse**(*Cr, Pl, rain, -*)
   e. **endorse**(*Cr, Pl, umbrella, -*)

(17) The president is pro-big business. He appoints industry lobbyists to public bodies. (EVIDENCE)
   a. **assert**(*Pl, Cr, pro − biz*)
   b. **challenge**(*Cr, Pl, pro − biz, -*)

c. **assert**(*Pl, Cr, lobbyists*)
d. **endorse**(*Cr, Pl, lobbyists, -*)
e. **endorse**(*Cr, Pl, pro − biz, -*)

(18) The president is going to veto the environmental bill. I read about it in *Mother Jones*. (JUSTIFY) That's a progressive monthly magazine. (BACKGROUND)

a. **assert**(*Pl, Cr, sign*)
b. **challenge**(*Cr, Pl, sign, -*)
c. **assert**(*Pl, Cr, MoJo*)
d. **query**(*Cr, Pl, MoJo*)
e. **assert**(*Pl, Cr, magazine*)
f. **endorse**(*Cr, Pl, magazine, -*)
   endorse(*Cr, Pl, MoJo, -*)
   endorse(*Cr, Pl, sign, -*)

(19) The president is going to sign the environmental bill, even though he's pro-big business. (CONCESSION) He's convinced by the scientific evidence of climate change. (CAUSE)

a. **assert**(*Pl, Cr, sign*)
b. **challenge**(*Cr, Pl, sign, pro − biz*)
c. **assert**(*Pl, Cr, science*)
d. **endorse**(*Cr, Pl, science, -*)
e. **endorse**(*Cr, Pl, sign, -*)

(20) Secure the print head by lining up the hole in the print head with the green post on the printer carriage. (ENABLEMENT/RESTATEMENT) (cf Larsson and Cooper (2000))

a. ```S: secure the print head.```
b. ```U: how?```
c. ```S: Line up the hole in the print head with the green post on the printer carriage.```
d. ```U: right, OK```

4. Conclusions and future work

This paper has tried to show how certain coherence relations in text, notably the Presentational relations of RST, can be modelled as by-products of an "inner" dialogue with a virtual agent. The inspiration for this work is the notion that human reasoning is a fundamentally social activity, and even the solitary reasoner must have some hypothetical discussant or student in mind. This leads to a conjecture that the various devices available for structuring coherent text have their counterparts in habitual sequences of dialogue moves, and that competence in the latter is a prerequisite for constructing a reasoned monological argument. The particular dialogue model employed belongs to the Information State family, but has particular characteristics stemming from the influence of Walton and Krabbe (1995) and Brandom (1994) in that it is designed to use the same data structures to keep track of both *practical* and *propositional* commitments.

This paper has not discussed details of the text planning algorithms which determine the order in which the constituent propositions are realised in a text. Other work (Kibble 2006a; Kibble 2006c) presents algorithms for generating text in different orders while preserving the underlying rhetorical structure as in (21) below:

(21)   a.   It's going to rain. I heard it on the BBC. You should take an umbrella.
           b.   You should take an umbrella. I heard the BBC weather forecast. It's going to rain.
           c.   You should take an umbrella. It's going to rain. I heard it on the BBC.

Although I hope to have made a plausible case for the particular set of RST relations discussed above, the research questions raised at the start of Section 3 remain open. It is practically certain that not every dialogue can be transformed into a monologue, but it remains to be seen whether the methods of this paper can be applied to other relations, in particular the "semantic" or *Subject Matter* relations.

As mentioned in the Introduction, the idea of modelling monologue in terms of an underlying implicit goes back at least to (van Kuppevelt 1993; van Kuppevelt 1995). I believe the proposals in this paper to be largely complementary to this earlier work; some key differences are:

- van Kuppevelt's primary concern is to account for the overall topic-comment structure of a text, while this paper addresses a lower-level task of reconstructing particular rhetorical relations in terms of specific dialogue moves;

- part of van Kuppevelt's argument is that the syntactic and prosodic characteristics of a text remain intact when topic-forming questions are removed, whereas in this paper the outcome of the inner dialogue is taken to be an abstract discourse plan which may be re-ordered, pruned or otherwise modified prior to linguistic realisation;

Finally, the notion of "disputed commitments" is inescapably reminiscent of Ginzburg's *Questions under Discussion* or *QUD* (Ginzburg 1996) and a detailed comparison will be undertaken in future work.

References

Brandom, Robert
- 1994 *Making it Explicit*. Cambridge, Massachusetts and London: Harvard University Press.
- 2000 *Articulating Reasons*. Cambridge, Massachusetts and London: Harvard University Press.

Cohen, Philip, and Hector Levesque
- 1990 Rational interaction as the basis for communication. In *Intentions in Communication*, Philip Cohen, Jerry Morgan, and Martha Pollack (eds.), 221 – 55. Cambridge, Massachusetts and London: MIT Press.

Davidson, Donald
- 1982/2001 Rational animals (1982). In *Subjective, Intersubjective, Objective*, 95 – 105. Oxford University Press.

Deligiorgi, Katerina
- 2002 Universalisability, publicity and communitcation: Kant's conception of reason. *European Journal of Philosophy*, vol. 10.2.

Ginzburg, Jonathan
- 1996 Dynamics and the semantics of dialogue. Chapter 15 of *Logic, Language and Computation vol. 1*, Jerry Seligman, and Dag Westerstahl (eds.), 221 – 237. Stanford: CSLI Publications.

Hamblin, Charles
- 1970 *Fallacies*. London: Methuen.

Kibble, Rodger
- 2006a Dialectical text planning. Floriana Grasso, Rodger Kibble, and Chris Reed (eds.), *Proceedings of 6th Workshop on Computational Models of Natural Argumentation*. Riva del Garda, Italy.
- 2006b Reasoning about propositional commitments in dialogue. *Research on Language and Computation* 4: 179 – 202.
- 2006c Generating coherence relations via internal dialogue. Rodger Kibble, Paul Piwek, and Ielka van der Sluis (eds.), *Proceedings of the ESSLLI 2006 workshop: Coherence in Generaton and Dialogue*. University of Malaga, Spain. Extended version under review for journal publication.

Larsson, Staffan, and Robin Cooper
- 2000 An information state approach to natural interactive dialogue. *Proceedings of LREC 2000*. Athens.

Mann, William C., and Maite Taboada
- 2006 RST website. `http://www.sfu.ca/rst`. Visited Feb 27th 2006.

Mann, William C., and Sandra A. Thompson
    1987   Rhetorical structure theory: A theory of text organization. Technical Report, Marina del Rey, CA: Information Sciences Institute.

Taboada, Maite, and William Mann
    2006   Rhetorical Structure Theory: Looking back and moving ahead. *Discourse Studies* 8(3): 423 – 459.

van Kuppevelt, Jan
    1993   Intentionality in a topical approach of discourse structure. Owen Rambow (ed.), *Proceedings of ACL Workshop: Intentionality and Structure in Discourse Relations*.
    1995   Discourse structure, topicality and questioning. *Journal of Linguistics* 31: 109 – 147.

Walton, Douglas, and Eric Krabbe
    1995   *Commitment in dialogue*. Albany: State University of New York Press.

A question of cost

Ian Lewin

Did you threaten to overrule him?
I was not entitled to instruct Derek Lewis and I did not instruct him.
Did you threaten to overrule him?
The truth of the matter is that Mr. Marriot was not suspended-
Did you threaten to overrule him?
I did not overrule Derek Lewis-
Did you threaten to overrule him?
-I took advice on what I could or could not do-
Did you threaten to overrule him?
-and acted scrupulously in accordance with that advice. I did not overrule Derek Lewis-
Did you threaten to overrule him?
-Mr. Marriot was not suspended
Did you threaten to overrule him?
I have accounted for my decision to dismiss Derek Lewis-
Did you threaten to overrule him?
-in great detail before the House of Commons-
I note you're not answering the question whether you threatened to overrule him.
Well, the important aspect of this which it's very clear to bear in mind-
I'm sorry. I'm going to be frightfully rude but, I'm sorry, it's a straight yes or no question and a straight yes or no answer, Did you threaten to overrule him?
I discussed this matter with Derek Lewis. I gave him the benefit of my opinion. I gave him the benefit of my opinion in strong language, but I did not instruct him because I was not, er, entitled to instruct him. I was entitled to express my opinion and that is what I did.
With respect, that is not answering the question of whether you threatened to overrule him.
It's dealing with the relevant point which was what I was entitled to do and what I was not entitled to do, and I have dealt with this in detail before the House of Commons and before the select committee.
But with respect you haven't answered the question of whether you threatened to overrule him.
Well, you see, the question is...

(Extract of Paxman versus Howard: *BBC Newsnight* May 13th 1997)

1. Introduction

In a famous televised political interview, Michael Howard, former British Home Secretary, avoided answering a question put to him on twelve successive occasions. Howard succeeded in never directly addressing the question of threat, but the overall cost of the interview is a matter of some dispute. Howard failed in his immediate party leadership bid in 1997. Memories of the interview were revived during his subsequent unsuccessful bid to become Prime Minister in 2005.

Howard could have answered the question on any one of those twelve occasions. He simply chose not to. Assuming this was a rational calculation, of sorts, then, on each occasion, the utility of the direct answer was simply outweighed by other considerations. The interviewer, Paxman, presumably also made a series of rational calculations. Perhaps the answer to this particular question was simply of supreme importance; perhaps there was no reasonable chance of obtaining the answer by a more roundabout route; perhaps the value of highlighting the refusal to answer was just too great; perhaps the appearance of rudeness through insistent repetition was of insufficiently great consequence. Conversation is a calculated and cost-conscious activity.

2. Information states in dialogue modelling

The Information State Update approach to dialogue modelling is a highly abstract characterization of dialogue semantics. Contributions to a dialogue are treated like programs in dynamic logic: they both *update* a dialogue state and are *interpretable* in the light of a previous state. What is a state? In an ecumenical spirit which characterizes much of Robin Cooper's work, a state *can* be almost anything you like. But the very comparison and contrast of the different sorts of state that different theories give rise to enables their real differences to be brought to light, under one umbrella, and away from the murky rain that pours on all outside. The state characterization may also lead to computer implementations.

Agents have two main roles in this abstract picture: to use state in interpreting contributions; and to make state by generating contributions. A great deal of research has concentrated on the former question. What must a state look like if I am to be able to interpret *this* sort of conversational offering? And what will it look like once I have both interpreted and incorporated it? I want to ask: what must a state look like, if I am to choose to make *this* sort of conversational offering? And what will it look like once I have made it? My focus

$$\begin{bmatrix} \text{FROM} \\ \text{DEPARTURE-TIME} \\ \text{TO} \\ \text{MODE OF TRAVEL} \end{bmatrix}$$

Figure 1. Travel Frame

1. [S] When do you want to leave?
2. [U] *I want to be in Gothenburg at 8.*

Figure 2. Unsolicited information

will be on the role of the dialogue state in spoken dialogue systems, partly because this is a useful (and largely externally imposed) constraint on the extent of the material to consider, partly because the results may be practically useful and partly because designing and building programs to hold conversations (in highly restrictive domains) is almost as much fun as deriving truth conditions and entailments of sentences (in highly restrictive domains).

Although the simplest dialogue systems are encodable directly in a network formalism with states and transitions, and choices over dialogue moves could be encoded in a nondeterministic network, it is actually more enlightening to begin with a frame based (or slot-and-filler) architecture. This is traditionally the "next step up" from a network formalism. The commercially employed VoiceXML dialogue specification uses one version of frames (Oshry et al. 2006). An example frame for the travel planning scenario is shown in figure 1. In VoiceXML, a question is associated with each attribute. The question can be put if a value for the attribute is required. The whole frame may also be associated with a question, to be put when the frame first comes into focus. The frame stays in focus until all attributes have received values. The VoiceXML question selection algorithm is: if the frame is already in focus, ask the first question (from top to bottom) whose value is unknown else ask the question associated with the whole frame.

3. Non-answers to questions

One merit of this scheme is that it easily permits appropriate future dialogue behaviour upon encountering unsolicited relevant information, as in figure 2. This assumes the information can be recognized and processed, of course, but if it can be understood as a possible answer to "How can I help you?" or even as an initiating exchange utterance on its own, then it ought also to be processable as a response to "When do you want to leave?". The user response is not an answer, not a direct one at least, but it can be used to fill in the value of an attribute nonetheless. Then, the next question to be asked can be calculated as before on the basis of what else the system needs to know. Of course, the VoiceXML selection algorithm will end up repeating the very same question.

What is required for an agent to select more intelligently amongst the options it actually has available? In what circumstances would an agent move on to a different question, or even a different frame? An agent reasonably just repeats the original question if the answer is either *essential* for progress; or if, more mundanely, it just remains the best bet for making progress. What led Paxman finally to give up his questioning? Did he weigh the likelihood of success of the twelfth repetition against the possible success of an alternative dialogue path? "Essential" and "progress" are terms that need cashing out. A general characterization of 'dialogue progress' is rather hard to give. One advantage in concentrating on a typical task for a spoken dialogue system is that reasonable measures are easier to come by. One common assumption underlying a frame based dialogue manager, as in the travel agency domain, is that the first goal of the dialogue is to construct a database query whose results can subsequently be presented to the user and evaluated relatively easily. An "essential" piece of knowledge is therefore one without which no query can be made. A dialogue manager which insists on asking a particular question even though the underlying query system does not require it is therefore deficient. If the question is not essential, then we need to weigh the likelihood of making progress by repeating it. Dialogue progress can be measured by how close we believe we are to having an executable query that can deliver a (smallish) set of results. One very good reason for not repeating is simply that the previous attempt failed to get an answer; and this might have been the result of an underlying cause that has not changed. The goal may be achievable in different ways, however, and perhaps not all of them will include finding out the departure-time. Therefore, it may be simply practical as well as polite not to insist on settling the original question when the user does not answer it.

A simple addition to the Information State to enable more intelligent selection in this scenario is to define a preference ordering over all the subsets of possible attributes, $A : Sel : Pow(A) \to Z^+$. The selection algorithm then becomes: choose the attribute whose addition to those already known maximizes the value of *Sel*. Such a function is also easily implemented. Depending on the particular *Sel* function defined, a dialogue manager may now repeat its original question, ask a different one or indeed execute a query straight away and move onto the next stage of the dialogue. If we add in a simple cost function which progressively penalizes repetitions of questions, then we essentially have the system of Lewin (2001).

A variety of constraints might be imposed on the preference ordering. In general, more query constraints are better than fewer, because the set of satisfiers will likely be smaller and it will be easier to discuss and evaluate a small set of alternatives later; but a query that is likely to return no answers (because the query is overly specified) might receive a very low value indeed. In particular, if the system knows X and requests M, but receives N, then (X+M+N) might be considerably lower than (X+N+O) for some other O. Indeed, X+N might be the better than any extension of it, in which case the query can be made now.

The analysis is not restricted to this particular scenario in which progress is evaluated by anticipated results of a database query. One might, for example, be able to execute a query after every new piece of information from the user and thereby have access to the actual travel possibilities given what the user has said so far. In this case, the next question might be calculated using Information Theoretical considerations: which question is the best next one to ask to identify the right travel option out of this set of possibilities?

When the dialogue manager interprets the user's unsolicited offering and calculates his next move, need it note that a question was asked but not answered. Do we pop the question off a stack? The system knows of course which goals remain unsatisfied so the issue here is not whether to put the question again or not; just whether to note that there is an outstanding question that has not been answered. The distinction between public shared parts of dialogue state and private personal ones becomes particularly important here. There is an intuition that the putting of a question is a public act that alters a shared linguistic environment; and this is independent of any mental states that might have led to its putting. Unfortunately the public or private status of a question as remaining outstanding or not is far less clear. If we examine what an agent might infer whilst interpreting, then the issue appears really quite fine. The offering might be (or result from) a simple rejection of our question, in which case it would not be outstanding. Alternatively, perhaps the offering is an answer to the general topic of travel times which subsumes the particular question that was asked. Perhaps the user does intend to return to the original question at some point in the future and has placed the issue on a mental stack. Cooper and Larsson note how subtle the factors might be in enabling one to come to the best hypothesis on this kind of question (Cooper and Larsson 2005).

I want to make two points about this issue. The first is that whatever our *best* interpretation of the user's offering, our next action should not simply be determined by that interpretation plus our own plans and goals. A rational cost calculation must include not only the risk of our best interpretation being incorrect but the possible cost of the next action calculated on its basis. At best, we will only have a probability distribution over interpretations since the actual state of the user is of course unobservable. To the extent that interpretations also influence next moves, then the anticipated cost of those next moves must also be factored in. Williams and Young (2005) have recently been exploring the use of partially observable Markov decision processes in the settings of spoken dialogue systems.

The second, and strongly related, point is to emphasize that whether the dialogue "needs" to pop a stack or not is partly a matter of what strategic calculations about dialogue progress the dialogue manager *can* make. The dialogue manager, when interpreting the user's unsolicited offering, is of course also just about to make another contribution to the dialogue itself. If it is really only capable of asking questions at this point, then whatever the current state, the new most salient outstanding question will be the one it now chooses to make. Could the original question be required as context for a subsequent elliptical utterance? This is perhaps not impossible although it is perhaps unlikely given that the original question was not answered and has now been superseded by a new one. The original question is otiose as context if the question is just repeated of course. It is true that a re-formulation in the re-raising may be better than a straight repetition (Cooper and Larsson 2005). The information necessary for this may already be available via the mechanism that penalizes question repetition during next move calculation.

The most important reason to record the original question on a stack is if the moves available to the dialogue manager include one that hands the initiative to the user. It is a common enough human strategy, if a non-answering response is made to a question, simply to acknowledge the response. One might either signal, perhaps through intonation, that more input is expected or just wait to see what turns up next. What is important here is that this is not just a result of a protocol that humans happen to have. It is also not just a characteristic of chit-chat conversations, in which it doesn't particularly matter what happens next. It can be a calculated move in a strictly goal-driven interchange. In a chess game, one player might believe he understands his opponent's plan of attack, but play an inconsequential move to allow his partner the opportunity of making a more revealing move. However, in a state of the art spoken dialogue system, such a move represents a rather luxury item. The important point is that "only acknowledging" is itself a particular dialogue move with consequences that need to be weighed; and this possibility of weighing needs to be built in from the start. If a dialogue manager is to be *capable* of just acknowledging a user assertion, then it ought also to be sensitive to the cost of doing that versus something else. It should not simply be written in as part of a protocol of interaction. Dialogue managers with this sort of capability have yet to be fully experimented with.

Chu-Carroll and Nickerson (2000) and Litman and Pan (2002) present explorations of parts of the space. They also describe experiments showing that online adaptation in dialogue strategy is beneficial to users. Litman and Pan's TOOT system monitors predicted speech recognition error rates and can change strategy twice. The system begins by not confirming user utterances at all. If problems are detected, it can start implicitly confirming utterances ("I heard you say Sunday. What time would you like to leave?"); and if problems continue, it can move to explicit confirmation ('On which day of the week do you want to leave", "Sunday", "Do you want to leave on Sunday?"). Simultaneously, the open-endedness of the prompts and the range of acceptable responses is degraded. For example, at the middle stage (entitled *mixed initiative*, somewhat bizarrely) the system will not let the user ignore its question but insists on an answer. Chu-Carroll and Nickerson's MIMIC system also monitors interpretation difficulties, though this is not restricted to speech recognition problems but includes within-domain, perhaps vague or ambiguous, utterances which do not advance the dialogue. A binary global switch can be set causing the system to offer less open-ended prompts. The switch may also be reset if sufficient cue evidence of success can be found. One cue is whether the user subsequently adds unsolicited information to an answer.

The bundling of different elements of dialogue strategy and the concentration on whether to prompt the user more or less explicitly is almost inevitable given the actual performance levels of today's speech recognition engines, not to mention the costs involved in building systems and conducting empirical experiments with users. Nevertheless, the general perspective of the Information State Update approach does promise the possibility of a much more systematic investigation in the area of move selection strategy; one grounded in a semantically inspired theory of what dialogue is.

1. [S] Do you want the train or the plane?
2. [U] *What time do they arrive?*

Figure 3. Dependent questions

1. [S] Do you want the train or the plane?
2. [U] *What time do they arrive?*
3. [S] The train arrives at 3 and the plane at 4
4. [U] *The train please*

Figure 4. Long distance short answers

4. Questions, questions

So far we have only considered the case where the user supplies the answer to a question not yet asked. But the user can also supply questions in response to questions, as in figure 3. Classically, these cases are ones where the answer to 1 somehow depends on the answer to 2. If it is analysed as being dependent, then the first question may be put on a stack; or perhaps a nested conversational game is begun, or possibly an outstanding obligation to answer it is recorded (Ginzburg 1996; Lewin 2000; Matheson, Poesio, and Traum 2000). Shifting the focus of our attention onto next move selection again urges rather the importance of weighing the possible next moves. If the goal motivating the original question is still of interest to us, then we can re-ask it, as well as answering the original question. If it isn't we can ask something else. But the tactic of *only* answering the new question is also a specific move with its own specific advantages and disadvantages

Again, the original question *might* remain useful. It might function as a context for a possible ellipsis resolution; but this is again most likely only given an agent that also chooses just to answer the last question (Figure 4). In spoken dialogue systems, it is also worth remembering that correct ellipsis resolution is any case not a simple operation, increasingly hard the longer the distance grows between context and ellipsis and that, in many situations, there may often be other ways to achieve the right interpretation. Perhaps "the train" will only ever mean "I'd like to travel by train" in this type of dialogue.

Ginzburg, in his careful analysis (Ginzburg 2007), notes that dialogue stack structures do not arise as the results of seemingly arbitrary rules of dialogue syntax but from underlying dependencies amongst issues. That is, the answer to "train or plane" may depend upon arrival times. He goes further and states

1. [S] Välkommen till resebokningstjänsten. Hur jan jag hjälpa dig?
   [Welcome to the travel bureau, How can I help you?]
2. [U] Jag vill ha en resa till Göteborg från Stockholm.
   [I want to travel from Stockholm to Gothenburg.]
3. [S] Vilket datum vill du resa?
   [What day will you travel on?]
4. [U] Jag vill vara framme i Göteborg den elfte i åttonde.
   [I want to be in Gothenburg on August 11th.]
5. [S] Vill du resa med tåg eller flyg?
   [Will you travel by plane or train?]
6. [U] Vilken tid kommer dom fram?.
   [What time do they get there?]
7. [S] Vilken tid vill du resa ungefär?
   [What time will you leave?]
8. [U] Jag vill vara framme i Göteborg före klockan åtta.
   [I want to be in Gothenburg for eight o'clock]
9. [S] Det finns ett flyg som avgår klockan sju noll noll och ankommer klockan åtta noll noll. Det är det tidigaste flyget.
   [There is a flight that leaves at seven zero zero and arrives at eight zero zero. That is the earliest flight.]

Figure 5. Progress without Answers

that "Since B can be assumed to attempt to provide information about $q1$ were she able to do so, the fact that she has not done so must mean that B cannot do so without (attempting to) resolve $q2$". It seems to me that this is not true, or at least the force of the *cannot* demands careful elucidation. In educational contexts, a teacher may respond to a question with another because this is just the best way to further the underlying educational objective even though a direct answer could have been given. Is this somehow uncooperative behaviour and does it really matter if we deem that it is or isn't? Is it that this is not a "suitably simple" dialogue? The point I want to stress is that such considerations arise even in ordinary form-filling travel agency dialogues in spoken dialogue systems. There is after all a perfectly plausible alternative strategy on being asked "Do you want the train or plane?" which is just to give an answer and then see how the dialogue turns out from there.

278   Ian Lewin

5. Cooperation and cost

A rather richer example occurs in the dialogue illustrated in Figure 5, a genuine extract from a travel agency dialogue conducted between a human and a human (or "wizard") simulating a computer system. The wizard uses a script to determine the next computer action, although the script is not necessarily complete for all conceivable circumstances. This is a rather complex dialogue after utterance 4. It is an interesting exercise to try to discern which questions remain open for discussion at which points and which cues we expert human language users might use to help us decide. Could the behaviour be reproduced by a wholly automatic computer system in conversation with a human? What structures would it need to do it? How much inference would it need to employ? The answer is simple: it only requires the simple resources we have already sketched. Let us suppose the wizard is actually issuing a database query after each user utterance and choosing what to say next based partly on the results of that query. Starting at 5, the system determines that an answer to the question of travel mode will most likely reduce the size of the solution set the most; but the user does not answer this question. Unfortunately, his offering, 6, does not reduce the size at all; although had he asked "How much do they cost?", the story might be different. The system already knows the times that they all arrive but there are too many to announce. What should the system do next? Repeating the travel mode question is a possibility; and is still presumably optimal with respect to solution set size; but there is a penalty for repeats. So, in this case, the next best question, 7, is decided upon. The user now offers 8 which does not answer the question either. But 8 does in fact reduce the size of the solution set sufficiently and this phase of the dialogue can close through 9.

It is noteworthy that none of the three questions posed was actually answered. Yet the dialogue has succeeded. The suggested flight in 9 is not, I think, an answer to questions 5, 6, and 7. Indeed, even if the user follows up with "I'll take it", it is far from clear that that is a response to 5, 6, and 7, as well as 8. Why should the user follow up question 5 with his own question but then question 7 with a non-answering statement? It appears that the user's motivating goal was probably all along the desire to be in Gothenburg by eight o'clock on August 11th. He was happy to play along with the system's questioning so long as progress was made towards this goal. Question 5 put this in jeopardy but by asking for arrival times, he planned to pick one before eight o'clock. When this tactic failed, he decided not to play along with the system's strategy anymore and decided to override the system's question entirely and state the hard constraint he had in mind. That is one possible interpretation at any rate.

Does the dialogue instantiate *uncooperative* behaviour? Certainly questions were left unanswered; but each agent did at all times attempt to advance his own goals and, as the two sets of goals were indeed related, a mutually agreeable path forwards could be found. Co-operation is simply something that can exist at different levels of activity and at different times. One can answer a question in a way that does not advance the task; just as one can advance the task by not answering a given question. Cooperation is not a complete package that one just buys into or not in any given conversation. Besides, a robust system needs to be able to cope with a mildly uncooperative human it encounters.

Would a dialogue manager with a fixed cost model as above and which always asks questions in order to keep the initiative actually permit users to navigate through most dialogues of this type? When can "only acknowledging" be usefully added to the dialogue model? Could the parameters for a cost model be learnt from examples, or perhaps via an online training methodology? I do not know. But I think this kind of development of the Information State Update model looks a most interesting and practically useful research area.

So, what sort of a cost model was Paxman employing during his protracted series of exchanges with Howard? Paxman later claimed that he was informed mid-interview through his earpiece that the next item on the programme was not ready yet and he just couldn't think of anything else to ask.

Acknowledgments

Thanks to Telia Research AB, Vitsandsgatan 9, S-123 86 Farsta, Sweden for permission to use their corpus of travel dialogues.

References

Chu-Carroll, J., and J. Nickerson
    2000   Evaluating automatic dialogue strategy adaptation for a spoken dialogue system. *Proc. 1st NAACL.* 202–209.

Cooper, R., and S. Larsson
    2005   Accommodation and reaccommodation in dialogue. R. Bäuerle, U. Reyle, and T.E. Zimmerman (eds.), *Presuppositions and Discourse.* Elsevier.

Ginzburg, J.
    1996   Interrogatives: Questions, facts, and dialogue. In *The Handbook of Contemporary Semantic Theory*, Shalom Lappin (ed.), 385–422. Blackwell Publishers.

2007 *Semantics and Interaction in Dialogue*. Studies in Computational Linguistics. CSLI Publications.

Lewin, I.
2000 A formal model of conversational game theory. *Fourth Workshop on the Semantics and Pragmatics of Dialogue: Gotalog 2000*. 115–122.
2001 Limited enquiry negotiation dialogues. *Eurospeech 2001: Proceedings of the 7th European Conference on speech communication and technology*. 2333–2336.

Litman, Diane J., and Shimei Pan
2002 Designing and evaluating an adaptive spoken dialogue system. *User Modeling and User-Adapted Interaction* 12 (2-3): 111–137.

Matheson, C., M. Poesio, and D. Traum
2000 Modelling grounding and discourse obligations using update rules. *Proceedings of NAACL 2000*.

Oshry, Matt, RJ Auburn, Paolo Baggia, Michael Bodell, David Burke, Daniel C. Burnett, Emily Candell, Jerry Carter, Scott McGlashan, Alex Lee, Brad Porter, and Ken Rehor
2006 Voice Extensible Markup Language (VoiceXML) 2.1.

Williams, J. D., and S. Young
2005 Scaling up pomdps for dialog management: The "summary pomdp" method. *Automatic Speech Recognition and Understanding, 2005 IEEE Workshop on*, pp. 177–182.

To be or not to be, isn't that a question?

Lars Ahrenberg

1. Introduction

Seemingly, the notion of a question is a simple and uniform one. Most speakers can recognize a question when they hear one, and most orthographies find it sufficient to use a single symbol to indicate questions. Yet the linguistic and philosophical literature on questions is rich in analyses and controversies, and there exist a large number of subtypes of questions, both as regards form and function.

The two major types in most taxonomies of questions are *polar questions*, also referred to as yes-no questions or nexus-questions, and *x-questions*, also called wh-questions or questions of identity. A third type is the *alternative question*, whose characteristic feature is that it provides two or more alternatives from which one should be selected. In (1) we give one example of each kind:

(1)   a.   *Is today Monday?* (Polar question)
       b.   *What day is it today?* (X-question)
       c.   *Is today Monday or Tuesday?* (Alternative question)

While these examples also illustrate typical question constructions, it is clear that there is more than one way to express questions of a similar function, and, conversely, the same type of structure can be used with varied functional impact. For instance, all of the following can be interpretred as x-questions, in the appropriate context:

(2)   a. *What time will she arrive?* (*wh*-clause)
       b. *She will arrive at what time?* (in situ *wh*-clause)
       c. *And she will arrive:?* (paused construction)
       d. *Her arrival time?* (noun phrase)

A recent attempt to capture both the uniformity in kind, and the variation in use and forms of expression is (Ginzburg and Sag 2000). This work, henceforth referred to as G&S, provides a well-argued analysis of the syntax and semantics of questions in English within a HPSG framework. In addition to the types already illustrated above, they include *multiple x-questions* as in (3a)

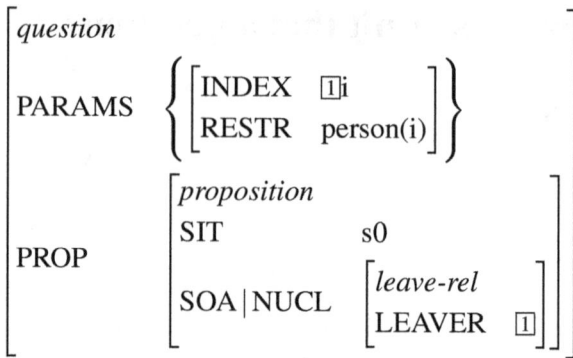

Figure 1. Analysis of the sentence *Who left?*

and *question fragments* as in (3b). The latter type is handled within a fairly elaborate model of the way questions, and, more generally, other dialogue acts, function in context, to which we will return later.

(3) a. *Who arrived when?*
     b. *Who?*

Alternative questions, however, are conspicuously absent from this work. We suspect that this may be due in part to a lack of a well-developed model of coordination in HPSG, but the absence is noteworthy nevertheless. This paper will provide some observations on alternative questions and other types of questions that are not so well covered in G&S' work, notably deliberative questions. This will lead us to suggest some changes to the model.

In the next section I give a condensed overview of some central aspects of the G&S model. It should be stressed that this is not a review of the entire work, but meant as background information for a discussion of the mentioned question types.[1] In section 3 I discuss alternative questions and polar questions, and section 4 considers deliberative questions. Section 5, finally, offers my conclusions.

2. The G&S model

2.1. Questions as propositional abstracts

The central idea as regards the semantic analysis of questions in the G&S model is that questions are propositional abstracts. Polar questions, simple x-questions[2] and multiple x-questions are all claimed to share internal structure in terms of a proposition that they are constructed out of, and a set of parameters. The difference lies in the make-up of the set of parameters: a multiple wh-question has more than one parameter, a simple wh-question has exactly one, and a polar question has an empty set of parameters. Using Typed Feature Structures (TFS), G&S provides the analysis in Figure 1 for the question *Who left?* and the analysis shown in Figure 2 for *Did Bo leave?*.

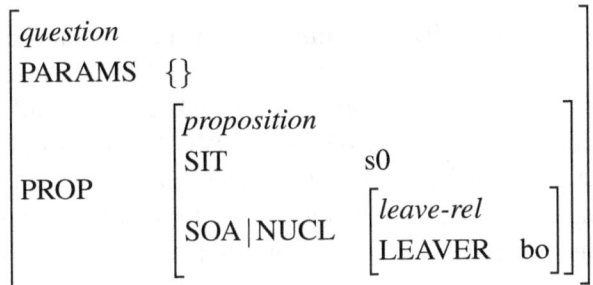

Figure 2. Analysis of the sentence *Did Bo leave?*

Thus, the model provides a unified account of questions as semantic objects. In addition, G&S show how syntactic and semantic properties of different types of questions follow from general assumptions about English phrase types and expressions such as wh-words and negative particles. As grammar is not in focus in this paper, I leave this part of the model aside.

2.2. Questions in dialogue

It has become increasingly popular in recent years to model dialogue in terms of changes of information states (Traum et al. 1999; Larsson 2002). Each dialogue participant maintains an information state, divided into a private part and a shared part. Every new contribution to the dialogue results in updates of the information states, and, conversely, new contributions are phrased according to what the speaker's information state considers as shared information. A short exchange between two participants are assumed to develop along the following lines:

- A wants to communicate C1 to B
- A says U1 to communicate C1
- A updates her information state with C1 and U1
- B perceives and grounds U1 understanding C1'
- B updates her information state with C1' and U1
- B wants to communicate C2 to A

- B says U2 to communicate C2
- ...

There is in general no guarantee that B will interpret A's utterance in the way intended by A. This is why we distingish C1 and C1' in the stages above. However, for the simple cases we will discuss, we will assume no conflicts of interpretation.

Following (Ginzburg 1996) the information state contains at least the following information: A set of shared facts, called FACTS, a set of questions that are currently under discussion, called QUD, and a record of the content of the latest contribution, called LATEST-MOVE. Later works have developed more elaborate information states, but the QUD has enjoyed a fairly stable existence. An important aspect of the QUD is that it is partially ordered in terms of conversational precedence, with one question possibly being the highest ordered in terms of this relation. As is common we will refer to this question as the MAX-QUD. This question is of special importance, since this is the contextual item that is assumed to licence and provide information relevant to the interpretation of short answers such as *Bo* or *Yes*.

2.3. Accommodation

In the case of simple question-answer exchanges, the relation between the question uttered and the MAX-QUD is straight-forward in normal circumstances. Once the question is grounded by the addressee, its content can be integrated as the MAX-QUD. In some developments of the model, assertions being made also give rise to a new MAX-QUD, viz. the question of whether they are true or not (Ginzburg and Cooper 2004). If the addressee accepts this, the proposition asserted will then be recategorized as belonging to the set of FACTS. Similarly, volunteered information, expressed as a word or a short phrase, can be accommodated by assuming that it relates to a question, that the participants expect to be raised in the course of the dialogue. (Larsson 2002)

Accommodation may be seen as part of the inferencing that a dialogue participant (or, in fact, reader of a text) needs to perform. In Larsson's words (Larsson 2002: 161): "Accommodation is one type of reasoning involved in understanding and integrating the effects of dialogue moves". Accommodation obviously has to be restricted somehow. Not any information can be accommodated. There are at least two restricting factors. One is relevance to the current dialogue, and the other is that the question inferred has a tight relationship with the information given. For example, as a question abstracting over a proposition at the place where the contributed information would fit.

3. Alternative questions

An alternative question is a question that contains two or more phrases that are coordinated by a disjunction and embedded in some other marker of questionhood, such as a polar interrogative, a question intonation or a question mark. Some examples are given below:

(4) a. *Did Bo or Mo leave?*
     b. *Did Bo leave or stay?*
     c. *Today is Monday or Tuesday?*

Alternative questions admit two types of answers. On the one hand they may be answered by *yes* or *no* as an ordinary polar question, but normally a choice of one of the mentioned alternatives is what is required. For instance, the first question above may be answered with a short answer as in (5), i.e., in the same way as the wh-question *Who left*:

(5) a. *Bo (did)*
     b. *No, but Jo (did)*

Since alternative questions admit of short answers, it could be asked whether the relation of a short answer to an alternative question is substantially different from its relation to an x-question. In my view, the difference is not very large; one would expect answers to an alternative question to be drawn from the expressed set of alternatives, but as illustrated in (5b), other short answers are also possible. Unlike alternative questions, however, x-questions do not license *yes* or *no* as part of the response.

It would be possible to introduce a special rule to account for the relation of short answers to alternative questions. However, a better option is that an alternative question adds an x-question to the QUD, and actually to the MAX-QUD. This would account for the possibility of short answers in the same way as it does for proper x-questions. Moreover, the relation of an alternative question to the corresponding x-question is tight enough to be treated as accommodation, by abstracting over the position in the sentence structure where the disjunction appears. Thus, an utterance of (4a) would cause the addressee to place the question *Who left?* on her information state.

We must note, though, as in (5b) that a rejection of the mentioned alternatives seems to require a *no* before other answers can be given. This sug-

$$\begin{bmatrix} \text{MAX-QUD} & \begin{bmatrix} \textit{question} \\ \text{PARAMS} & \left\{\begin{bmatrix} \text{INDEX} & \boxed{1}i \\ \text{RESTR} & \text{person(i)} \\ \text{AOI} & i\in\{b,m\} \end{bmatrix}\right\} \\ \text{PROP} & \begin{bmatrix} \textit{proposition} \\ \text{SIT} & s0 \\ \text{SOA}|\text{NUCL} & \begin{bmatrix} \textit{leave-rel} \\ \text{LEAVER} & \boxed{1} \end{bmatrix} \end{bmatrix} \end{bmatrix} \\ \text{BACKGRD} & \{\text{named(b,Bo), named(m,Mo)}\} \end{bmatrix}$$

Figure 3. Representation of the MAX-QUD resulting from the question *Did Bo or Mo leave?*

gests that the representation cannot be exactly the same as for an ordinary x-question.

The effect of accommodating the x-question as a QUD could be seen as similar to updating an information state from two explicit consecutive questions, as in (6). The first of these questions actually provide a context for the interpretation of the short expressions that follow. For this reason it will be called a framing question. We use the same term whether this question is the result of direct integration or accommodation.

(6)   a.   *What day is it? Is it Monday or Tuesday?*
       b.   *Who left? Bo or Mo?*

The expressed alternatives must also be part of the interpretation, however. I will refer to them as answers-of-interest and represent them with an attribute AOI. Given that we can identify an appropriate abstract, the contents of the alternatives can preferably be represented as further restrictions on the parameter of the abstract, as in Figure 3. This makes the representation different from an ordinary x-question, which has an empty set of answers-of-interest.

The alternatives raised by an alternative question may be discussed at more or less length following the question. This is another motivation for making them explicit in the information state. Larsson (2002), makes this point in his model of negotiative dialogues, but we hold that alternative questions generally have this potential.

3.1. Polar alternative questions

A specific case of an alternative question is when the second conjunct is a negation:

(7)   a. *Did Bo leave or not?*
      b. *Are you coming or not?*

It has in fact been argued by many that a polar question should be treated as a kind of abbreviated alternative question of this kind. Bolinger (1978) argued forcefully against this view, however, and I see little reason to oppose him. Bolinger's major argument is that the addition of *or not* either adds insistence which otherwise would be absent, or, in other contexts, impartiality or neutrality where a positive expectation is associated with the simple polar question. To see how this kind of alternative question would fit into the framework presented so far, we must first say something about polar questions.

3.2. Polar questions

According to G&S, polar questions differ from x-questions in that the set of parameters is the empty set. A drawback of this analysis is that it does not account for the fact that many polar interrogatives need more than just a *yes* or a *no* to be resolved. In many cases what is required is either a confirmation (i.e., a *yes* or some equivalent), or a correction, as in the following examples:

(8)   *A: Is today Monday?*
      B: No, (it's) Tuesday.

(9)   *A: Did Bo leave?*
      B: No, he just went out to have a smoke.

Thus, an utterance of a polar interrogative often implies a QUD with a non-empty set of parameters such as, for the examples above, *What day is it today?*, and *What did Bo do?*, what we called a framing question above. In addition, the polar question raises a possible answer "for discussion", in a way which is quite similar to the way an alternative question raises more than one answer candidate. This is quite parallel to the case of two consecutive questions as in (10).

(10) a. *What day is it today? (Is it) Monday?*
      b. *Who left? Bo?*

The difference between (8) and (10) is that, in (8), the framing question is the result of accommodation, whereas in (10) it can be derived compositionally and integrated. Moreover, in (10), the second question already has a frame for its interpretation.

It may be argued against this proposal that polar questions will be ambiguous, i.e., that there are several different framing questions that can be derived from them. For instance, an utterance of (9) can be interpreted as relating to the framing question *Who left?* rather than to *What did Bo do?* as implied by B's answer. This is true, but in spoken language intonation will often differentiate. Usually only one constituent receives pitch accent and this will be the constituent that gets abstracted from to create the QUD. In other cases, one component is markedly non-informative or underspecified. This is the case with alternative questions, but also with, for example, indefinites. Thus, (11) implies the question *What did you see at the Zoo?* rather than *Where did you see something exciting?*

(11)   *Did you see something exciting at the Zoo?*

Apart from the linguistic indicators, making an utterance relevant is part of the interpretation process. Grounding at the constitutent level has been shown to be important for the analysis of reprise clarifications in e.g. in (Ginzburg and Cooper 2004; Purver 2006), but surely grounding at the move level is equally important. Determining the framing question can be seen as a part of grounding the speaker's move which draws on knowledge of the discourse context in addition to knowledge of the grammar.

3.3.   Zero abstraction

G&S defines their semantic universe as encompassing, among other things, propositional abstracts. In particular they make sure that the abstracts, representing questions, and the propositions that constitute their bodies, are formally different. The relation between an abstract and a proposition is mediated by so called place holders. The role of place holders is to identify components of the body of an abstract that can be the locus of abstracting. However, in the case of polar questions, the place-holder must not pick out a component, it must pick out something outside of the body.

A problem I can see with this construction is that the association between the formal object, the abstract, and the polar question that it represents, becomes arbitrary. The empty set of parameters seems not to add anything to the representation except the gain of treating all questions alike formally. But unlike the case of component place-holders, we do not get a parameter to place restrictions on as we do with x-questions.

Polar questions allow many types of answers that need the proposition part of the question as a contextual parameter, e.g., *yes*, *may be*, or *I think so*, all of which contract some answerhood relation with respect to the question.[3] Many of these can be used also if the proposition is asserted. Thus, it is sufficient to relate the answer to the proposition to arrive at an interpretation, something which speaks in favour of the model. Some of the words and phrases that can accompany the proposition when it is asserted cannot be used with polar questions, however, or it least not with the same interpretation. For example:

(12)   A: *Has Bo left?*, B: **Already

(13)   A: *Bo has left*, B: *Already?*

(14)   A: *Has Bo left?*, B: *?I know.*

(15)   A: *Bo has left*, B: *I know.*

With (12) one could assume that *Already* would imply an affirmative answer in the same way as other answers such as *regrettably* or *unfortunately* but for some reason it cannot. However, it can be used with the corresponding assertion, as in (13). The adverb *really* seems to behave in the same way.

In (15) B's utterance can be construed as 'I know that Bo has left'. This is not possible in (14), however, where *know* may pick up the question as in *I don't know*, meaning 'I don't know whether Bo has left'. or, with stress on the first word, as an answer to an accommodable question *Who knows whether Bo has left?*.

The point is that if the occurrence of short utterances is to be explained with reference to some aspect of a MAX-QUD, we need some parameter that the utterance can pick up. If this parameter is not the proposition, or some part of the proposition, it must be somewhere else. Conversely, if a short utterance can pick up a proposition when it is asserted, but not when it is the base of a question, some value with which the utterance can clash seems to be required. But an empty set of parameters does not fulfil this requirement. It does not tell us in what way the proposition is 'open' nor does it provide a parameter to constrain.

3.4. Polar alternative questions revisited

In essence, we are suggesting that all questions contribute a question with a non-empty set of parameters to the information states. From the point of view of the G&S model, this is not necessarily controversial, since, after all, it has its focus on compositionally derived meanings.

However, polar questions vary with respect to the answers that they seek, that is with respect to the information needs of their speakers. There are polar questions that seem to indicate no interest in any other answers than a *yes* or a *no*. Polar alternative questions are of this kind. Simple polar questions such as *Will you be there?* if asked in connection with some future event like a conference or a party can also be of this kind. If the answer is no, there may be no interest in, and hence no discussion on, the potentially abstracted x-questions *Where will you be?* or *Who will be there?*. But when this interest is more likely, as with *Is today Monday?*, the related x-question *What day is it?* invites itself in a more direct manner. This is so because knowledge of the day is considered to be important for everybody (above a certain age) and it is known that there are, basically, seven alternatives values. Thus, whether a framing question is considered as part of an information state at all, depends largely on relevance factors, whereas the term of existence for it depends on the next and following moves.

The polar alternative questions using *or not* seem to be problematic for the G&S model, however. The option that the disjunction is part of the base proposition, or rather that the base is taken to be the disjunction of some proposition p, and its negation, does not give the right interpretation. A *yes*-answer would pick out the disjunction as a whole rather than the positive alternative. Thus, it seems necessary to "lift" the alternatives to something akin to our AOI attribute, with only the positive proposition as a body. If the set of parameters is required to be empty, this attribute need to be placed outside the parameters, at the top level as it were, but then it is not clear what is being constrained.

A variant of a polar alternative question is the following, where the answers that the speaker displays her interest in are again restricted to the the two alternatives accept/agree or reject/disagree.

(16)   *Are you coming? Yes or no?*

Again, an attribute representing answers of interest seems appropriate. Whether the value of this attribute should be the words themselves or some expression of their content, say functions from propositions to propositions is a question that I leave open.

4. Deliberative questions

A deliberative question is a question about the future actions of some agent, perhaps most often the speaker herself or some group to which she belongs.

(17) a. *What are we to do?*
b. *How can this conflict be settled?*

A deliberative question can also be alternative, i.e., provide two or more specific alternative actions of interest. The most famous example of such a question is probably the one appearing in Hamlet's soliloqui, which is in fact a polar, alternative, deliberative question.

> To be, or not to be: that is the question: whether 'tis nobler in the mind to suffer the slings and arrows of outrageous fortune, or to take arms against a sea of troubles, and by opposing end them?
> *Hamlet, Act 3, Scene 1*

The interest of deliberative questions in the context of the G&S model concerns the nature of their bodies. Is it a proposition or not? G&S makes three claims that bear on this issue. The first one is that all questions are related to propositions, they all have a part that semantically is a proposition. The second claim is that propositions (and questions) must be distinguished from a type of semantic object they call an outcome. An outcome is a message-type that is characteristically associated with imperative and subjunctive clauses, and with some infinitive VP's. Another feature of outcomes is that notions such as true and false do not apply to them, a feature which makes them distinct from propositions. Yet a third characteristic is that they are based on non-real state-of-affairs; in particular they are not anchored in time. In their universe, G&S model them with abstracts over the temporal parameter of a state-of-affairs.

It follows from this that questions cannot be constructed out of outcomes, a conclusion that is supported by the claim that questions in English cannot use imperative or subjunctive verb forms (p. 78). This seems to be true for imperatives and the subjunctive form *be*, but Nerbonne questions this claim in his review (Nerbonne 2005) with respect to the use of *were* with third-singular subjects.

Now, deliberative questions are usually formed with auxiliary verbs, having infinitival complements, as in the examples above. Deliberative questions with *to*-infinitives, such as *What to do?* or *Where to go for advice?* are also fairly common, so to make the semantic claim hold up, it must be assumed that in these sentences the infinitive actually expresses a proposition.

G&S (p. 216) analyses the sentence *I wonder whether to leave* as expressing a proposition in the *whether*-clause. This fits with their theory, but is not quite consistent with their analyses of the difference between infinitives that express outcomes and infinitives that express propositions. They give the following examples.[4]

(18)   a.   Lee wants [to be happy] (outcome)
            b.   They claimed [to know the answer to that question] (proposition)

Moreover, they say that outcomes go together with what they call mandatory predicates and they mention *demand, require, prefer,* and *instruct* as examples. These are verbs where one agent "mandates" something of another agent. But verbs such as *want* or *wish* that do not necessarily involve another agent but solely the wants or hopes of a single agent are implied by the example above to relate to outcomes.

What then with more salient examples of deliberation verbs such as *wonder* or *ponder*? Media provides several examples of sentences with these verbs followed by an infinitive as in (19).

(19)   a.   *Under surveillance, three security police wonder whether to ask for autograph.*[5]
            b.   *Opposition parties ponder whether to combine or go it alone in the fight for seats in parliament.*[6]

In the overall majority of these cases the *to*-infinitive VP expresses a future event with no fixed time argument, which is one of the features of an outcome. Nor is its truth-value at stake. Sometimes the clause could be taken to denote a norm of some sort as if the question concerns the right or proper thing to do, in which case a propositional reading might be preferred. But often it is clear that the resolution of the question will happen through a decision in much the same way as mandatory events are resolved by decisions. The difference is that, in the case of deliberations the agent making the decision is the same as the agent that deliberates, whereas in the case of mandatory events the decision falls on somebody else to whom the mand is directed. We may add that often the problem of indecision that accompanies a deliberation has its source in a conflict of the agent's will with the demands of others. As another piece of evidence, we can note that it is often possible to follow on a deliberative question with a sentence carrying a mandatory predicate. For example,the second sentence may be followed by *What (outcome) would you prefer?* which indicates that it at least makes an outcome interpretation available from the VP's.

The G&S model assumes that the content of the *whether*-clause is unified with that of the complementizer itself and the content of its complement. If the VP denotes an outcome, whereas the clause denotes a question, two options are possible. Either we allow questions to be constructed out of outcomes in some circumstances, or we would have to find a way of coercing the embedded SOA into a proposition or an outcome depending on the item it is a complement to. The first alternative definitely seems the more appropriate. After all, propositions and outcomes are sub-types of the same superordinate message type, so it is not surprising that they could share properties. If so, what is required is that finer semantic distinctions are made to the outcomes, so that subjunctive and imperatives, on the one hand, denote different subtypes of outcomes than infinitive VP's.

5. Conclusions

To conclude, let us return to the question posed in the title. It is of course meant to be rhetorical, but a theory of questions should be able to tell us what makes those words a question, and how it should be properly represented. As for the first issue I believe we are forced to say that it is a question because Hamlet says so, and this is in itself a support for having message types in the grammar, and in the lexicon.

As for the second issue, Hamlet's question is obviously alternative and polar. I have argued that the framework provided by G&S can not incorporate alternative questions without some augmentation. Alternative questions allow short answers in much the same way as x-questions. By assuming that alternative questions give rise to x-questions that frame the alternatives, and that such framing questions are maximal, we get an explanation for this fact. But the alternatives themselves must also be represented. When they relate to a component utterance parameter, it is natural to assume that they apply to the parameter's values and represent them accordingly. I have used an attribute AOI, answers-of-interest, for this purpose.

If we wish to handle polar alternative questions, such as Hamlet's or those that simply add *or not* to the end of a polar, interrogative clause, we face a problem: the G&S model has no explicit parameter representing the likelihood or truth value of a proposition. Instead, polar questions are represented with an empty set of parameters. Hence, when the explicit alternatives are *yes* and *no*, in whatever way expressed, there is no parameter which the alternatives can be related to. While there may be good reasons to keep truth-values out of the underlying semantic theory, the truth-false dimension (or, if one prefers, accept-reject dimension), could still be allowed as a topic, or question-under-discussion, in the modelling of information states.

Ordinary polar questions may also give rise to framing questions. They differ from alternative questions in that only one answer-of-interest is being proposed. Thus, all questions can be said to give rise to framing questions. While x-questions do so by straight-forward integration into information states, polar and alternative questions do so via accommodation of a suitable abstract. In addition, x-questions do not explicitly propose any answers-of-interest.

Hamlet's question is also deliberative. In general, all three basic types of questions may be deliberative, i.e., concerning future actions of an agent that are dependent on the agent's decisions. I have argued that deliberative questions relate to outcomes rather than to propositions, and, hence that the claim that questions can only relate to a body expressing a proposition, is too strong.

Notes

1. For proper reviews, see e.g. (Koenig 2004; Nerbonne 2005)
2. G&S use the term wh-question, but for consistency I stick to the term I myself prefer.
3. G&S recognize a scale of answerhood relations including exhaustive answers, resolving ansers and answers that are merely about the question.
4. examples 84a and 84b, p. 52 in (Ginzburg and Sag 2000).
5. In other words ... David Bowie. London: Omnibus Press, 1986, cited from BNC, section AB5.
6. Part of a heading from an ArmeniaNow.com news article, Issue 3 (222), January 19, 2007.

References

Bolinger, Dwight
    1978   Yes-no questions are not alternative questions. In *Questions*, H. Hiz (ed.), 87–105. Dordrecht: Reidel.

Ginzburg, Jonathan
    1996   Interrogatives: Questions, facts, and dialogue. In *The Handbook of Contemporary Semantic Theory*, S. Lappin (ed.), 385–422. Oxford: Blackwell.

Ginzburg, Jonathan, and Robin Cooper
    2004   Clarification ellipsis and the nature of contextual updates in dialogue. *Linguistics and Philosophy* 27: 297–365.

Ginzburg, Jonathan, and Ivan Sag
    2000   *Interrogative Investigations: The Form, Meaning and Use of English Interrogatives*. Stanford, CA: CSLI Publications.

Koenig, Jean-Pierre
    2004   Any questions left? review of Ginzburg & Sag's Interrogative Investigations. *Linguistics* 40: 131–148.

Larsson, Staffan
    2002   Issue-based dialogue management. Ph.D. diss., Department of Linguistics, Goteborg University, Goteborg.

Nerbonne, John
    2005   Review of Jonathan Ginzburg and Ivan Sag (2000) Interrogative Investigations: The Form, Meaning and Use of English Interrogatives. *Language* 81(4): 989–992.

Purver, Matthew
    2006   Clarie: Handling clarification requests in a dialogue system. *Research on Language and Computation* 4: 259–288.

Traum, David, Johan Bos, Robin Cooper, Staffan Larsson, Ian Lewin, Colin Matheson, and Massimio Poesio
    1999   A model of dialogue moves and information state revision. Deliverable 2.1, Task Oriented Instructional Dialogue (TRINDI), Gothenburg, University of Gothenburg.

Attitude reports in spontaneous dialogue: Uncertainty, politeness and filled pauses

Merle Horne

1. Attitude reports in dialogue

Integrating information in dialogue interaction is a complex process that involves multimodal reasoning. Building on work in situation semantics (Barwise and Perry 1983), Cooper and colleagues (e.g. Cooper 1996; Cooper and Ginzburg 1996) have developed a model for the analysis of dialogue meaning which incorporates different information sources. One aspect of dialogue semantics that has received particular attention is the role of information states and their relationship to the analysis of propositional attitudes. Attitude reports are important in the analysis of spontaneous discourse and in practical applications such as automatic speech recognition and understanding. They give important information as to the speaker's attitude to his/her utterance in relation to the listener. The present contribution focuses on attitude reports in Swedish spontaneous speech.

1.1. Attitude reports in spontaneous speech: pragmatic particles

When investigating the meaning structure of spontaneous speech, it becomes clear that the expression of attitude reports related to mental states like believe and know is not always coded exclusively by attitudinal predicates like believe, doubt, etc. In spoken spontaneous dialogue, where the speaker and addressee(s) interact in real time, propositional attitudes are often modulated by other means than just lexical predicates. For example, pragmatic mood-related particles such as Swedish liksom 'like' in spoken language (see Anward 1999; Andersen and Fretheim 2000, Aijmer 2004) add a modulating, interactive dimension to the speaker's propositional attitude:

(1)   Man **tror liksom** att man nått botten, men det blir bara sämre och sämre
        'You think like you've reached the bottom, but it only gets worse and worse' <www.slowfat.com/pblog.php?dec=7>

1.1.1. Hedges, uncertainty and politeness

Pragmatic particles, in combination with attitudinal predicates like *believe* are related to the immediate interactive dimension of dialogue semantics. The mood-related pragmatic particle *liksom* 'like' is what has been referred to as a *hedge* (Lakoff 1972), a mechanism used to modulate the assertive force of an utterance. Hedging has been observed to be an important communicative device used to soften the modal attitude or illocutionary force of a statement. In Japanese, for example, hedges have been shown to be realized both lexically (e.g. with verbs and adverbs) and through non-lexical hedging devices (e.g. syntactic and prosodic devices) (Nittono 2003). Glottalized filled pauses can thus be interpreted as a kind of hedging mechanism related to politeness phenomena and modality. Hedging functions as a means for realizing what has been termed *positive politeness*, i.e. a strategy for maintaining a positive relationship or *face* between parties (Brown and Levinson 1987). Hedges can in other words be associated with face-saving, politeness and indirectness. The propositional attitude *uncertainty* is related to politeness in the sense that a speaker can be uncertain as to how to best formulate an utterance so as not to lose face (Aijmer 2004). The uncertainty attitude of the speaker uttering (2) is expressed through the use of the glottalized filled pause *EH~* (glottalization will be represented as (~)) :

(2)   *Jag ser ju att EH~ PAUSE tiden räcker ju liksom inte till ändå för mig*
        'I see you know that UH~ PAUSE the time just you know like isn't long enough anyway for me'

It can be assumed that it is not the truth value of the proposition that the speaker is uncertain about in this case, but rather the optimal way of coding the message for the addressee who she has never spoken to before. The other interactional devices used by the speaker, the pragmatic particles *ju* 'you know' (twice) and *liksom* 'like', are further evidence for the very listener-oriented speech coding that the speaker is involved in.

1.1. Attitude reports and prosody: uncertainty, politeness and intonation

In addition to lexical predicates and pragmatic particles, attitude reports can further be realized by prosodic means. For example, an intonation contour with a final rise in declaratives has been associated with an attitude of uncertainty on the part of the speaker (Pierrehumbert and Hirschberg 1990; Ohala 1983; Gussenhoven 2004; House 2003).

Speaking with a high level of fundamental frequency has also been associated with politeness according to the Frequency Code (Ohala 1983; Gussenhoven 2004). The example in Figure 1 is an assertion with a high-rising question-like intonation which could have been uttered as a hedging answer to a question such as: Where would you like to live? This intonation pattern signals an attitude of uncertainty on the part of the speaker, both as regards the utterance's assertive/illocutionary force, i.e. the degree of speaker commitment to the truth associated with the proposition, as well as the speaker's attitude as regards the hearer's background knowledge, e.g. uncertainty as regards the addressee's knowledge as to the whereabouts of Ottawa.

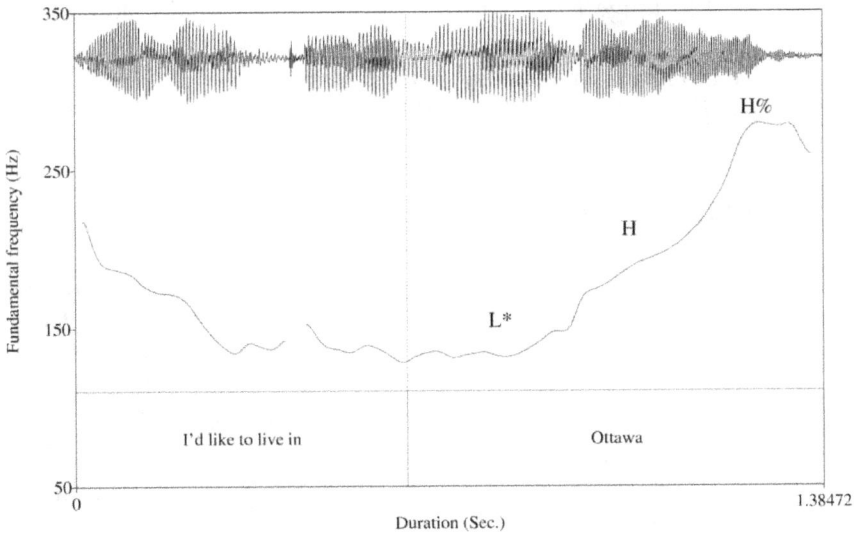

Figure 1. Wave form and fundamental frequency (pitch) curve for the utterance *I'd like to live in Ottawa* with a final question-like intonation: a rising pitch accent (L*+H) on Ottawa and a high phrase accent (H%).

2. Uncertainty, politeness and glottalized filled pauses

In the present contribution, drawing on data from Swedish spontaneous speech, it will be illustrated how another voice-related cue, the parameter glottalization or creaky voice used in the production of filled pauses in spontaneous speech can also be interpreted as signalling the speaker attitude uncertainty.

2.1. The filled pause *EH*

In speech technology studies, the filled pause or filler *EH* 'UH' has often been termed a *disfluency* (e.g. Shriberg 2001), since it constitutes a delay in the flow of speech associated with lexical meaning. Despite their lack of referential or lexical meaning, filled pauses have, nevertheless, been associated with clear discourse functions, such as signaling an upcoming focussed word (Strangert 1991; Bruce 1998), or the intention to continue speaking. Since *EH* can therefore be associated with relatively clear discourse or pragmatic meanings, it has sometimes been classified as a *word*, an *interjection* (Allwood et al. 1990; Clark and Fox Tree 2002).

2.1.1. Distribution of EH in spontaneous dialogue

Using spontaneous speech in spontaneous interview situations involving speakers who had never met before (data from *SweDia* database), Horne (2006) showed that *EH* occurred in this material almost exclusively as a clitic to a preceding function word or discourse marker: 127 of the 137 instances of *EH* occurred in this environment. *EH* occurred most often after *och* 'and' and *men* 'but' which often function as discourse markers, e.g. introducing new topics, topic continuations, etc. 52 cases of *EH* occurred after these two function words. *Och EH* 'and UH' was the most common function word + *EH* construction. The second most frequent function word category preceding *EH* was the subordinate conjunction *att* 'that' which also can function as a discourse marker introducing a non-subordinate clause. 24 instances of *EH* occurred after *att*. The other instances of *EH* were found after the following function words:

preposition (n=13), articles (n= 9), pronouns (Subject) (n= 9), basic verbs or auxiliary verbs (n=9), demonstrative article (n=5), indefinite adjective (n=3), subordinate conjunction (other than *att* 'that') (n=2), Negation (n=1). Content words preceded *EH* in only 7 cases. Finally, there was 1 case where *EH* was a repetition. Thus, the dominating discourse context for filled pauses is after a discourse marker, in clause-initial position. *EH* is thus intimately associated with a context where it can be assumed to be related to the coding of clauses in working memory.

2.1.2. Phonetic realization of EH

Three basic realizations of the filled pause *EH* were observed in Horne (2006): a middle-high front or central vowel: e.g. [ɵ] (see Fig. 2), a nasalized vowel or vowel + nasal consonant: e.g. [əm] (see Fig. 3), and a glottalized or creaky vowel: e.g. [ə̰] (see Fig. 4).

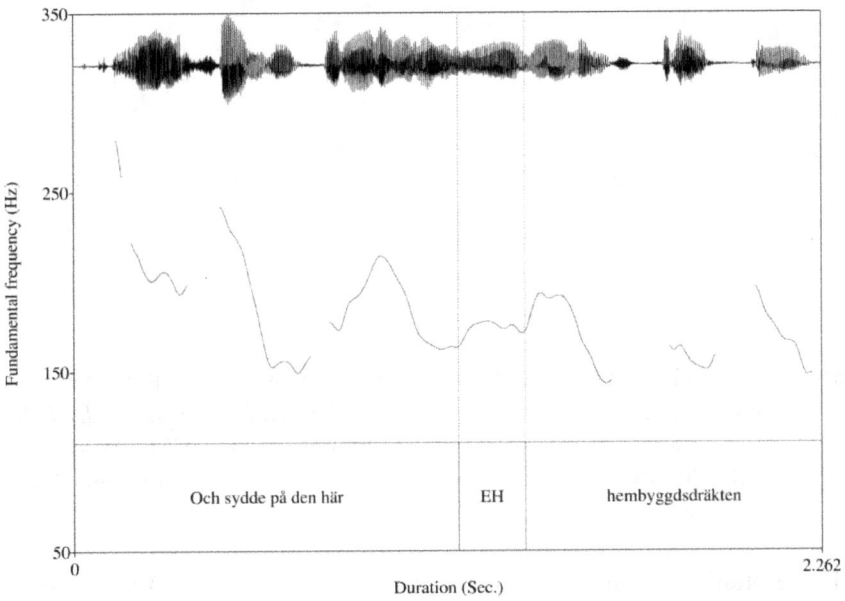

Figure 2. Example of the realization of *EH* as the middle high vowel [ə] in the utterance *och sydde på den här EH hembyggdsdräkten* 'and sewed this UH folk dress'

The vowel realizations of *EH* were the most frequent (n=61) and had a mean duration of 268 ms and a SD of 136 ms. The nasalized or vowel+nasal realizations were second in frequency (n=43), and had a mean duration of 436 ms and a SD of 185 ms. These showed a distribution like the vowel+nasal fillers in English that Clark and Fox Tree (2002) analyzed, i.e. they were always followed by other kinds of 'delays', sometimes several in sequence as in Figure 3 with SWALLOW, SMACK, INHALE following *EH*.

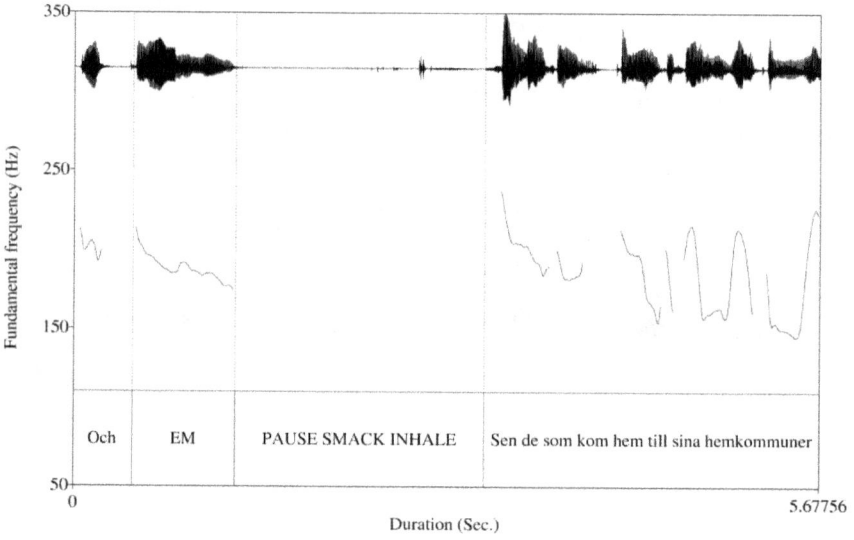

Figure 3. Example of the realization of *EH* as a vowel+nasal [⌷m] before a relatively long delay in speech: *Och EM SWALLOW SMACK INHALE sen de som kom hem till sina hemkommuner* 'and UM SWALLOW SMACK INHALE then the ones that came back to their home municipalities...

The glottalized realizations of *EH* were the fewest (n=31) had a mean duration of 310 ms and a SD of 150 ms. Their duration thus overlaps with the durations of the vowel and vowel+nasal realizations. Unlike the vowel+nasal realizations, the only other delay that was observed to follow the glottalized filled pause was a silent pause.

2.3. Glottalization and dialogue interaction

Glottalized filled pauses in dialogue are in some sense unexpected, since EH is often assumed to be a signal that the speaker wants to hold the floor, whereas glottalization or creaky voice, on the other hand, is assumed to be a signal of finality (Ladefoged, 1982). Ogden (2001) shows for example, that in Finnish, creaky voice in utterance-final position functions in dialogue to signal the end of a speaker's turn. Grivičić and Nilep (2004) have observed creaky voice quality in the pronunciation of English *yeah* as feedback in telephone speech and suggest that it is a signal on the part of the listener for a change of the discourse topic. Duncan and Fiske (1977) observed that when creaky voice is coupled with low pitch, it can signal the end of a conversational turn.

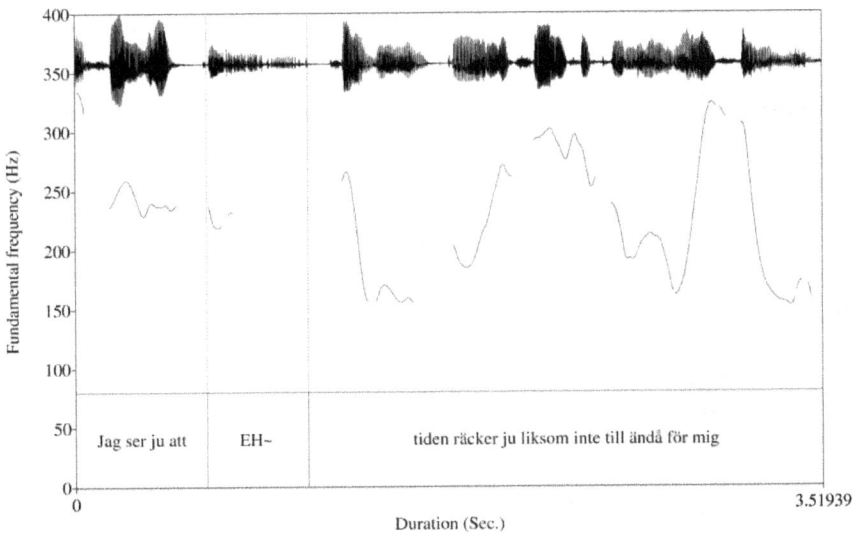

Figure 4. Example of the realization of *EH* as the creaky/glottalized vowel [ə̰] in the utterance: *Jag ser ju att EH tiden räcker ju liksom inte till ändå för mig* 'I see you know that UH time just like isn't enough you know anyway for me'.

2.3.1. Glottalization and attitude reports: uncertainty

Associated with a filled pause, however, glottalization or creak seems to have other functions than signaling turn change (Shriberg 2001). Bear et al. (1992), Lickley (1994), Nakatani and Hirschberg (1994) have observed that glottalization is not uncommon before a speech repair. Glottalized *EH* could, therefore, be interpreted as a juncture signal for an upcoming pause in speech that is *not* to be interpreted by the listener as a TRP (Transition Relevance Place). When it occurs *within* a non-completed turn, glottalization seems to function as a signal that the speaker wishes to continue but is somewhat uncertain as to how to encode the upcoming speech:

(3)   *men den såg ju inte ut EH~ det var någon*
      'but it did not look like UH~ it was somebody'

2.3.2. Glottalized filled pauses as procedural markers

Glottalized filled pauses thus can be considered to be procedural markers of speaker attitude. They occur in environments where the speaker seems to be uncertain about how he or she should code a proposition for a listener who the speaker is not well acquainted with, such as in the example in (4):

(4)   *Jag ser ju att EH~ PAUSE tiden räcker ju liksom inte till ändå för mig*
      'I see you know that UH~ PAUSE the time you know just isn't like long enough anyway for me'

Notice in this example (see also Figure 4) involving the filled pause *EH~*, the cooccurrence of the 'softener' *liksom* 'like' as well as the intensifying positive feedback seeking particle *ju* 'you know' (2 occurrences), which constitute further evidence of the interactional, hedge-related interpretation of the glottalized filled pause. The speaker's fundamental frequency is also relatively high in the context of the filled pause. This high pitch constitutes additional support for a hedge interpretation of the glottalized filler, since, as mentioned above, high F0, according to the *Frequency Code,* is associated with uncertainty and politeness. The uncertainty, however, is not related to the truth value of the proposition being coded but rather to procedural encoding of the message (Blakemore 1987), i.e. it is related to the speaker's mental state as to how the message should be encoded in the most relevant way given the speaker-addressee relationship.

Thus, we propose that glottalized filled pauses signal the speaker attitude uncertainty related to the assertive force of the utterance, more specifically as to how the message should be coded linguistically in a dialogue situation where the speaker is not sure of the optimal way to code a message. The data we have used to illustrate this assumption come from dialogues where the speaker and listener have never met before and therefore have very little common ground. We assume the attitude associated with glottalized filled pauses is related to that associated with the pragmatic particle *liksom* 'like'. However, glottalized EH~ is not associated with uncertainty as regards the referential meaning of the proposition but rather to uncertainty regarding what the speaker determines to be the optimal way of coding the utterance being planned. This attitude can be thought to arise due to the paucity of the common ground established in the current discourse. It is associated with the interactive dimension of the discourse, in the sense that it involves the speaker's degree of awareness of the need to code his or her utterance in a way that best suits the context, given the background knowledge that the addressee has or seems to have. Since it is a kind of uncertainty related directly to speech planning/performance in a dialogue setting, it is therefore a procedural related attitude report.

Nonglottalized EH, on the other hand, is not readily associated with this uncertainty. Nonglottalized filled pauses occur in contexts generally associated with prominence in discourse such as signalling an upcoming focussed word (new information) (Strangert 1991). In this type of context, the speaker is not perceived as being uncertain about how the utterance is to be coded. Notice that in the example in Figure 2, *och sydde på den här EH hembyggdsdräkten* 'and sewed this UH folk dress' one could not add the hedge *liksom*: **och sydde på den här hembyggdsdräkten liksom* '*and sewed like this folkdress', since the presence of the demonstrative determiner den här 'this' indicates that the referent *hembyggdsdräkten* is known to the speaker and the listener. One could, however, have said *och sydde på en hembyggdsdräkt liksom* 'and sewed like a folkdress' where the indefinite article en 'a' indicates a referent, which is new in the discourse and thus assumed by the speaker to be relatively inaccessible for the listener. The use of a glottalized EH~ at the beginning of the clause would make the interactive nature of the utterance more apparent and the speaker attitude more uncertain as regards the procedural encoding of the utterance: *och EH~ sydde på en hembyggdsdräkt liksom* 'and UH~ sewed like a folkdress'.

3. Summary and conclusion

The glottalized realization of the filled pause EH has been hypothesized to have a function related to that of the 'hedging' particle *liksom* 'like'. It is assumed to be an interaction-related hedge signal like liksom in the sense that it is intimately associated with the speaker's cognitive activity in speech planning, i.e. it is a procedural cue to the speaker's attitude.

The data discussed here suggest that glottalized filled pauses would appear to be related to attitude reports that involve uncertainty and positive politeness. Glottalized *EH* is thus assumed to constitute a procedural cue to the speaker's mental state as regards the most relevant way to code the current message, given the dialogue situation where the common ground for speaker and addressee is minimal. The analysis is based on data from discourse situations where the speaker and listener have never met before.

The uncertainty attitude associated with glottalized filled pauses is supported by the fact that other cues to uncertainty and politeness are sometimes present in the utterances containing a glottalized *EH*, for example, pragmatic particles such as the hedge *liksom* 'like' as well as a relatively high fundamental frequency. These cues have independently been associated with the same speaker attitude of uncertainty as well as to politeness. In order to strengthen the present analysis, however, more data from more dialogue situations has to be analyzed and compared.

Acknowledgements

This research was supported by a grant from the Swedish Research Council *(VR)*.

References
Aijmer, Karin
    2004   Pragmatic markers in spoken interlanguage. *Nordic Journal of English Studies* 3: 173–190.

Allwood, Jens, Joakim Nivre, and Elisabeth Ahlsén
1990   Speech management – On the non-written life of speech. *Nordic Journal of Linguistics* 13: 3–48.
Andersen, Gisle, and Thorstein Fretheim (eds.)
2000   *Pragmatic Markers and Propositional Attitude*. University of Bergen/University of Trondheim Pragmatics and Beyond NS 79. Amsterdam: John Benjamins.
Anward, Jan
1999   Allt du önskar kan du få? Om SAG och talspråket. *Svenskans Beskrivning* 24: 329–353.
Barwise, Jon, and John Perry
1983   Situations and attitudes. Cambridge, Mass.: MIT Press.
Bear, John, John Dowding, and Elizabeth Shriberg
1992   Integrating multiple knowledge sources for detection and correction of repairs in human-computer dialog. *Proceedings of the 30th Annual Meeting of the Association for Computational Linguistics*, 56–63.
Blakemore, Diane
1987   *Semantic Constraints on Relevance*. Oxford: Blackwell.
Brown, Penelope, and Stephen Levinson
1987   *Politeness. Some Universals in Language Usage*. Cambridge: Cambridge University Press.
Bruce, Gösta
1998   *Allmän och Svensk Prosodi*. Lund: Dept. of *Linguistics* and Phonetics, Lund University.
Clark, Herb, and Jean Fox Tree
2002   Using *uh* and *um* in spontaneous *speech*. *Cognition 84*: 73–111.
Cooper, Robin
1996   The attitudes in Discourse *Representation* Theory and Situation Semantics. In Logic, Language and Computation, Vol. 1, Jerry Seligman and Dag Westerståhl (eds.), 137–150. Stanford: CSLI Publications.
Cooper, Robin, and Jonathan Ginzburg
1996   A compositional situation semantics for attitude reports. In Logic, Language and Computation, Vol. 1, Jerry Seligman and Dag Westerståhl (eds.), 101–113. Stanford: CSLI Publications.
Duncan, Starkey, and Donald Fiske
1977   Face to Face Interaction: Research Methods and Theory. Hillsdale, N.J.: Lawrence Erlbaum Associates.
Grivičić, Tamara, and Chad Nilep
2004   When phonation matters: the use and function of *yeah* and creaky voice. *Colorado Research in Linguistics* 17 <http://www.colorado.edu/ling/CRIL/Volume17_Issue1/index.htm>

Gussenhoven, Carlos
2004   *Phonology of Tone and Intonation*. Cambridge: Cambridge University Press.

Horne, Merle
2006   The filler EH in Swedish. In Proceedings of Fonetik 2006, Working Papers (Dept. of Linguistics and Phonetics, Lund University) 52: 65–68.

House, David
2003   Perceiving question intonation: the role of pre-focal pause and delayed focal peak. *Proceedings of the 15th International Conference of the Phonetic Sciences* (Barcelona): 755–758.

Ladefoged, Peter
1982   The linguistic use of different phonation types. *University of California Working Papers in Phonetics* 5: 28–39.

Lakoff, George
1972   Hedges: A study in meaning criteria and the logic of fuzzy concepts. *Journal of Philosophical Logic* 2: 458–508.

Lickley, Robin
1994   *Detecting disfluency in spontaneous speech*. Ph.D. dissertation, University of Edinburgh.

Nakatani, Christine, and Julia Hirschberg
1994   A corpus-based study of repair cues in spontaneous speech. *Journal of the Acoustical Society of America* 95: 1603–1616.

Nittono, Miharu
2003   Japanese hedging in friend-friend discourse. Ph.D. dissertation, Columbia University.

Ogden, Richard
2001   Turn transition, creak and glottal stop in Finnish talk-in-interaction. Journal of the International Phonetic Association 31: 139–152.

Ohala, John
1983   An ethological perspective on common cross-language utilization of f0 in voice. Phonetica 41: 1–16.

Pierrehumbert, Janet, and Julia Hirschberg
1990   The meaning of intonational contours in the interpretation of discourse. In Intentions in Communication, Philip Cohen, Jerry Morgan and Martha Pollack (eds.), 271–311. Cambridge, Mass.: MIT Press.

Shriberg, Elizabeth
2001   To 'errrr' is human: ecology and acoustics of speech disfluencies. *Journal of the International Phonetic Association* 31: 153–169.

Strangert, Eva
1991   Phonetic characteristics of professional news reading. Proceedings from Fonetik 1991, *PERILUS* XIII: 39–42. Stockholm: Stockholm University.

Modelling speech synthesis for human interaction

Rolf Carlson

1. Introduction

"... han talte med bönder på bönders vis, och med lärde män på latin ..."
("... he talked to peasants as peasants do, and to learned men in Latin ...")
(Erik Axel Karlfeldt "Sång efter skördeanden", *Fridolins visor*, 1898)

Human-human interaction can be characterized by many features such as context dependent adaption to the domain, the speakers, the relation between speakers, and the dialog flow such as miscommunications. During a normal human-human interaction the speaker or listener uses extra linguistic cues to signal for example understanding or non-understanding. Disfluencies can be natural cues to display closeness, uncertainty, or a speaker's emotive state. Current human-machine systems rarely explore such features, but we see a growing and exciting research direction to address human-like behaviour in dialog systems, (Carlson et al. 2006).

Current work shows that, on the one hand, people's interactions with computers are fundamentally social; users apply "overlearned" social rules to computers such as politeness. Furthermore, users appear to prefer synthesized speech with a "prosodic personality" similar to their own (Nass and Lee. 2000; Nass and Moon 2000). On the other hand, as argued by Callaway (2003), the naturalness of synthesized speech needs further improvement in order to meet higher demands on human-computer interaction. Thus, one specific research goal is to build synthesis models which are able to produce spontaneous speech including natural breaks and disfluencies. In addition to the general challenge to understand and model the features of spontaneous speech, such models can then be explored in human-like spoken dialogue systems.

In this contribution we will briefly review some research efforts on human perception of upcoming boundaries in spontaneous dialog and a sequence of synthesis experiments to model disfluencies based on this knowledge. These efforts are in line with our vision that a conversational dialog system, using speech synthesis as an output device, should follow human behaviour as much as possible to be accepted by human users.

The work has been carried out as joint efforts between KTH, Sweden; Umeå University, Sweden; University of Tilburg, The Netherlands; and Columbia University, USA. Some perceptual data have have been collected at the University of Tokyo, Japan and the Chinese University of Hong Kong, China.

2. Prediction of upcoming prosodic boundaries

In our initial effort and as a base for the synthesis development we studied perceptual aspects of boundaries in spontaneous speech. The work was carried out within the GROG-project (Carlson et al. 2002). Previous studies have shown that listeners are not only sensitive to the absence or presence of a boundary, but that the strength of the boundary is also important (e.g. Dutch (Sanderman 1996) and Swedish (Fant, Kruckenberg and Liljencrants 2000; Strangert and Heldner 1995; Hansson 2003). These studies found that perceived boundary strength is heavily dependent on the occurrence of a silent pause, even to the extent that it may overrule the contribution of other parameters. In addition, we know from previous work on prosody modeling that there are other features such as F0 change, voice quality, and final lengthening which presignal upcoming breaks (e.g. Baronet al. 2002; Ferrer, Shriberg and Stolcke 2002; Swerts, Collie and Terken 1994). These studies are important in that they suggest how listeners may be able to process speech input in real time, while phrases are being produced.

Recently we described a sequence of studies of listener perceptions of prosodic boundaries in spontaneous Swedish. In these experiments the presented stimuli lacked pausal cues, (Carlson, Hirschberg and Swerts 2005). The specific hypothesis tested was that speakers not only encode prosodic breaks locally at the places where they occur (e.g. in the form of silent pauses), but that they also signal these breaks in advance. The general result was that listeners were able to make boundary predictions with considerable accuracy, when compared with hand-labeled breaks. We also reported on additional studies of non-Swedish speaking listener judgments of the same Swedish data. This was done to test whether listeners without access to lexical and grammatical information in the data would exhibit the same ability to identify prosodic boundaries. The data presented in this contribution are expanded to include not only Swedish and American but also Chinese and Japanese listeners.

3. Experiment

For our studies we conducted a variant of the gating paradigm, in which spontaneous Swedish utterance fragments of two different lengths were presented to Swedish and non-Swedish listeners, who were instructed to guess whether or not the fragments are followed by a break, and, if so, to rate its strength on a scale from 1 to 5. Our goal was to test whether upcoming boundaries could be identified under conditions in which pausal information is not present. Furthermore, lexical and grammatical information is not available for the non-Swedish listeners.

The speech corpus was selected from one interview of a female politician that was originally broadcast on public Swedish Radio. The entire interview was prosodically labeled by three independent researchers (Heldner and Megyesi 2003) with respect to boundary presence and strength, with a majority voting strategy used to resolve disagreements. 60 utterance fragments (each about 2 seconds long) were selected for the experiments. The exact initial cutting point was moved to the nearest word boundary, whereas the final cutting point was fixed. The fragments all preceded the word "och" (and) in their original context, and were cut just before the silent interval (if any) preceding that word. The decision to use the word "och" was partly motivated by syntactic considerations, given that the fragments then all occurred in comparable syntactic positions before an identical conjunction. The fragments differed with respect to the presence or absence of a break between the end of the fragment and the word "och". In about one third of the cases, labellers found a strong intervening break at the end of the fragment; in about one third they identified a weak break; and in the remainder they judged there was no break at all after the fragment. From these longer fragments, we then constructed shortened versions consisting of only the final word of the fragment.

Native speakers with four different language backgrounds were used as subjects: 13 Swedish, Umeå University; 29 American, Columbia University; 15 Chinese, Chinese University of Hong Kong and Columbia University; 12 Japanese, University of Tokyo. The subjects had the task to identify whether the stimulus was followed by a strong, a weak or no break.

4. Results

Results revealed that the Swedish, American and Japanese listening groups were indeed able to predict whether or not a boundary (of a particular strength) followed the fragment, see Figure 1. This suggests that acoustic and prosodic, rather than lexico-grammatical and semantic information was being used by listeners as a primary cue. However, Chinese listeners tended to need more than one word to be able to predict an upcoming boundary.

The results indicate that it is the final part of the fragment that in fact contains the critical acoustic or prosodic features which facilitate the prediction of upcoming breaks. Descriptive studies in fact support this possibility, finding important boundary predictors located in the final word, including type of boundary tone preceding the break, final lengthening, loudness patterns, and possible effects of voice quality (e.g. creaky voice). Acoustic and prosodic correlates of the judgments were examined, with significant correlations found between judgments and the presence/absence of final creak, and phrase-final F0 level and slope. In Figure 2 the results for Swedish listeners are presented together with observed final creak. In the next section we will evaluate these findings in synthesis experiments of spontaneous speech.

5. Synthesis experiments of disfluencies

Disfluencies are a recurrent feature in spontaneous speech and occur for reasons such as problems in lexical access or in the structuring of utterances or in searching feedback from a listener. With a few exceptions, relatively little effort has so far been spent on research on spontaneous speech synthesis with a focus on disfluencies. Methods based on unit selection can naturally include some of the hesitation features present in spontaneous speech but this is mostly by accident. In recent work (Sundaram and Narayanan 2003) new steps are taken to predict and realize disfluencies as part of the unit selection in a synthesis system.

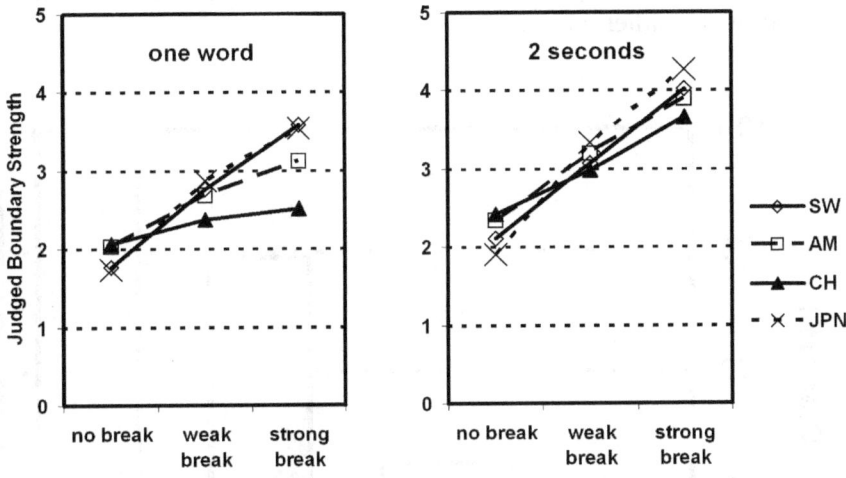

Figure 1. Perceived upcoming boundary strength (subject scores on a 5-point scale). Data grouped according to expert labeled boundary strength (no, weak or strong break), fragment size and native language. Data for Swedish (SW) and American (AM) speakers presented in Carlson, Hirschberg and Swerts 2005 have been expanded with data for Chinese (CH) and Japanese (JPN) speakers.

The focus in the current work is on one type of disfluency, hesitations. The aim is to gain a better understanding of what features contribute to the impression of hesitant speech on a surface level. The work has been carried out through a sequence of experiments using Swedish speech synthesis. In Carlson, Gustafson and Strangert 2006a a study exploring the perceptual signalling of hesitation using parametric synthesis was presented. The manipulations were made in two positions (phrase-internal and phrase external) in a short utterance and were based on observations of the distribution and acoustic manifestations of perceived hesitations in spontaneous speech. This study showed pause duration to be a strong cue to perceived hesitation together with final lengthening. This is a result supported by previous studies showing pauses and retardations to be among the acoustic correlates of hesitations (Eklund 2004; Horne et al. 2003) and also that pause insertion is a salient cue to the impression of hesitation (Lövgren and van Doorn 2005). Most important, however, was the result that it was the total increase, the combination of both pause duration and final lengthening, that was the valid cue rather than the contribution by either factor.

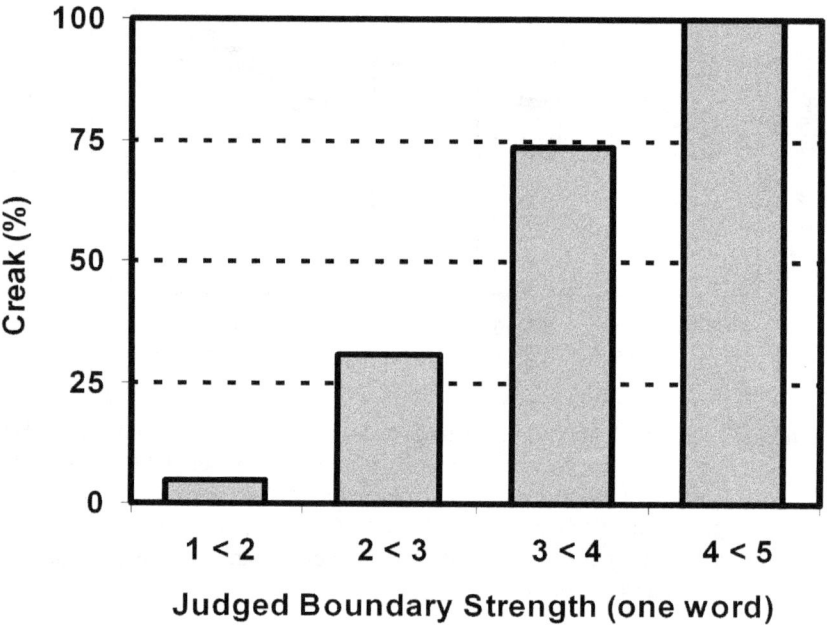

Figure 2. Number of stimuli with creaky voice (in %) for different judged boundary strength intervals (one word). Swedish listeners.

Surprisingly variation of F0 slope, which was also investigated, had almost negligible effects. Whether F0 in effect plays a role can be considered an open question in the light of what is known up till now, as there are results going in both directions. The results reported above and Edlund and Heldner (2005) point to F0 as a cue for hesitation, while the results in Horne et al. 2003 reveal no significant F0 differences between fluent and disfluent contexts. A factor, on the other hand, that appeared to have an influence was syntactic position; different results were obtained in phrase-internal and phrase-external positions.

6. Experiment

Starting out from the findings described above, new potential cues to hesitation (creaky voice) as well as modifications of earlier parameter settings (temporal parameters and F0 slope variation) were included in a new experiment using synthetic speech (Carlson, Gustafson and Strangert 2006b). The stimuli was synthesized using the KTH formant based synthesis system (Carlson and Granström 1997), giving full flexibility for prosodic adjustments, see Figure 3. A hesitation was placed either in the first part of the utterance (F) or in the middle (M) of the Swedish utterance: *I sin F trädgård har Bettan M tagetes och rosor*. (English word-by-word translation: 'In her F garden has Bettan M tagetes and roses.' Tagetes is, like roses, a type of flower.) The stimuli were manipulated with respect to duration features, F0 slope and presence versus absence of creaky voice. Since the total increase in duration is the most important cue rather than each factor separately (Carlson, Gustafson and Strangert 2006), pause and final lengthening were combined in one "total duration increase" feature. In addition, there were stimuli without inserted hesitations.

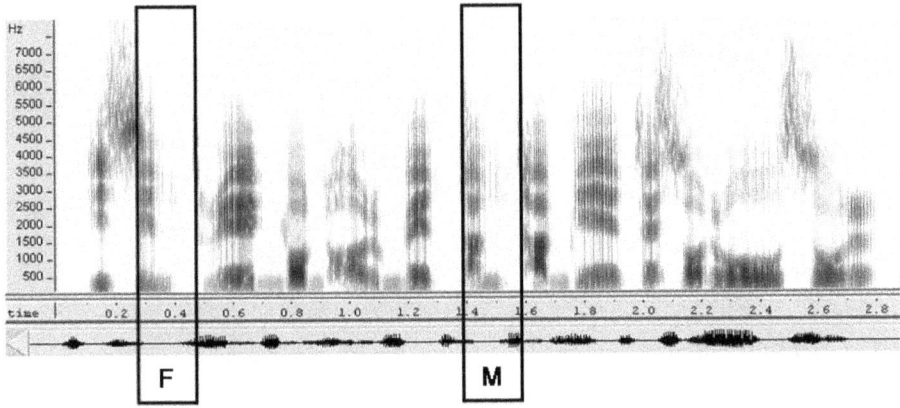

Figure 3. Default synthesis *I sin F trädgård har Bettan M tagetes och rosor*. with the two possible positions for hesitation marked with F and M.

The two positions were chosen to be either inside a phrase (F) or between two phrases (M). The hesitation points F and M were placed in the unvoiced stop consonant occlusion and were modelled using three parameters: a) total duration increase combining retardation before the hesitation point and pause, b) F0 slope variation and c) presence/absence of creak.

The intonation was modelled by the default rules in the TTS system. At the hesitation point the F0 was adjusted to model slope variation in 5 shapes with rising contours (+20, +40 Hz) a flat contour (0) and falling contours (-20, -40 Hz). The pivot point before the hesitation was placed at the beginning of the last vowel before the hesitation. See Figure 4 for an illustration of maximally falling and maximally rising contours.

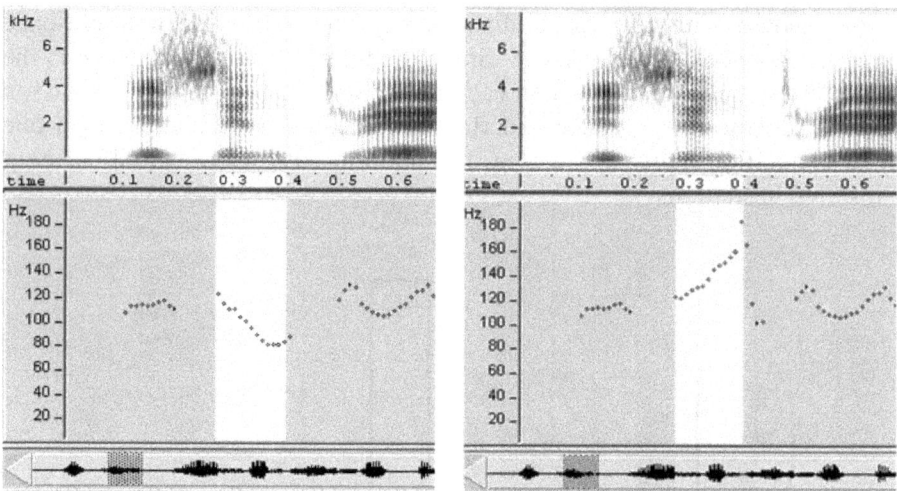

Figure 4. Illustration of intonation contours for the two extreme cases in position F.

Creaky voice was set to start three quarters into the last vowel before the hesitation and to reach full effect at the end of the vowel. The creak was modelled by changing every other glottal pulse in time and amplitude (Klatt and Klatt 1990).

The synthesized stimuli were presented to 14 Swedish subjects. During the test the subjects listened to an individually randomized list. The subjects evaluated each stimulus, noting whether they perceived a hesitation, and, if so, where it was positioned. Each stimulus could be repeated until they were satisfied with their judgment.

7. Results

In Figure 5 hesitation perception is plotted as a function of total duration increase (across variation of F0 slope and creak). The strong effect is similar to and confirms the previous result that the combined effect of pause and retardation is a very strong cue to hesitation. The detection is easier with greater total duration increase (p<.001). The perception of hesitation further depends on syntax, as reflected in the difference between the two curves, a difference of about 25% in the cross-over area. That is, it is easier to detect hesitation in the first (phrase-internal) position than in the second (phrase-external) position (p<.001). Furthermore, there is a significant interaction of position and total duration increase. The detection is easier with an intermediate duration increase in F position (p<.001).

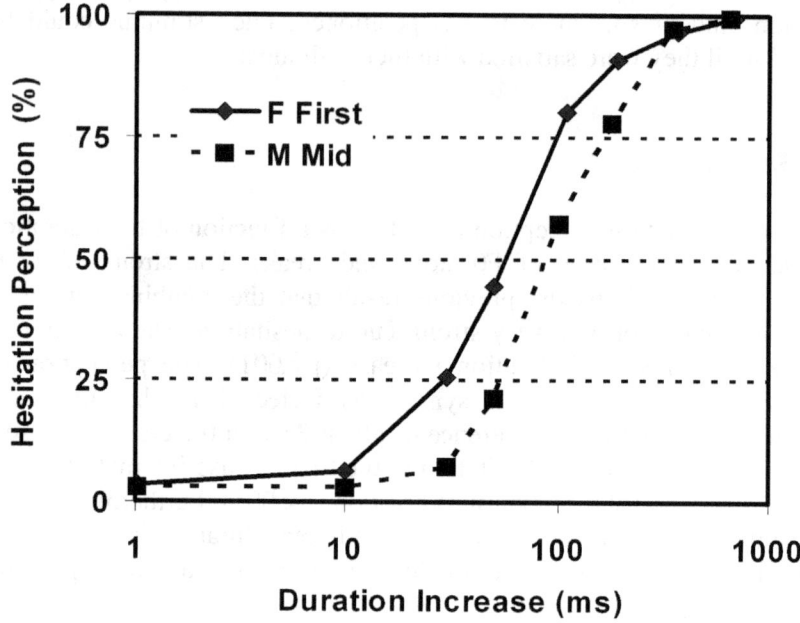

Figure 5. Detection of hesitation as a function of duration increase across variation of F0 slope and creak. Data separated depending on position of hesitation (phrase-internally=F, phrase-externally=M).

The F0 slope seems to have some influence on the hesitation detection and compensate for weak duration cues. Falling F0 contours make the perception of hesitation easier in the cross-over area for duration (Figure 6). F0 tends to interact both with position and duration making detection easier with falling F0 combined with shorter total duration increase in F position, approaching significance (p=.093).

The change in hesitation perception due to the presence of creak is plotted against total duration increase in Figure 7. The two curves represent the phrase-internal and phrase-external positions, respectively. Here, a compensatory pattern is revealed, in particular in the phrase-internal (F) position; in the cross-over area (at, or close to, a total duration increase of about 100 ms), creak has a strengthening effect, making detection easier. Significant interaction of creaky voice and position indicate that the detection is easier with presence of creak in F position (p<.05) i.e. creak tends to compensate for weak duration cues.

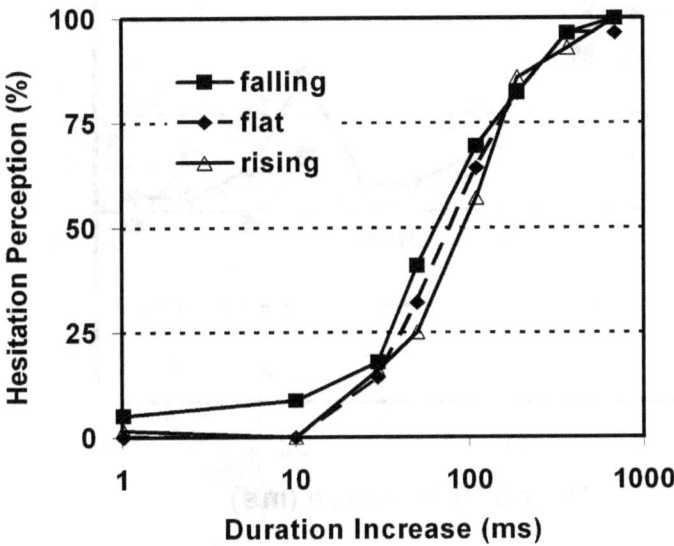

Figure 6. Hesitation perception depending on F0 slope. Phrase-internal and phrase-external data are pooled.

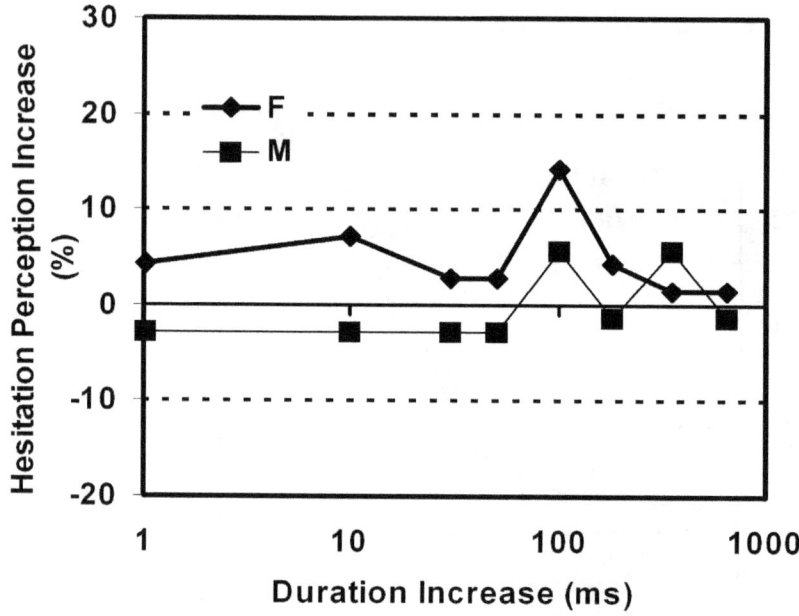

Figure 7. Change of hesitation perception depending on presence of creak. Phrase-internal (F) and phrase-external (M) data are separated.

8. Discussion and concluding remarks

Our perceptual studies of upcoming boundaries in spontaneous Swedish speech show that listeners are in fact able to predict upcoming boundaries based on properties of the preceding word or phrase alone, without access to a following pause. Furthermore, reliable judgments can be made by non-Swedish listeners without access to lexical or syntactic information.

The synthesis results support the conclusion that duration increase, achieved by the combined effects of retardation and pause, is an extremely powerful cue to a perceived break, in this case a hesitation. People apparently have expectations on the temporal structuring of an utterance and react to even modest deviations from this structuring.

F0 slope variation and creak play a role, too, but both are far less powerful compared to the duration cues, being more of supporting cues.

Their greatest effects apparently occur in the cross-over area, when the decision hesitation/no hesitation is the most difficult.

The assumption that subjects are less sensitive to modifications in the middle position (M) than in the first position (F) is also borne out. We relate this to the difference in syntactic structure; in the F position the hesitation occurs in the middle of a noun phrase ("I sin F trädgård"), whereas in the M position it occurs between two noun phrases, functioning as subject and object respectively. A reasonable assumption is that the subjects expected some kind of prosodic marking in the latter position and that therefore a greater lengthening was required in order to produce the percept of hesitation.

This assumption and even more the corollary, that subjects do not expect boundary signalling cues within phrases, get support from how the subjects reacted to the other two features investigated. Both intonation and creaky voice have the capacity to signal an upcoming boundary. Therefore it is not surprising that both intonation (negative F0 slopes) and presence of creak made detection of hesitance easier in the phrase-internal than in the phrase-external position. This dependence on syntax is not unexpected in the light of vast numbers of production studies showing the strength of prosodic signalling to depend on the strength of the syntactic boundary.

In conclusion, our results indicate that the perception of hesitation is strongly influenced by deviations from an expected temporal pattern. In addition, different syntactic conditions have an effect on how much changes in prosodic features like the F0 contour and retardation and the presence of creaky voice contribute to the perception of hesitation. In view of this, the modelling of hesitation in speech technology applications should take account of the supporting roles that F0 and creak can play in achieving a realistic impression of a break. In the future also, more global aspects of hesitant speech should be covered. It might be worth while to consider other modifications than those occurring at or before the hesitation point. Also, hesitation is not a binary feature; therefore, a generic model of hesitation should include different degrees of hesitance.

An important step in the modelling of spontaneous speech would be to include predictions of hesitations depending on the utterance structure. To do this, data are required, not only of the realization of hesitant speech, but also of the distribution of hesitations, see e.g. Strangert 2004. The long-term goal to build a synthesis model which is able to produce spontaneous speech on the basis of such data, and to integrate the model in a conversational dialogue system still requires considerable further research.

Acknowledgements

The work has been carried out as a number of joint efforts between Rolf Carlson and Kjell Gustafson, Centre of Speech Technology (CTT), KTH, Sweden; Eva Strangert, Umeå University, Sweden; Marc Swerts, University of Tilburg, The Netherlands; and Julia Hirschberg, Columbia University, USA. Perceptual data have also been collected by Keikichi Hirose, University of Tokyo, Japan and Tan Lee, Chinese University of Hong Kong, China. We thank Jens Edlund, CTT, for designing the test environment for the synthesis experiment, and Thierry Deschamps, Umeå University, for technical support in performing the experiments. This work was supported by The Swedish Research Council (VR) and The Swedish Agency for Innovation Systems (VINNOVA).

References

Baron, Don, Elizabeth Shriberg and Andreas Stolcke
   2002   Automatic Punctuation And Disfluency Detection In Multi-Party Meetings Using Prosodic And Lexical Cues, ICSLP 2002, Denver, USA.

Callaway, Charles
   2003   Do we need deep generation of disfluent dialogue? In: AAAI Spring Symposium on Natural Language Generation in Spoken and Written Dialogue. AAAI Press, Menlo Park, CA.

Carlson Rolf, Julia Hirschberg and Marc Swerts
   2005   Cues to upcoming Swedish prosodic boundaries: Subjective judgment studies and acoustic correlates. Speech Communication 46, pp 326-333.

Carlson, Rolf and Björn Granström
   1997   Speech synthesis. In: Hardcastle W. J. and Laver J. The Handbook of Phonetic Science. Oxford: Blackwell Publ., pp 768-788.

Carlson, Rolf, Jens Edlund, David House, Mattias Heldner, Anna Hjalmarsson, and Gabriel Skantze
   2006   Towards human-like behaviour in spoken dialog systems. In Proceedings of Swedish Language Technology Conference (SLTC 2006). Gothenburg, Sweden

Carlson, Rolf, Björn Granström, Mattias Heldner, David House, Beata Megyesi, Eva Strangert and Marc Swerts
   2002   Boundaries and groupings – the structuring of speech in different communicative situations: A description of the GROG project. Proc. Fonetik 2002, 65-68.

Carlson, Rolf, Kjell Gustafson and Eva Strangert
2006a   Modelling hesitation for synthesis of spontaneous speech. In Proceedings of Speech Prosody 2006. Dresden, Germany.
2006b   Cues for Hesitation in Speech Synthesis. In Proceedings of Interspeech 06. Pittsburgh, USA.

Edlund, Jens and Mattias Heldner
2005   Exploring prosody in interaction control. Special issue of Phonetica: Progress in Experimental Phonology, 62 (2-4)

Eklund, Robert
2004   Disfluency in Swedish human-human and human-machine travel booking dialogues. Dissertation 882, Linköping Studies in Science and Technology.

Fant, Gunnar, Anita Kruckenberg, and Johan Liljencrants
2000   Acoustic-phonetic Analysis of Prominence in Swedish. In A Botinis (ed.), Intonation, Analysis, Modeling and Technology (Kluwer).

Ferrer, Luciana, Elizabeth Shriberg and Andreas Stolcke
2002   Is the speaker done yet? Faster and more accurate end-of-utterance detection using prosody, ICSLP – 2002, Denver, USA.

Hansson, Petra
2003   Prosodic Phrasing in Spontaneous Swedish. Travaux de l'institut de linguistique de Lund 43, Dept. of Linguistics and Phonetics, Lund University, Sweden.

Heldner, Mattias and Beata Megyesi
2003   Exploring the prosody-syntax interface in conversations. In: Proc. 15th ICPhS, Barcelona, pp. 2501-2504.

Horne, Merle, Johan Frid, Birgitta Lastow, Gösta Bruce, and Adina Svensson
2003   Hesitation disfluencies in Swedish: Prosodic and segmental correlates. In: Proc. 15th ICPhS, Barcelona, pp. 2429-2432.

Klatt, Dennis and Laura Klatt
1990   Analysis, synthesis and perception of voice quality variations among female and male talkers. JASA 87, pp 820-857.

Lövgren, Tobias and Jan van Doorn
2005   Influence of manipulation of short silent pause duration on speech fluency. In: Proc. DISS2005, pp. 123-126.

Nass, Clifford and Kwan Min Lee
2000   Does computer-generated speech manifest personality? CHI2000, 329-336.

Nass, Clifford and Youngme Moon
2000   Machines and mindlessness: Social responses to computers. Journal of Social Issues, 60(1):81-103.

Sanderman, Angelien
1996   Prosodic phrasing. Production, perception, acceptability and comprehension. PhD thesis, Eindhoven University of Technology.

Strangert, Eva
 2004 Speech chunks in conversation: Syntactic and prosodic aspects. In: Proc. Speech Prosody 2004, Nara, pp. 305-308.

Strangert, Eva, and Mattias Heldner
 1995 Labelling of boundaries and prominences by phonetically experienced and non-experienced transcribers. In PHONUM 3, pp. 85-109. Umeå: Department of Phonetics, Umeå University.

Sundaram, Shiva and Shrikanth Narayanan
 2003 An empirical text transformation method for spontaneous speech synthesizers, In: Proc. Interspeech 2003, Geneva, Switzerland.

Swerts, Marc, Rene Collier and Jacques Terken
 1994 Prosodic predictors of discourse finality in spontaneous monologues. Speech Communication 15, 79-90.

Conversational Interactions: Capturing Dialogue Dynamics[1]

Arash Eshghi, Julian Hough, Matthew Purver (QMUL, London), Ruth Kempson, Eleni Gregoromichelaki (KCL, London)

1. The scope of grammar

In this paper, we set out the case for combining the Type Theory with Records framework (TTR, Cooper (2005)) with Dynamic Syntax (DS, Kempson, Meyer-Viol, and Gabbay (2001); Cann, Kempson, and Marten (2005)) in a single model (DS-TTR). In a nutshell, this fusion captures a phenomenon inexpressible in any direct way by frameworks grounded in orthodox sentientialist assumptions – the dynamics of how, in ordinary conversations, we build up information together, incrementally, bit by bit, through half starts, suggested add-ons, possible modifications to the emergent structure which we are apparently collaborating on, all the while allowing that we might be uncertain as to the final outcome, or even in fierce disagreement. To this hybrid, TTR brings representations of content which, through its rich notion of subtyping, allows for highly structured models of both content and context. DS contributes a grammar framework in which syntax is defined as the progressive building of representations of content via update mechanisms following real-time dynamics. Together they provide a framework in which the interactive dynamics of conversational dialogue is an immediate consequence. And the data we present below show that such a model is essential if core syntactic properties of natural language are to be fully captured.

1.1. Incrementality, radical context-dependence and dialogue phenomena

1.1.1. The (non-)autonomy of syntax

Evidence for incrementality in conversation comes from the widespread use of utterances that are fragmentary, subsentential, yet intelligible, all in virtue of ongoing interaction between interlocutors and their physical environment:

(1)   Context: Friends of the Earth club meeting

A: So what is that? Is that er... booklet or something?
B: It's a [[book]]
C: [[Book]]   (*Answer/Acknowledgement/Completion*)
B: Just ... [[talking about al you know
alternative]]   (*Continuation*)
D: [[On erm... renewable yeah]]   (*Extension*)
B: energy really I think...   (*Completion*)
A: Yeah   (*Acknowledgment*)   [BNC:D97]

Moreover, the placing of items like inserts, repairs, hesitation markers etc. follows systematic patterns that show subtle interaction with grammatical principles at a sub-sentential level (Levelt 1983; Clark and Fox Tree 2002):

(2)   "Sure enough ten minutes later the bell r-the doorbell rang" *(Schegloff, Jefferson, and Sacks 1977)*

(3)   "I-I mean the-he-they, y'know the guy, the the pathologist, looks at the tissue in the microscope..." *(Schegloff, Jefferson, and Sacks 1977)*

The heart of the incrementality challenge is that people can make perfect sense of and systematically manipulate not only their own sub-sentential utterances as they produce them, but also others'. Even very young children can seamlessly take over from an adult in conversation. Participants may seek to finish what someone else has in mind to say as in (4), but equally, they may interrupt to alter what someone else has proffered, taking the conversation in a different or even contrary direction, as in (5) :

(4)   Gardener: I shall need the mattock.
      Home-owner: The...
      Gardener: mattock. For breaking up clods of earth.[BNC]

(5)   (A and B arguing:)
      A: In fact what this shows is
      B: that you are an idiot

Yet, this phenomenon of *compound contributions* is by no means restricted to one party completing someone else's utterance according to their own sense of the required outcome. Participants may, in some sense, "just keep going" from where their interlocutor had got to, contributing the next little bit. Such exchanges can indeed be indefinitely extended without either contributor knowing in advance the end-point of the exchange:

(6) (a) A: Robin's arriving today
(b) B: from?
(c) A: Sweden
(d) B: with Elisabet?
(e) A: and a dog, a puppy and very bouncy
(f) B: but Robin's allergic
(g) A: to dogs? but it's a Dalmatian.
(h) B: and so?
(j) A: it won't be a problem. No hairs.

The upshot is that it is hard to tell where one sentence stops and the next starts.

This phenomenon is not a dysfluency of dialogue. The forms of such 'fragments' are not random: with only very isolated exceptions, they follow exactly the licensing conditions specified by the NL grammar, with syntactic dependencies of the most fundamental sort holding between the subsentential parts.[2]

(7) A: I'm afraid I burned the buns.
B: Did you burn
A: myself? No, fortunately not.

(8) A: D'you know whether every waitress handed in
B: her taxforms? A: or even any payslips?

People can take over from one another at any arbitrary point in an exchange (Purver et al. 2010), setting up the anticipation of possible dependencies to be fulfilled. We have already seen that it can be between a preposition and its head, (6b-c), between a head and its complement (6f-g), between one conjunct and the next (6d-j), between a reflexive pronoun and its presented antecedent (7), determiner and noun (4), quantifier and expressions it binds (8) etc. So, unless the grammar reflects the possibility of such dependencies to be set and fulfilled across participants, not a single grammatical phenomenon will have successfully been provided with a complete, uniform characterisation. Moreover, any attempt to reflect this type of context-dependence, and the attendant sense of continuity it gives rise to, through grammar-internal specifications will have to involve constraints on fragment construal that go well beyond what is made available in terms of denotational content: such constraints will have to include the full range of syntactic and morphosyntactic dependencies (Ginzburg and Cooper 2004; Ginzburg 2012).

Amongst the proposed solutions to capturing such dependencies is the stipulation of a salient antecedent utterance, whose syntactic characterisation is projected into context and taken to constrain the form of the following fragment (see e.g. Ginzburg's approach (2012)). However, even in the absence of any linguistic antecedent, where the derivation of speech act content is achieved purely pragmatically, such fragments need to respect the morphosyntactic requirements of the relevant NL:

(9)   Context: A and B enter a room and see a woman lying on the floor:
      A to B: Schnell, den Arzt/*der Arzt   [German]
      "Quick, the doctor$_{ACC}$ /*the doctor$_{NOM}$"   [command]

(10) A is contemplating the space under the mirror while re-arranging the furniture and B brings her a chair:
      tin karekla tis mamas?/*i karekla tis mamas? Ise treli?
      [Greek]   [clarification]
      the chair of mum's$_{ACC}$/*the chair$_{NOM}$ of mum's. Are you crazy?

(11) A is handing a brush to B:
      A: for painting the wall?   [clarification]

(12) A is pointing to Bill:
      B: No, his sister   [correction]

Thus no account that relies on rules that require reference to some salient linguistic form of antecedent utterance will be general enough (even Ginzburg's invocation of genre-specific scripts does not provide the relevant licensing for such cases). In particular, these data suggest that the grammar needs to be defined as part of a general model of action/perception so that common representations can be retrieved and manipulated both from the linguistic and extra-linguistic context (see e.g. Larsson (2011)). A crucial ingredient in such integration would be licensing mechanisms that operate at a subsentential level with fine-grained sensitivity to the time-linear process of interaction among agents and the evolving context in which such interaction takes place.

1.1.2. Pragmatic/semantic "competence" and radical context-dependence in dialogue

These data are also significant to pragmatists. Almost all pragmatists assume that the supposedly isolatable sentence meaning made available by the grammar should feed into a theory of performance/pragmatics whose burden it is to explain how, relative to context, both full sentences and fragments are uttered on the presumption that the audience will come to understand the propositional content which the speaker has (or could have) in mind. But, contrary to this view, participants understand what each other is saying and switch roles well before any such propositional content could be interpreted to constitute the object relative to which the speaker or other party could hold a propositional attitude:

(13)   Daughter: Oh here dad, a good way to get those corners out
         Dad: is to stick yer finger inside.
         Daughter: well, that's one way (Lerner 1991)

(14)   M: It's generated with a handle and
         J: Wound round?   [BNC]
         M: Yes, wind them round and this should, should generate a charge

There is negotiation here as to the best way to continue a partial structure, with intentions of either party with respect to the resulting content possibly only emerging after the negotiation. Utterances may also be multi-functional, with more than one speech act expressed by a single utterance:

(15)   Lawyer: Do you wish your wife to witness your signature, one of your children, or..?
         Customer: Joe.

So there is no single proposition/speech act that the individual speaker may have carried out which has to be grasped in order for successful exchanges to have taken place. Participants rely on the setting up of grammatical dependencies which both speaker and hearer are induced to fulfil, so as to perform possibly composite speech acts (Gregoromichelaki et al. forthcoming):

(16)   Jim: The Holy Spirit is one who ...gives us?
         Unknown: Strength.
         Jim: Strength. Yes, indeed. .... The Holy Spirit is one who gives us? .....
         Unknown: Comfort. [BNC HDD: 277-282]

(17)   Therapist: What kind of work do you do?
         Mother: on food service
         Therapist: At ...
         Mother: uh post office cafeteria downtown main point office on Redwood
         Therapist: Okay (Jones & Beach 1995)

The commitment to recovering any such content as a precondition for successful communication has therefore to be modified; and so too does the presumption of there having to be specific intended propositional plans on the part of the speaker (Grosz and Sidner 1986; Poesio and Rieser 2010; Carberry 1990). Such cases show, in our view, that "fragmentary" interaction in dialogue should be modelled as such, i.e. with grammar defined to provide mechanisms that allow participants to incrementally update the conversational record without at each step requiring reference to some propositional whole. Even though participants can reflect and reify such interactions in explicit propositional terms (Purver et al. 2010), the ongoing metacommunicative interaction observable in dialogue is achievable via the grammatical mechanisms themselves without commitment to deterministic speech-act goals.

The problem current frameworks have in dealing with such data can be traced to the assumption that it is sentential strings that constitute the output of the grammar, over which some propositional content is to be defined, along with the attendant methodological principle debarring any attribute of performance within the grammar-internal characterisation. In this respect, Cooper and colleagues (see e.g. Ginzburg (2012)) have achieved significant advance in defining an explicit semantic model that is not so restricted, exploring ontologies required to define how speech events can cause changes in the mental states of dialogue participants. However, the syntax of that system is defined independently as an HPSG grounded module which precludes a principled modelling of the evolving subsentential (syntactic) context-relativity in these compound contributions with their seamless shifts between parsing and generation. It is within the composite DS-TTR system that their natural modelling emerges, in virtue of both content and context being defined for both parties in the same terms of evolving partial structures.

2. DS-TTR for dialogue modelling

In turning to details of this model, we will need concepts of incrementality applicable to both parsing and generation. Milward's (1991) two key concepts of *strong incremental interpretation* and *incremental representation* apply to semantic incrementality. *Strong incremental interpretation* is the ability to make available the maximal amount of information possible from an unfinished utterance as it is being processed word by word, particularly the semantic dependencies of the informational content (e.g. a representation such as $\lambda x.like'(john',x)$ should be available after processing "John likes"). *Incremental representation*, on the other hand, is defined as a representation being available for each substring of an utterance, but not necessarily including the dependencies between these substrings (e.g. having a representation such as $john'$ attributed to "John" and $\lambda y.\lambda x.like'(y,x)$ attributed to "likes" after processing "John likes"). There are two further concepts of incrementality. In order to model *compound contributions*, the representations produced by parsing and generation should be *interchangeable*, e.g. by defining parsing and generation as employing the same update mechanisms (section 3.1). Finally, the notion of an incrementally constructed and accessible *context* becomes important for modelling self-repair, but also independently motivated for a range of other elliptical phenomena such as stripping and VP-Ellipsis. As we will see in sections 2.2, 3.2 (see also Cann, Kempson, and Purver (2007)), the appropriate concept of context for DS is a *procedural* one since it is by means of conditioned procedures for update that interpretations are incrementally constructed.

2.1. Combining Dynamic Syntax and TTR

DS is in the spirit of Categorial Grammars in directly modelling the building up of interpretations, without presupposing or indeed recognising an independent level of syntactic processing. Thus the output for any given string of words is a purely semantic tree representing its predicate-argument structure; words and grammatical rules correspond to actions which incrementally license the construction of such representations in tree format, employing a modal logic for tree description which provides operators able to introduce constraints on the further development of such trees (LOFT, Blackburn and Meyer-Viol (1994)). However, unlike categorial grammars, it achieves this while also respecting time-linear incrementality, with the left-right progressive build-up of information directly modelled through the incorporation of structural underspecification plus update as a core syntactic device. In particular, analysis of long-distance dependencies and other noncontiguous dependencies are defined in such terms (see Cann, Kempson, and Marten (2005), ch. 2 for details). The DS lexicon consists of *lexical actions* keyed to words. There is also a set of globally applicable *computational actions*. Both constitute packages of monotonic update operations on semantic trees, and take the form of IF-THEN action-like rules which when applied yield semantically transparent structures. For example, the lexical action corresponding to the word *john* has the preconditions and update operations in (18):

(18) IF $?Ty(e)$
      THEN put($Ty(e)$)
            put($[\ x\ :\ john\ ]$)
      ELSE abort

The trees upon which actions operate represent terms in the typed lambda calculus, with mother-daughter node relations corresponding to semantic predicate-argument structure (see Figure 1 below). The pointer object, ◊, indicates the node currently under development. In DS-TTR, tree nodes are annotated with a node type (e.g. $Ty(e)$) and semantic formulae in the form of TTR *record types* (Cooper 2005). In this incorporation of TTR into DS (Purver et al. 2010; Purver, Eshghi, and Hough 2011), following Cooper (2005), TTR *record types* consist of fields of the form $[\ l\ :\ T\ ]$, containing a unique label l in the record type and its type T; the type of the final field corresponds to the node type of the DS tree at which a record type formula is situated. Functional nodes have node types which correspond to the final field types of argument and functor in the TTR function decorating them. Fields can be *manifest* (i.e. have a singleton type such as $[\ l_{=a}\ :\ T\ ]$). Within record types there can be *dependent* fields such as those whose singleton type is a predicate as in $[\ p_{=like(x,y)}\ :\ t\ ]$, where x and y are labels in fields preceding it (i.e. are higher up in the graphical representation). Functions from record type to record type in the variant of TTR we use here employ paths, and are of the form $\lambda r : [\ l1\ :\ T1\ ]\ [\ l2_{=r.l1}\ :\ T1\ ]$, an example being the formula at the type $Ty(e_s \to t)$ node in the trees in Figure 1 below, giving DS-TTR the required functional application capability. Parsing intersperses the testing and application of both lexical actions triggered by input words and the execution of permissible sequences of computational actions, with their updates monotonically constructing and the tree and compiling decorations for its nodes: functor node functions are applied to their sister argument node's formula, with the resulting β-reduced record type added to their mother.[3] Seen in these terms, successful processing sequences are those in which applied actions lead to a tree which is complete (i.e. has no outstanding requirements on any node, and has type $Ty(t)$ at its root node as in Figure (1). Incomplete *partial* structures are maintained in the parse state on a word-by-word basis.

We further adopt an event-based semantics along Davidsonian lines (Davidson 1980). So we include an event node (of type e_s) in the representation: this allows tense and aspect to be expressed,[4] allowing incremental modification to the the record type on the $Ty(e_s)$ node during parsing and generation after its initial placement in the initial axiom tree.

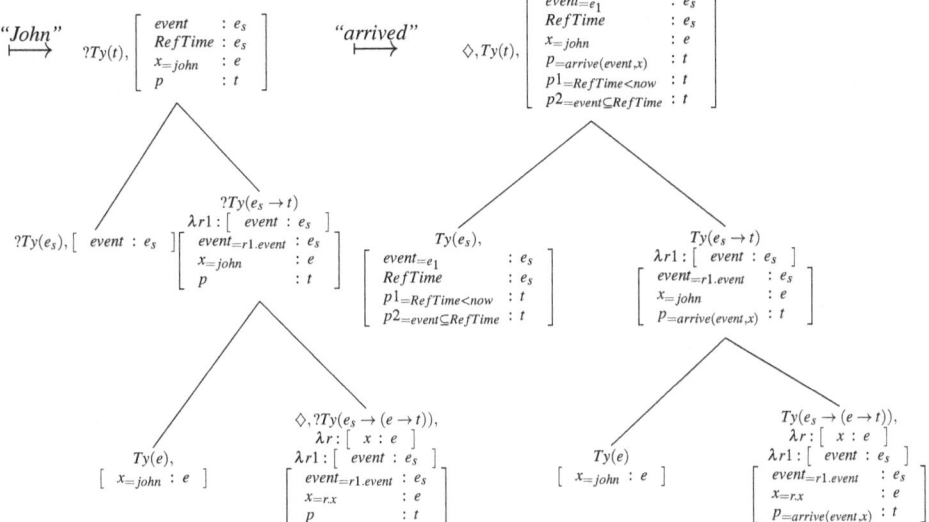

Figure 1. Parsing "John arrived"

This event node specification also permits a straightforward analysis of adjuncts as extensions by the addition of fields from an independently constructed semantic representation (see section 3.1 and Appendix 1 for examples). To achieve this, independent predicate-argument structures are induced via construction of a so-called LINKed tree, an adjunct tree, whose dependency on some host tree despite this structural independence is ensured through a sharing of formula terms at nodes in the two trees in question. A computational action is defined to licensing the appropriate transition from a node of one partial tree to the initiation of this LINKed tree, imposing on its development a dictated co-sharing of terms (see Kempson, Meyer-Viol, and Gabbay (2001)). This device applies to adjunct processing in general (Cann, Kempson, and Marten (2005), ch. 3, also Gregoromichelaki (2006)). In DS-TTR, such LINKs are evaluated as the intersection/concatenation (the *meet* operation, as in Cooper (2005)) of the record-type accumulated at the top of a LINKed tree and the matrix tree's root node record type (see Appendix 1 for example derivations). So construal of adjuncts boils down to the progressive specification of richer record types.

Through a simple tree compiling algorithm (Hough 2011), the DS-TTR composite now makes available a root record type which gives the maximal amount of semantic information available for partial as well as complete trees (Figure 1). This is achieved by performing all possible functional applications from functor nodes to argument nodes, using underspecified record types as necessary for nodes which have not yet been decorated with semantic content (see e.g. the $Ty(e \rightarrow (e_s \rightarrow t))$ node on the left tree in Figure 1 above, where the functional type corresponding to an upcoming verb does not yet contain an overt predicate to be applied to the subject $john'$, this being simply the unmanifest/underspecified field $p : t$).

This root record type compilation via functional application and type intersection meets the requirement of strong incrementality of interpretation, only implicit in DS, as now maximal record types become available as each word is processed. Yet the LOFT underpinning to the mechanisms of tree-growth means that the DS insight that core syntactic restrictions emerge as immediate consequences of the LOFT-defined tree-growth dynamics is preserved without modification (Cann, Kempson, and Marten 2005; Cann, Kempson, and Purver 2007; Kempson and Kiaer 2010; Kempson, Gregoromichelaki, and Howes(eds.) 2011; Chatzikyriakidis and Kempson 2011).

2.2. DS-TTR procedural context as a graph

Aside from the strong incremental interpretation that DS-TTR representations afford, the model provides incremental access to *procedural context* as required not only for modelling the phenomena reviewed above, but independently motivated for phenomena such as VP-Ellipsis and stripping. In DS, this context is taken as including not only the end product of parsing or generating an utterance (the semantic tree and corresponding string), but also information about the dynamics of the parsing process itself – the lexical and computational action sequence used to build the tree (Cann, Kempson, and Purver 2007). This procedural context is modelled as a Directed Acyclic Graph (DAG) (a representation originally used to characterise the parsing process (Sato 2011)), in which edges correspond to DS actions and nodes to (partial) *trees* (Purver, Eshghi, and Hough 2011). This model now satisfies the criterion of *strong incremental representation*: we get a transparent representation of not only the maximal interpretation for the utterance so far, but also for which sub-utterances contributed which sub-parts of this interpretation. Aside from our model of self-repair set out below, this is required for modelling clarification as well as confirmation behaviour in dialogue. This context DAG can be tightly coupled with a word hypothesis graph (or "word lattice") as obtained from a standard speech recogniser, resulting in ease of integration in modern incremental dialogue systems (Purver, Eshghi, and Hough (2011)).

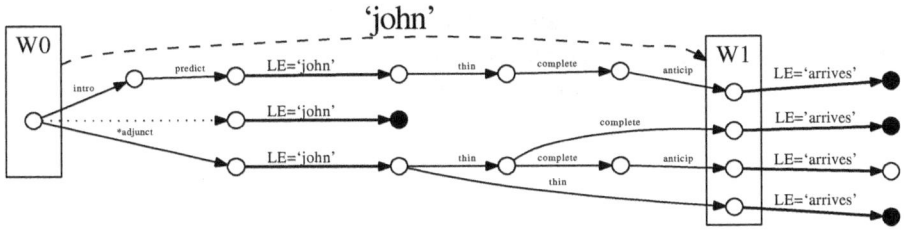

Figure 2. DS context as DAG, consisting of a parse DAG (circular nodes=trees, solid edges=lexical(bold) and computational actions) subsumed by the corresponding word DAG (rectangular nodes=tree sets, dotted edges=word hypotheses) with word hypothesis 'john' spanning tree sets W0 and W1.

The resulting model of context is thus a hierarchical model with DAGs at two levels (figure 2). At the action level, the parse graph DAG (shown in the lower half of figure 2 with solid edges and circular nodes) contains detailed information about the actions (both lexical and computational) used in the parsing or generation process: edges corresponding to these actions are connected to nodes representing the partial trees built by them, and a path through the DAG corresponds to the action sequence for any given tree. At the word level, the word hypothesis DAG (shown at the top of figure 2 with dotted edges and rectangular nodes) connects the words to these action sequences: edges in this DAG correspond to words, and nodes correspond to sets of parse DAG nodes (and therefore sets of hypothesized trees). For any partial tree, the context (the words, actions and preceding partial trees involved in producing it) is now available from the paths back to the root in the word and parse DAGs. Moreover, the sets of trees and actions associated with any word or word subsequence are now directly available as that part of the parse DAG spanned by the required word DAG edges. This, of course, means that the contribution of any word or phrase can be directly obtained, fulfilling the criterion of incremental representation.

2.3. DS-TTR Generation as Parsing

The goal for the generation module must then, equally, reflect the incremental behaviour that yields confirmations as in (16), (14), continuations as in (4), (16), user interruptions without discarding the semantic content built up so far to provide for realistic clarification and *self-repair* capability such as in (2), (3) and possibly the presumption that the fragment may contribute more than one such attribute as in (15). The same requirements for parsing apply also to generation, viz: *strong incremental interpretation*; *incremental representation* on a word-by-word basis; continual access to *procedural context* to implement all information made available by selected expressions without delay. As noted above, there is the extra requirement in generation of *representational interchangeability* enabling the switch between parsing and production activities. DS-TTR can meet these criteria elegantly in virtue of the DS decision to model generation in terms of the same tree-growth mechanisms as in parsing (Purver and Kempson 2004) with the simple addition of a *subsumption check* against a so-called *goal tree* (but see below for how in DS-TTR this has been replaced with TTR goal concepts).[5] The DS generation process is thus made word-by-word incremental with maximal tree representations continually available, effectively combining lexical selection and linearisation into a single action due to word-by-word iteration through the lexicon.

While no formal model of self-repair was proposed in DS (but see section 3.2), self-monitoring is inherently part of the generation process, as each word generated is parsed. Notwithstanding the degree of incrementality so achieved, the Purver and Kempson (2004) model of generation did not meet the criterion of *strict incremental* interpretation, as maximal information about the dependencies between the semantic formulae in the tree did not need to be computed until the tree is complete. On the other hand, the goal tree needs to be constructed from the grammar's actions, so any dialogue management module must have full knowledge of the DS parsing mechanism and lexicon, and so interchangeability of representation becomes difficult. In moving to the DS-TTR framework, several adjustments were therefore incorporated.

2.3.1. TTR goal concepts and subtype checking

One straightforward modification to the DS generation model enabling representational interchangeability is to replace the previously defined *goal tree* with a *TTR goal concept* which takes the form of a record type e.g.:

(19) $\begin{bmatrix} event_{=e1} & : e_s \\ RefTime & : e_s \\ p1_{=today(RefTime)} & : t \\ p2_{=RefTime \bigcirc event} & : t \\ x1_{=Sweden} & : e \\ p3_{=from(event,x1)} & : t \\ x_{=robin} & : e \\ P_{=arrive(event,x)} & : t \end{bmatrix}$

The goal concept may be *partial* as required for such data as (1)-(4), and the dialogue manager may further specify it, but even then it need not correspond to a complete sentence in incremental dialogue management strategies (Guhe 2007; Buß and Schlangen 2011). This move also means a dialogue manager may input goal concepts directly to the generator; and no considerations of the requirements of the DS grammar are needed (contra Purver and Kempson's (2004) approach). The tree subsumption check in the original DS generation model can now be characterised as a TTR subtype relation check (see p.96, Fernández (2006)) between the goal concept record type and the current parse state's root record type.

Figure 3 displays a successful generation path,[6] where the incremental generation of "john arrives" succeeds as the successful lexical action applications at transitions $\boxed{1} \mapsto \boxed{2}$ and $\boxed{3} \mapsto \boxed{4}$ are interspersed with applicable computational action sequences at transitions $\boxed{0} \mapsto \boxed{1}$ and $\boxed{2} \mapsto \boxed{3}$, at each stage passing the subtype relation check with the goal (i.e. the goal is a subtype of the top node's compiled record type), until arriving at a tree that *type matches* the assigned goal concept in $\boxed{4}$ in the rich TTR sense of *type*. In implementational terms, there will in fact be multiple generation paths in the generation state, including incomplete and abandoned paths, which can be incoporated into the DS notion of context as a DAG.

Another advantage of working with TTR record types rather than trees during generation is that selecting relevant lexical actions from the lexicon can take place before generation begins through comparing the semantic formulae of the actions to the goal concept. Subtype checking makes it possible to reduce the computational complexity of lexical search through a pre-verbal lexical action selection.

3. Incremental processing of dialogue phenomena

We can now see how the resulting DS-TTR model deals with compound contributions; this has been implemented in the publicly available DyLan dialogue system[7] (Eshghi, Purver, and Hough 2011; Purver, Eshghi, and Hough 2011).

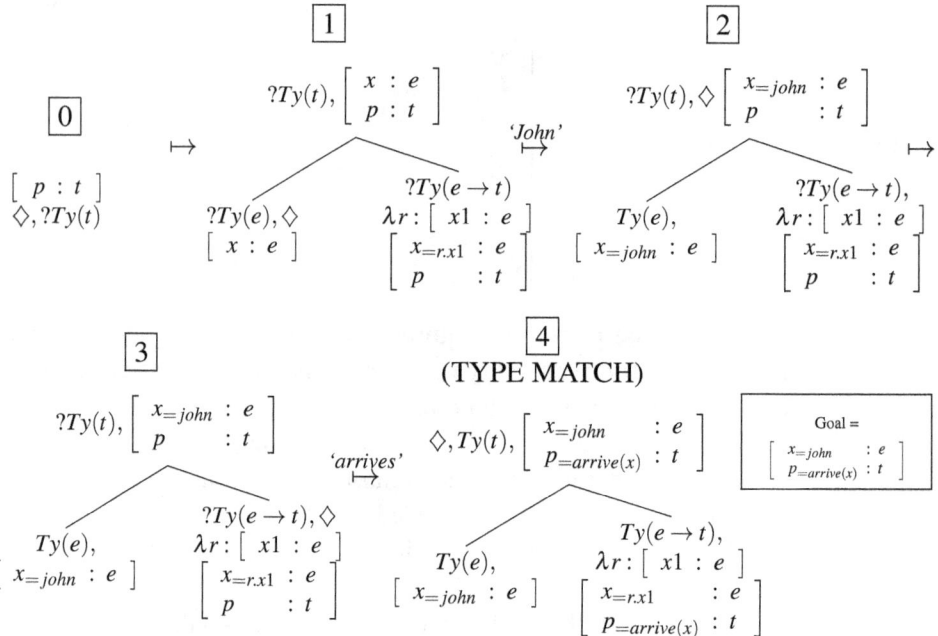

Figure 3. Successful generation path in DS-TTR

3.1. Compound contributions

Previous formal and computational accounts of compound contributions (CCs) have focussed on a sub-category of CCs, so-called *completions,* where a responder succeeds in projecting a string the initial speaker had intended to convey. The foremost implementation is that of Poesio and Rieser (2010), using the PTT model for incremental dialogue interpretation (Poesio and Traum 1997; Poesio and Rieser 2003) in combination with LTAG (Demberg and Keller 2008). The approach is grammar-based, incorporating syntactic, semantic and pragmatic information via the lexicalised TAG, providing an account of the incremental interpretation process incorporating lexical, syntactic and semantic information.[8] This model meets many of the criteria defined here. Both interpretation and representation are incremental, with semantic and syntactic information being present; the use of PTT suggests that linguistic context can be incorporated suitably. However, while reversibility might be incorporated by choice of suitable parsing and generation frameworks, this is not made explicit;

and the extendability of the representations seems limited by TAG's approach to adjunction. The use of TAG also restricts the grammar to licensing grammatical *strings*, problematic for some CCs (e.g. examples (7) in which *semantic* dependencies hold between the two parts of the CC); and the mechanism may not be sustainable for all compound contributions where participants make no attempt to match what the other party might have in mind. So the account is at best incomplete.[9]

The broad range of CCs follows as an immediate consequence of DS-TTR. The use of TTR record types removes the need for grammar-specific parameters; and the interchangeability of representations between parsing and generation means that the construction of a data structure can become a collaborative process between dialogue participants, permitting a range of varied user input behaviour and flexible system responses. This use of the same representations by parsing and generation guarantees the ability to begin parsing from the endpoint of any generation process, even mid-utterance; and to begin generation from the end-point of any parsing process. Successive sequential exchanges between participants leading to a collaboratively completed utterance as in (6) are directly predicted. Both parsing and generation models are now characterised entirely by the parse context DAG with the addition for generation of a TTR goal concept. The transition from generation to parsing becomes almost trivial: the parsing process can continue from the final node(s) of the generation DAG, with parsing actions extending the trees available in the final node set as normal. Transition from parsing to generation also requires no change of representation with the DAG produced by parsing acting as the initial structure for generation, though we require the addition of a goal concept to drive the generation process. The same record types are thus used throughout the system: as the concepts for generating system plans, as the goal concepts in NLG, and for matching user input against known concepts in suggesting continuations. Possible system transition points trigger alternation between modules in their co-construction of the shared parse/generator. A goal concept can be produced by the dialogue manager at a speaker transition by searching its domain concepts for a suitable subtype of the TTR record type built so far, guaranteeing a grammatical continuation given the presence of appropriate lexical actions. This extends the method for CC modelling described in (Purver and Kempson 2004): now the dialogue manager has an elegant decision mechanism for aiding content selection. And, given the presumption of context, content and goal specifications all in terms of record types, the ability to construct goals in a scenario without linguistic antecedents as in (9) and (10).

The data of CCs thus follows in full, even when either the goal record type for the interrupter does not match that of the initiator as in (5), or when the goal record type does not correspond to a complete domain concept, as in the successive fragment exchanges such as (6). This is achieved through progressive extensions of the partial tree so far, either directly, or by adding adjunct LINKed trees. This results in the word-by-word further specification of the record type at the root of the matrix tree representing the maximal interpretation of the string/utterance so far. In Figure 4 we give the progressive record-type specification for the exchange (20), a simplification of (6), showing how incomplete structures may serve as both input and output for either party:

(20) A: Today Robin arrives B: from A: Sweden

Details of the tree derivations are omitted in Figure 4, but we have included these in Appendix 1, which contains a fuller tree derivation for (20). As noted,

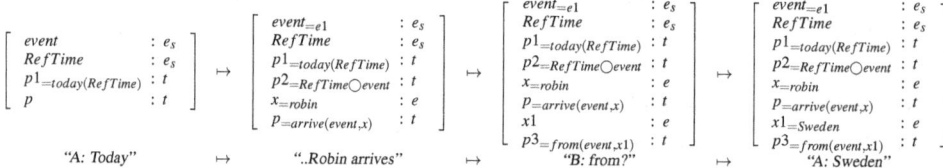

Figure 4. Incremental interpretation via TTR subtypes

more complex forms can be generated by incorporating LINKed trees, as is presumed in the characterisation of the many extensions by the addition of an adjunct, as in (8) (See Appendix 1), without any of these having to involve any extension of the formal DS vocabulary.

3.2. Self-repair

In this section, we present our initial model of self-repair. Specifically, there are two types of repair that we address here: type 1, where the repair involves a local, and partial restart of the reparandum, as in (2) and type 2 where the repair is simply a local extension, i.e. a further specification of the reparandum as in (3).

In our DS-TTR model of generation set out above, a type 1 repair arises due to an online revision of a record type goal concept, whereby the new goal concept is not a sub-type of the one the speaker had initially set out to realise. We model this via backtracking along the incrementally available context DAG as set out above. More specifically, repair is invoked if there is no possible DAG extension after the semantic filtering stage of generation (resulting in no candidate succeeding word edge). The repair procedure proceeds by restarting generation from the last realised (generated) word edge. It continues backtracking by one DAG vertex at a time until the root record type of the current partial tree is a subtype of the new goal concept. Generation then proceeds as usual by extending the DAG from that vertex. The word edges backtracked over are not removed, but are simply marked as repaired, following the principle that the revision process is on the public conversational record and hence should still be accessible for later anaphoric reference (see Figure 5).

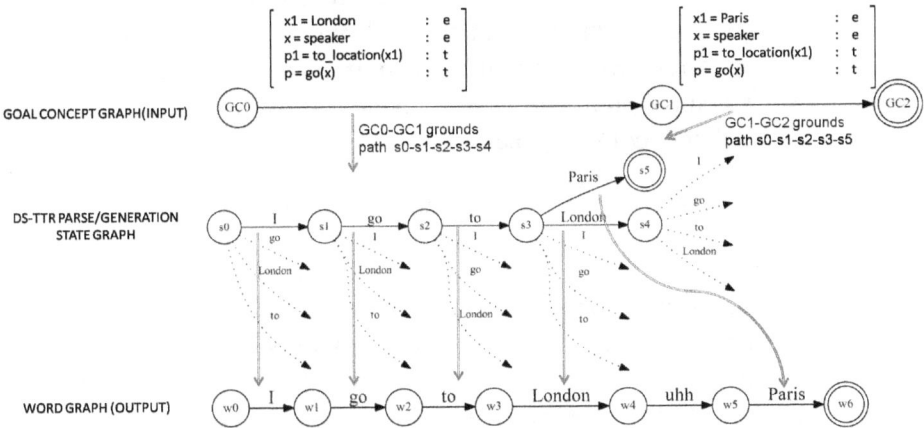

Figure 5. Incremental DS-TTR generation of a self-repair upon change of goal concept. Type-matched record types are double-circled nodes and edges indicating failed paths are dotted.

Our protocol is consistent with Shriberg and Stolcke's (1998) empirical observation that the probability of retracing N words back in an utterance is more likely than retracing from N+1 words back, making the repair as local as possible. Utterances such as "I go, uhh, leave from Paris" are generated incrementally, as the repair is integrated with the semantics of the part of the utterance before the repair point, maximising re-use of existing semantic structure.

Type 2 repairs on the other hand, i.e. *extensions*, where the repair effects an "after-thought", usually in transition relevance places in dialogue after apparently complete turns, are also dealt with straightforwardly by our model. The DS-TTR parser simply treats these as monotonic extension of the matrix tree through LINK Adjunction to it (see Cann, Kempson, and Marten (2005), but also Appendix 1 for an example of such extensions) resulting in subtype extension of the root TTR record type. Thus, a change in goal concept during generation will not always put demands on the system to backtrack, such as in generating the fragment after the pause in "I go to Paris ... from London". Backtracking only operates at a semantics-syntax mismatch where the revised goal concept is no longer a subtype of the root record type for the (sub-)utterance so far realised, as in Figure 5.

Unlike string-based *speech plan* approaches such as that of Skantze and Hjalmarsson (2010), there is no need here to regenerate a fully-formed string from a revised goal concept and compare it with the string generated thus far to characterise repair. Instead, repair is driven by attempting to extend existing parse paths to construct the new target record type, *retaining* the semantic representation and the procedural context of actions already built up in the generation process to avoid the computational demand of constructing syntactic structures from afresh where possible. Also, importantly, unlike string-based approaches which are bound to be very domain specific, we note that our approach is completely domain-general.

3.3. Speech Acts and speaker/hearer attributions in DS-TTR

A further bonus of combining DS mechanisms with TTR record types as output decorations is the allowance of a much richer vocabulary for such decorations, as empirically warranted. In particular, it provides a basis from which speaker and hearer attributes may be optionally specified. In this connection, (Purver et al. 2010) propose a specification of fields with sub-field specifications, one a *context* sub-field for speaker-hearer attributions and micro utterance events, and the second, *content*, for familiar lambda-terms, a modification which allows a record of speaker-hearer attributions to be optionally kept alongside function-argument content record type specifications so that the different anaphor-dependency resolutions across switch of participant roles can be modelled as in (7)-(8) without disturbing content compilation of the lambda terms:

With intersection of record types available for record types of arbitrary complexity, such specifications are unproblematic. As Purver et al. (2010) demonstrate, speech act content can also be derived optionally as a later step of inference over such structures by addition of LINKed trees (see *ibid.* for details). We note, nevertheless, that this isn't essential for an explanation of the interactional patterns observable in conversation, even meta-communicative interaction. Instead, we suggest, conversational interaction is buttressed by mechanisms intrinsic to grammar itself, as we have set out. This of course raises issues of what constitutes successful communication, in particular for Gricean and neo-Gricean models in which recognition of the content of the speaker's intentions is essential: Poesio and Rieser (2010) are illustrative. We do not enter into this debate here, but merely note that this stance is commensurate with the data of section 1 in which participants' intentions may only be emergent or be subject to modification during the course of a con-

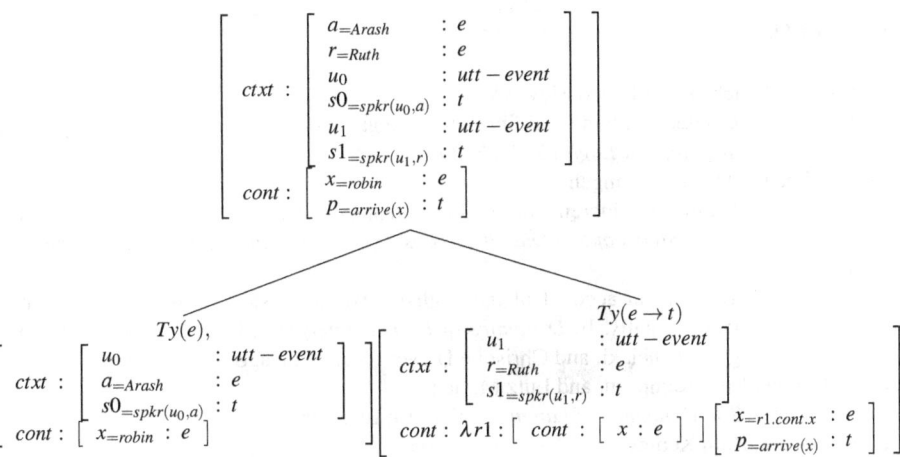

Figure 6. Processing 'Arash: Robin.. Ruth: ..arrived', with micro utterance events and speaker/hearer attributions, adapted from Purver et al. (2010)

versation without jeopardising its success (Gregoromichelaki et al. 2011; Gregoromichelaki et al. forthcoming).

4. Conclusion

We have presented a formal framework for modelling conversational dialogue with parsing and generation modules as controlled by a dialogue manager, both of which reflect word by word incrementality, using a hybrid of Dynamic Syntax and Type Theory with Records. The composite framework allows access to record types incrementally during generation, providing strict incremental representation and interpretation for substrings of utterances that can be accessed by existing dialogue managers, parsers and generators equally, allowing the articulation of syntactic and semantic dependencies across parser and generator modules. Several avenues of research now open up. But most important of all, there is a radical shift of perspective, with the defined "competence" model now securely grounded in its articulation of mechanisms for interactive language performance that it makes possible. And with this move, the nesting of the language faculty into a coherent cognitive system at last becomes possible, opening up radical new perspectives on philosophy of language, psychology and cognition.

References

Blackburn, Patrick, and Wilfried Meyer-Viol
    1994   Linguistics, logic and finite trees. *Logic Journal of the Interest Group of Pure and Applied Logics* 2 (1): 3–29.

Buß, Okko, and David Schlangen
    2011   Dium : An incremental dialogue manager that can produce self-corrections. *Proceedings of SemDial 2011 (Los Angelogue), Los Angeles, CA.* 47–54.

Cann, Ronnie
    2011   Towards an account of the english auxiliary system: building interpretations incrementally. In *Dynamics of Lexical Interfaces*, Ruth Kempson, Eleni Gregoromichelaki, and Christine Howes (eds.). Chicago: CSLI Press.

Cann, Ronnie, Ruth Kempson, and Lutz Marten
    2005   *The Dynamics of Language*. Oxford: Elsevier.

Cann, Ronnie, Ruth Kempson, and Matthew Purver
    2007   Context and well-formedness: the dynamics of ellipsis. *Research on Language and Computation* 5 (3): 333–358.

Carberry, S.
    1990   *Plan recognition in natural language dialogue*. the MIT Press.

Chatzikyriakidis, Stergios, and Ruth Kempson
    2011   Standard modern and pontic greek person restrictions: A feature-free dynamic account. *Journal of Greek Lingusitics*, pp. 127–166.

Clark, Herbert H., and Jean E. Fox Tree
    2002   Using *uh* and *um* in spontaneous speaking. *Cognition* 84 (1): 73–111.

Cooper, Robin
    2005   Records and record types in semantic theory. *Journal of Logic and Computation* 15 (2): 99–112.

Davidson, Donald
    1980   *Essays on Actions and Events*. Oxford, UK: Clarendon Press.

Demberg, V., and F. Keller
    2008   A psycholinguistically motivated version of tag. *Proceedings of the International Workshop on Tree Adjoining Grammars*.

Eshghi, A., M. Purver, and Julian Hough
    2011   Dylan: Parser for dynamic syntax. Technical Report, Queen Mary University of London.

Fernández, Raquel
    2006   Non-sentential utterances in dialogue: Classification, resolution and use. Ph.D. diss., King's College London, University of London.

Ginzburg, Jonathan
    2012   *The Interactive Stance: Meaning for Conversations*. Oxford University Press.

Ginzburg, Jonathan, and Robin Cooper
    2004   Clarification, ellipsis, and the nature of contextual updates in dialogue. *Linguistics and Philosophy* 27 (3): 297–365.

Gregoromichelaki, E.
    2006   Conditionals: A dynamic syntax account. Ph.D. diss., King's College London.

Gregoromichelaki, E., R. Cann, and R. Kempson
    forthcoming On coordination in dialogue: subsentential talk and its implications. In *On Brevity*, Laurence Goldstein (ed.). OUP.

Gregoromichelaki, Eleni, Ruth Kempson, Matthew Purver, Greg J. Mills, Ronnie Cann, Wilfried Meyer-Viol, and Pat G. T. Healey
2011   Incrementality and intention-recognition in utterance processing. *Dialogue and Discourse* 2 (1): 199–233.

Grosz, Barbara J., and Candace L. Sidner
1986   Attention, intentions, and the structure of discourse. *Computational Linguistics* 12 (3): 175–204.

Guhe, Markus
2007   *Incremental Conceptualization for Language Production*. NJ: Lawrence Erlbaum Associates.

Hough, Julian
2011   Incremental semantics driven natural language generation with self-repairing capability. *Recent Advances in Natural Language Processing (RANLP)*. Hissar, Bulgaria, 79–84.

Kempson, R., and J. Kiaer
2010   Multiple long-distance scrambling: Syntax as reflections of processing. *Journal of Linguistics* 46 (01): 127–192.

Kempson, Ruth, Eleni Gregoromichelaki, and Christine Howes(eds.)
2011   *The Dynamics of Lexical Interfaces*. CSLI - Studies in Constraint Based Lexicalism.

Kempson, Ruth, Wilfried Meyer-Viol, and Dov Gabbay
2001   *Dynamic Syntax: The Flow of Language Understanding*. Blackwell.

Larsson, Staffan
2011   The TTR perceptron: Dynamic perceptual meanings and semantic coordination. *Proceedings of the 15th Workshop on the Semantics and Pragmatics of Dialogue (SemDial 2011 - Los Angelogue)*. 140–148.

Levelt, W.J.M.
1983   Monitoring and self-repair in speech. *Cognition* 14 (1): 41–104.

Milward, David
1991   Axiomatic grammar, non-constituent coordination and incremental interpretation. Ph.D. diss., University of Cambridge.

Poesio, Massimo, and Hannes Rieser
2003   Coordination in a PTT approach to dialogue. *Proceedings of the 7th Workshop on the Semantics and Pragmatics of Dialogue (SEMDIAL)*. Saarbrücken, Germany.
2010   Completions, coordination, and alignment in dialogue. *Dialogue and Discourse* 1: 1–89.

Poesio, Massimo, and David Traum
1997   Conversational actions and discourse situations. *Computational Intelligence* 13, no. 3.

Purver, Matthew, Arash Eshghi, and Julian Hough
2011   Incremental semantic construction in a dialogue system. J. Bos, and S. Pulman (eds.), *Proceedings of the 9th International Conference on Computational Semantics*. Oxford, UK, 365–369.

Purver, Matthew, Eleni Gregoromichelaki, Wilfried Meyer-Viol, and Ronnie Cann
2010   Splitting the 'I's and crossing the 'You's: Context, speech acts and grammar. P. Łupkowski, and M. Purver (eds.), *Aspects of Semantics and Pragmatics of Dialogue. SemDial 2010, 14th Workshop on the Semantics and Pragmatics of Dialogue*. Poznań: Polish Society for Cognitive Science, 43–50.

Purver, Matthew, and Ruth Kempson
2004   Incremental context-based generation for dialogue. A. Belz, R. Evans, and P. Piwek (eds.), *Proceedings of the 3rd International Conference on Natural Language Generation (INLG04)*, Lecture Notes in Artifical Intelligence no. 3123. Brockenhurst, UK: Springer, 151–160.

Sato, Yo
2011   Local ambiguity, search strategies and parsing in Dynamic Syntax. In *The Dynamics of Lexical Interfaces*, E. Gregoromichelaki, R. Kempson, and C. Howes (eds.). CSLI Publications.

Schegloff, Emanuel A., Gail Jefferson, and Harvey Sacks
1977   The preference for self-correction in the organization of repair in conversation. *Language* 53 (2): 361–382.

Shriberg, Elizabeth, and Andreas Stolcke
1998   How far do speakers back up in repairs? A quantitative model. *Proceedings of the International Conference on Spoken Language Processing*. 2183–2186.

Skantze, Gabriel, and Anna Hjalmarsson
2010   Towards incremental speech generation in dialogue systems. *Proceedings of the SIGDIAL 2010 Conference*. Tokyo, Japan: Association for Computational Linguistics, 1–8.

5. Appendix

This appendix provides a derivation for a split dialogue in which both input and output of intermediate generation and parsing steps involve partial structures: "A: Today Robin arrives B: from? A: Sweden". Notice how the event node on the matrix tree is represented as EVENT in the two step derivation for A's first utterance. The matrix tree is then omitted from the rest of the steps of the derivation for reasons of space, and represented just as EVENT (but see Figure 4 for the progressive specification of the matrix tree root record type)[10].

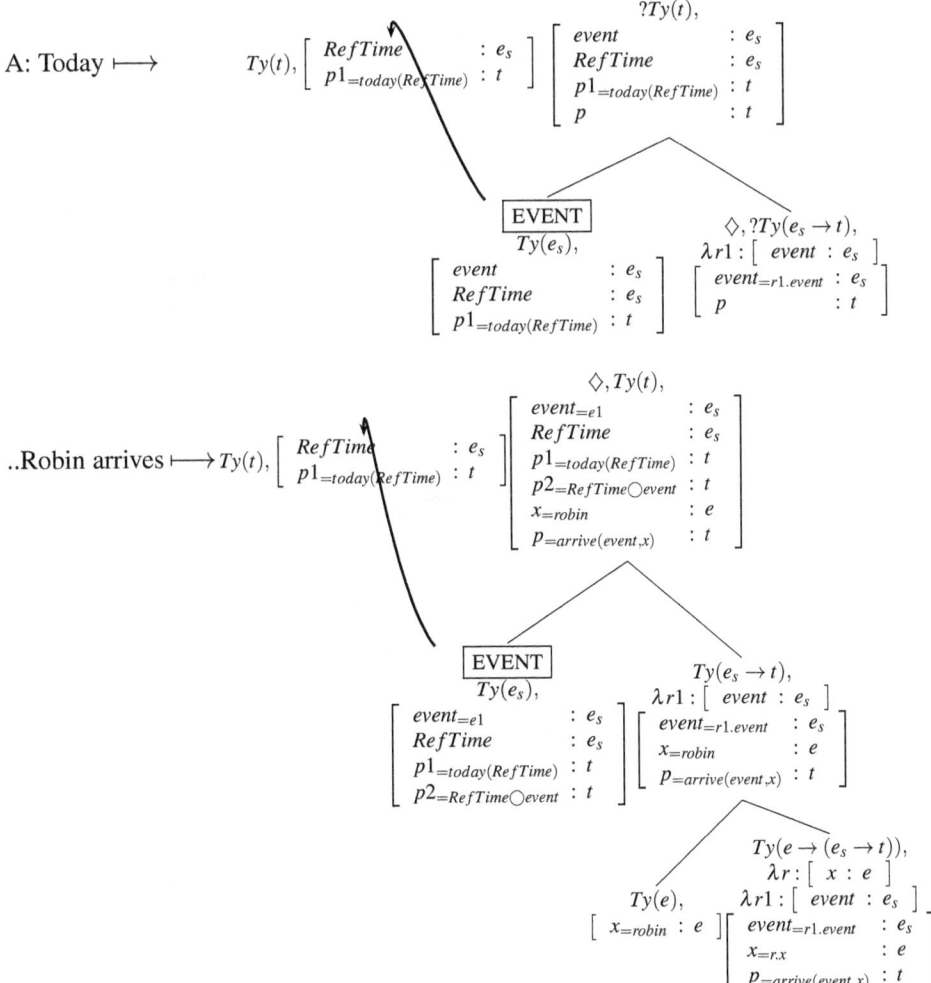

Figure 7. Processing "A: Today, Robin arrives"

348 Eshghi et al.

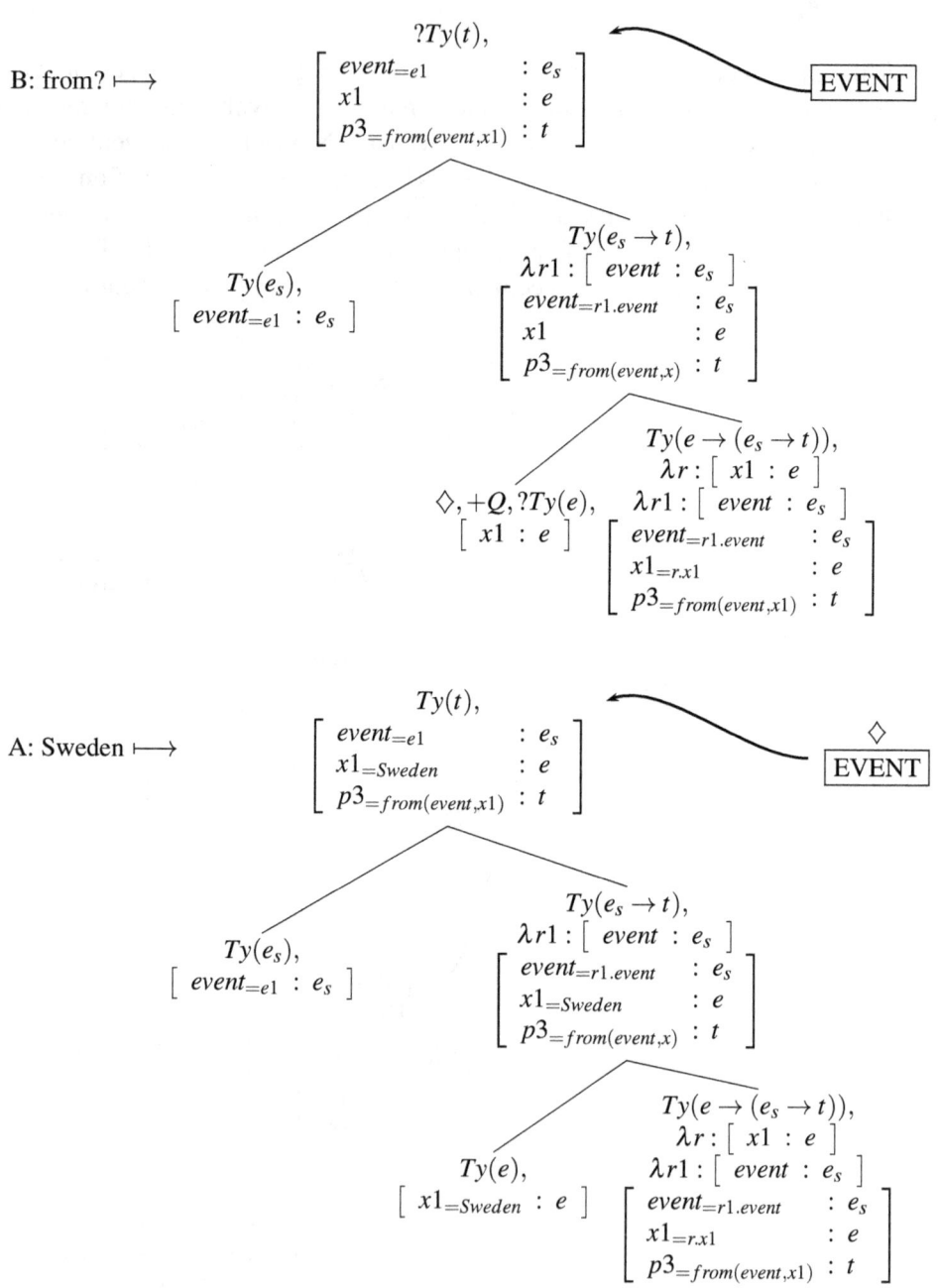

Figure 8. Processing "B: from? A: Sweden"

Notes

1. This paper in part reports work done under the ESRC project RES-062-23-0962, The Dynamics of Conversational Dialogue, and also under the current EPSRC project EP/J010383/1, Robust Incremental SEmantic Resources for Dialogue, who we thank for financial support. This interdisciplinary work has involved a number of colleagues to whom we are profoundly grateful for their input: Patrick Healey, Wilfried Meyer-Viol, Ronnie Cann, Christine Howes, Yo Sato, Graham White. This research would not have been the same without them. There is also a broader set of colleagues from whose work and comments we have greatly benefited, primary amongst whom are Robin Cooper, Staffan Larsson and Jonathan Ginzburg. And finally there are other colleagues who over the years have offered helpful input and stimulus. However, we absolve any of these from errors in this particular offering.
2. English has one such exception, in its use of the accusative case in fragments such as *Who is taking this class? Me?*.
3. For functional application and Link-Evaluation (see ch. 3, Cann, Kempson, and Marten (2005), but also Appendix 1 for example DS-TTR derivations involving Link-Evaluation), which require the intersection/concatenation of two record types, *relabelling* is carried out when necessary to avoid leaving incorrect variable names in the record types in the manner of Cooper (2005) and Fernández (2006).
4. See Cann (2011) for the detailed Reichenbachian treatment of tense/aspect used here.
5. This ease of matching incrementality in both generation and parsing is not matched by other models aiming to reflect incrementality in the dialogue model while adopting relative conservative grammar frameworks, some matching syntactic requirements but without incremental semantics (Skantze and Hjalmarsson 2010), others matching incremental growth of semantic input but leaving the incrementality of structural growth unaddressed (Guhe 2007).
6. Since Figure 3 is given to display the generation path dynamics, event term specifications are omitted for simplicity.
7. Available from http://dylan.sourceforge.net/
8. Poesio and Rieser provide a detailed account of how a suggested collaborative completion might be derived using inferential processes and the recognition of plans: by matching the partial representation at speaker transition against a repository of known plans in the relevant domain, an agent can determine the components of these plans which have not yet been made explicit and make a plan to generate them.
9. The calling up of the requisite mechanisms would also lead directly to predictions of processing complexity that we have strong reason to believe will not be met.
10. Each of these steps involves attaching a LINKed tree by way of adjunction to this event node in the (omitted) matrix tree, so that in the final derivation there are in fact two LINKed trees linked to the EVENT node on the matrix tree.

www.ingramcontent.com/pod-product-compliance
Lightning Source LLC
Chambersburg PA
CBHW050123170426
43197CB00011B/1689